THE POLITICS
OF POWER

*A Critical Introduction to
American Government*

THE POLITICS
OF POWER

*A Critical Introduction to
American Government*

FOURTH EDITION

IRA KATZNELSON
Columbia University

MARK KESSELMAN
Columbia University

ALAN DRAPER
St. Lawrence University

WADSWORTH
™
THOMSON LEARNING

Australia • Canada • Mexico • Singapore • Spain
United Kingdom • United States

WADSWORTH
™
THOMSON LEARNING

Political Science Editor: David Tatom
Development Editor: Stacey Sims
Editorial Assistant: Dianna Long
Marketing Manager: Laura Brennan
Project Manager, Editorial Production: Barrett Lackey
Permissions Editor: Shirley Webster
Production Service: Clarinda Publication Services

Photo Researcher: Lili Weiner
Copy Editor: Sheralyn Goldbecker
Cover Image: A/P World Wide Photos
Cover Printer: Lehigh Press, Inc.
Compositor: The Clarinda Company
Printer: Quebecor Printing Fairfield

Printed in the United States of America
1 2 3 4 5 6 7 05 04 03 02 01

For more information about our products, contact us at:
Thomson Learning Academic Resource Center
1-800-423-0563

For permission to use material from this text, contact us by: **Phone:** 1-800-730-2214
Fax: 1-800-730-2215
Web: http://www.thomsonrights.com

Library of Congress Control Number:
2001094652

ISBN 0-15-501698-9

Asia
Thomson Learning
60 Albert Street, #15-01
Albert Complex
Singapore 189969

Australia
Nelson Thomson Learning
102 Dodds Street
South Melbourne, Victoria 3205
Australia

Canada
Nelson Thomson Learning
1120 Birchmount Road
Toronto, Ontario M1K 5G4
Canada

Europe/Middle East/Africa
Thomson Learning
Berkshire House
168-173 High Holborn
London WC1 V7AA
United Kingdom

Latin America
Thomson Learning
Seneca, 53
Colonia Polanco
11560 Mexico D.F.
Mexico

Spain
Paraninfo Thomson Learning
Calle/Magallanes, 25
28015 Madrid, Spain

To Ephraim and Sylvia Katznelson,
Robert and Clarice Draper,
and the memory of
Paul and Anne Kesselman

———————————■———————————

PREFACE

"Times change." So began the last edition of *The Politics of Power*, published in 1987, one year before President Ronald Reagan's Vice President, George H. W. Bush, was elected president of the United States. This new edition has been published during the presidency of his son, former Texas Governor George W. Bush. An entire political generation has passed between the two editions.

The world and American society have changed in fascinating and important ways since 1987. *The Politics of Power* has changed with it. The book has been reorganized and rewritten completely. With the addition of Alan Draper to the team of authors, each chapter has been recast and revised in order to keep up with the quickening pace of events and a burgeoning scholarly literature. Faculty familiar with previous editions of *The Politics of Power* will find much that is new within this book. We hope that students and faculty unfamiliar with past editions will be pleasantly surprised as well. Each section of the book, covering political economy, participation, institutions, and policy, now begins with an introduction to those topics. Each chapter now contains more vignettes to vivify our points and help students see the relevance of the arguments we make. Material within the chapters has been updated through and beyond the 2000 elections. This material highlights what we believe to be the major changes in American politics since publication of the last edition of *The Politics of Power* in 1987: the emergence of the United States as the lone superpower in a more interconnected world; the increasing importance of money in American politics; the more ideological, partisan, confrontational nature of American politics; and the growing acceptance of the virtue of markets.

While *The Politics of Power* has been renovated thoroughly, its aim remains the same: to introduce students to a critical perspective on American politics by highlighting how political institutions and processes are influenced by deep inequalities generated by the country's political economy. The text underscores the mutually supportive but uneasy relationship joining American democracy and American capitalism. We try to clarify this multifaceted association in the hope that our perspective and analytical framework, even if controversial, will provoke thought and discussion. In so doing, we aim to assist students in developing not only their own approaches to the study of American politics but also their role as citizens.

Following the Introduction, which provides a theoretical framework that analyzes key issues in democratic theory, the book divides into four parts. Part I explores ties linking politics and economics. Part II examines the political participation of citizens seeking to influence the institutions and public policies that affect their lives. Part III investigates the federal government's executive, legislative, and judicial institutions. Part IV turns to how domestic and foreign policy have been shaped and limited by these institutions and by capitalism and democracy. The book concludes with an assessment of the Clinton presidency and a discussion of future directions in American politics. Throughout, we have aimed to be direct without being simplistic, engaging without being flippant, and critical without being cynical. We will be pleased if our discussions animate students new to the study of American politics, engage more advanced students, and challenge professors who assign the book.

We continue to be assisted by numerous people. Librarians at St. Lawrence University and Columbia University were enormously helpful in locating difficult sources and information (the SLU Library plays bigger than its size; Columbia's maintains agility despite its proportions). Fred Cocozzelli, Matt Fellowes, Suzy Kim Lee, and Jessica Olsen provided able research assistance. We also profited from the insightful criticisms of fellow political scientists, including John Coleman, Roy Flemming, Daniel P. Franklin, Joel Krieger, Cathie Jo Martin, Gerald Rosenberg, and Stephen Skowronek. Ira Katznelson and Mark Kesselman remain indebted to the family, friends, and colleagues warmly acknowledged in earlier editions. New to the enterprise, Alan Draper would like to thank Jeffrey Burstein, Liz Donoghue, Gerry Ducharme, Edward Edelman, Fred Exoo, Wally Malakoff, Sheila Murphy, Ansil Ramsay, Bob and Verna Schwartz, and Josh Tankel for first aid when needed most. He also wishes to thank Pat Ellis for taking over from there . . . and ever since. His brother Douglas and his children, Rachel and Sam, remain a thorn in his side; he would not have it any other way. Collectively, we remain thankful for the professionalism of our editors at Wadsworth.

CONTENTS

PART II: THE MANY FACES OF POLITICAL PARTICIPATION 99

CHAPTER 4
MOVEMENT FOR CHANGE: WORKERS AND WORK 101

CHAPTER 5
POLITICAL PARTIES, ELECTIONS, AND MOVEMENTS 133

PART III: POLITICAL INSTITUTIONS   177

CHAPTER 6
THE PRESIDENCY: IMPERIAL OR IMPERILED?   181

CHAPTER 7
CONGRESS   217

CHAPTER 8
THE JUDICIARY   265

PART IV: PUBLIC POLICY   297

CHAPTER 9
CORPORATE CAPITALISM, FOREIGN POLICY, AND THE GLOBAL POLITICAL ECONOMY   299

THE POLITICS OF POWER

A Critical Introduction to American Government

Democracy's Challenge

Located on northern Florida's Treasure Coast, Vero Beach is a prosperous small city of 107,000. Over 240 doctors practice there, many in lovely townhouses in the community's island section. On the less affluent mainland sits the Health Department Clinic, home to We Care, a program staffed by volunteer doctors, many retired, who see uninsured patients. At the start of the twenty-first century, 44 million Americans lack health coverage. Most of them earn too much to qualify for Medicaid, the government's program of insurance for the poor, but too little to afford private insurance (this number is up from 34 million ten years earlier). The patients served by We Care have modest means. To qualify, their income cannot exceed 150 percent of the national poverty level (in 2000, $8,240 for a single person and $16,700 for a family of four).

Jodi Duff, a 35-year-old waitress, was told by a We Care clinic doctor she needed to see a cardiologist. Months passed before a volunteer could be found who recommended she undergo an angiogram to see if her coronary artery was blocked. The procedure would cost $2,000. No local doctor would do it for free. Her only hope, she was told, was to apply as a charity case to a responsive hospital, the Deborah Heart and Lung Center in New Jersey, where a minor blockage was treated with a new medicine.

Alma Almanza, a seasonal orange picker, discovered a large lump in her breast. It proved cancerous, and a top-flight volunteer surgeon performed a mastectomy. The chemotherapy that followed so weakened Ms. Almanza that she could not work. With unpaid bills, her phone was shut off, but hospital invoices, totaling over $5,000, continued to arrive. Soon she was poor enough to qualify for Medicaid, and the hospital recouped its expenses. Ms. Almanza began radiation treatment. As she grew stronger, she could look forward to returning to the harvest. She knew, however, that if she earned too much, she would lose her health insurance.[1]

———————————————— ■ ————————————————

---

[1]*Wall Street Journal*, November 30, 1999.

The Center for Security Policy is a tax-exempt research organization, directed since its founding in 1988 by Frank Gaffney, Jr., who served as Assistant Secretary of Defense for International Security Policy during the administration of President Ronald Reagan. The center is known for its opposition to the campaign to ban anti-personnel landmines and especially for its efforts to support the deployment of ballistic missile defenses. Its World Wide Web site quotes the magazine Human Events as saying the center is "referred to by some as the 'real National Security Council' in Washington" [emphasis in original].

The center's budget is $1.2 million a year. Approximately one-third is supplied by military contractors dedicated to building an anti-missile system. Eight members of the industry are on the center's board of directors, including six from Lockheed Martin, which is one of the three main contractors, along with Boeing and TRW, on the Pentagon's missile defense program. These firms have been steady supporters of the center. So have such other military contractors as Rockwell International, Northrop Grumman, and General Dynamics. Their contributions are tax-deductible. Thus, much of the cost of the center's activities is borne in the form of lost revenue by the federal government, the target of the center's lobbying efforts, and by American taxpayers at large.

Some $60 billion in potential business is at stake in the controversial decision as to whether to build this kind of defense system. Specialists disagree about whether it can work and whether it will lead to a more or less stable nuclear balance. They also disagree about whether it makes sense for the United States to cancel or violate the Anti-ballistic Missile Treaty it signed in 1972 with the Soviet Union. This debate, however, has not taken place entirely on the merits. As with the Center for Security Policy, the firms with the most to gain have spent considerable sums to shape the debate about security policy. In the 1990s, the military industry contributed $49 million to the two major political parties ($21 million to the Democrats, $28 million to the Republicans), primarily in "soft money," the unrestricted donations permitted under federal finance laws.[2] Opponents of anti-missile defense system expenditures have no such deep pockets to draw on. The playing field on which the debate is conducted is highly uneven.

———————————————— ■ ————————————————

Many Americans do not participate in the political process. In 1998, when all the seats in the House of Representatives and one in three seats in the Senate were contested, slightly over 200 million Americans had reached voting age. Of these, some

---

[2]*New York Times,* June 13, 2000.

73 million chose to vote. If we set aside aliens who lack citizenship, felons who are serving time in prison (and ex-felons who are permanently struck from the voting rolls), and a small number of people who are deemed incompetent for reasons of mental incapacity, nearly 120 million eligible adults failed to go to the polls. Two years earlier President Clinton was reelected. For the first time since the 1920s, fewer than half the electorate cast a vote. More than half the children in the United States live in homes where neither parent votes. Indeed, one in three Americans is not even registered to vote. This degree of abstention from one of the key activities of democratic politics is unusual. In many other democratic countries, the vast majority of citizens cast a ballot. Many countries automatically register citizens when they reach the age of eighteen. Others conduct house-to-house surveys to find eligible voters.

Even though turnout rates in the United States have been historically low, the decline to 36 percent in 1998 represents a new, embarrassing low in modern American elections. Young citizens, in particular, are less disposed to vote. A recent national survey of 18- to 25-year-olds found that fewer than half said they "definitely will" vote, compared to two in three older adults. The younger adults displayed less information about public issues, paid less attention to civic affairs, and expressed more distrust in all levels of government, with only 9 percent trusting the federal government.[3] Participation rates are also lower for citizens who belong to minority groups and for those earning less than $30,000 a year.

Politicians are aware that many people do not vote—and that voters from some groups will be less receptive to their message. The technology of targeting voters has become sophisticated. Specialist firms, using Census and survey information, map information onto the national zip code grid. They sell their services to parties and candidates who want to tailor their appeals, say, to college-educated white young women with children who live in homes valued above $250,000. One of the most successful of these firms, GeoVoter, processes "vast amounts of data to sort desirable from undesirable voters—right down to the individual household." The company can generate "walk lists, complete with maps, for canvassers who want to crisscross a neighborhood visiting only selected voters who meet specified criteria, as well as phone lists and mailing lists." This Wisconsin-based company is not shy in touting its successes: "GeoVoter," one ad reads, "A liberal candidate's worst nightmare."

---

[3]Project Vote Smart, "General Population and Youth Survey on Civic Engagement," www.vote-smart.org/yip, September 14, 1999. The survey, based on 1,326 detailed interviews, was funded by the Pew Charitable Trusts and was a collaborative effort of Project Vote Smart, the Thomas S. Foley Institute for Public Policy and Public Service at Washington State University, and the Program for Governmental Research and Education at Oregon State University.

Another ad boasts: "When people say the NRA [National Rifle Association] has an unfair political advantage, they're absolutely right. The NRA has GeoVoter."[4]

———————————————■———————————————

The vignettes illustrate some important features of American politics that we will explore in this book. In diverse ways, they suggest, at a general level, the link between inequalities in economic resources and the kinds of political decisions that get made and, at a personal level, the link between inequalities in people's economic and other resources and their ability to obtain favorable outcomes. The fact that access to medical care in the United States depends on the size of one's pocketbook is not inevitable, but rather the result of political decisions (and nondecisions) about how health care is organized. In most other industrialized countries, citizens are entitled to adequate medical care as a matter of right. In the United States, medical care (and insurance entitling one to health care) is treated as a commodity that most people must purchase. Similarly, laws regulating taxes and lobbying enable wealthier individuals and corporations to exert vastly greater influence over political decisions than most citizens do. And when voting turnout is low, and unequally distributed among those of different generations, social classes, and racial and ethnic groups, those Americans who vote and are mobilized enjoy considerable political influence.

TITANIC INEQUALITIES

The *Titanic* was the biggest, fastest, most luxurious ocean liner ever constructed when it left the dock in 1912. The owners were so sure of what they had built that they said the ship was unsinkable. Life on board the ship was good when the *Titanic* set sail on its maiden voyage. As the boat cruised toward New York, first-class passengers enjoyed elegant parties, drank fine wine, and ate gourmet meals. Even those in less comfortable quarters below appeared to enjoy themselves, although they had to bring their own food, had less living space, and enjoyed far fewer amenities. As the ship crossed the Atlantic, everything appeared calm. When notified that the ship was entering treacherous waters off Newfoundland, the captain dismissed the warnings, confident in the ship's power and invincibility. Then disaster struck. An iceberg tore a hole in the ship's hull, and the *Titanic* began to

———————————————

[4]Robert Dreyfuss, "The Turnout Imperative," *American Prospect* 9 (July–August 1998), 76–81.

An ad announcing the maiden voyage of the *Titanic*.

sink. Bedlam broke out on board. People in third class demanded the same access to lifeboats as those in first class. Under orders from the ship's owners, the *Titanic*'s crew acted to enforce the class system aboard ship. First-class passengers were evacuated, while those in steerage were locked in the holds, consigning them to die in the icy waters of the Atlantic. Just as class influenced how people lived on board ship, it influenced who would die.

There are many ways in which the tale of the *Titanic* offers a powerful metaphor for key features of American society and politics even today. Like that great ship, the United States is the most powerful, richest, and strongest nation in the world. No other country is as militarily powerful, economically wealthy, or politically influential. It also is characterized by massive disparities in wealth, income, and political resources. Like the divisions between first- and third-class passengers on board the *Titanic*, deep inequalities based especially on race and on class (which often intertwine) divide the population. These divisions determine not only which Americans live better in terms of access to the good things in life, but also, as on the *Titanic*, who lives at all. Membership in a higher social class reduces the risk of heart attack, diabetes, infectious disease, arthritis, and some cancers and is a more powerful predictor of health and mortality than genetics, exposure to carcinogens, and smoking.[5] Wealthier citizens can afford good medical care, while those who are poor or earn marginal incomes often have to take their chances in the open seas and hope for the best.

The long arm of inequality even reaches into the voting booth, affecting whose vote is tallied. In Florida, where votes were undercounted in the 2000 presidential election, voters located in poorer precincts were more likely to have their votes thrown out. Voters in these precincts used older voting machines that failed to record accurately how citizens cast their ballots because the county could not afford more modern, more accurate models.

In almost every decade since the *Titanic* sailed, the gap between first-class passengers in the United States and those in steerage narrowed as more and more Americans were helped by increasingly widespread schooling, government programs, and economic growth to join a growing middle class. Yet in the past two decades, and especially in the 1990s, the gap between the top and bottom of the society widened. The metaphor of the *Titanic* again is all too credible. The average income of the top quintile has grown, and despite the longest economic boom in American history, that of the bottom quintile actually has shrunk. By the end of the 1990s, the average income for families in the top 20 percent of the income distribution was $137,000. That was more than ten times the average income of the poorest 20 percent, which was only $13,000. In some states, the gap was even wider. The top fifth of families in New York earned 14 times the bottom fifth; in California, 12 times.[6] Ironically, nowhere is the gap between the top and bottom 20 percent larger than in the nation's capital, Washington, D.C., where the average income for the top group was over $203,000, but the bottom 20 percent earned on average just $7,500.[7] Race and ethnicity magnify inequalities in wealth. In 1998, the median net worth for minority families—including Latinos, Asians, and African Americans—was $16,400, only a fifth of the $94,900 for non-Hispanic white families.[8] Whites and minorities, the rich and the poor, may all be passengers on the *Titanic,* but their experience on board ship is going to be very different given their disparities in income.

With political participation by ordinary American citizens going down and the lobbying effort by those with the means on the increase, public policy often reinforces these trends. Tax policy, for example, has had very powerful effects. In recent years, corporations have begun to pay enormous sums to their top executives by giving them the right to buy stock in their companies at no cost to themselves. Increasingly, companies are rewarding top-level employees in this way, putting vast potential wealth in their hands,

---

[5]*New York Times,* June 1, 1999.

[6]Even states with the smallest gaps between income groups were characterized by big differences. In Utah, Indiana, and Iowa, the most equal of the country's states, the best-off earned about seven times what the poorest did.

[7]*Wall Street Journal,* January 18, 2000.

[8]*Wall Street Journal,* March 14, 2000.

often at levels even the first-class passengers on the *Titanic* could only dream about. These gains are subsidized by the tax system in what amounts to a remarkable welfare system for the very rich. When company stocks owned by top employees increase in value, they can be sold for large profits. When this happens, the companies receive tax deductions equal to the taxes that are paid by the individuals on the gains the stocks have made. As a result of this tax write-off, some of the country's richest corporations, including Microsoft, owed no federal tax in 2000.[9]

At a time when the leaders of the business class have been reaping unprecedented benefits with this federal assistance, the country's children have grown more and more unequal. Those at the bottom of the income spectrum tend to be trapped there. Commenting on a recent study of children in poverty, the *New York Times* reported that "[a]bout 6 in 10 of the children in the lowest group—the poorest 20 percent . . . were still in the bottom income group 10 years later. About 9 in 10 children in the bottom group remained in the bottom two income groups 10 years later."[10]

Of the roughly 120 million tax returns filed each year, the 110,000 wealthiest households, those with taxable incomes of $200,000 a year or more after subtracting deductions, composed one-tenth of 1 percent of the total. This group alone was responsible for 14 percent of all income reported in 1994 and just under 20 percent in 2000. Curiously, the Internal Revenue Service in the 1990s shifted its attention from audits on the wealthy to investigations into the income tax returns of the working poor. In 1992, 1 in every 36 tax returns filed with gross incomes of $100,000 or more was audited; by 1999, this number had dropped to fewer than 1 in 150. There also has been a sharp decline in scrutiny of corporate tax returns. "The percentage of corporate returns that are audited," the *New York Times* reported at the end of 1999, "is expected to fall just above 1 per cent for the current fiscal year from just under 3 per cent in 1992."[11] By contrast, the agency has increased its audits of working Americans earning just enough to escape poverty.

From Vero Beach health care to growing income and wealth inequality to high-powered lobbying to efforts to target only some members of the eligible electorate, politics and public policy make a vital difference. The framework for health care is established by many pieces of national legislation. Lobbyists work hard to convince national politicians to legislate in ways that affect the shares of income and wealth of those who pay their bills. Citizens who lack a political voice—because they possess little money, fail to vote, or remain uninterested or uninformed—almost always end up below deck. The politics of power, and powerlessness, thus matters profoundly. The task we have set ourselves in this book is to ask how. To do so, we must begin with the manner in which capitalism and democracy intertwine.

---

[9] *New York Times*, June 13, 2000.

[10] *New York Times*, February 18, 2000.

[11] *New York Times*, December 15, 1999.

DEMOCRACY AND CAPITALISM

The metaphor of the *Titanic* breaks down at a crucial point. The United States is a democracy, the world's oldest. The *Titanic* was not. The captain of the *Titanic* was accountable to the owners who employed him; the passengers did not elect him. By contrast, all adult American citizens today (with the exception of prisoners and some ex-felons) have the right to vote. Democrats and Republicans, as well as a host of minor political parties, compete actively to win the support of the electorate. Organized groups lobby to defend the interests of their members. In few countries is there as much freedom to engage in political debate. Citizens can mobilize to make demands others find uncomfortable. Newspapers and television provide regular reports of government activities, debate the wisdom of public policies, and expose wrongdoing by high government officials, including presidents. Perhaps more than ever, the American political system is a global beacon. When young people, at great risk, fought for democracy in China in 1989, they raised a model of the Statue of Liberty in Beijing's main square. More political refugees fleeing oppressive conditions seek asylum in the United States than anywhere else. Compared to those in nondemocratic countries, public authorities are accessible and responsive. Their rule is not arbitrary. Citizens are protected by rights and by laws that prevent public authorities from acting in arbitrary ways. Government is accountable to the people, who are invited into the political process as participants. In the last resort, the people are sovereign.

Without citizen rights, lawful procedures, and institutions where social decisions can be made, no meaningful democracy is possible. Yet even if the rules of democracy are fully enforced (which is not the case, as we shall see), democracy cannot be judged only by its formal rules. What happens when we combine the democratic features of American government with the inequalities that were so rife aboard the *Titanic?* To what degree does the unequal distribution of wealth and life prospects between first-class passengers and those in steerage affect their ability to influence public policy? What shall we make of uneven voting; the massively unequal distribution of wealth, income, and life prospects; the disparate capacities of citizens to influence public policy; and the impact of monied interests on elections and the political process? More generally, to what extent is popular sovereignty possible in a society organized within a capitalist economic framework characterized by large inequalities of resources? In the pages that follow, we show both how American democracy is distorted by vast economic and political inequalities and how democratic institutions make it possible for ordinary citizens to effect change.

Our starting point is the special status possessed by the country's major business firms. Those who own the means to produce goods and services have disproportionate power not only because they have more money and the ability to secure access and influence, but also because governments must act in ways that promote the prosperity of the private economy, the country's great engine of wealth and employment. The well-being of everyone in terms of jobs and income depends on the investment decisions and the profits of private firms, and corporate executives decide the "nation's industrial technology, the pattern of work organization, location of industry, market structure, resource allocation, and, of course, executive compensation and status." As a result, as political economist Charles Lindblom shrewdly observed, "business leaders thus become a kind of public official and exercise what, on a broad view of their role, are public functions."[12] The leaders of the private economy cannot be ordered to invest or perform effectively. They have to be prompted and persuaded to do so. Public policies concerned with taxation, trade, and regulation, among other matters, are the instruments the government utilizes to achieve this goal.

Business thus commands a privileged position in public life. "In the eyes of government officials," Lindblom notes, "businessmen do not appear simply as the representatives of a special interest, as representatives of interest groups do. They appear as functionaries performing functions that government officials regard as indispensable."[13] The result is twofold. Business leaders in general, but especially the leaders of major corporate firms, have a double advantage in the country's democracy. With more money, they craft access to decision-makers and influence debates about public policy. Even more important, holding a key structural position—the economy will not work without their investment decisions and economic judgments—they become key partners of government in what might be called a corporate complex.

One consequence of this close relationship is that, although the Constitution provides ample protection for expressing the most unpopular opinions, many political views are, in fact, not adequately represented in public debate. Key issues of manifest public significance, such as what to produce (computer chips or potato chips?), where to produce it (in the United States or abroad?), how to produce it (repetitive assembly-line work or multitask jobs?), and what to do with the surplus generated by production (distribute it to shareholders in the form of higher dividends or to workers in the form of higher wages?), are decided privately, with little public discussion. The result is a public sphere more limited than the cacophony of debate might suggest. The principle of majority rule, the very centerpiece of representative democracy, thus applies to a confined range of questions.

It is impossible to understand the politics of power, and powerlessness, in the United States without attention to the way democracy and inequality intertwine to affect virtually every aspect of American life, including the place of race and gender, the quality of city neighborhoods, the provision of services, and political choices made by government officials and citizens. These

---

[12]Charles E. Lindblom, *Politics and Markets: The World's Political-Economic Systems* (New York: Basic Books, 1977), pp. 171, 172.

[13]Ibid., p. 175.

are the issues we place front and center in this critical introduction to American government. We wrote this book to highlight both the remarkable aspects of political democracy and the recurring problems that distort it, such as inequalities rooted in class, gender, and race that make the country's political system less democratic than it might be. We define democracy not only in terms of its formal rules, but also by the more demanding yardstick of whether all citizens have relatively equal chances to influence and control the making of decisions that affect them.

Although formal, legal, democratic procedures and institutions are essential to this standard of democracy, they do not guarantee it. Just as the quality of democracy may be compromised when power is concentrated in the hands of a single elite combining economic with political power, it also may be diminished when many key issues are not considered appropriate for public discussion and when public policies are influenced by social inequalities. To assess American democracy, we thus must grasp how political institutions operate, often with a bias that limits democracy itself. Understanding this politics of power and comprehending how political and social change within its ambit is possible through the use of democratic rights and procedures compose our central themes.

STANDARDS OF DEMOCRACY

What standards should we apply to assess American democracy in the face of these patterns and changes? In 1961, political scientist Robert Dahl published a brilliant and influential study of politics in New Haven, Connecticut. By commonly accepted standards, he argued, the city was a democracy, since virtually all its adult citizens were legally entitled to vote, their votes were honestly counted, and "two political parties contest elections, offer rival slates of candidates, and thus present the voters with at least some outward show of choice." Although the city's residents were legally equal at the ballot box, they were substantively unequal. Economic inequality in New Haven contrasted sharply with its formal political equality. Less than one-sixteenth of the taxpayers owned one-third of the city's property. In the wealthiest ward, one family out of four had an income three times the city average; the majority of the families in the poorest ward earned under $2,000 per year. Only 1 out of 30 adults in the poorest ward had attended college, as contrasted to nearly half of those in the richest ward.[14]

Is the combination of legal equality and class inequality democratic? Dahl put the question this way: "In a system where nearly every adult may vote but where knowledge, wealth, social position, access to officials, and other

---

[14]Robert Dahl, *Who Governs? Democracy and Power in an American City* (New Haven, Conn.: Yale University Press, 1961), pp. 3–4.

resources are unequally distributed, who actually governs? . . . How does a 'democratic' system work amid inequality of resources?"[15] He placed quotation marks around the term *democratic* because its meaning in this situation is unclear. Should a democratic system be measured only by legal standards of equality, such as fair and open election procedures, or should it be measured by substantive standards, according to the control and distribution of resources? What, in short, is the relationship of capitalism and democracy?

In his study of New Haven, Dahl argued that, rather than one elite group making political decisions, different groups determined policy in different issue areas, such as urban renewal, public education, and the nomination of candidates for office. In each area, however, there was a wide disparity between the ability of politically and economically powerful people and that of average citizens to make decisions. As a result of such disparities, Dahl noted, New Haven was "a long way from achieving the goal of political equality advocated by the philosophers of democracy and incorporated into the creed of democracy and equality practically every American professes to uphold." Nevertheless, he concluded that "New Haven is an example of a democratic system, warts and all,"[16] because it met key procedural tests denied to the majority of humankind. Not only could the city's citizens vote, but also they had a choice between candidates in elections that were conducted honestly and freely.

The United States clearly is a democracy, warts and all. We prefer, however, a higher standard both recognizing, and cherishing, the procedures essential to democracy and insisting on a reckoning with the extent, character, and effects of inequality. Broadly, from this perspective, we distinguish three aspects of democracy. The first stresses popular participation in decision making; the second, the representation of interests; and the third, the modification of advantage and the diminution of disadvantage.

Citizen participation in decision making traditionally has been regarded as a centerpiece of democracy. In the famous view of eighteenth-century French political theorist Jean Jacques Rousseau, when citizens exercise control by participating in making decisions, they subjectively feel like active citizens and thus develop loyalty to their society. In addition, by participating, citizens learn how to do so effectively. As social theorist Carole Pateman put it in her interpretation of Rousseau's *The Social Contract*, "the more the individual citizen participates, the better he is able to do so. . . . He learns to be a public as well as a private citizen."[17]

Direct participation is much easier to achieve in small groups and settings, like New England town meetings, than in society as a whole, especially one as large and complex as that of the United States. Hence the first

---

[15]Ibid., pp. 1, 3.

[16]Ibid., pp. 86, 311.

[17]Carole Pateman, *Participation and Democratic Theory* (Cambridge: Cambridge University Press, 1970), p. 25.

key standard of democracy with regard to participation concerns the ability and propensity of citizens to participate in politics via elections and also through various channels of influence like political parties, interest groups, and social movements.

A second standard concerns the concept of political representation. Since, as citizens, we cannot all participate simultaneously in making political decisions, especially in legislative bodies like Congress, we depend on having our preferences and interests literally "re-presented" by others inside the political process. There are four dimensions of representative democracy that provide us with an immediately useful yardstick against which to test present realities. The first is *procedures*. It is essential in a democracy that individuals and groups be able to make their views known and fairly select their leaders and public officials. In this regard, civil liberties and civil rights are essential. Freedom of speech, freedom of assembly, freedom of the press, and the absence of discriminatory barriers to participation are the basic hallmarks of procedural representation. When these procedural guarantees are suppressed, it is extraordinarily difficult for people to formulate and express their interests.

The electoral mechanisms available to citizens for selecting their representatives are also an important factor in procedural representation. How wide is the electorate? How is party competition organized? What, in short, are the rules of the electoral process? The discussion of procedures of representation cannot be limited to elections, however. Rather, we must consider the nature of all of the rules that determine whether an individual or group has access to the political system and whether that access is likely to have an effect on decision making. Are workers permitted to join unions? How are congressional committee chairs selected? How does an elected mayor exercise control over unelected city bureaucrats? To whom and how are a school system's personnel formally accountable? How are key foreign policy decision-makers chosen? How, if at all, are they formally held accountable? What are the procedures for representation in areas such as the space program, where expertise is available to only a few? Who selects the experts and to whom are they accountable? What are the procedures of leadership selection in interest groups (unions, farmers' organizations, professional associations)?

The list could easily be extended. The procedural dimension of representative democracy depends not only on equitable electoral procedures, but also more broadly on the mechanisms of access, influence, and accountability in government and in organizations that claim to represent the interests of their constituents. It is essential that the "rules of the game" ensure that the line that divides representatives and represented does not harden and that access to ruling positions is open to all and not limited by racial, class, sexual, or other forms of discrimination.

A second dimension of representation concerns *personnel*. Irrespective of the way in which representatives have been selected, those who govern may or may not accurately reflect the characteristics of class, race, ethnicity, sex, and geography of those they formally represent. This demographic representativeness of those who make political decisions is important not just to fulfill abstract numerical quotas of representation. Rather, the personnel dimension of representation is important because the more demographically representative a political system is, the more likely it is that the interests of the basic groups of the social structure will be adequately and substantively represented. It is highly unlikely, for example, that a group of business leaders will accurately represent the interests of workers or that the interests of blacks will be better represented by whites. Group members are much more likely than others to vigorously represent their own interests. It is not surprising, therefore, that workers in unions earn better wages than those whose wage levels are entrusted to the discretion of their employers; nor is it surprising that southern blacks have been treated more equitably by police since the passage of the Voting Rights Act of 1965 than they had been when they had to depend on the goodwill of the white community.

To represent group interests adequately, representatives also must satisfy the criterion of *responsiveness.* They must be aware of, and responsive to, their constituents' concerns. In this respect, ordinary citizens often find it much more difficult than the most privileged to achieve representation of their interests, since those with more resources tend to perceive and promote their interests more accurately and effectively than others do. Thus, representation concerns not only *who* rules, but also the *uses* to which power is put by those who rule. The first two dimensions of representation—procedures and personnel—refer to the first of these two issues. But the dimension of responsiveness asks how representatives see the interests of their constituents and how they act on behalf of these interests. To satisfy the requirements of representative democracy, those who formally represent the population must use the power conferred by their positions to promote the interests of the citizens they represent.

But even where the first three dimensions of representation are satisfied, political democracy cannot be said fully to be in operation. The last dimension that must be realized is *effectiveness*—the ability of representatives to produce the results they desire. A system cannot be democratically representative if effectiveness is distributed unequally among representatives. Thus, representative democracy can be said to have been achieved only when all four dimensions of representation are satisfied: when leaders are selected by regular procedures that are open to all people and all groups have relatively equal access to the political system; when representatives reflect the composition of the population as a whole; when they are conscious of and responsive to their constituents' interests; and when they can effectively act on behalf of those interests.

Unlike a purely procedural approach to democracy, this standard of representative democracy does not simply endorse present practices as democratic when they meet a procedural test. Rather, it allows us to measure the degree of representative democracy that exists. Conversely, it shows us how much needs to be done to achieve a fully representative democracy. It is not enough that all Americans enjoy freedom of expression when those who own the media can express their views to millions, while most Americans lack the means to disseminate their opinions. It is not enough that all Americans enjoy political rights when those who are wealthy can make lavish campaign contributions and can afford to run for office, while most Americans find such expenditures beyond their means. It is not enough that all Americans enjoy basic rights and civil liberties when the rich can use their wealth to take advantage of such rights in ways other citizens cannot conceivably afford, such as by gaining access to the best lawyers. Procedural rights are important, but inadequate. Substantive democracy takes us beyond these limits and is the best available standard to test the democratic content of existing political institutions and processes. It represents a demanding, yet realistic yardstick to measure the extent of democracy in America. Sadly, when we apply this yardstick, we find that America does not measure up in many key respects.

Nevertheless, even our more demanding standard by which to assess democracy is too limited. For it does not address the basic dilemma posed earlier in the chapter: in Dahl's words, "How does a 'democratic' system work amid inequality of resources?"

The answer to this question is that the two systems may coexist in varied and changing ways, as they have in much of the West for more than the past century. Even as this duality is a fact of life, however, its character and content have been, and continue to be, contested. It is clear that high degrees of inequality stand as a barrier to achievement of the fullest degree of democracy, of what we designate here as substantive democracy, a situation in which all citizens have relatively equal chances to influence the making of decisions that affect them. Indeed, the limits of procedural democracy help perpetuate the idea that what exists is democratic and therefore does not need reform. The more demanding, more critical standard of substantive democracy is based not only on the various political dimensions of representation, but also on social equality.

CHANGE, AND MORE CHANGE

The interplay of these dimensions of democracy with inequality raises pressing questions about political life not only in the United States and industrial societies in Western Europe, but also in Russia and other former Communist countries, in Latin American nations that have moved from authoritarian rule to democracy, and in postapartheid South Africa—indeed, in most of the entire world. Many of the most significant questions of social theory and political philosophy in the past century have concerned the tension inherent in societies that are simultaneously capitalist and democratic. Even when these issues are not openly on the agenda, the relationship between the inequalities generated by the routine operation of the market economy and the equal rights and responsibilities of citizens in a democratic polity shape major features of political life.

These questions are not new. The particular conditions in which they are being probed and explored in American politics, however, have changed enormously in the past two generations. Over the course of this book, we will grapple with a good many of these transformations linked to changes in technology and communications; to global movements of population, trade, and finance; to shifts in the climate of opinion; and to the end of the Cold War. These are massive alterations to the ground on which politics stands. Most of these trends transcend the scope of American politics, since they cross national boundaries.

Standing between these immense changes and what the government in the United States seeks to do about them is the contested terrain of the politics of power. Here—where policy ideas compete, political parties act, citizens mobilize, and politicians decide inside the country's major institutions of the presidency, Congress, and the courts—is where American politics takes place. As we look at these sites of politics, we discover that here, too, ground has been shifting under our feet.

Of the many trends we discuss below, four stand out at the start of the twenty-first century as especially important for their effects on the politics of power.

1. THE UNITED STATES IS THE LONE SUPERPOWER IN A MORE INTERCONNECTED WORLD. The end of the Cold War in 1989 left the United States as the only superpower in the world. Its military power is unrivaled. It has the most technologically sophisticated, best-equipped military in the world, bar none. Economically, it is the largest market in the world, home to more of the biggest, most profitable corporations than any other country. Its economic record of low inflation, high employment, and productivity growth is the envy of other countries, and the American dollar continues to be the international medium of exchange, the currency in which the rest of the world does business. Its military power and economic power combine to give the United States extraordinary influence in international affairs. There are few significant places or issues around the world where the United States does not project its power, from sending humanitarian aid to Africa to negotiating trade agreements with China, from mediating the Arab-Israeli conflict to sending troops to the Balkans, from signing defense treaties with Europe to fighting drug smugglers in South America.

Yet even as the United States outdistances all other rivals, the world has become a more complicated stage. There are now more countries with atomic weapons that can cause vast damage than ever before. Small conflicts now have a greater chance of escalating into larger ones that draw surrounding countries into the turmoil. And more of our economy is engaged in international trade, exporting or importing goods from abroad. As the globe has grown more interdependent, considering politics at home without reference to these factors has become less and less possible. Throughout American history, the country has been shaped by war and trade, but the scope and velocity of today's movements of people, ideas, money, goods, and weapons across borders are unprecedented.

2. MONEY HAS BECOME VASTLY MORE IMPORTANT TO POLITICAL DEBATE AND OUTCOMES. "Indisputably," one veteran Washington journalist writes, "the greatest change in Washington over the past twenty-five years . . . has been in the preoccupation with money. . . . The culture of money dominates Washington as never before."[18] In the 1996 presidential election year, $2.2 billion was spent to persuade voters to support federal candidates and parties. The effort to raise funds has accelerated since then. In 1999, Ken Parmelee, vice president of the National Rural Letter Carriers' Association, a Democratic-leaning union, noted that, just after the last election, "I just came back from New York on the train, and the first thing I had to do was go through about four inches of faxes and fund-raising invitations that had accumulated since I'd left a few days before." Only three months after the 1998 congressional elections, "no less than 75 members have already sent invitations." Likewise, Glenn B. LeMunyon, a Republican-oriented lobbyist who headed a political action committee, noted that "[t]he day after the election, I was getting invited to several fund-raisers, and that kind of caught me off-guard."[19] The total spent on all campaigns for federal offices in 2000 reached $3.5 billion, an increase of 66 percent from four years earlier.

The money chase has become a constant feature of political life for politicians and donors alike. Monied interests clearly have an advantage in securing access and influence on the outcomes of elections and the political process. Soft money spending, which political parties and groups can use to press their views on issues, exploded from $86 million in the 1992 presidential elections to $260 million in 1996 to some $750 million in 2000.

In 1998, Common Cause, a citizens group advocating campaign finance reform, released a report on the sources of soft money. Of the 50 corporate and union soft money donors giving from $1 to $6 million, 6 were union-based (the AFL-CIO plus 5 individual labor unions), and 44 were corporate givers. The largest donor was Philip Morris, whose cigarette business was under challenge. Other leading contributors included the Walt Disney Company, RJR Nabisco, Federal Express, Bell Atlantic, Atlantic Richfield, and AT&T. Virtually all the corporate donors supported both political parties, but with a decisive Republican tilt (of Philip Morris's $5.9 million, $4.9 million was given to Republican causes; in all, 60 percent of soft money went to Republicans and 40 percent to Democrats). The rate of spending increase has been dramatic. The transportation industry donated $1.4 million

---

[18]Elizabeth Drew, *The Corruption of American Politics: What Went Wrong and Why* (Woodstock, New York: Overlook Press, 2000), p. 61.

[19]*National Journal*, February 27, 1999.

in soft money to both parties in 1995 and $5.0 million in 1999. Banking contributions jumped in this period from $1.45 to $3.7 million. Gifts from the electronics industry moved from $1 to $4 million. Donations from organized labor increased from $2.2 to $6.9 million. Further, issue advocacy groups of all kinds spend enormous sums to affect the public's views of candidates. In each election season, the Christian Coalition spends millions of dollars to produce and distribute voter guides supporting issues that Republican candidates favor. Likewise, liberal groups like Handgun Control and the Sierra Club target ads to vulnerable Republican districts in order to elect their Democratic opponents.

Political spending matters. In 1996, in a race in California's Second District, which includes Santa Barbara and San Luis Obisbo, the incumbent freshman Republican, Andrea Seastrand, raised $1.2 million, while Walter Capps, her Democratic opponent who unseated her, raised $970,000. But at least $1 million, and by some estimates up to $4 million, was spent by advocacy groups in the district in order to put Capps over the top. Seastrand lost by 10,000 votes.[20] In 1996 and 1998, the candidates who outspent their opponents won in 96 percent of contested House races and 91 percent of contests for the Senate.

3. POLITICS HAS BECOME MORE POLARIZED IN TERMS DEFINED BY THE INTERPLAY OF PARTY, CLASS, RACE, AND REGION. Commenting on the differences between politics today and politics from a quarter of a century ago, one Washington insider told journalist Elizabeth Drew, "Everything is much more personal, much more partisan, and much more confrontational—and ideological."[21]

For a very long time, one of the standard truisms of American politics was that the country's political parties were broad tents, covering a wide array of groups and interests. During the period spanning the 1910s to the early 1960s, for example, the Democratic Party housed liberal and progressive politicians who supported unions, civil rights, and social equality. It also sheltered the country's leading segregationist politicians from the South, where Jim Crow defined the law of the land. The Republican Party, likewise, was quite heterogeneous, including internationally minded, relatively liberal members and isolationist, more conservative party leaders. Today, though there are quite a few conservative Democrats and some moderate to liberal Republicans, liberals are grouped nearly exclusively in the Democratic Party and conservatives, in the main, in the Republican. Compared to the situation that prevailed just two decades ago, liberal Republicans and conservative Democrats are endangered political species.

The most significant cause of these developments has been the partisan realignment of the South. While the South was once solidly Democratic in its

---

[20]Robert Dreyfuss, "Harder than Soft Money," *American Prospect,* January–February 1998, 30–37.

[21]Quoted in Drew, *Corruption of American Politics,* p. 35.

voting patterns, today it ordinarily votes Republican in national elections and, increasingly, in more local contests as well. The realignment of the South—a region whose population continues to grow—from a Democratic stronghold to a Republican fortification has created a strong pro-Republican bias in presidential elections and the prospect of a long-term run for a Republican House and Senate.[22] The South, in short, has become the main instrument for a strong tilt in national politics in a conservative direction.

4. *AMERICANS DEMONSTRATE A STRONGER BELIEF IN THE VIRTUE OF MARKETS.* The last two changes—the increased power of money in politics and the resurgence of the Republican Party due to partisan change in the South—are both cause and consequence of yet another large transformation in American politics. The election of Ronald Reagan as president in 1980 signaled the triumph of a more conservative ideology. Four years before the election, Robert Bartley, in charge of the editorial page of the politically conservative *Wall Street Journal,* observed that liberalism as an "establishment . . . has ordered our political and intellectual lives for the past two generations." He predicted that "over the next few years we will see an increasing challenge to the very heart of liberal . . . thinking."[23] The new ideology he and other conservative intellectuals advocated as a distinctly minority position at the time was thought to be well outside the political mainstream. It held that government should do less, not more; that government should be smaller, not bigger; that more decisions should be left to the marketplace, not to elected officials; that the welfare state hurts people, especially its clients, more than it helps; and that society should seek to provide more opportunity, not more equality. Just four years later President Reagan, drawing on the ideas of a new generation of conservative intellectuals promoting these ideas, began to implement this design for a more modest government and more reliance on the marketplace. As a result of the Reagan revolution, conservatives now set the main terms of public debate. Even moderate Democrats like President Bill Clinton have felt obliged to justify their policies by invoking the virtues of smaller government, balanced budgets, and the marketplace.

CONCLUSION

The tension between democracy and capitalism, the manner in which formal, legal equality and real, substantive inequality interact, is the subject of

---

[22]Walter Dean Burnham, "Realignment Lives: The 1994 Earthquake and Its Implications," in *The Clinton Presidency: First Appraisals,* ed. Colin Campbell and Bert A. Rockman (Chatham, N.J.: Chatham House, 1996), p. 363.

[23]Robert L. Bartley, "Liberalism 1976: A Conservative Critique" (paper prepared for the Conference on the Relevance of Liberalism, Columbia University Research Institute on International Change, New York, January 1976).

this book. Earlier we saw how the experience of the *Titanic* provides a useful, if incomplete, metaphor for the meaning of inequality in America. To conclude, we draw on *The Grapes of Wrath*, the Pulitzer Prize–winning novel by John Steinbeck that poignantly describes the hardships migrant workers experienced in the Depression of the 1930s. In an early scene in the 1940 movie version, Tom Joad, Sr., a poor dirt farmer in Oklahoma, shouts defiantly, "Don't come any closer," to the sheriff who has come to evict him from his land. Joad then levels his gun at the sheriff, a friend of his, and with determination in his eyes again warns him not to come any closer. But the sheriff, unimpressed by this threat, tells Joad that killing him would be senseless because the bank would simply send another man in his place. "Well, I'll kill him, too," says Joad. The sheriff replies that the bank would send another and then another, and Joad could not possibly kill them all. Still determined, Joad proclaims that he'll go into town and kill the banker if that is what he must do to protect his family and his farm. The sheriff explains that this won't do any good either because the bank in town owes money to a bank in Tulsa, which owes money to a bank in St. Louis, which owes money to a bank in Chicago. Joad retorts that he will go to Chicago to shoot the banker there. But his voice is now less sure and his eyes less steady. Still patient, the sheriff shakes his head in sympathy and sorrow that this poor farmer, his friend, still does not get it. He explains that the bank in Chicago owes money to a bank in New York and that bank probably owes money to five other banks, some not even in the country. Just a minute ago Joad was filled with righteous anger and determination. But now he stands on his porch broken and defeated, sensing himself in the grip of some powerful, impersonal, and unseen force that decides his fate. Where he once spoke with determination to the sheriff, he now lowers his gun and beseeches him for answers. "Who do I shoot?" he asks the sheriff plaintively, even desperately. "Who do I shoot?"

We hope this book will sufficiently inform readers about the politics of power so that they can learn who is responsible, grasp the forces that affect their lives, and thus avoid the sense of helplessness that defeated Tom Joad.

Here is our plan: In Chapters 2 and 3, we consider the close relationship between the national government and the country's capitalist economy. In Chapters 4 and 5, we turn to the main mechanisms, social movements and political parties, by which citizens are linked to the government and can press their demands. In Chapters 6, 7, and 8, we address the interplay of political economy and popular participation in the institutional settings of the presidency, Congress, and courts. In Chapters 9 and 10, we assess the public policy outcomes produced by this process in foreign policy and the welfare state. Finally, in our conclusion, Chapter 11, we ask about sources of persistence and change in American politics and society.

INTRODUCTION TO AMERICAN POLITICAL ECONOMY

A Tale of Two Cities

In the 1960s, Flint, Michigan, was a prosperous city. The town was built around automaker General Motors (GM), the world's largest corporation. GM employed over 40,000 workers in Flint, and the roads in town bore such names as Chevrolet Highway and Buick Freeway—an indication of Flint's connection to two of GM's automotive divisions. Work in the auto plants throughout the city was hard, but the union, the United Automobile Workers (UAW), helped to ensure that workers were rewarded for their efforts.[1] In 1969, average earnings in the county where Flint is located were roughly $2,000 above average earnings across the rest of Michigan and $7,000 higher than average income throughout the United States.[2] Unemployment was low and poverty was negligible. In one of the first quality-of-urban-life surveys ever conducted, Flint ranked 18th out of 66 medium-sized cities.[3]

Michael Moore, who grew up in Flint, left home in the 1970s to pursue a career in journalism and filmmaking. When he returned to Flint years later, he found a city on its knees. In 1980, Flint led the nation's cities in joblessness, with an unemployment rate of 20.7 percent, causing Moore to dub his hometown "the unemployment capital of America." While Flint's unemployment rate subsequently declined from that depressing level, it remained twice as high as the unemployment rate in Michigan throughout the 1980s. Nor did the picture improve much in the 1990s. In 1993, private-sector

---

[1]Changes in Flint can be analyzed by comparing Ronald Edsforth's *Class Conflict and Cultural Consensus: The Making of a Mass Consumer Society in Flint, Michigan* (New Brunswick, N.J.: Rutgers University Press, 1987), which covers the 1930s, with Ben Hamper's *Rivethead: Tales from the Assembly Line* (New York: Warner Books, 1991), which describes the lives of Flint's autoworkers in the 1980s, and with Steven P. Dandaneau's *A Town Abandoned: Flint, Michigan Confronts Deindustrialization* (Albany: State University of New York Press, 1996).

[2]Don Pemberton and Robert Schnorbus, *Genessee County and the Transformation of the Auto Industry* (Chicago: Federal Reserve Bank of Chicago, 1996).

[3]Ben-Chieh Liu, *Quality of Life Indicators in United States Metropolitan Areas: A Statistical Analysis* (New York: Praeger, 1976).

employment in the area was actually 6 percent below the 1986 level, even as employment grew in the rest of the state by 12 percent.[4]

As jobs disappeared, so did people. Flint's population fell from 190,000 in 1970 to 140,000 in 1990, a decline of over 25 percent in just 20 years. Depopulation left its mark on Flint, as once-proud, stable neighborhoods were defaced by abandoned buildings and dilapidated housing. Public services declined.[5] Crime skyrocketed.[6] Earnings fell. By 1990, more than a quarter of the families in Flint had income levels below the poverty line. Aggregate real earnings in the area slumped 9 percent between 1969 and 1993, as the high-wage industrial jobs that disappeared when auto plants shut down were replaced by low-paying service-sector work. With considerable understatement, a 1996 Federal Reserve Bank of Chicago study reported, "From a peak in 1977 to 1993, average real wage gains per job in Genessee [the county in which Flint is located] fell by $9,500 (about 28%), a significant decline in a community's standard of living over a six year period."[7]

Efforts to revive the city failed. A luxury hotel opened in 1979, but declared bankruptcy in 1991. An $80 million theme park extolling the virtues of automobiles opened in 1984, but filed for bankruptcy within two years. Two major retail projects that were supposed to spark Flint's renewal also failed. All these indignities—the poverty, the unemployment, the poor business climate, the crime, and the urban decay—combined to earn Flint last place in *Money Magazine*'s 1987 quality-of-urban-life survey of 300 cities.[8]

Flint's decline began when GM decided to disinvest, closing factories and moving product lines out of the city. GM closed plants in Flint not out of malevolence, but because its share of the U.S. auto market declined from 45.8 percent in 1980 to under 30 percent by 2000. GM lost market share because it responded too late to the challenge of the more efficient cars imported from Japan, experienced turmoil within the ranks of its board of directors, had the worst labor relations of any of the Big Three car companies, had greater administrative overhead than its competitors, and pursued an expensive and failed strategy of replacing workers with robots. GM employees were forced to absorb the costs of GM's strategic mistakes. In 1983, GM merged its Buick and Fisher Body divisions, reducing employment in the two plants by 3,600 people.[9] In 1986, GM announced it was closing 11 plants

---

[4]Pemberton and Schnorbus, *Genessee County and the Transformation of the Auto Industry*, p. 3.

[5]*New York Times*, October 26, 1980.

[6]See *Crime in the United States* (Washington, D.C.: U.S. Department of Justice, 1971), p. 1981, for 1970 crime statistics, and *State, Metropolitan Area Data Book* (Washington, D.C.: Department of Commerce, 1989) for 1988 crime statistics.

[7]Pemberton and Schnorbus, *Genessee County and the Transformation of the Auto Industry*, p. 9.

[8]George F. Lord and Albert C. Price, "Growth Ideology in a Period of Decline: Deindustrialization and Restructuring, Flint Style," *Social Problems* 39, no. 2 (May 1992): 155–69.

[9]*New York Times*, January 20, 1983.

nationwide, affecting 29,000 workers. Flint was hit harder by this new round of plant shutdowns. Two of the plants slated for closure, employing over 7,000 workers, were located in Flint.[10]

But Flint's troubles were far from over. In 1987, GM shuttered Fisher Body plants 1 and 2, which had a special place in labor history. Exactly 50 years earlier, in 1937, during the height of the Great Depression, which had thrown millions out of work, autoworkers shut down their machines and occupied the Fisher Body plants to force GM to accept their right to join the fledgling UAW. This historic sit-down strike contributed to the rise of industrial unionism and the Congress of Industrial Organizations (CIO) in the 1930s.[11] But in 1987, the plants were closed, and another 3,000 workers were unemployed.[12] By the end of the decade, Flint had lost 30,000 manufacturing jobs, over 20,000 of them attributable to GM plant closings alone. The 1990s brought Flint no relief from plant closures. As plants shut down, Flint collapsed around them.

When Michael Moore decided to make a film about Flint, he went looking for the person whose decisions were key in producing the tragedy affecting his beloved hometown. He did not go looking for the mayor of Flint or the city council. Nor did he go looking for the governor of Michigan or any other public official. Instead, he went looking for Roger Smith, the Chairman and Chief Executive Officer of General Motors. Moore believed that decisions made by General Motors had more consequences for the city than any action taken by any public official. The rest is history: *Roger & Me*, released in 1990, is the most popular documentary ever distributed and provides a graphic and tragicomic description of how Flint's dependence on its corporate sponsor led to the city's ruin.

Roger & Me describes Moore's futile attempt to impress on Roger Smith the tragic consequences his company's policies had for Flint. The movie ends with Roger Smith presiding at a lavish Christmas celebration in Detroit, reminding the global "General Motors family" of the "individual worth of each human being." While Roger Smith is praising the dignity of each individual, Moore is back in Flint filming the local sheriff as he evicts yet another family from its home during the holiday season.[13]

Roger Smith's decision to close plants in Flint was not the result of callousness or venality on his part. GM's decisions were dictated more by the imperatives of profit seeking in a capitalist economy than by the moral

[10]*New York Times*, November 8, 1986.

[11]A dramatic account of the sit-down strike can be found in Sidney Fine, *Sit-Down: The General Motors Strike of 1936–37* (Ann Arbor: University of Michigan Press, 1969).

[12]*New York Times*, January 2, 1987.

[13]Ronald Edsforth, "Review of Roger and Me," *American Historical Review* 96 (October 1991): 1145–47.

character of management.[14] The costs GM's decisions imposed on Flint were invisible from the perspective of GM's balance sheet. They were an unfortunate, unintended by-product of management's attempt to maximize profits.

Because Flint's decline is so extreme, it is atypical of economic change in most communities. However, Flint's history outlines in stark relief a key feature of American politics. To illustrate that political action can make a difference, we highlight an opposite development in another American city.

A year after Flint finished dead last in a quality-of-urban-life survey, Burlington, Vermont, was voted "The Most Livable City in America" in the under-100,000 population category by the U.S. Conference of Mayors. While Flint succumbed to the power of General Motors, Burlington, under the direction of Mayor Bernie Sanders, an avowed socialist, sponsored reforms, sometimes over the objections of business, that significantly improved the quality of city life and provided additional services to residents most in need.

Sanders was first elected mayor of Burlington by ten votes in 1981 in a shocking upset. He ran a grassroots campaign as an independent, defeating a Democratic Party machine that had ruled Burlington for over three decades. Sanders polled very well among working-class and liberal voters— the groups that form the constituency of major Socialist parties in Western Europe.[15]

Sanders tried to shape economic reform in a way that would be of greatest benefit to the community. For example, he promoted waterfront development that included parks, fishing piers, and restaurants that could be used by all city residents, as opposed to luxury condominiums available only to the rich.

Sanders demonstrated the possibilities of political power in other areas as well. Under the Sanders administration, Burlington became the first municipality in the United States to fund a community land trust, designed to make home ownership more affordable for low- and middle-income people.[16] The Sanders administration also shifted some of the tax burden from low- and middle-income residents by finding alternatives to the property

---

[14]Capitalism requires people to act not immorally, but amorally. That is, people respond to the market without regard for the moral consequences of their actions. This point was expressed best in the movie *You've Got Mail,* when Tom Hanks, whose new superstore threatens to bankrupt Meg Ryan's small, independent bookstore, tells her, "It's not personal, it's business." The same applies to GM: It argued that its decision to close plants in Flint was dictated by the market. It was business, not personal. But to Meg Ryan in the movie, it was very personal, not just business, whether she lost her store, just as it was very personal, not just business, to the workers in Flint whether they lost their jobs.

[15]Tom W. Rice, "Who Votes for a Socialist Mayor?: The Case of Burlington, Vermont," *Polity* 17 (Summer 1985): 795–805.

[16]Essentially, a land trust separates the cost of land, which can be as much as 25 percent of the purchase price for a home, from the cost of buying a home.

tax. In addition, his administration sponsored an ambitious program of concerts, festivals, and exhibits that increased local appreciation of the arts, reached new audiences, and energized the local arts community.

All these initiatives sparked a new interest in politics and civic affairs in Burlington. Voter interest and turnout in municipal elections increased, and the Progressive Coalition behind Sanders's candidacy broke the mold of two-party politics in the city. Electoral options in Burlington were no longer defined by a choice between Democrats and Republicans, but by a choice between the Progressive Coalition, identified with Sanders's supporters, and the Conservative Coalition, which was a fusion of the Democratic and Republican parties.

One observer claimed, "In Burlington, a strong argument can be made that poor and working people have been the prime beneficiaries" of the Sanders administration.[17] But Sanders was constrained by the larger framework of the American political economy.[18] The Vermont state government blocked many of Sanders's proposals that required its approval. The Burlington Board of Aldermen and the local bureaucracy tried to thwart his agenda. The courts also blocked reform at times. And Sanders's need to obtain the cooperation of the local business community further limited the scope of possibilities.

However, Sanders's administration did reveal that a determined, progressive coalition could make a difference. The city was enriched culturally, civic involvement increased, working-class neighborhoods received more services at the same time that their share of the local tax burden was reduced, and economic development was tempered by broader social concerns.

This tale of two cities is quite revealing. The manner in which GM held the fate of Flint in its hands illuminates basic features of capitalist democracy and how power is exercised in the United States. GM's decisions to disinvest from Flint not only tragically affected the workers who were laid off, but also harmed the entire community. But Burlington's experience indicates that politics can make a difference. Sanders and the voters who supported him disrupted politics as usual in Burlington. Certainly, the courts, the federal structure of government, the system of checks and balances, and the power of business set limits as to how far reform could go. Still the Progressive Coalition was able, within these constraints, to overturn the two-party system, redirect city services to working-class residents, and politicize and enrich the local community.[19]

---

[17]Steven Soifer, *The Socialist Mayor: Bernard Sanders in Burlington, Vermont* (New York: Bergin & Garvey, 1991), p. 60.

[18]By political economy, we mean the interaction between the political and economic arenas. Chapter 2 highlights how the organization of a capitalist political economy has an important impact on politics; chapter 3 focuses more squarely on the relationship of the state to the American economy.

[19]This analysis of Mayor Sanders's administration in Burlington draws heavily on Soifer, *The Socialist Mayor*, which is critically supportive of Sanders. For a bit less sympathetic treatment of the Sanders administration from a left perspective, see W. J. Conroy, *Challenging the Boundaries of Reform: Socialism in Burlington* (Philadelphia: Temple University Press, 1990).

The lesson that emerges from this tale of two cities is that, to understand how power is distributed in the United States, we need to understand not only how the government operates, but also who controls the economy— which means focusing front and center on the power of large corporations. This is the task of Chapter 2. We analyze the relationship of the economy to the government in Chapter 3.

2

GLOBAL CAPITALISM
AND AMERICAN POLITICS

INTRODUCTION

Because large corporations exercise power over workers and communities, we suggest that our economic system—that is, capitalism—can be considered a system of *private government*. It is *private* in the sense that those who own and control capital—the financial resources and factories, machines, and raw materials used to produce commodities for sale—are not elected by the public through democratic procedures. Key economic decisions, notably what, where, and how to produce, are made privately, without public debate. However, this system resembles *government* in the sense that corporate policies have profound consequences for all citizens. More than almost any action taken by government, people's lives and their communities are affected greatly by the decisions that private corporations make.

Corporations are far from all-powerful. They compete with each other and are influenced by the actions of a variety of private and public groups, including their employees, consumers, and the state. (By state, we mean government in its broadest sense, including the president and the executive branch, Congress, the judicial system, and the armed forces.) Further, we are not suggesting that market-based production, in which production is privately organized, does not provide important benefits, such as material abundance. But rather than dwell on the features that are so widely known and praised, we focus on the less discussed tendencies for privately organized production to generate extensive inequalities and for the private government of capitalism to limit and distort democratic processes and government policies.[1]

[1]For a penetrating critique of markets and their inadequacies, see Robert Kuttner, *Everything for Sale: The Virtues and Limits of Markets* (New York: Knopf, 1997).

THE SYSTEM OF CAPITALISM

Capitalism is commonly defined as a system in which production is privately controlled and carried on for sale or profit rather than directly for consumption and use. Those who own and control capital set the process in motion by hiring workers to carry out the actual work. Their aim in doing so is to make a profit, which can be used for further investment and the accumulation of additional profits. Firms compete with each other to expand in value, to grow. If they do not, they may become uncompetitive, be the target of a hostile takeover, or go out of business.

In capitalist economies, most people earn their living by going to work for employers who own and control the means of production. Others, constituting a much smaller proportion of the population, own and run small businesses. Unless they do, they must hire themselves out to employers, as is the case with the vast majority of Americans. This participation in the labor market is a form of freedom. Unlike feudalism, where peasants were tied to a lord's domain, workers are able to contract for work with any employer. But this freedom obscures a lack of alternatives. Without joining the labor market, hiring themselves out to employers, workers have no way to sustain themselves. Workers cannot earn the necessities of life except through wage labor.

Not only is wage labor the characteristic form that labor takes within a capitalist society, but also relations within the workplace and the economy as a whole are highly undemocratic. Within the workplace, employers have the right to hire and fire, to set wages and salaries, to determine what jobs workers do, and to tell them how to do it. They even have the right to dictate when workers can go to the bathroom![2] Within the entire economy, those who own and control companies decide what to produce, where to produce it, and how to produce it. It is often claimed that this authoritarian situation is the price that must be paid to achieve maximum efficiency. However, there is compelling evidence that more democratic relations in the workplace not only provide benefits to workers, but also contribute to productivity.[3]

The long-run consequence of this situation, in which workers produce commodities at capitalists' direction, is a society whose core sector is exploitative and undemocratic. This harsh fact is rarely noted. It is only at unusual moments, like the demise of Flint, which Michael Moore captured so vividly in *Roger & Me*, that the reality of capitalism becomes transparent and exposed. Much of the time, it appears to most people as the only possible way to organize an economy and the product of free choice.

---

[2]Marc Linder and Ingrid Nygaard, *Void Where Prohibited: Rest Breaks and the Right to Urinate on Company Time* (Ithaca, N.Y.: Cornell University Press, 1998).

[3]See, for example, Samuel Bowles, Herbert Gintis, and Bo Gustafsson, eds., *Markets and Democracy: Participation, Accountability and Efficiency* (New York: Cambridge University Press, 1993); Jon Elster and Karl Ove Moene, eds., *Alternatives to Capitalism* (Cambridge: Cambridge University Press, 1989); and Robert B. Reich, *The Work of Nations: Preparing Ourselves for 21st Century Capitalism* (New York: Vintage Books, 1992), pt. 3.

GM workers in Flint line up to file unemployment claims at their union local.

So long as capitalism as a system of production remains in place, capitalists will possess extraordinary influence over the entire political economy. The day-to-day strategic decisions that capitalists make affect the fate of local communities like Flint, entire regions, and the whole nation. Such strategic decisions include whether to invest, where to invest, what to invest in, and how to organize production. These decisions, which have far-reaching consequences for society, are the prerogative of capitalists because they own and control the means of production. A fuller picture of capitalism as a system of private government can be gained by analyzing the rights conferred on capitalists by their control over capital.

WHETHER TO INVEST

Investment decisions by giant corporations determine the level of production and are made on the basis of what promises to fetch the highest profit. Whole communities can be affected by capitalist investment decisions, as Flint discovered to its dismay when GM decided to disinvest from the city. When investment lags, then production lags, wages stagnate, and workers are unable to find jobs. When investment booms, then production booms, jobs are plentiful, and wages rise as employers compete for workers.

A profoundly important consequence of this process is that citizens tend to identify their individual welfare with the welfare of capitalism. This helps explain the widespread support for capitalism in the United States. In addition to the intensive propaganda on behalf of capitalism generated by schools, businesses, political parties, the media, and other institutions, there is a rational basis for pro-capitalist beliefs. Capitalism is the goose that lays the golden eggs, on which the livelihood of workers depends. Society's dependence on business to generate jobs and prosperity makes plausible the arguments of business representatives that their specific interests are the interests of the wider society; that high profits for business are necessary for the rest of society to enjoy higher growth, less inflation, and more jobs. This situation creates a terrible paradox for workers. Their jobs depend on the profitability of their firm, which, perversely, depends on workers' own exploitation. As one autoworker wrote to his union with some irony: "Believe me—we know how hard it is to make a profit—we spend 50 to 60 hours a week at the company, working to make a profit for our employers."[4] Workers in Flint recognized the awful horns of this dilemma when, in the midst of the crisis afflicting them, they joked in an often repeated phrase, "The only thing worse than working for General Motors is not working for General Motors."

This does not mean that citizens do not perceive conflicts between their interests and those of the companies where they are employed. Again, workers in Flint hardly needed to be reminded of this as GM sacrificed their jobs because of its declining competitive position. Nor does widespread support for capitalism mean that workers and other citizens do not struggle against specific features of capitalist domination. Environmental activists protest industrial pollution and demand stricter environmental controls on business. Voters elect candidates who stretch the boundaries of reform and oppose corporate power. Tenants organize rent strikes demanding that landlords maintain their buildings. Women demand an end to sexual discrimination inside and outside the workplace, and unions seek to improve working conditions, which employers resist fiercely.

In fact, Americans tend to support capitalist values, such as individualism and minimum state interference, mostly in the abstract. When questioned as to their support for specific government programs to assist the poor, help the sick, and feed the hungry, Americans tend to express broad approval for such activities. Political scientist Elizabeth Sanders writes that, "whatever their reservations about government power," non-elite Americans "have shared a powerful belief in community, collective action, and the government's responsibility to remedy market 'defects.'"[5] Even during the heyday of conservatism in the 1980s, when Republican presidents were regularly denouncing the sins of big government, the public continued to support social programs by large and stable majorities.[6] Similarly, when

---

[4]Kim Moody, *Workers in a Lean World: Unions in the International Economy* (New York: Verso Press, 1999), p. 12.

[5]Elizabeth Sanders, *Roots of Reform: Farmers, Workers, and the American State, 1877–1917* (Chicago: University of Chicago Press, 1999), p. 387.

[6]Thomas Ferguson and Joel Rogers, "The Myth of America's Turn to the Right," *Atlantic Magazine*, May 1986, 43–53.

President George W. Bush denounced environmental regulation as costly and unnecessary in 2001, there was a firestorm of protest.

WHERE TO INVEST

In a capitalist system, corporate leaders are free to decide where to locate their facilities. These decisions are made on the basis of which location will minimize production costs and maximize sales. Such factors as proximity to suppliers, raw materials, and markets are taken into account when corporations consider where to invest. Corporations also take into account whether the local community is sympathetic to their needs. States and local governments compete with each other in order to attract investment and the jobs it brings. They fear that, if they do not prostitute themselves in an attempt to lure capital, then another state or community will. States and local communities woo business with special tax incentives, loans, anti-union laws, and weak environmental regulations.[7] Alabama holds what might be the dubious record of offering $300 million in incentives to attract a small Mercedes car factory that would employ only 1,500 people, in effect paying $200,000 for each job. State leaders in Oregon were so embarrassed at the financial incentives they offered Nucor Corp. to invest in their state that they began to reconsider the whole strategy of pursuing firms in this manner.[8]

In the end, the financial incentives offered by local governments are rarely the deciding factor in plant location decisions. Indeed, rather than contributing to a region's economy, such incentives as low tax rates and abatements on property taxes may actually retard it. Tax revenue lost due to such incentives offered to corporations could leave a community without enough money to support basic services and amenities that make an area attractive. Moreover, some corporations take the concessions and then cut their workforce or relocate anyway. After an exhaustive analysis of the effect these incentives have on plant location decisions, political scientist Peter Eisinger concluded, "The positive effects of such incentives have not been established incontrovertibly, and there are even potentially perverse effects."[9]

Corporations also consider the characteristics of the local workforce when they decide where to invest. Companies search for areas where workers will accept low wages, are not militant, or are unlikely to join labor unions that might challenge management. Corporations are not above putting workers into competition with each other to see who could offer business the

---

[7]This section draws heavily from Peter Eisinger, *The Rise of the Entrepreneurial State: State and Local Economic Development Policy in the United States* (Madison: University of Wisconsin Press, 1988), pp. 128–73. See also James C. Cobb, *The Selling of the South: The Southern Crusade for Industrial Development, 1936–1980* (Baton Rouge: Louisiana State University Press, 1982), pp. 229–54.

[8]*Wall Street Journal*, October 1, 1999.

[9]Eisinger, *Rise of the Entrepreneurial State*, p. 224.

most concessions before they decide where to invest, in the same way they play one state off against another. In 1991, GM announced it would close its assembly plant in either Ypsilanti, Michigan, or Arlington, Texas. GM chose to close the Ypsilanti assembly plant even though it had a $74 million cost advantage over the Arlington site. The Ypsilanti workforce had a reputation for militance and offered fewer work-rule concessions. In contrast, the union local in Arlington promised GM—in defiance of the United Auto Workers' (UAW's) national leadership—that it would run three daily shifts, instead of the normal two, if the company kept the plant open.[10] (The result was night work for the plant's employees.)

Finally, corporations may choose to invest abroad, beyond American borders. For example, from 1920 through 1950, the textile industry moved from New England to the South, which offered special tax incentives, lower wages, and an anti-union climate to firms that relocated. But in the 1960s and 1970s, those same firms left the South to invest in Third World countries that offered still lower wages, more subsidies, and an even more anti-union climate than the southern states in the United States could offer.

WHAT TO INVEST IN

Investment decisions by giant corporations also determine the kinds of goods available in society. Companies decide whether to develop a "new, improved" deodorant or a vaccine for a rare disease; they decide whether to invest in improving a product or marketing the old one more aggressively; they decide whether to produce guns or butter. Corporations make these decisions according to what is most profitable to produce and not what society needs, and these decisions shape decisively the consumption patterns of society.

Corporate investment may take the form of what former Secretary of Labor Robert Reich calls "paper entrepreneurialism." This form of investment does "not create wealth, but merely rearranges industrial assets."[11] A prime example of paper entrepreneurialism is the boom in mergers and acquisitions.[12] While mergers and acquisitions increase corporate earnings and produce mega-corporations with even greater power, they also usually increase corporate debt and lead to layoffs. Such strategic decisions are made by corporate executives who are accountable solely to the corporation's investors, not to the workers and communities who experience the unemployment and plant closings their decisions create.

---

[10]*New York Times*, September 7, 1992.

[11]Robert B. Reich, *The Next American Frontier* (New York: Times Books, 1983), p. 141.

[12]Incisive, biting exposés of Wall Street's frenzied dealings appear in Bryan Burrough and John Helyar's *Barbarians at the Gate: The Fall of RJR Nabisco* (New York: Harper & Row, 1990), and Tom Wolfe's wicked novel, *The Bonfire of the Vanities* (New York: Farrar, Straus & Giroux, 1987).

Generic and brand-name drugs.

The pharmaceutical industry is a prime example of how production deci-sions are made with corporate profits and not the public interest in mind. Drug companies use patents to protect profitable brand-name drugs and prevent the marketing of low-cost generic equivalents. In a case that came to light in 2000, Abbott Laboratories sued to prevent Zenith Goldline Pharma-ceuticals from marketing a generic version of Abbott's Hytrin, a drug used to treat high blood pressure and enlarged prostates. The average monthly dose of Hytrin costs $53, while the generic version sold for only $23. Zenith's lawyer protested that "Abbott makes a million dollars a day for every day it keeps us off the market."[13]

Abbott soon devised a more effective way than a lawsuit to prevent Zenith from competing. Abbott offered to pay Zenith up to $2 million a month if Zenith would agree *not* to market a low-cost generic alternative to Hytrin! On the day that Abbott announced the agreement with Zenith, its stock rose 5 percent. As the investigative reporters who broke the story wrote, "The good news for Wall Street was bad news for Main Street, where customers without health insurance were paying full freight for Hytrin."[14] As for the reasons why Americans pay more for drugs than con-sumers in other countries, the reporters noted, "The United States is the last free market for pharmaceuticals: other developed nations control drug prices, as in Japan, Canada, and France, or drug company profits, as in England. So Americans typically pay higher prices for new medications

---

[13]Quoted in *New York Times*, July 23, 2000.
[14]Ibid.

than people anywhere else in the developed world."[15] Pharmaceutical companies often defend high prices and profit margins on the grounds that they must spend vast sums to develop and test new drugs. However, a Kaiser Family Foundation study found that drug companies spend three times more on marketing and administrative expenses than they do on research and development.

How Production Is Organized

In a capitalist society, the workplace is not organized democratically. Private managers decide who will be hired, fired, and promoted; what kind of technology will be utilized; and how the process of production will be organized. Workers are paid to take orders, not take initiative. The rights of citizens end at the factory gate and the office door. Once workers step through those portals, they are at the disposal of management. Profits depend, in part, on how efficiently—from the standpoint of the capitalist—labor can be put to work. But capitalists have a difficult time translating their formal control over the labor process into actual control of the shop floor or office. While management views the issue of the pace of work through the lens of productivity and production costs, workers perceive it as an issue of health and endurance. Consequently, workers have devised various strategies to resist capitalist efforts to maximize how long and how hard they work.

Here is where the political sphere of democracy and the private sphere of the market connect—and often collide. For example, workers have used their political power as citizens to limit the length of the workday and to press for the passage of laws that require employers to meet certain health and safety standards at work. Workers have also limited the power that capitalists exercise over the labor process through collective bargaining agreements that employers sign with unions who represent workers. Such agreements often include work rules that set some limits to management's otherwise unlimited power on the shop floor.[16] Workers have also used informal means to limit the power that employers exercise over the process of production. Workers often conspire among themselves to restrict output by setting their own standard of what constitutes a fair day's work, as opposed to what management might consider an appropriate level of effort.[17]

---

[15]Ibid.

[16]For a powerful account that describes the struggle over work rules in two textile plants, see Daniel J. Clark, *Like Night and Day: Unionization in a Southern Mill Town* (Chapel Hill: University of North Carolina Press, 1996).

[17]The literature on this is fascinating and important. See, for example, the essays in David Montgomery, *Workers' Control in America* (New York: Cambridge University Press, 1979); Michael Buroway, *Manufacturing Consent: Change in the Labor Process Under Monopoly Capitalism* (Chicago: University of Chicago Press, 1979); and Donald Roy, "Quota Restriction and Goldbricking in a Machine Shop," *American Journal of Sociology* 57 (1952),: 427–42.

THE MOBILIZATION OF BIAS

Respect for the rights of private property gives corporations who own and control capital significant power over the lives of ordinary citizens. Their decisions on what level of investment to make, where to invest, what to invest in, and how to organize production affect the entire society. As political economist Charles Lindblom pointed out, "Because public functions in the market [capitalist] system rest in the hands of businessmen, it follows that jobs, prices, production, growth, the standard of living, and the economic security of everyone all rest in their hands."[18] Capitalist control over these decisions gives business a unique advantage in the political arena. Elected officials are dependent on business to invest, create jobs, and increase the standard of living. In a capitalist system, where production is privately organized, these decisions are made by those who own and control the means of production. And capitalists will do the things society needs them to do only if they can make a profit.

Elected officials, therefore, have an enormous stake in ensuring that the needs of business are satisfied. They have an incentive to create conditions under which business can make a profit so that business will continue to invest and generate employment. If business does not do those things—if it stops investing, it fails to generate jobs, and a recession or depression occurs—politicians risk being held responsible and voted out of office. Elected officials' political careers are, therefore, dependent on continued prosperity, which is heavily influenced by business decisions. Moreover, prosperity means more revenue, more tax money flowing into government coffers, to pay for programs that might earn politicians credit with voters. Consequently, it is in politicians' self-interest to offer inducements to businesses, to anticipate and respond positively to businesses' political demands, in order "to motivate them to provide jobs and perform their other functions," according to Lindblom.[19]

The special political advantage business enjoys by virtue of its economic power can be described by the term coined by political scientist E. E. Schattschneider, "the mobilization of bias." Political scientists Peter Bachrach and Morton S. Baratz have argued that a mobilization of bias occurs when "the rules of the game" tend to favor one group over another. Their point is not that the resources groups have in the struggle over policy may be unequal—that may be true, too!—but that the playing field may unfairly favor one group over all others. How the game is set up may have as much to do with the outcome as the relative strengths of the players on the field. Bachrach and Baratz describe the mobilization of bias as "the second face of

---

[18]Charles Lindblom, *Politics and Markets: The World's Political-Economic Systems* (New York: Basic Books, 1977), p. 172.

[19]Charles Lindblom, "The Market as Prison," *Journal of Politics* 44 (1982): 327.

power," in which power operates behind the scenes, in contrast to "the first face of power," in which power is open and observable.[20]

We suggest that our economic and political system contains a mobilization of bias in favor of business that is built into the political framework and limits the extent of American democracy. That is, even before the first vote is cast, the first campaign contribution is made, or the first lobbyist contacts a member of Congress, business starts with an advantage in the political arena based on its control over the means of production. Take an important illustration of how the mobilization of bias operates: Presidents constantly look over their shoulder to see how their proposals register with the stock and bond markets. They worry that, if investors oppose their policies, these investors will pull their money out of the market, causing stock and bond prices to fall. Business confidence will sink and companies will not invest, with consequences that are all too reminiscent of what happened to Flint, Michigan, in the 1980s.

James Carville, Bill Clinton's campaign strategist in 1992, acknowledged this mobilization of bias during the presidential campaign that year. "The damned bond market," he said with some surprise. "Who the hell knew it was so powerful? If it gets nervous, everybody has to calm it down. If I'm ever reincarnated, I want to come back as the bond market. Then everybody will be afraid of me and have to do what I say."[21]

Democratic presidents are not the only ones susceptible to the mobilization of bias. It affects officeholders from every party, regardless of their ideology. Newt Gingrich, the conservative Republican Speaker of the House from 1994 to 1999, once asked a room full of corporate executives "under what circumstances you'd put the next thousand high value-added jobs in the U.S. What do we need to do to regulation, taxation, litigation, education, welfare, the structure of the bureaucracy? You tell us how to make this the best place on the planet to invest."[22] It is hard to find the mobilization of bias expressed better than in Gingrich's appeal to business leaders.

The fact that business begins with a special political advantage does not guarantee that government policy will always reflect capitalist interests. Just because business begins the race with a head start does not mean it will reach the finish line first. Other groups may press their claims and overcome the advantage of business. As Neil J. Mitchell explains, business must engage in policy struggles characterized by unreliable politicians, "a shifting set of adversaries, and volatile public preferences."[23] Despite its advantages,

[20]Peter Bachrach and Morton S. Baratz, *Power and Poverty: Theory and Practice* (New York: Oxford University Press, 1970). For a brilliant discussion of the different dimensions of power, see John Gaventa, *Power and Powerlessness: Quiescence and Rebellion in an Appalachian Valley* (Urbana: University of Illinois Press, 1980), pp. 1–33.

[21]*New York Times*, September 15, 1996.

[22]Gingrich is quoted in E. J. Dionne, *They Only Look Dead: Why Progressives Will Dominate the Next Political Era* (New York: Simon & Schuster, 1996), p. 206.

[23]Neil J. Mitchell, *The Conspicuous Corporation: Business, Public Policy and Representative Democracy* (Ann Arbor: University of Michigan Press, 1997), p. 167.

business's success in the policy struggle is highly contingent and no sure thing. The mobilization of bias in favor of business is not constant across the entire agenda of issues or equally powerful at all times.

Public officials enjoy considerable room to maneuver despite the presence of a mobilization of bias for two reasons.[24] First, capitalists have different political interests and continually struggle with each other. Capital or business is rarely united and cohesive. On many issues, business firms have different interests depending on the region in which they are based, whether they produce for local or international markets, whether they are capital- or labor-intensive, and so on. Political struggles among different business groupings have occurred in American history from the time slaveholders and manufacturers fought over the tariff in the 1800s to more contemporary struggles over trade policy between domestic producers and export-oriented firms. The capitalist class is riven with political conflicts. These conflicts enable elected officials to play one business interest off against another and give them more latitude to respond to other interests. For example, journalists Jeffrey H. Birnbaum and Alan S. Murray attribute the passage of the 1986 Tax Reform Act, which included the largest corporate tax increase in history, to conflicts within the business community. In the 1990s, big business was intensely divided over President Clinton's attempt to reform health care. Some corporations, at least initially, saw Clinton's plan as a way to contain their rising health care costs. Others, notably insurers and pharmaceutical companies, perceived it as a threat to their business.[25]

Second, democratic procedures require policy-makers to take into account the larger public. Movements from below have achieved significant political victories over the opposition of a united capitalist class, which threatened that reform would undermine business confidence. For example, in President Clinton's first term, the popular Family Medical Leave Act, which permits employees to take unpaid family or medical leave, was passed over business's objections. Public support for the measure offset business threats that the bill would reduce profits, hurt employment, and erode management's autonomy. During President Clinton's second term, another popular measure, an increase in the minimum wage, sailed through Congress despite threats from business that passage of the bill would be inflationary and hurt the economy. The labor movement flooded Congress with letters of support for the bill. With the 1996 election just three months away and polls indicating that four out of five Americans supported an increase in the minimum wage, the bill passed easily, even receiving a majority of votes from Republicans, who normally oppose such measures.[26]

---

[24]This issue is treated meticulously in Hal Draper, *Karl Marx's Theory of Revolution,* vol. 1, bk. 1, *State and Bureaucracy* (New York: Monthly Review Press, 1977), pp. 311–39.

[25]Cathie Jo Martin, "Nature or Nurture? Sources of Firm Preference for National Health Reform," *American Political Science Review* 89 (December 1995): 898–913.

[26]*New York Times,* August 3, 1996.

In each case, democratic pressure from below was sufficient to overcome the mobilization of bias that operates in favor of business. Elected officials cannot simply ignore popular challenges, but must respond to them. Sometimes such challenges are sufficiently powerful that policy-makers must recalculate the risks of conceding to business and instead support alternative interests and values. When the public is mobilized and organized, politicians redefine their self-interest and will oppose business despite the mobilization of bias in its favor.[27] While the political burden of proof is much greater for movements from below than it is for business interests, the power of democratic pressure to influence state policy cannot be dismissed.

Politics matters. If, as Mitchell argues, the "house" always won, then citizens would think the game is fixed and lose interest. Instead, citizens play with gusto because business does not always win. The "house" sometimes loses.[28] The state stretches and bends in response to the political pressures exerted on it. Even though business derives an enormous advantage from the mobilization of bias, political struggles matter. The advantage that business derives from the mobilization of bias depends on whether groups opposed to business are mobilized and united.

What distinguishes the American case from those of other industrialized democracies is the relative weakness of such groups in the United States. All business sectors enjoy the same mobilization of bias in their favor. But American business derives more political benefits from it than do its counterparts elsewhere because the opposition it faces here is that much weaker. The result has been a different mix of government policies, such as a less extensive and less generous welfare state (see Chapter 10), which helps to produce more inequality in the United States than in other industrialized democracies.

Just because American business has faced weaker political challenges, permitting it to exploit the mobilization of bias more effectively, so that policy generally reflects the interests of business, does not mean that such political challenges will remain weak. Political struggle is highly variable. Contingency rules. The future is always open.

This book examines the sometimes tense, sometimes smooth, relationship between democratic politics and the undemocratic private government of capitalism. The character of American democracy is affected by the capitalist organization of the economy, and the capitalist organization of the economy is affected, in turn, by the fact that the political system is democratic. We believe that, in order to understand American politics, one must appreciate both that the mobilization of bias constitutes a powerful pressure in favor of business and that democratic pressure is capable of mitigating, if not counteracting, it. Our aim in this book is to describe both sides of this complicated coin. In the next section, we review the overall characteristics of the private government exercised by corporate capitalism in the United States.

---

[27]Mitchell, *Conspicuous Corporation*, pp. 167–89.

[28]Ibid., p. 11.

CORPORATE CAPITALISM

Suppose it was learned that a small group had gained control over vast concentrations of economic resources and political power in the United States. Imagine that, in a country with a population of 270 million people, several thousand Americans—unrepresentative, not democratically chosen, not even known to most people—controlled key aspects of American economic life. This small group determined what the level of investment would be, where investment would occur, what would be produced, and how production would be organized. It owned and controlled the offices and factories in which production occurred, as well as the media that influenced the values and attitudes of many Americans. It hired, fired, and promoted a large proportion of Americans and produced the goods and services that they depended on. Because members of this group controlled much of the country's productive capacity, their decisions affected every American. Yet they based their decisions not on what the country needed, but on what would be most profitable for them. This small group was obscenely wealthy, acquiring expensive clothes, driving luxury cars, and living in stately homes in various cities and fashionable vacation spots. At the same time, millions of other Americans just managed to obtain basic necessities, such as medical care and adequate housing and food, while still others failed to do so and fell through the cracks entirely.

Further, the small group at the top of the wealth pyramid had enormous political influence. Candidates and political parties shaped their agendas around its concerns in exchange for campaign contributions. Members of Congress responded to lobbyists representing the group's interests, and a number of policy-makers needed no introduction to the group's needs because they were members of the group themselves.

One can imagine the outcry that would greet the announcement that such a group existed. Its existence and power would be a betrayal of American democracy. And yet such a group does exist. All that has been described is fact, not fiction. A convenient shorthand label for the group that controls the process of production and derives immense political power from its control of the economy is corporate capitalism.

Corporate capitalism includes the largest mining and manufacturing companies, investment banks, financial services firms, retail chains, utilities, high-technology companies, media companies, and corporate law firms. The giant companies listed in the Fortune 500 are the core of corporate capitalism. The corporate sector is characterized by large firms that tend to be capital-intensive, highly productive, highly bureaucratic, and diversified; enjoy easy access to credit; sell in national and international markets; and have geographically dispersed production centers.

The corporate sector of the economy is distinguishable from the competitive sector, which includes the 22 million other businesses that exist in the United States. These firms range from convenience stores to car repair shops to locally owned restaurants. Firms in the competitive sector of the economy not only are smaller in terms of profits, sales, assets, and number of employ-ees, but also operate only in local markets and are more labor-intensive than firms in the corporate sector.[29]

One of the distinctive characteristics of the American economy is the high rate of business start-ups, highlighted in recent years by the dot.com phe-nomenon. In some cases, these firms have flourished and have even, in the case of a favored few like Microsoft and Cisco Systems, soared to become worldwide leaders. What is mentioned less often is that most start-up com-panies are not in the high-tech vanguard (the most common start-up is buy-ing your own taxi). Further, the vast majority of new businesses, including the dot.coms, fail within a few years.

Firms in the competitive sector are not independent of the corporate sec-tor. Small businesses act as suppliers to the corporate sector, are dependent on it for orders, provide retail sales outlets for its products, and repair what large firms produce. They also act as shock absorbers for the corporate sec-tor: They are the first firms to fail when recessions occur because they lack the resources of the larger firms to withstand them. In the cosmos of capital-ism, the small, competitive-sector firms are planets that rotate around and rely on the heat and light of the corporate sun, which sustains them.

The large number of small firms in the competitive sector of the economy contrasts sharply with the small number of very large firms that comprise the corporate sector. In 1994, 98 percent of all corporations in the United States had assets below $5 million. The almost 4 million corporations in the competitive sector of the economy controlled only slightly over 5 percent of all corporate assets. In contrast, a tiny group of corporations, each with more than $250 million in assets—.001 percent of all corporations in the United States—controlled 83 percent of all corporate assets.[30]

Some idea of the raw power and wealth concentrated within the corpo-rate sector is conveyed by the following figures.

SIZE.   The total corporate revenues of the Fortune 500—which amounted to $6.3 trillion in 1999—constitute over half the gross domestic product (GDP) of the entire American economy.[31] The 20 largest U.S. firms have higher cor-porate revenues than the GDP of all but a few of the world's wealthiest coun-tries. The Fortune 500 employ about one-seventh of the American workforce. The 20 largest Fortune 500 firms in 1999 are listed in Table 2–1.

While differences in firm size between the corporate and competitive sectors are immense, differences between firms at the top of the Fortune 500 and those at the bottom are also noteworthy. The largest firm, General

[29]Robert Averitt, *The Dual Economy: The Dynamic of American Industrial Structure* (New York: Norton, 1968).

[30]*Fortune*, May 15, 1995, 213.

[31]*Fortune*, April 17, 2000, F-19.

Motors (GM), had revenue 63 times that of Reliastar Financial, which came in at 500 on *Fortune's* list, with revenue of "only" $3 billion. While the Fortune 500 is a select club, some members clearly tower over others.

CONCENTRATION.   Economists call an industry concentrated if a few large firms dominate production and sales. The extent of industrial concentration in the United States can be gleaned from the following figures from the 1992 Census of Manufacturers. The Census listed 9,158 firms in the transportation equipment industry, with combined sales of over $332 billion. The 4 largest firms in the industry accounted for more than half of all sales in the industry; the 50 largest firms in the industry accounted for 85 percent of all sales. The four largest firms in the textile mill industry divided 82 percent of a $20 billion market among themselves. Just eight companies command more than half of a huge $118 billion market in petroleum refining, and just four companies shared 90 percent of an even bigger market, worth $133 billion, in motor vehicles.[32] And with the number and size of corporate mergers and acquisitions growing, industrial concentration is increasing. The merger of Mobil and Exxon partially restored the old Rockefeller Standard Oil empire, while the merger of telephone companies has resurrected big pieces of the old Bell telephone system. The Clinton administration presided over the largest, most expensive merger wave in history in the 1990s, with over 166,000 deals valued at $9.8 trillion. Big companies used to eat small companies. Now they eat each other.

When production becomes concentrated, in brief, control over society's productive resources becomes centralized in fewer hands. As industries become more concentrated, economic power becomes more centralized and integrated around a cluster of privately owned companies who can squeeze their suppliers as well as their customers. More dangerous, democracy is threatened because such a concentration of economic power tends to promote the concentration of political power.

Consider the news media. In recent years, the already large media companies have become fewer and larger. Cases in point: Disney purchased Capital Cities/ABC, resulting in a $16 billion communications empire; Time Warner merged with CNN, which resulted in a $20 billion conglomerate; and Westinghouse Electric Corporation bought CBS for $5.4 billion.[33] But these deals were dwarfed in 2000 when America Online, the Internet company, purchased Time Warner, the media empire, for $165 billion.

These media mergers not only fuel corporate concentration, but also affect the news we get and the character of public discourse and debate. For example, "[w]ithin weeks of the announced merger between ABC and Disney,

---

[32]These figures are drawn from "Concentration Ratios in Manufacturing," *1992 Census of Manufacturers* (Washington, D.C.: U.S. Department of Commerce, 1996).

[33]Eric Alterman, *Who Speaks for America: Why Democracy Matters in Foreign Policy* (Ithaca, N.Y.: Cornell University Press, 1998), p. 156.

■ TABLE 2-1

Rank 1999	1998		Revenues	
			$ millions	% change from 1998
1	1	**GENERAL MOTORS** Detroit	189.058.0	17.2
2	3	**WAL-MART STORES** Bentonville, Ark.	166,809.0	19.8
3	4	**EXXON MOBIL** Irving, Texas	163,881.0	62.7
4	2	**FORD MOTOR** Dearborn, Mich.	162,558.0	12.6
5	5	**GENERAL ELECTRIC** Fairfield, Conn.	111,630.0	11.1
6	6	**INTL. BUSINESS MACHINES** Armonk, N.Y.	87,548.0	7.2
7	7	**CITIGROUP** New York	82,005.0	7.3
8	10	**AT&T** New York	62,391.0	16.4
9	8	**PHILIP MORRIS** New York	61,751.0	6.8
10	9	**BOEING** Seattle	57,993.0	3.3
11	11	**BANK OF AMERICA CORP.** Charlotte, N.C.	51,392.0	1.2
12	35	**SBC COMMUNICATIONS** San Antonio	49,489.0	72.0
13	13	**HEWLETT-PACKARD** Palo Alto	48,253.0	2.5
14	36	**KROGER** Cincinnati	45,351.6	—
15	14	**STATE FARM INSURANCE COS.** Bloomington, Ill.	44,637.2	0.0
16	15	**SEARS ROEBUCK** Hoffman Estates, Ill.	41,071.0	(0.6)
17	22	**AMERICAN INTERNATIONAL GROUP** New York	40,656.1	22.1
18	27	**ENRON** Houston	40,112.0	28.3
19	18	**TIAA-CREF** New York	39,410.2	9.8
20	28	**COMPAQ COMPUTER** Houston	38,525.0	23.6

the ABC Radio Network canceled 'Hightower Radio,' the country's only nationally left-wing populist talk-radio show."[34]

EXPANSION. Corporate capitalism not only is more concentrated and centralized, but also now burrows deeper into our lives through the process of

---

[34]Ibid. Jim Hightower had previously analyzed Disneyland's exploitation of homeless workers in his talk show.

FORTUNE 500 LARGEST U.S. CORPORATIONS

Profits			Assets		Stockholders' Equity	
$ millions	Rank	% change from 1998	$ millions	Rank	$ millions	Rank
6,002.0	12	103.0	273,921.0	12	20,059.0	20
5,377.0	15	21.4	70,245.0	52	25,848.0	14
7,910.0	4	24.2	144,521.0	27	63,466.0	2
7,237.0	11	(67.2)	276,229.0	11	27,537.0	12
10,717.0	1	15.3	405,200.0	5	42,557.0	8
7,712.0	7	21.9	87,495.0	39	20,511.0	18
9,867.0	2	69.9	716,900.0	1	49,700.0	5
3,428.0	30	(46.4)	169,406.0	23	78,927.0	1
7,675.0	9	42.9	61,381.0	57	15,305.0	33
2,309.0	43	106.2	36,147.0	90	11,462.0	48
7,882.0	5	52.6	632,574.0	2	44,432.0	7
8,159.0	3	102.8	83,215.0	44	26,726.0	13
3,491.0	27	18.5	35,297.0	92	18,295.0	22
955.9	114	—	16,266.1	167	2,683.4	253
1,034.1	102	(21.6)	119,143.5	30	45,793.6	6
1,453.0	70	38.6	36,954.0	88	6,839.0	93
5,055.4	16	34.3	268,238.0	14	33,306.0	9
893.0	119	27.0	33,381.0	94	9,570.0	63
1,024.1	105	21.9	289,248.0	9	7,025.4	85
569.0	178	—	27,277.0	112	14,834.0	34

SOURCE: *Fortune*, April 17, 2000, F-1.

capitalist expansion. Capitalist expansion occurs when more and more goods and services take the commodity form; that is, they are produced for sale on the market. The market has become ubiquitous today. Everything from human organs to live babies can be purchased in the commercial bazaar. The market has invaded activities that were previously off-limits, turning them into new profit centers. Capitalist expansion has proceeded to such a degree that it has breached the defenses thrown up around activities where money is not supposed to count. For example, activities that were once the exclusive domain of government are now run as profit-making businesses. Today private firms educate schoolchildren, provide fire protection, process welfare applications, and run prisons—all for a profit. The market has even intruded into our most intimate spheres, weakening the bonds of family. New branches of production, including day-care centers and nursing homes that provide services for a profit, have emerged to fill the gap left by eroding family ties and obligations. Families that were previously self-servicing now fulfill their needs in the marketplace.[35]

WHO OWNS AMERICA'S PRIVATE GOVERNMENT?

The answer to this question begins with identifying who owns stock in giant corporations. People who invest money in corporations receive shares in the assets—called stocks—of that corporation. Stockholders are entitled to a share of the corporation's profits in proportion to the amount of stock they own. Stockholders are also entitled to vote for the board of directors of the corporation, which chooses the corporation's top management and reviews its performance and decisions. The number of votes that investors cast depends on the amount of stock they own in the corporation.

If corporate stock ownership was widely and equally distributed, then the following frequently heard claim would be valid: "In our system of free enterprise, the capitalist system, industry is owned by the American public."[36] In fact, only about half of all American households own stock in any form, either directly or indirectly through a mutual or pension fund. Among those households that report owning stock, a tiny group owns the lion's share. As Table 2–2 makes clear, people's capitalism, or what is sometimes called shareholder democracy, is a myth. In 1998, the top 1 percent of households in terms of wealth held 42 percent of the value of all the stock in the United States; the wealthiest 5 percent owned about two-thirds; the top 10 percent, more than three-quarters; and the top 20 percent (or "quintile," meaning one-fifth), about nine-tenths. "Unsurprisingly," economist Edward N. Wolff notes, "people with the highest salaries own the most stock."[37] The very rich and the tier right below them owned most of the stock, while middle-class and poor people owned little or none at all.

The stock market soared in the 1990s, although a downturn in 2000–2001 provided a reminder of the ever-present risk of instability. The Dow Jones Industrial Average, a leading benchmark of the stock market's performance,

---

[35]Gosta Esping-Andersen, *Social Foundations of Postindustrial Capitalism* (New York: Oxford University Press, 1999).

[36]William Lynch, an executive of the stockbrokerage house Dean Witter Reynolds, interviewed by the Voice of America, February 3, 1985. Note that this statement was broadcast around the world as a description of the American system.

[37]Edward N. Wolff, "The Rich Get Richer . . . and Why the Poor Don't," *American Prospect*, February 12, 2001, 15.

■ TABLE 2–2

CONCENTRATION OF STOCK OWNERSHIP BY
U.S. WEALTH CLASS, 1998

Wealth Class	Value of Stock Holdings			National Share of All Stock Owned	
	Any Amount	$5,000 or More	$10,000 or More	Total	Cumulative Total
Top 1 percent	93.2%	92.9%	91.2%	42.1%	42.1%
Next 4 percent	89.0	87.0	86.1	25.0	67.1
Next 5 percent	83.9	80.4	78.9	10.6	77.7
Next 10 percent	78.7	74.0	71.6	11.1	88.8
Second quintile	58.9	49.8	45.4	7.7	96.5
Third quintile	45.8	32.7	25.9	2.6	99.1
Fourth quintile	35.1	15.1	8.6	0.7	98.8
Bottom quintile	18.6	4.6	1.8	0.2	100.0
All U.S. households	48.2	36.3	31.8	100.0	

NOTE: Stock holdings include directly owned stock and shares owned indirectly through mutual funds, trusts, and retirement accounts. Data from the U.S. Bureau of the Census. Found in Edward N. Wolff, "The Rich Get Richer . . . and Why the Poor Don't," *American Prospect* (February 12, 2001), p. 15.

increased by over 400 percent over the course of the decade. This remarkable achievement was trumpeted on the evening news and in innumerable political speeches as evidence of American prosperity. However, the enormous gains from the surge in stock prices were distributed very unevenly and very narrowly. Since over half of all Americans do not own stock in any form, they received no direct financial benefit from the stock market's unprecedented performance. The 5 percent at the top of the wealth pyramid garnered fully three-quarters of the capital gains from the market's remarkable growth. The fact that a small group of wealthy Americans captured most of the vast increase in wealth generated by the stock market's spectacular rise in the 1990s further increased already great economic inequality in the United States.

THE PROFESSIONALIZATION OF CAPITAL

In the 1800s, the ownership and control of a business were united in the same person. Robber barons, such as John D. Rockefeller, Jay Gould, and J. P. Morgan, managed their own businesses, from which they derived their reputations for ruthlessness and their great wealth.

But as firms became larger and multidivisional, operated in a range of industries, and needed more capital to expand, many firms sold shares and became public corporations.[38] Ownership and control of the corporation increasingly split apart. Owners, now transformed into large stockholders, no longer performed day-to-day operations, but oversaw the work of corporate managers who carried out these tasks. Today's corporate executives tend to be faceless and unknown to the general public, unlike yesterday's titans of industry. In fact, in *Roger & Me*, Michael Moore never does complete his quest and get to talk to Roger Smith, the head of GM, who is protected from the public by an army of receptionists, security guards, and publicists. The protective cocoon surrounding "corporate decision makers . . . who have the power to make or break a community, insulate[s them] from the injuries, the pain, and the anger their policies create."[39]

Many corporate executives come from upper-class families, attended the most selective colleges, are graduates of either business or law school, or both, and are generally white and male, although there has been a tiny increase in minority members and women within the top ranks of the business elite.[40]

Corporate executives are rewarded lavishly for their efforts. The average salary and bonus of corporate chief executive officers (CEOs) in 2000 amounted to $10.9 million, an increase of 16 percent from the previous year.[41] Chief executive compensation has more than doubled since 1995, when they received on average "only" $4.4 million. Such averages, however, obscure the reality that executives at the very top receive far more. For example, Michael Eisner, CEO of Walt Disney, garnered over half a billion dollars in pay, stock options, and bonuses in 1999. But Eisner was outdone by Charles Wang, of Computers Associates International, who brought home $702,822,000 that year.[42] These inflated costs are passed along to the rest of us, since executive salaries increase the cost of goods we buy. And they amount to a corporate tax break, since executive salaries are considered a business expense and can be deducted from the company's taxable income.

Although top management in the United States has always earned much more than the workers they employ, there has been a dramatic increase in inequality between the top and bottom of the corporate pyramid. In 1980, the CEO of the typical major U.S. corporation received 42 times the compensation of an average factory worker; by 1990, the ratio had doubled. By the

---

[38]The most significant work on this process is Alfred D. Chandler, *The Visible Hand: The Managerial Revolution in American Business* (Cambridge: Harvard University Press, 1977).

[39]Ronald Edsforth, "Review of Roger & Me," *American Historical Review* 96 (October 1991): 1145.

[40]Michael Useem and Jerome Karabel, "Pathways to Corporate Management, *American Sociological Review* 51 (April 1986): 184–200."

[41]*New York Times*, February 26, 2001.

[42]*Business Week*, April 17, 2000, 102.

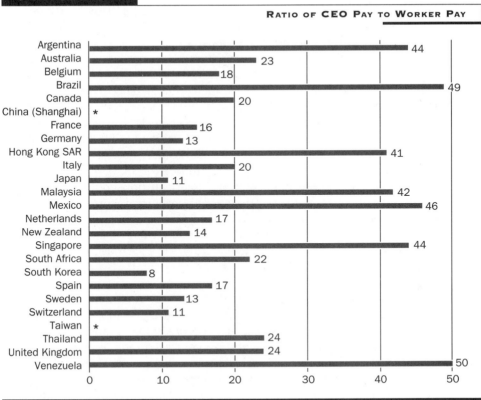

FIGURE 2-1

RATIO OF CEO PAY TO WORKER PAY

Argentina	44
Australia	23
Belgium	18
Brazil	49
Canada	20
China (Shanghai)	*
France	16
Germany	13
Hong Kong SAR	41
Italy	20
Japan	11
Malaysia	42
Mexico	46
Netherlands	17
New Zealand	14
Singapore	44
South Africa	22
South Korea	8
Spain	17
Sweden	13
Switzerland	11
Taiwan	*
Thailand	24
United Kingdom	24
Venezuela	50

*N.A.

SOURCE: Towers Perrin. Compiled at *www.aflcio.org/paywatch/ceopay.htm.*

time the decade ended, the average CEO made a whopping 475 times more than the typical factory worker.[43] Corporate executives are paid more in one day than the average worker in their firm earns in one year.

Although chief executives elsewhere are also rewarded generously, and receive many times what the average worker does, Figure 2–1 demonstrates that the United States is exceptional with respect to the vast gulf between executive compensation and that received by average manufacturing workers. The country with the next most unequal ratio is Venezuela—where the ratio is 50 compared to 475 in the United States. It is 11 in Japan and 13 in Germany—the world's second and third largest economies, respectively. These figures suggest a far greater degree of inequality in the U.S. corporate structure than in corporations abroad.

---

[43]The data in this paragraph, reported by the AFL–CIO Executive Paywatch Organization, are available at *www.paywatch.org.*

Data on executive compensation suggest that "managers" are not merely salaried employees, but also part of the wealthy elite. This is one reason why the separation of ownership from control within corporations is far from complete. Large stockholders often sit on the board of directors of corporations, where they oversee management's performance. Managers, for their part, often own large blocs of stock in the firms they direct. For example, Bill Gates, the chief executive of Microsoft, owns $35 billion worth of Microsoft stock; Philip Knight, the head of Nike, owns stock worth $3.68 billion in his company; and Michael Eisner, who runs Walt Disney, owns stock worth $1.2 billion in his company. One study of the 200 largest publicly traded companies found that chief executive officers owned an average of $57.8 million worth of their company's equity in 1997. (For some perspective, in 1995, the median net worth of American households, taking into consideration the total value of all personal property, including cars, financial investments, and houses, was $45,630.[44]) Grants of large blocs of stock to executives help align the interests of management with those of other large stockholders. This alliance is then sealed by the fact that many corporate executives not only actively manage the company, but also sit on the firm's board of directors.

Below the very top ranks of shareholders and corporate management, there has been an explosion of professions that assist top management in directing the firm. When we speak of the professionalization of capital, we refer to the army of middle managers, lawyers, accountants, engineers, market researchers, product developers, advertising specialists, and others who have specialized skills and command good salaries in return for helping corporate managers maximize corporate profits. The boundaries of this large group extend from corporate executives down toward the ranks of semi-skilled clerical and service workers. There are enormous variations in the occupational positions of the group members, so one cannot generalize much about their membership or interests. But they occupy a central, if subordinate, position in corporate capitalism.

THE STRUCTURE OF EMPLOYMENT

The professionalization of capital has not, we argue, changed the behavior of firms, but it has altered the shape of the workforce within them. An industrial occupational order based on manual, blue-collar, and often male factory workers has been replaced by a new postindustrial order that relies on white-collar office workers, who are often female.

Industry first began to overtake agriculture as the basis of employment after the Civil War. Workers employed in manufacturing increased from just

---

[44]*New York Times*, February 15, 1998.

2.5 million in 1870 to over 11 million by 1920. Labor historian Melvin Dubof-sky writes, "Both in its growth and its distribution, then, the American labor force from 1865 to 1920 became concentrated in the primary (extractive) and secondary (manufacturing) sectors of the economy."[45] Hand tools were replaced by machines, workshops were replaced by factories, artisans were replaced by unskilled manual workers, and crafted items were replaced by standardized products. Foreign immigrants and native farmers took jobs as industrial workers in factories, transforming villages into towns and towns into cities. Pittsburgh grew up around steel, Akron around rubber, and De-troit around cars. But nowhere was the industrial transformation as rapid as it was in Flint. Flint was transformed from a sleepy town of 13,000 in 1900 into a bustling city of 150,000, where over 60,000 industrial workers were employed—many of them in GM factories—by 1929.[46]

As the industrial workforce grew and defined its era, it created the need for a new postindustrial occupational order based on the growth of white-collar occupations that would eventually overtake it. As productivity in industry increased, firms hired salespeople and market researchers to find and create new outlets for their growing productive capacity. As capitalists discovered the benefits of applying science to production, firms hired scien-tists and technical experts to develop new products and improve existing methods. As companies took the skill out of jobs, firms hired engineers to design the labor process and supervisors to manage it. As companies in-creased in size and became more bureaucratic, the number of office workers and levels of management increased to coordinate the flow of work within the firm. As the advance of industry broke down traditional social relations, the demand for service workers increased as people turned to the market to purchase what they previously provided themselves. Finally, as industrial capitalism grew, so did the white-collar public-sector workforce in order to provide essential services and cope with the escalating costs of capitalist development. That is, the growth of a postindustrial workforce did not occur separately or independently from the grimy world of material pro-duction, but emerged in response to the demands of industry and the changes it provoked in social life.

The shift from an industrial to a postindustrial workforce is reflected in Table 2–3 from the U.S. Department of Labor's *Report on the Workforce*. In 1996, the traditional industrial proletariat, consisting of craft workers and operatives, comprised just 25 percent of the total workforce. These occupa-tions have declined in the face of the dramatic growth of white-collar occu-pations, which have absorbed many of the married women entering the labor market.

---

[45]Melvin Dubofsky, *Industrialism and the American Worker, 1865–1920*, 2nd ed. (Arlington Heights, Ill.: Harlan Davidson, 1985), p. 3.

[46]Ronald Edsforth, *Class Conflict and Cultural Consensus: The Making of a Mass Consumer Soceity in Flint, Michigan* (New Brunswick, N.J.: Rutgers University Press, 1987), pp. 39–71.

■ TABLE 2–3

OCCUPATIONAL DISTRIBUTION, ANNUAL AVERAGES,
1983–96 (IN THOUSANDS)

Occupation	1983	1996
TOTAL	101.8	126.7
Managers	10.7	17.7
Professionals	12.8	18.7
Technicians	3.1	3.9
Sales	11.8	15.4
Administrative support, including clericals	16.4	18.3
Services	13.8	17.2
Crafts	12.3	13.6
Operatives	16.1	18.2
Farming, forestry and fishing	3.7	3.5

SOURCE: Table 10, *Report on the American Workforce* (Department of Labor, 1997), p. 160.

As the postindustrial occupational order emerged, so have disturbing signs that the occupational structure is bifurcating. That is, both good and bad jobs are growing at the expense of the middle. According to Table 2–3, such good jobs as manager, professional, and technician—jobs that are well compensated and require education—have increased in number. Indeed, the increase in managers has led economist David M. Gordon to argue that American corporations are top-heavy with managers compared to their foreign counterparts. Managers comprise 13 percent of total nonfarm employment in the United States compared to 3.9 percent in Germany, 4.2 percent in Japan, and 2.6 percent in Sweden. Moreover, contrary to recurrent news reports that corporate downsizing thinned managerial ranks in the 1990s, they have actually grown. Between 1989 and 1994, the number of managers grew by 1.4 million, and their share of total nonfarm employment increased from 12.6 percent of the workforce to 13.2 percent.[47]

While good jobs have increased, bad jobs have, too, right alongside of them. These jobs, concentrated in the service and sales occupational categories, tend to be poorly paid, offer few fringe benefits, and require menial and routine labor. The increase in the number of bad jobs is highlighted by the fact that GM, which has traditionally provided its workers with solid wages and benefits, has been replaced as the country's largest private employer by Walmart, which offers part-time, low-wage work without benefits. In effect, the middle, represented by General Motors' full-time jobs at union

---

[47]David M. Gordon, *Fat and Mean: The Corporate Squeeze of Working Americans and the Myth of Managerial "Downsizing"* (New York: Free Press, 1996), pp. 33–61.

wages, is giving ground steadily to both good jobs at the top and, in larger measure, to bad jobs at the bottom.

The bifurcation of the occupational order into good and bad jobs helps explain why wage disparities are higher in the United States than elsewhere. Economist Richard B. Freeman found that the distribution of wages (and income) is more unequal in the United States than in any other advanced country.[48] A comparison of the wages that the top 10 percent receives with those received by the lowest 10 percent shows that the United States has the highest degree of wage dispersion among industrialized democracies.[49] Wage inequality is double what it is in Sweden, which has the most egalitarian wage structure. The fact that inequalities vary so much among comparably affluent countries suggests that the reasons are political, not economic. That is, in the absence of a political force to check the tendency of the market to generate winners and losers, inequality will intensify.

Another reason why wage dispersion is larger in the United States than in Europe and Japan is that managerial ranks are fatter here. Further, what are considered junk jobs here are compensated better elsewhere due to the greater power of unions and government regulations that raise wages at the bottom to above-market rates. While all advanced countries are making the same transition from an industrial to a postindustrial workforce, the consequences are different in each country depending on its politics. Because the United States has let the unfettered market shape the occupational order, the quality of work and the distribution of wages and benefits are more unequal here than in comparable advanced industrial economies.[50]

CONFLICT AND COHESION

Capitalist economies are dynamic and in constant motion. The engine of change is competition among firms for markets and profits. But corporate capitalism is characterized by cooperation and coordination among firms, as well as rivalry and competition. In 1935, political scientist E. E. Schattschneider noted, "Businessmen collectively constitute the most class-conscious group in American society. As a class they are the most highly organized, more easily mobilized, have more facilities for communication, are more like-minded, and are more accustomed to stand together in defense of their privileges than any other group."[51]

---

[48]Richard B. Freeman, "How Labor Fares in Advanced Economies," in *Working Under Different Rules*, ed. Richard B. Freeman (New York: Russell Sage Foundation, 1995), p. 12.

[49]OECD, *Employment Outlook* (Paris: OECD, July 1996).

[50]The interpretive framework employed here draws heavily on Gosta Esping-Andersen, *The Three Worlds of Welfare Capitalism* (Princeton, N.J.: Princeton University Press, 1990), and his *Social Foundations of Postindustrial Economies* (New York: Oxford University Press, 1999).

[51]E. E. Schattschneider, *Politics, Pressures and the Tariff* (New York: Prentice-Hall, 1935), p. 287.

Capital is linked together through a dense organizational network. Managers are united in their desire to protect their firm's autonomy and to pursue its economic and political interests with minimal interference from the state or popular movements. One mechanism through which capitalist class cohesion occurs is exclusive social clubs, such as the Links and Century clubs in New York, the California Club in Los Angeles, and the Pacific Union Club in San Francisco. Social clubs promote capitalist class cohesion by creating information and friendship networks among the elite. The exclusive social club is the last step in a long process of elite socialization that begins in prep school, is reinforced at prestigious private colleges, is strengthened at the best law schools, and is polished at corporate headquarters.[52]

Peak business associations are another source of capitalist class cohesion. At the very top of the industrial pyramid is the Business Roundtable, which tries to find consensus on public issues among the managers of the largest corporate firms in the United States. Membership in the Business Roundtable is limited to the chief executives of the 200 largest corporations. The Roundtable employs no support staff or lobbyists. Instead, the chief executives themselves convey the Roundtable's position on public issues to legislators and policy-makers directly in one-to-one exchanges. At a broader, less elite level, thousands of large and small firms are members of the U.S. Chamber of Commerce and the National Association of Manufacturers. These peak associations seek to represent the collective interests of business across industries. At the level of specific industries, one finds countless trade associations, such as the Society of the Plastics Industry and the Association of Home Appliance Manufacturers, which express the interests of firms in a particular sector.

A third source of capitalist class cohesion is corporate interlocks, in which the member of one corporate board of directors also serves on the board of another corporation. Interlocks facilitate communication between firms. According to sociologist Michael Useem, interlocks promote "the flow of information throughout the [corporate] network about the practices and concerns of most large companies, companies that are operating in virtually all major sectors of the economy and facing the full range of economic and political problems confronting business generally."[53] Directors who sit on multiple corporate boards comprise what Useem identified as the "inner circle" of capital. Those in the inner circle form the leading edge of the capitalist class because their perspective goes beyond the interests of any particular firm or industry to encompass the interests of corporate capitalism as a whole. Capitalist class cohesion results from the activities and transcendent corporate perspective of the inner circle.

---

[52]For a list of exclusive social clubs, see G. William Domhoff, *The Higher Circles: The Governing Class in America* (New York: Random House, 1970).

[53]Michael Useem, *The Inner Circle: Large Corporations and the Rise of Business Political Activity in the U.S. and U.K.* (New York: Oxford University Press, 1984), p. 56.

President George W. Bush emerging from a meeting with business leaders following his election.

Given the fact that corporate capitalism increasingly operates on a transnational level, as we describe in chapter 9, new mechanisms to promote cohesion among businesses on a global level are developing. For example, every winter top business leaders from around the world assemble in Davos, Switzerland, an Alpine resort, to meet with government officials and socialize. This kind of informal occasion is invaluable in providing the opportunity to develop common positions and exchange views.

No single organization enforces discipline and unity among the firms that comprise corporate capitalism. Yet social clubs, peak business associations, and corporate interlocks form the infrastructure that promotes classwide understandings, if not specific positions on policy. Unified political action by capital is rare. But it is more likely to occur when managerial authority is threatened than at any other time. Ironically, the threat posed by the emergence of unions was responsible for molding employers into a cohesive, effective political force. In 1906, one leader of the newly formed National Association of Manufacturers (NAM) admitted, "It is surprising how many of our members take issue with us on everything except the labor question. . . . On that the manufacturers are a unit. The minute you get away from it there is no unity."[54]

---

[54]Quoted in Julie Greene, *Pure and Simple Politics: The American Federation of Labor and Political Activism, 1881–1917* (New York: Cambridge University Press, 1998), p. 92.

The government sometimes poses another threat to managerial authority against which capitalists may ally and unite. An important example occurred in the 1970s with the passage of social legislation that limited managerial prerogatives and affected firms in a variety of industries. Management now had to abide by regulations that governed its workplace (health and safety laws), its products (consumer protection laws), its workforce (employment discrimination laws), and its place of business (environmental laws). According to David Vogel, "[F]irms in different industries [now] found it in their interest to cooperate with one another" in order to resist these regulations and restore managerial authority.[55]

Relations within corporate capitalism are characterized by both conflict and cooperation. Some issues provoke conflict within the business community. Other issues might politically mobilize firms in one industry, while the rest of the business community remains indifferent and inactive. And on issues that challenge managerial autonomy, such as social regulations and labor law reform, the business community stands armed and united. Overall, according to political scientists Kay Lehman Schlozman and John T. Tierney, "[C]ooperation within the business community is far more commonplace than conflict." Members of the business community were more likely to identify other business interests as political allies than as antagonists.[56]

THE UNSTABLE CHARACTER OF CAPITALISM

Capitalism is extraordinarily dynamic. It is constantly transforming itself as the competitive drive for profits forces firms to improve efficiency, create new technologies, and explore new markets. But the dynamism of capitalism, its revolutionary thrust, is also the source of its instability. Supply and demand are not coordinated. Markets fail to clear, and investment, production, and consumption fail to equilibrate. Consequently, business cycles occur, in which periods of economic growth, measured by output, employment, and profits, are followed by periods of economic contraction, in which production declines, unemployment increases, and bankruptcies rise.[57] Capi-

---

[55]David Vogel, *Fluctuating Fortunes: The Political Power of Business in America* (New York: Basic Books, 1989), p. 201.

[56]Kay Lehman Schlozman and John T. Tierney, *Organized Interests and American Democracy* (New York: Harper & Row, 1986), p. 401. These impressions were confirmed statistically by Jeffrey M. Berry, who found twice as many cases of no conflict within and across industries on bills pending in Congress as examples of inter- or intra-industry disagreement. See Jeffrey M. Berry, *The New Liberalism: The Rising Power of Citizen Groups* (Washington, D.C.: Brookings, 1999), p. 79.

[57]Of course, the major alternative to capitalist production in modern times, the command or socialist economies found in the Soviet Union and its allies in the twentieth century, proved even more unstable. Only Cuba continues to organize its economy in this fashion. This is not to claim that radical, desirable, and feasible alternatives to capitalist production cannot be devised. But none has yet proved itself by the test of history.

talist economies tend to oscillate between expansion and recession, with each period pregnant with the conditions that will produce its opposite. That is, just as economic growth creates the conditions for a new period of contraction to follow, so does recession clear the ground for a new period of growth.

One reason that business cycles occur is that there is a constant tendency for productive capacity to outstrip demand. During periods of economic growth, capitalists estimate that the chances of making a profit are high, and they invest in new equipment to expand output. But this eventually leads to overproduction because workers cannot afford to purchase enough of the commodities that the economy is able to produce. As economist Roger E. Alcaly points out, "The small incomes of the majority of the population limit their ability to consume the output that the economy is increasingly capable of producing."[58] When production exceeds demand, factories begin to run at partial capacity, and workers are laid off, thus further reducing the demand for goods, and a downward spiral toward recession begins.

A second way in which an economic boom turns into a recession is through the workers' demand for higher wages. When the economy is expanding, more workers are hired in order to produce more goods. As the number of people looking for work goes down, employers are forced to raise wages to attract new employees. Increased production costs result, thus squeezing profits. After profits are squeezed beyond a certain point, workers are laid off, contributing to a new downward spiral.

A third way prosperity generates recession under capitalism is by replacing workers with machines. Technological unemployment contributes to the problem of inadequate demand, as workers who are replaced by machines cannot afford to buy all that capitalists can now produce more efficiently. Workers left unemployed by machines can no longer purchase what the machines that replace them produce. This poses a dilemma for capital, which was vividly captured in a celebrated exchange between a Ford Motor Company executive and former UAW President Walter Reuther. The executive took Reuther on a tour of the new Oak Brook engine plant that Ford had just built. He showed Reuther all the new machines the plant was equipped with, reminding Reuther that those machines never went on strike, they were extremely efficient, and "not one of those machines pays union dues." Reuther replied, "And not one of those machines buys new Ford cars, either."[59]

In a society where all share in the gains from technological innovation, it is socially beneficial to replace labor with capital. Technological innovation

---

[58]Roger E. Alcaly, "An Introduction to Marxian Crisis Theory," in Union for Radical Political Economics, *U. S. Capitalism in Crisis* (New York: Economic Education Project, 1978), p. 18. This section draws heavily on Alcaly.

[59]Nelson Lichtenstein, *Walter Reuther: The Most Dangerous Man in Detroit* (New York: Basic Books, 1995), p. 291.

can reduce work time and free workers to enjoy more leisure. But in a capitalist society, technological innovation often spells unemployment, and workers displaced by machines are forced to absorb the costs of the change.

The business cycle, the alternation of boom and bust, is a universal characteristic of capitalism. The tendency for the economy to contract is as central to a capitalist economy as its tendency to expand. Thus, a recession is part of the capitalist process and, within limits, even beneficial to it. A recession sets the stage for a new period of profitable investment and economic growth by weeding out inefficient firms. Companies that cannot withstand the rigors of a recession are forced out of business. A recession also weakens the working class. Unemployment weakens workers' bargaining power, making them more compliant and willing to give concessions to management in order to keep their jobs.

THE CURRENT SITUATION

Throughout the 1990s, the business cycle was in a prolonged expansionary phase. By most standard measures, the American economy performed extremely well during the last decade of the twentieth century. Growth was remarkably steady, with the economy experiencing its longest expansion ever. Stock market prices soared to new heights, breaking new records along the way. The federal deficit was reduced, with surpluses projected into the coming years. While much of Europe was mired in double-digit unemployment, the U.S. unemployment rate was around 4 percent, lower than at any time since the 1970s. In 1996, the "misery index"—the combination of inflation and unemployment—was the lowest it had been in four decades.

The American economy performed so well that it was held up as a model for the rest of the world to emulate. American policy-makers began to lecture the leaders of other countries that the American model was the only route to success in the jungle of the new global economy. Other countries were told that they must adopt the American economic model or risk being left behind in the race for competitiveness and global markets. One leader complained that the American model, which is based on the notion that the "market can do no wrong, is sacrosanct, is your benefactor, savior and the ticket to prosperity is now as extreme as was the Communism and socialism of yesteryear."[60]

The American economic model has five parts: (1) deregulation—removing state restrictions on business; (2) privatization—shifting activities from the public to the private sector, where they will now be subject to the logic of the market; (3) labor flexibility—giving management a free hand in deploying

---

[60]Quote by Prime Minister Mahatir Mohammed of Malaysia in *New York Times*, November 26, 1997.

labor by removing union work rules and government regulations from the workplace; (4) low taxes—letting the market and not the state direct the flow of society's income; and (5) a small safety net—reducing welfare state expenditures and making each citizen's welfare dependent on the market.[61] (We review these elements in later chapters.)

There is no dismissing the success of the American model in the 1990s. But, as the following years have demonstrated, that success was more fragile than its boosters claimed. Further, the expansion generated a rising tide of inequality. According to a study released in 1999 by the Center on Budget and Policy Priorities, based on Congressional Budget Office data, the share of income going to families in the wealthiest fifth of the income pyramid increased from 44.2 to 50.4 percent between 1977 and 1999, while the share going to the poorest income fifth declined from 5.7 percent to 4.2 percent. The wealthiest fifth thus now receives 1/2 of all household income; the bottom fifth receives 1/25. Moreover, during this period, the income of the poorest fifth declined (in constant dollars) by over 10 percent, while the share of the wealthiest fifth increased by 38 percent.[62] Table 2–4 shows that the group that has done by far the best is the richest 1 percent: the share of national income received by members of this group increased to 12.9 percent during this period, while their after-tax income doubled. Commenting on the results of the economic boom of the late twentieth century, economist Paul Krugman notes, "It's not just that the top 20 percent have gotten richer compared with the rest. The top 5 percent have gotten richer compared with the next 15 percent; the top 1 percent have gotten richer compared with the next 4 percent, and there is pretty good evidence the top .25 percent have gotten richer compared with the next .75 percent."[63]

Moreover, there appears to have been a sea change in economic patterns during the 1990s. Periods of full employment usually empower labor to demand higher wages. Yet, despite steady productivity growth in the 1990s and the longest economic expansion in history—with record levels of

---

[61]Journalist Thomas L. Friedman provides a more precise description of the American model, which he describes, tellingly, as "the golden straitjacket." The "golden rules" include "making the private sector the primary engine of its primary growth, maintaining a low rate of inflation and price stability, shrinking the size of its state bureaucracy, maintaining as close to a balanced budget as possible, if not a surplus, eliminating and lowering tariffs on imported goods, removing restrictions on foreign investment, getting rid of quotas and domestic monopolies, increasing exports, privatizing state-owned industries and utilities, deregulating capital markets, making its currency convertible, opening its industries, stock, and bond markets to direct foreign ownership and investment, deregulating its economy to promote as much domestic competition as possible, eliminating government corruption, subsidies and kickbacks as much as possible, opening its banking and telecommunications systems to private ownership and competition, and allowing its citizens to choose from an array of competing pension options and foreign-run pension and mutual funds." Thomas L. Friedman, *The Lexus and the Olive Tree* (New York: Farrar, Straus and Giroux, 1999), p. 87.

[62]*New York Times*, September 5, 1999.

[63]*New York Times*, August 21, 1995.

■ TABLE 2–4

SHARE OF NATIONAL INCOME BY INCOME GROUPS,
1977–1999

Household Groups	Share of All Income*		Average After-Tax Income (Estimated)		Change
	1977	1999	1977	1999	
One-fifth with lowest income	5.7%	4.2%	$ 10,000	$ 8,800	▼ 12.0%
Next lowest one-fifth	11.5	9.7	22,100	20,000	▼ 9.5%
Middle one-fifth	16.4	14.7	32,400	31,400	▼ 3.1%
Next highest one-fifth	22.8	21.3	42,600	45,100	▲ 5.9%
One-fifth with highest income	44.2	50.4	74,000	102,300	▲ 38.2%
1 percent with highest income	7.3	12.9	234,700	515,600	▲ 119.7%

*Figures do not add to 100 due to rounding.

SOURCE: Isaac Shapiro and Robert Greenstein, "The Widening Income Gulf," *Center on Budget and Policy Priorities,* September 5, 1999.

employment and an intense demand for labor—wages barely inched upward. Intensified global competition, weaker unions, and rapid technological change have proved remarkably effective in deterring workers from exploiting their potential power in a tight labor market.

If one views the wages of American workers in a longer perspective, the record is even more dismal. As the graph in Figure 2–2 shows, although the productivity of American workers has increased by 30 percent since the mid-1970s, hourly wages (in constant dollars) have decreased by 9 percent. So much for the value of hard work!

In the boom following World War II, wages kept pace with productivity growth. Not so today. In the 1990s, the wealth created by increasing productivity was captured by corporations in the form of rising profits, not by workers in the form of rising wages. As economist Edward N. Wolff observes, "Average wages have been stagnant now for almost 25 years, and the share of income going to owners of capital has been rising dramatically in the last 10 years particularly."[64]

In addition, while American employment figures are the envy of the world, their superiority has been exaggerated. For example, part of the rea-

---

[64]Quoted in *New York Times,* January 19, 2000.

■ **FIGURE 2-2**

CHANGES IN PRODUCTIVITY AND WAGES 1974–1999

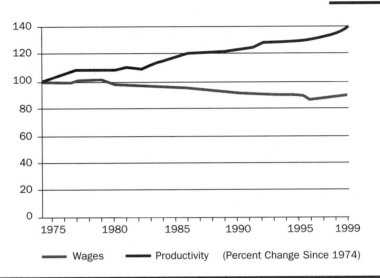

SOURCE: Modified from Lawrence Mishel, Jared Bernstein, and John Schmitt, *The State of Working America 1998–1999* (Ithaca: ILR Press, 1999), p. 154; additional data from Bureau of Labor Statistics.

son why employment statistics are so much more favorable in the United States than in Europe is that countries define the unemployed in different ways. Different definitions and methods of counting exaggerate differences in the unemployment rate between Europe and the United States. The United States also has more institutions that can soak up excess labor, especially among the young, who otherwise might be unemployed. The military, prisons, and colleges absorb a larger proportion of potential workers in the United States than in Europe.

Still there is no disputing that the United States stands alone as the preeminent economic power at the beginning of the twenty-first century. But powerful as it is, it is still subject to the vagaries of the business cycle that govern the rise and fall of capitalist economies. (The dramatic decline in prices of many high-tech stocks in 2000–2001 provided sober corroboration of this point.) And quite apart from the question of its stability, important concerns remain concerning how equitably our economy functions and what impact it has on the quality of American democracy.

CONCLUSION

Capitalism does not simply distribute money and wealth unequally. It also distributes economic power unequally. People who own and control the means of production have the power to make decisions about whether to invest, where to invest, what to invest in, and over the working lives of their employees that have consequences for the entire society. Decisions by capitalists are not subject to democratic accountability even though they affect all citizens profoundly. Capitalists make these decisions based on what will yield the greatest profit, not the greatest good. Their economic wealth and power enable them to wield great political influence. Their wealth provides them with the ability to organize in support of their interests, contribute money to political campaigns, and influence public opinion. Meanwhile, their economic power creates a mobilization of bias in their favor. If the former gives them more powerful weapons with which to wage political combat, the latter tilts the rules of combat in their favor.

Yet the results of political struggle remain open depending on a host of factors. Chief among them are how unified capitalists are, which cannot be taken for granted, and the extent of popular opposition they encounter. The grim story of Flint, Michigan, and the possibilities of Burlington, Vermont, are each available within the limited range of capitalist futures. The result depends on political struggle. The tale of two cities remains unfinished.

3

THE AMERICAN STATE AND CORPORATE CAPITALISM

INTRODUCTION

We described in Chapter 2 the mobilization of bias that integrates corporate capitalism into the fabric of American politics. The rights and powers capitalists enjoy by virtue of owning and controlling the means of production include the right to manage the workforce, organize production, make investment decisions, and retain profits. Such decisions are typically considered beyond political debate and beyond the reach of democratic decision making. We focus on the relationship between capitalist production and the political sphere because understanding this problematic relationship is central to understanding the character and limits of American democracy. The focus of Chapter 2 was the organization of American capitalism—capitalism as private government. The present chapter examines the relationship between the American state and corporate capitalism.[1]

Capitalism is often described as a system in which production for private profit is organized and coordinated through markets that are free of political direction. But the free market was and remains a fiction. Markets cannot exist without a government to maintain order, enforce contracts, create currency, and provide a host of other public goods without which the "free market" could not last for a single day. Markets require a protective, facilitating political order in order to function.

Even in the United States, where the state's role within the economy has been less extensive than elsewhere, the state has been deeply implicated in the economy from the very start. Soon after the founding of the United States, following ratification of the Constitution in the late eighteenth century, state

---

[1]By state, we mean the totality of public institutions that form the government of a country. The core of the state is the executive—in the United States, the president, the office of the presidency, and the executive branch or bureaucracy, along with the military. But the state also includes Congress, the courts, and, in a federal system such as ours, state and local governments. The use of the term *state* for both state governments and the more inclusive state as defined here complicates descriptions of American politics. However, the text should be clear as to which of the two referents is intended.

and local governments developed a commercial code and legal framework to bring order and stability to economic activity, created a common currency to facilitate trade and exchange, employed a military and police to secure property and markets, financed the building of roads and bridges to facilitate production and trade, and provided rudimentary social services. As capitalism matured, the different forms of state assistance increased. The invisible hand of the market has always been supplemented and supported by the visible hand of the state.

Capitalism has developed not at the expense of government, but alongside it. Historian Karl Polanyi writes, "[State] regulation and markets, in effect, grew up together."[2] The relationship of government to the capitalist economy contains elements of both mutual antagonism and mutual dependence. On the one hand, the government restricts the play of markets by issuing regulations. On the other hand, the government supports markets by creating conditions in which they can function and protects them from their own excesses. If left to themselves, markets would create unacceptable levels of inequality, exploitation, and unemployment.

The relationship between the state and market-based production for private profit (or capitalism) is especially complicated in those countries, such as the United States, in which capitalist production exists alongside democratic political institutions. In those settings, the state needs to sponsor measures that foster profitable capitalist production while at the same time responding to popular demands, as expressed in elections and other ways. The problem is that the two goals may conflict.[3] A tension may exist between capitalism, an economic system based on profits for the few, and democracy, a political system based on democratic rights for the many.

This tension is resolved only through political struggle and conflict, the outcome of which is always open and contingent. But that is not to say there have not also been clear and regular winners. For example, employers, workers, and farmers have often been in conflict throughout American history as each group tried to impose its own vision of the proper balance between free markets and state regulation. Business has been unusually successful in these struggles. As a result, the steering capacity of the government regarding production and investment decisions is weaker here than elsewhere. Historically, other advanced capitalist states (notably, in Western Europe) have at their command more powerful and more numerous levers than the American government enjoys to affect the overall development of the economy. Business has successfully limited the government's ability to influence the behavior of private firms, shaped the institutions through

[2]Karl Polanyi, *The Great Transformation* (Boston: Beacon Press, 1957), p. 68.

[3]For classic analyses of these dilemmas, see Charles Lindblom, *Politics and Markets: The World's Political-Economic Systems* (New York: Basic Books, 1977), and Claus Offe, *Contradictions of the Welfare State* (Cambridge: Cambridge University Press, 1984).

which intervention would occur, and heavily influenced the policies those institutions would implement. Business has been able to take advantage of the mobilization of bias we described in Chapter 2, as well as deploy extensive political and ideological resources to win these struggles.

But under popular pressure, state policy has also diverged at times from business interests. While the relative weakness of the American state's steering capacity has been a durable aspect of American history, business interests have constantly needed to defend it against insurgent groups who envisioned a different role for the state in the economy.

One can discern periodic swings throughout American history in which the tendency for state intervention to be directed against the logic of the market has waxed and waned. Since World War II, as we shall describe in more detail below, there have been two long swings of the pendulum. In the postwar period, building on the expansion of government during the Great Depression of the 1930s and the government's enormous success in steering the economy during World War II, the state played a more expansive role than in the past. From the 1930s through the 1970s, the government's size and scope increased enormously.

Beginning in the late 1970s, especially following the election of Ronald Reagan to the presidency in 1980, the pendulum shifted in the opposite direction. Now the principal aim was to free markets from the "shackles" imposed during decades of government regulation. As a result of the "Reagan Revolution," business has enjoyed much greater freedom since the 1980s, and groups seeking to restrict market forces in order to defend the environment, help the less affluent, protect consumers, and safeguard the interests of workers have been thrown on the defensive. But Stephen Roach, chief economist of Morgan Stanley, the Wall Street investment company, believes the pendulum may be shifting once again. Roach warned his colleagues in the investment community that a backlash to the triumph of markets is gathering momentum. Investors, Roach warned, have deceived themselves into believing that they have discovered the equivalent of the capitalist fountain of youth in unregulated markets. The pendulum is beginning to swing away from markets, according to Roach, and "trapped in their comfort zones, few will ever see it coming."[4] While the future direction of state involvement in the economy is unclear at this point, it will depend heavily on the course of political struggles.

In this chapter, we study the state's changing relationship to the economy, focusing on the change ushered in by President Franklin Delano Roosevelt's New Deal in the 1930s, the policy instruments that government uses to influence the economy, the reversal of the New Deal policy paradigm by President Ronald Reagan in the 1980s, and its aftermath in the Clinton administration of the 1990s.

---

[4]Stephen Roach, "Angst in the Global Village," *Challenge*, September–October 1997, 95–108.

THE FIRST WAVE OF EXPANSION

The first expansionary phase in American history, starting in the 1840s, was based on a revolution in transportation.[5] New roadways, canals, and railroads allowed farmers in the Ohio and Mississippi valleys to ship their products more quickly to seaboard cities like New York, Baltimore, and Philadelphia. Shipping midwestern grain to New York by wagon took almost two months; by canal, it took three weeks; by rail, it took just seven days.[6] Regional and even national markets in labor and commodities soon developed as a result of these efficiencies in transportation. Railroads especially were a dynamic force propelling the entire economy forward with them. Their demand for massive inputs of labor and material created new markets, encouraged new technologies, and produced new corporate forms.

But the revolution in transportation would not have had nearly the impact attributed to it had it not been for the role of government. Almost a century ago one historian wrote that, despite popular images of the United States as "the land of private enterprise *par excellence;* the place where 'State interference' has played the smallest part, and individual enterprise has been given the largest scope, it is a fact that this country was one of the first to exhibit the modern tendency to extend the activity of the State into industry."[7] This impression of minimal state interference in the economy persists partly because people often look for the state in the wrong place. Historians Oscar and Mary Handlin warned over 50 years ago that, "[I]n America, the peculiar complexity of federalism has often, in the last half-century, misled those who have touched upon the subjects of government and business enterprise."[8] *State governments,* far more than the federal government, were involved in shaping the contours of the pre–Civil War political economy.[9] State governments had the authority to regulate labor relations, including slavery; determine public policy regarding corporations; collect their own taxes; plan and build their own public works; and expropriate private property under laws of eminent domain.

---

[5]We focus here on the development of what became the industrial base of the American economy in the North and Midwest. The story of southern economic development, based on a semifeudal plantation economy dependent on slave labor, highlights one of the most shameful aspects of American history. But since the southern economy was increasingly marginal to national economic development, our focus in this chapter will be on the development of the industrial base.

[6]Bruce Laurie, *Artisans into Workers: Labor in Nineteenth Century America* (New York: Noonday Press, 1989), pp. 15–47.

[7]Guy S. Callender, "The Early Transportation and Banking Enterprises of the States in Relation to the Growth of Corporations," *Quarterly Journal of Economics* 77 (November 1902): 111–62. Quoted in Colleen A. Dunlavy, *Politics and Industrialization: Early Railroads in the United States and Prussia* (Princeton, N.J.: Princeton University Press, 1994), p. 97.

[8]Quoted in ibid., p. 26.

[9]See the important article by Harry N. Scheiber, "Federalism and the American Economic Order, 1789–1910," *Law & Society Review,* Fall 1975, 57–119.

Nowhere was the influence of state governments more apparent than in their contribution to railroad development. For example, a number of state governments built and operated railroads themselves. Where they did not own and operate railroads, state governments invested in them. State and local governments financed almost 30 percent of the more than $1 billion invested in railroads before the Civil War. In addition, state governments regulated railroads through charters they issued to private railroad companies, through appointments to railroad commissions, and through the railroad rates they set.[10]

During this classic era of competitive capitalism, prior to the rise of giant corporations, the federal government's role was quite limited. Political scientist Stephen Skowronek found that "[t]he national government throughout the nineteenth century routinely provided promotional and support services for the state governments and left the substantive tasks of governing to these regional units."[11] The national government's jurisdiction in economic matters was limited basically to establishing tariff policy and banking and monetary policy, managing public lands, and maintaining order.

The activities pursued by state and national government in the early nineteenth century were essential to creating a framework within which business could grow. They challenge the common belief that, prior to the twentieth century, government did little to influence the economy. But the economic role governments played prior to the Civil War paled in comparison to the range and level of activity that governments pursued in the twentieth century, as they tried to respond to the challenges posed by industrialization, the rise of corporate capitalism, and economic instability.

STAGNATION AND CHALLENGE

The first wave of economic expansion, which was initiated by the transportation revolution, ended in 1873. The competitive nature of early capitalism led to an accelerating downturn. Prices fell throughout the last quarter of the nineteenth century as fierce competition drove entrepreneurs to introduce new, efficient production methods in an attempt to cut costs and prices. The downturn initiated a wave of business consolidations and acquisitions, creating large corporations that could dominate their markets. Citizens were at their mercy, forced to accept the wages corporations offered and the prices they charged. Labor historian Melvin Dubofsky quotes a Pennsylvania coal miner who lamented: "The working people of this country . . . find monopolies as strong as government itself. They find capital as rigid as absolute

[10]See Dunlavy, *Politics and Industrialization*, pp. 45–98.

[11]Stephen Skowronek, *Building a New American State: The Expansion of National Administrative Capacities, 1877–1920* (Cambridge: Cambridge University Press, 1982), p. 23.

monarchy. They find their so-called independence a myth."[12] These grievances soon found expression in organized political movements. In the 1870s,
farmers mobilized through the Grange to put pressure on state legislatures
and on Congress to demand fairer rates from the railroads. Workers also
mobilized in what became known as the Great Uprising of 1877. Railway
workers from Baltimore to San Francisco struck to protest wage cuts. Local
governments were either sympathetic to the workers' demands or so overwhelmed by their protests that the federal government had to dispatch
troops to crush the first national strike in U.S. history. The Great Uprising
was followed in 1886 by the Great Upheaval, when another labor organization, the Knights of Labor, emerged from obscurity to lead a series of strikes
by workers for the eight-hour day. At the same time that workers manned
picket lines, farmers in the South and the West joined the Populist Party. The
Populists challenged both major political parties and criticized their ties to
banks and large corporations.

All of these disparate movements opposed the growth of large corporations able to dominate their markets, at the expense of farmers, workers, and
consumers. They shared a belief in equality; a sense that labor, not capital,
created wealth; a fear that business had captured political power; and an op-
timism that the majority could tame the corrupting influence of capital. This
general critique was embodied in specific proposals for change. For example,
these social movements proposed cooperatives owned and managed by
farmers and workers themselves as an alternative to the traditional privately
managed firm. They also demanded specific changes in government policy
to reflect the power of the "producing classes," of workers and farmers, as
opposed to the selfish influence of merchants, bankers, and capitalists. For
the Grange, this meant government regulation of the railroads; for the
Knights of Labor, government regulation of the terms of labor; and for the
Populists, government measures to promote cheap and easy-to-obtain credit.

While these broad-based social movements failed to recapture government from the capitalists they believed had usurped it, they did leave a
legacy. First, they challenged—sometimes successfully—existing urban-
rural and racial cleavages. The Populists reached out to workers in the cities
for support in the same way that the Knights of Labor defied racist traditions
and opened up their membership to black workers. Second, these movements left a local heritage of radicalism, which later generations could draw
on. For example, in the 1900s, the Socialist Party garnered remarkable support from farmers in the Southwest because it could draw on an earlier tradition of Populism in the region.[13] Third, the political program of these
groups became the basis for the regulatory reforms of the Progressive period

---

[12]Quoted in Melvin Dubofsky, *Industrialism and the American Worker, 1865–1920* (Arlington
Heights, Ill.: Harlan Davidson, 1985), p. 53.

[13]James R. Green, *Grass Roots Socialism: Radical Movements in the Southwest, 1895–1943* (Baton
Rouge: Louisiana State University Press, 1978), pp. 228–70.

in the early twentieth century, which sought to restrain corporate capitalism.[14] Finally, these movements created an alternative to the dominant culture. They articulated a different vision—one based on the dignity of labor, the benefits of a rough equality, a restrained individualism, and the virtues of self-sufficiency.[15]

THE SECOND WAVE OF EXPANSION

A second wave of expansion began at the turn of the century, sparked by the development of new power sources. The electric motor and the internal combustion engine now powered industry and increased productivity. These technological innovations contributed to the concentration and centralization of production. Historian David Noble points out that, in such varied industries as petroleum, steel, rubber, and transportation, "the systematic introduction of science as a means of production presupposed, and in turn reinforced, industrial monopoly."[16] Small firms that existed in competitive markets were being driven out of business or were combining with larger firms. The physical shape of business was changing under the impact of corporate mergers and industrial concentration.

The new wave of expansion depended as much on political support as it did on technological and economic changes. The critical election of 1896 cleared the political ground for the shift from competitive to corporate capitalism. Populists and other opponents of corporate capitalism rallied behind William Jennings Bryan, the Democratic candidate in the 1896 presidential election. But he was no match for the corporate money and political salesmanship that carried his Republican opponent, William McKinley, to victory. The Republican Party became the political handmaiden of industrial capitalism following the 1896 election. The Republican Party, during the Progressive era, which lasted from 1896 to 1916, laid the foundations for a new political economy.

The Progressive era marked a profound change in the American political economy. The rise of trusts—large corporations that had the raw power to dominate their markets and exploit consumers, farmers, and employees—generated popular demands for government action. In the past, state governments had intervened in the economy to promote business. Now citizens demanded that the federal government intervene to regulate business. Not

---

[14]Elizabeth Sanders, *Roots of Reform: Farmers, Workers and the American State, 1896–1917* (Chicago: University of Chicago Press, 1999).

[15]This point is made forcefully in Lawrence Goodwyn, *The Populist Moment* (New York: Oxford University Press, 1979).

[16]David F. Noble, *America by Design: Science, Technology, and the Rise of Corporate Capitalism* (New York: Oxford University Press, 1977), p. 6.

only did citizens now look to the federal government instead of state governments, but also within the federal government itself an institutional shift occurred. Policy formation moved from arenas sensitive to electoral politics, such as political parties and Congress, to executive agencies, independent commissions, and the courts, which were insulated from democratic pressures.

The central issue of the Progressive period was what to do about the power of large trusts. As large corporations with market power appeared first in the railroad industry and then in other industries, citizens demanded that a new relationship between business and government be constructed. Under popular pressure, the federal government assumed increased responsibility for regulating markets, but in a distinctively American way. The federal government would regulate markets in a way that still avoided big government and enabled large corporations to retain considerable freedom of action.[17] Historian Martin J. Sklar writes, "The corporate style of capitalism" entailed "a growing role for positive government . . . but . . . in a manner consistent with the greatest possible preservation of private initiative and private-property ownership as against state direction and state ownership."[18] Rather than closely scrutinizing corporate behavior, as many demanded, the federal government would simply seek to prohibit corporations from engaging in what was described as "unreasonable restraint of trade," such as price fixing. Hence firms would continue to enjoy a free hand and government's role would be limited to preventing unfair business practices.[19]

CORPORATE CAPITALISM UNRAVELS

Government intervention in the economy substantially increased during World War I (1917–1919) because of the pressing need to mobilize all available resources. The form that intervention took was very different from the earlier pattern of "negative regulation," that is, simply prohibiting certain forms of activity. This time the federal government formed tripartite committees, composed of representatives from business, labor, and the government, to develop policy that would coordinate production for the war effort. When the war ended, however, the tripartite committees were disbanded at business's insistence. Business could tolerate government direction during the wartime emergency. But when the emergency ended, business demanded

---

[17]Frank Drobbin, *Forging Industrial Policy: The United States, Britain and France in the Railway Age* (Cambridge: Cambridge University Press, 1994), pp. 28–91.

[18]Martin J. Sklar, *The Corporate Reconstruction of America* (New York: Cambridge University Press, 1988), pp. 38–39.

[19]Ibid., pp. 324–33.

The Stock Exchange in New York City on the day the market crashed in 1929.

that the government retreat and allow private capital to resume organizing and coordinating production.

The prosperity of the 1920s—like that of our own time—was deeply flawed. Inequality persisted and increased despite rising national income throughout the 1920s. In 1929, the top 1 percent of families on the income scale earned as much income as the bottom 42 percent. Moreover, income was rising faster for families at the top of the scale than for those at the bottom. A majority of families did not have sufficient income to reach "the American standard," a modestly defined standard of minimum comfort, and almost one-quarter of all families lived in severe poverty.[20]

The Roaring Twenties ended on October 21, 1929, when the stock market crashed. The Dow Jones Industrial Average, a barometer of the entire market, lost half its value in just two weeks. The "era of good feelings" was replaced first by gloom and then by despair. Unemployment rose steadily, from 4 million in January 1930, to 6 million by November, and then to 8 million by the following January. Employers increased the distress by cutting wages. Each line of defense against poverty—first family savings, next private charities, and then state and local government relief programs—was

---

[20]Irving Bernstein, *A History of the American Worker, 1920–1933: The Lean Years* (Boston: Houghton Mifflin, 1960), pp. 47–83.

overwhelmed by the demands for help placed upon it. Meanwhile, Republican President Herbert Hoover stubbornly remained faithful to the prevailing wisdom, which claimed that government could not and should not concern itself with the economy—even an economy mired in depression.

The depth and persistence of the Depression undermined people's faith in capitalism, in capitalists, and in a government that did nothing to help. Bread lines, soup kitchens, and the ever-present unemployed led people to demand large-scale change. Farmers struck, refusing to bring their crops to market because prices had dropped below production costs. Workers in the great manufacturing centers began to organize into unions. General strikes closed San Francisco and Minneapolis. Rubber workers in Akron, Ohio, and autoworkers in Flint, Michigan, held sit-down strikes and occupied factories until their demands for union recognition were met. A group of unions broke away from the American Federation of Labor (AFL), intent on organizing workers in the nation's great manufacturing centers into a new labor federation called the Congress of Industrial Organizations (CIO). By the end of the thirties, unions affiliated with the CIO boasted over 3.6 million members.

The Depression also weakened voters' faith in the Republican Party. From one end of the country to the other, from farms to factories, people demanded a fresh start. In 1932, a new electoral coalition of working people, Catholics, Jews, and southerners elected Democratic candidate Franklin Delano Roosevelt as president. In dramatic contrast to President Hoover's dithering, FDR promised a New Deal. He proposed that the government devise measures to end the Depression, provide relief, and manage the economy. For the half century after FDR's first election in 1932, political struggles in the United States revolved around how to give concrete meaning to Roosevelt's vision of a New Deal.

A NEW DEAL

Roosevelt believed that a fundamental restructuring of the economy and a new relationship of the state to the economy were necessary to restore economic growth, reduce unemployment, and satisfy voters. FDR was not hostile to capitalism, but believed that only great change could save it. However, there was intense disagreement among his advisers about what kinds of reforms were needed. Some advocated use of a much stronger regulatory hand by the government that would enhance public control over corporate institutions. Others advised letting business manage markets by encouraging business associations to form cartels that would set prices and production targets for industry. Still another group of New Dealers proposed just the opposite medicine. They suggested that the government use its power to enforce vigorous anti-monopoly measures that would promote competition and protect consumers and small businesses from unreasonable restraints of trade. Although these factions differed about how the government should reorganize the economy, they agreed that the federal government needed to restructure it in order to restore prosperity.

As the 1930s wore on, however, the issue of how to deal with the Depression—pressing as it continued to be—took back seat to an even greater emergency. Adolph Hitler came to power in Germany in 1933, a year after FDR was elected. In 1939, the Nazis invaded Poland, provoking World War II in Europe. Two years later the United States entered the war. As the Depression was superseded by a new emergency—World War II—a subtle shift in prevailing economic ideas occurred. The Roosevelt administration's priorities shifted from promoting growth through restructuring the economy to promoting growth through fiscal policy. Fiscal policy—that is, government's power to tax and spend—would be used to stimulate consumption by running budget deficits. Fiscal policy represented a less sweeping intervention by government in the economy than the other measures New Dealers had first proposed, since it entailed no change in the structure of the economy: not more government regulation, more cartels, or more anti-monopoly measures. According to historian Alan Brinkley, New Dealers now spoke less about redistributing economic power and more about increasing mass purchasing power.[21]

This new economic paradigm in which consumption drove the economy was based on ideas first developed by British economist John Maynard Keynes. Keynes claimed that the major cause of the Depression (which afflicted not only the United States, but European economies as well) was inadequate consumer demand. Private industry was caught in a vicious circle in which mass unemployment reduced the demand for goods. As inventories piled up for lack of consumers to purchase them, firms laid off even more workers. Private industry, by itself, was incapable of escaping from this downward spiral of unemployment, since private business firms were accurately reacting to signals indicating a lack of demand in the market. To break the vicious circle, government would have to step into the breach. By running a deficit in the federal budget—spending more money than it collected in tax revenue—the government would increase the total amount of money in circulation and thereby increase demand. Once people had money to spend again, business would react to the new consumer demand by rehiring workers and stepping up production. With workers back on the job earning and spending wages, demand would grow, and the economic recovery would become self-sustaining. Thus, Keynes argued that deficit spending by the government in times of slack demand was the key to transforming vicious circles into virtuous ones.

Corporations frightened by the potential radicalism of the New Deal found Keynes's emphasis on fiscal policy preferable to the earlier, more ambitious New Deal proposals. Fiscal policy required no change in the distribution of

---

[21] Alan Brinkley, *The End of Reform: New Deal Liberalism in Recession and War* (New York: Knopf, 1995), pp. 230–31.

economic power between government and business, whereas the initial proposals had involved more sweeping structural reforms. "Fiscal policy," according to Brinkley, "would not reshape capitalist institutions," but "would reshape the environment in which these institutions worked."[22] Thus, Keynesianism, as the new demand-side theory came to be called, represented the least threatening way to use government to counter tendencies toward recession and depression. For the next four decades, from the 1930s to the 1970s, both Democratic and Republican administrations followed Keynesian prescriptions of economic management.

THE ROAD NOT TAKEN

Keynesianism came to command such wide support in part because it was a safe alternative to more audacious proposals for state economic intervention. In many ways, the Depression and World War II emergencies represented a missed opportunity to regulate private economic power.[23] Certainly, the changes that occurred were substantial. For example, the outlines of the welfare state were forged during the New Deal, offering citizens some protection against the swings of the business cycle. Unemployment insurance and Social Security created at least a minimal safety net where none existed previously. The labor market also came in for a degree of regulation, as child labor was outlawed and a minimum wage law was passed. Labor unions grew from 3 million members in 1929 to 14 million by 1945, offering workers some protection against the unilateral power of management. These changes were consolidated after World War II and were accepted as legitimate by most Democrats and Republicans until the 1970s.

But set against comparable developments that occurred in Europe while these changes were being forged, the results were quite meager. In Europe, following World War II, governments developed a more expansive welfare state to cushion citizens from economic instability and more powerful administrative institutions to steer the economy, regulate the market, and influence the behavior of private firms. European governments did not rely predominantly on fiscal policy—that is, demand management by the government—to promote economic growth, but instead engaged in struc-

---

[22]Ibid., p. 268. This interpretation of the transformation of New Deal economic reform is based on Brinkley's work. A similar view is offered by John W. Jeffries, "The 'New' New Deal: FDR and American Liberalism, 1937–1945," *Political Science Quarterly* 105, no. 3 (1990): 397–418.

[23]Andrew Shonfeld writes, "The New Dealers . . . perceived the future as a new mixture of public and private initiatives, with the public side very much reinforced but still operating in the framework of a predominantly capitalist system. Considering the opportunities for radical experiment offered by twenty years of uninterrupted Democratic administration from 1933 to 1952, it is surprising how little follow-through there was from this original impulse into the postwar world." See Andrew Shonfeld, *Modern Capitalism* (London: Oxford University Press, 1970), p. 308.

tural reform. For example, basic industries, such as telecommunications, utilities, steel, railways, and airlines, which were privately held in the United States, were publicly owned in many European countries after the war. Public ownership gave European governments greater influence over the direction of the economy than was available to the U.S. government.

Interestingly, the United States had an opportunity to travel a similar path of public ownership following the war, but chose not to follow it. In order to meet wartime production requirements, the federal government built manufacturing plants and leased them to private industry, which operated the facilities. By the end of the war, the government owned 40 percent of all capital assets in the United States, including all the nation's synthetic rubber and magnesium production facilities, in addition to significant stakes in aircraft manufacturing and aluminum production. Continued ownership of the plants would have provided government with the potential to influence the postwar economy. But under pressure from conservative groups, wartime reconversion plans required the government to sell the plants in order to prevent the government from competing with private industry.[24]

The U.S. retreat from interventionist forms of economic management during and after the New Deal was due to a number of factors. First, liberals were already in political retreat by the 1936 elections. The ranks of Republicans and conservative Democrats grew in Congress after 1936, limiting political support for an ambitious program of structural economic reform.[25]

Second, opponents of an expansive role for government used the dramatic economic recovery during the war as a reason to avoid fundamental economic change—which was ironic in light of the government's leading role in creating that recovery. The war succeeded in ending the Depression, which eight years of the New Deal had failed to do. During the war years, gross national product grew by 50 percent, and full employment replaced mass unemployment. The economic emergency had passed and with it the argument for bold new measures.

Third, the onset of the Cold War had devastating consequences for domestic liberalism. Communism had to be rooted out at home as much as it did abroad. Cold Warriors put liberals on the defensive, claiming that liberals were soft on communism and that their proposals for more economic regulation led down the path to communism. Liberals had to renounce their program in order to prove their patriotism.[26]

---

[24]Brinkley, *End of Reform*, pp. 240–45.

[25]On the decline of liberalism in Congress, see James T. Patterson, *Congressional Conservatism and the New Deal* (Lexington: University of Kentucky Press, 1967); Shelley C. Mack II, *The Permanent Majority: The Conservative Coalition in the United States Congress* (Tuscaloosa: University of Alabama Press, 1983); Ira Katznelson, Kim Geiger, and Daniel Kryder, "Limiting Liberalism: The Southern Veto in Congress, 1933–1950," *Political Science Quarterly* 108, no. 2 (1993): 283–305.

[26]Robert Griffith and Athan Theoharis, eds., *The Specter* (New York: New Viewpoints, 1974).

CONSERVATIVE KEYNESIANISM

Keynesian theory was interpreted and applied in different ways in different places. The Keynesianism that governed American economic policy in the postwar years was the most conservative variant, and quite different from the Keynesianism that was implemented in Europe. For example, Keynes believed that full employment was essential to increasing aggregate—total—demand. Consistent with this belief, President Truman (who replaced President Roosevelt when the latter died in office) submitted the Full Employment Act to Congress in 1945, just two weeks after the end of World War II. Conservatives in Congress proceeded to dilute the bill beyond recognition. The original version of the bill proclaimed, "Every American able and willing to work has the right to a useful and remunerative job." But this pledge was transformed into "it is the policy of the United States to foster free competitive enterprise" in the version that was passed. Even the name of the bill was changed from the Full Employment Act to the Employment Act as it made its way through Congress.[27]

Keynes also believed that some kind of redistribution of income from the top to the bottom was required. He identified as one of the "outstanding faults of the [capitalist] economic society in which we live . . . its arbitrary and inequitable distribution of wealth."[28] But Keynes's prescription to redistribute wealth was rejected in America. Although governmental social spending grew, much of it was in the form of Social Security payments, which redistributed money from the young to the old, not from the rich to the poor. Welfare state spending pumped money into the economy, but did so in a way that did not disturb the underlying class structure.

While welfare state spending as a means to boost consumption was lower and less redistributive in the United States than in Europe, military spending was higher. Defense spending accounted for three-quarters of all discretionary spending by the federal government, generating military orders, jobs, and new technologies for the economy.[29] As *Business Week*, a management publication, pointed out, "There's a tremendous social and economic difference between welfare pump priming and military pump priming. . . . Military spending doesn't really alter the structure of the economy. It goes through regular channels. As far as a business man is concerned, a munitions order from the government is much like an order from a private customer."[30]

---

[27]Alan Wolfe, *America's Impasse: The Rise and Fall of the Politics of Growth* (Boston: South End Press, 1981), pp. 52–53.

[28]Quoted in ibid., p. 51.

[29]In the 1990s, with no Cold War to fight, national defense accounted for one-half of all discretionary spending by the federal government.

[30]Quoted in Robert M. Collins, *The Business Response to Keynes, 1929–1964* (New York: Columbia University Press, 1981), p. 199.

The conservative form Keynesianism took in the United States was also evident in the form that budget deficits took. Both Democratic and Republican administrations chose to pursue deficit spending through cutting taxes rather than increasing public spending. In 1964, President Lyndon Johnson defended his administration's tax cut in the very same terms that Republicans 20 years later used to defend their tax cuts. Johnson told an audience of business people, "We put some of the money back for the people to spend instead of letting the government spend it for them. We put some of the money back for business to invest in new enterprise instead of the government investing it for them."[31] A consequence of deficit spending through tax cuts was that, while many were well off in the United States, public facilities, such as schools and parks, were starved for funds. Economist John Kenneth Galbraith described the result as "private affluence amidst public squalor."[32]

In brief, Keynesianism became the new economic orthodoxy following the war, accepted not only by Democrats, but eventually by Republicans as well, because of the conservative way it was implemented. The American version of Keynesianism included only a symbolic commitment to full employment; economic stimulation through military spending, not redistribution; and deficit spending through tax cuts, not public investment. When recast in this form, even business, which was initially hostile to Keynesianism, came to appreciate its benefits. Although the Democratic Party was the first to embrace Keynesianism, by the 1970s even Republican President Richard Nixon could declare, "We are all Keynesians now."[33]

THE GOLDEN AGE OF CAPITALISM

Many feared that the economy would slide back into recession once the artificial stimulus of World War II was removed. Instead, the United States experienced the most prosperous 25 years in its history, often dubbed the golden age of capitalism. Median family income almost doubled between 1950 and 1970. As historian Jack Metzgar recalls in his memoir of the period, the affluence of the postwar years was "new, and surprising—like a first kiss."[34] Urban working families moved out of tenements and acquired new homes in the suburbs. Televisions, cars, washing machines, and telephones—beyond the reach of most families in 1940—were now owned by a majority of families just 20 years later.

---

[31]Quoted in Judith Stein, *Running Steel, Running America: Race, Economic Policy and the Decline of Liberalism* (Chapel Hill: University of North Carolina Press, 1998), p. 75.

[32]John Kenneth Galbraith, *The Affluent Society* (Boston: Houghton Mifflin, 1963).

[33]Herbert Stein, *Presidential Economies: The Making of Economic Policy from Roosevelt to Clinton* (Washington, D.C.: American Enterprise Institute, 1994), p. 135.

[34]Jack Metzgar, *Striking Steel: Solidarity Remembered* (Philadelphia: Temple University Press, 2000), p. 210.

Although Keynesianism is often given credit for making possible the postwar boom, its contribution is a matter of dispute. In fact, the success of the U.S. economy can be attributed to an unusual coincidence of national and international factors that distinguish this period from what came before—and after. First, pent-up consumer demand fueled the postwar economy. Production for the war effort restricted the supply of consumer goods at the same time it put people to work and money in their pockets. The combination of disposable income and pent-up demand led Americans to embark on a collective shopping spree.

Second, the huge demand for consumer goods led businesses to expand capacity and invest in new plants and equipment. Capital investment not only created jobs as a result of new plant construction, but also increased labor productivity as firms invested in new technology.

Third, labor relations simmered down following the 1946 strike wave, the largest in American history. Employers did not accept the legitimacy of unions, but now resentfully acknowledged them as a fact of life they could not avoid. Management prevented profits from being squeezed by tying wage increases to increases in productivity, while labor prevented inflation from eroding wage increases by negotiating cost-of-living adjustments in their contracts. The result was stable and predictable economic conditions, which boosted business confidence and thereby encouraged additional investment.

Fourth, big government contributed to the new affluence. Government spending climbed steadily from $47.1 billion in 1950, or 21 percent of gross domestic product (GDP), to $236.1 billion by 1970, or almost 27 percent of GDP. Public-sector employment more than doubled, increasing from 5.9 million in 1950 to 13 million by 1970.[35] Big government was not a drag on economic growth during the golden age of capitalism, but, rather, was essential to it.

Finally, the postwar economy profited from the emergence of U.S. global dominance. American firms not only were busy satisfying the voracious appetite of American consumers, but also were supplying war-torn Europe with food and clothes, as well as equipment and other supplies with which to rebuild its devastated economies. Moreover, American firms had the world market to themselves. The only potential competitors, in Europe and Japan, were heavily damaged from World War II and needed to devote their resources to wartime recovery.

By midcentury, the terms of the informal national bargain that had been struck between business and government were clear. Strategic decisions governing the American economy—how much to invest, where to invest, what to invest in, how to organize the work—would be made by corporate capital. Government would not intrude on corporate decision making or engage in economic planning that might interfere with business's right to manage. Instead, by smoothing out the business cycle, educating workers, stimulating consumption, funding research, and protecting corporate mar-

---

[35]By 1996, public-sector employment had grown to 19.7 million workers.

kets and investments abroad, government would create a political and economic environment that would encourage corporate investment and job creation.[36] President John Kennedy captured the essence of the bargain between business and government in a 1961 press conference: "The country cannot prosper unless business prospers. This country cannot meet its obligations and its tax obligations unless business is doing well. Business will not do well and we [will not] have full employment unless they feel there is a chance to make a profit. So there is no long run hostility between business and government. There cannot be. We cannot succeed unless they succeed."[37]

In the next section, we describe the federal government's economic policy-making institutions and processes, which developed in the postwar period and to a large extent remain in place in the present day. We then analyze why the golden age of capitalism ended in the 1970s and review the new pattern that has replaced it since the 1980s.

ECONOMIC POLICY MAKING

Policy-makers in the United States lack an extensive institutional capacity to manage the economy and influence the behavior of private firms. Deprived of powerful and direct levers, such as nationalized industries and banks with which to steer the economy, policy-makers must rely on weak and indirect mechanisms—notably, fiscal and monetary policy. But the ability of government to utilize effectively even these tools is undermined by its institutional design. Control over fiscal policy is fragmented between Congress and the president, which invites conflict and often produces incoherence. Control over monetary policy is vested in the Federal Reserve Board (popularly known as the Fed), a fiercely independent agency insulated from democratic pressure and electoral control. (Indeed, the Fed is informally designated as "the fourth branch of the federal government."[38]) Moreover, because responsibility for different kinds of economic policy is assigned to different institutions independent of each other, there is no assurance that fiscal and monetary policy will be coordinated—that is, that they will push in the same direction.[39]

The weak institutional capacity of the government makes it difficult for citizens to democratically control the economy through their elected representatives. The absence of direct controls, the fragmentation of authority

[36]Robert B. Reich, *The Wealth of Nations: Preparing Ourselves for 21st Century Capitalism* (New York: Knopf, 1991), p. 67.

[37]Quoted in Wolfe, *America's Impasse*, p. 67.

[38]James MacGregor Burns and Georgia J. Sorenson, *Dead Center: Clinton-Gore Leadership and the Perils of Moderation* (New York: Scribner, 1999), p. 101.

[39]William Greider, *Secrets of the Temple: How the Federal Reserve Runs the Country* (New York: Simon & Schuster, 1987), pp. 351–405.

over fiscal policy between Congress and the president; the independence of the Federal Reserve Bank, and the lack of mechanisms to ensure coordination between fiscal and monetary policy deprive the elected government of the means to influence greatly the "private government" that owns and controls capital. But the American pattern of economic policy making is not simply arbitrary or illogical. If it were, it would be astonishing that the United States has been the world's preeminent economic power for the past century. It is, in fact, well designed to let corporate capitalism flourish, escape democratic accountability, and preserve inequality.

FISCAL POLICY

Fiscal policy consists of taxation, which raises government revenue, and public spending. At the most general level, fiscal policy is a tool for managing the economy. Government can either stimulate the economy by running a budget deficit, as Keynes recommended should be done during a recession or depression, or restrain the economy by running a budget surplus. But the budget is more than a fiscal tool. It also establishes the priorities and values of the government. It is a blueprint of how the government intends to distribute costs and benefits among different social groups. Given that over one-quarter of America's GDP is collected in taxes and spent by government, fiscal policy plays a key role in deciding who the winners and losers in our society will be. The problems of our cities, the lack of public transportation, and the inadequacies of our welfare state can all be traced to the budget. The budget process is a long, difficult, and intensely political affair that involves partisan conflict between Democrats and Republicans and institutional conflict between the legislative and executive branches, as well as conflict within each of these branches. The budget is a window through which relations of power in society are revealed.

There is a common belief that government is too big, that it confiscates too much money in the form of taxes and spends too much money in the form of government programs. Indeed, government has grown tremendously since the New Deal of the 1930s. Government costs more, does more, and employs more people than it did 70 or even 10 years ago.

Yet when viewed comparatively, the public sector in the United States is relatively small. State, local, and federal employment accounts for just 15 percent of the nation's workforce, far less than the one-quarter to one-third of total employment that the public sector comprises in most other industrialized countries. In addition, the tax burden is considerably lighter on Americans than on citizens in other advanced capitalist democracies. As Table 3–1 indicates, the United States collects a lower share of taxes as a percentage of GDP than does any other major industrialized country with the exception of Japan.

State, local, and federal governments collected a total of $2.5 trillion in 1999. This was about 29 percent of GDP compared to a tax burden of 33 to

■ TABLE 3-1

TAX REVENUES AS PERCENT OF
GROSS DOMESTIC PRODUCT

	1970	1975	1980	1985	1990	1995	1999*	2000*	2001*
Australia	24.9	27.7	29.3	32.2	32.3	31.8	33.1	33.0	32.7
Austria	38.8	41.9	45.4	47.7	46.2	47.5	47.6	46.6	46.7
Belgium	39.3	45.3	48.1	51.3	47.9	49.2	49.9	49.1	48.8
Canada	34.6	36.7	36.5	38.7	42.1	42.0	42.8	42.5	42.2
Czech Republic	—	—	—	—	—	41.5	39.6	40.0	41.9
Denmark	—	—	—	—	55.0	56.8	57.4	56.3	56.0
Finland	34.3	42.8	40.3	46.0	49.9	50.7	50.0	49.6	48.6
France	39.1	40.7	45.6	48.8	47.7	48.0	50.2	49.8	49.3
Germany	37.4	41.6	43.7	44.5	41.8	45.0	46.0	45.6	45.3
Greece	27.2	28.9	32.0	35.2	34.9	44.5	47.7	47.2	46.8
Hungary	—	—	—	—	48.3	42.8	39.7	39.4	39.4
Iceland	—	—	—	—	33.3	36.0	37.0	36.7	36.6
Ireland	—	—	34.1	38.2	35.0	34.0	33.4	32.9	32.6
Italy	28.8	28.6	33.5	38.5	42.1	44.2	46.3	45.9	45.5
Japan	20.6	24.0	27.6	30.8	34.2	32.0	30.5	30.5	30.9
Korea	16.8	16.1	19.3	18.8	21.8	23.5	25.1	24.8	24.4
Luxembourg	—	—	—	—	—	—	—	—	—
Mexico	—	—	—	—	—	—	—	—	—
Netherlands	35.6	42.7	46.2	47.9	43.7	43.6	43.2	43.0	42.8
New Zealand	—	—	—	—	44.0	41.9	40.8	40.3	40.3
Norway	40.0	44.3	49.3	51.4	52.3	51.1	51.0	51.4	52.4
Poland	—	—	—	—	—	44.4	41.0	40.0	39.1
Portugal	22.1	22.6	28.7	32.8	35.5	38.8	42.4	42.5	42.6
Spain	20.8	22.8	28.0	32.2	35.6	35.5	37.2	36.9	36.8
Sweden	46.6	50.6	53.6	56.8	60.5	54.8	58.7	56.8	55.6
Switzerland	36.4	43.9	43.3	46.7	48.6	52.7	57.0	57.6	57.7
Turkey	—	15.9	17.4	12.9	14.6	18.7	20.5	20.5	20.4
United Kingdom	—	—	—	—	40.3	38.6	40.3	40.3	40.4
United States	27.6	27.1	28.7	28.7	29.3	29.8	31.0	30.8	30.6

*Estimates and projections. Source: *Economic Outlook,* no. 66, December 1999. OECD.

SOURCE: Analytical Databank, OECD.

■ FIGURE 3-1

COMPOSITION OF REVENUES

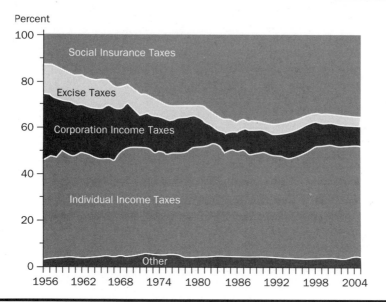

SOURCE: *A Citizen's Guide to the Federal Budget* (Washington, D.C.: U.S. Government Printing Office, 2001), p. 9.

50 percent in many European countries. State and local governments raise revenue primarily through property and sales taxes. The federal government raises revenue primarily through payroll or Social Security taxes, corporate income taxes, and individual income taxes. As Figures 3–1 and 3–2 make clear, the proportion of federal revenue raised through taxes on individual incomes has remained fairly constant over time. Payroll taxes have increased substantially as a percentage of total revenue, while corporate taxes have declined.

The United States also allocates a smaller proportion of its GDP to government spending than any other advanced capitalist democracy, as is clear from Figure 3–3.

Not only is the American government leaner, but it is also meaner. We spend a higher proportion of our budget on national defense and a lower proportion on social welfare than comparable European governments do.

The smaller public sector in the United States is reflected in the smaller number of public services available to Americans. As we will find in Chapter 10, which reviews social welfare policy, other countries have public programs to finance or directly provide such benefits as medical care to its citizens. In the United States, this and other services are considered commodities and must be purchased in the marketplace—if citizens can afford them.

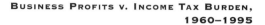

■ **FIGURE 3-2**

BUSINESS PROFITS v. INCOME TAX BURDEN, 1960–1995

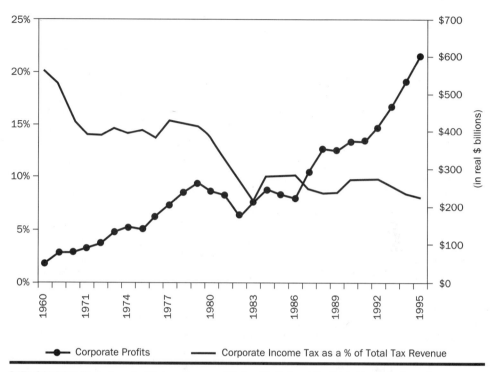

●— Corporate Profits   —— Corporate Income Tax as a % of Total Tax Revenue

DATA SOURCE: Department of Labor, Bureau of Labor Statistics, *http://stats.bls.gov/cpihome.htm.*

The difference has an appreciable impact on the quality of our social life, as measured by such indices as the extent of violent crime, child poverty, economic inequality, and drug addiction.

THE BUDGET PROCESS

Although the United States is toward the bottom of the league tables in terms of the size of the public sector, the extent of the tax burden, and the proportion of taxes raised through personal income taxes, President George W. Bush made tax and spending cuts his signature reform during his first year in office. In 2001, he succeeded in sponsoring a tax cut of about $1.35 trillion over eleven years. The president often proclaimed that the funds generated by the tax cut belonged to "the people," not to the government. However, the lion's share of the tax cut was captured by the wealthiest taxpayers,

■ FIGURE 3-3

REVENUES AS A PERCENT OF GDP—
COMPARISON WITH OTHER COUNTRIES

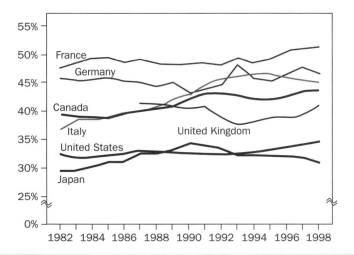

SOURCE: *A Citizen's Guide to the Federal Budget* (Washington, D.C.: U.S. Government Printing Office, 2001), p. 9.

who needed it the least. As a result, the reform—defended by the president on grounds of equity and fairness—will surely intensify economic inequality in the United States.

In tandem with cuts in personal income taxes, President Bush's first budget restrained federal spending, despite increases in population and public needs. Predictably, governments at all levels have been less able to ensure adequate education, infrastructure, and social services.

The place to begin our study of fiscal policy is the executive branch, especially in the office of the president. The president's annual budget proposal, sent to Congress each February, is the focal point of fiscal policy making. This is not to say that the president's preferences and priorities are accepted. Rather, they are the point of departure for a complex and conflictual process that eventually culminates in congressional passage of a budget.

Within the Executive Office of the President (which we describe in Chapter 6), the Office of Management and Budget (OMB) is in charge of formulating the president's budget. OMB negotiates with federal agencies to reconcile differences between their requests and the president's projections. It then submits a draft budget to the president for review and approval. Some presidents are more involved in preparing the budget than others. Bill Clinton, for example, was heavily involved in preparing the budget during his administration, while his predecessor, George H. W. Bush, preferred to leave negotiations and details to OMB Director Richard Darman.

Once Congress receives the president's proposed budget, an intensely political process begins. In recent years, Congress has displayed more budgetary independence, mainly as a result of "divided government" in which Congress and the presidency are controlled by different parties. For example, when President Clinton's 1996 budget was submitted to the Republican-controlled Congress, one leading Republican congressional representative dismissed it as D.O.A. (dead on arrival). Congress then proceeded to draft a budget that differed considerably from the president's requests.

Budget committees in both the House and the Senate first adopt a Budget Resolution that specifies the total amount of money the government intends to raise and spend, with expenditures distributed across 20 broad categories of government activity. A joint Budget Resolution is then negotiated between the House and the Senate, which sets spending and taxing totals for the government. Committees within Congress are then charged with amending existing law to reflect tax and spending changes consistent with the totals called for in the joint Budget Resolution. The Appropriations committees in both the House and the Senate review these changes and stipulate the actual funding levels for particular programs, with an eye to keeping total spending within the guidelines set by the joint Budget Resolution. Appropriations bills are then submitted to the president for his signature or veto.[40]

The significance of the budget, the degree to which its cold numbers embody and reflect the government's ruling philosophy, was never more clearly revealed than in the struggle between Congress and President Clinton over the 1996 budget. The question surrounding the 1996 budget was whether it would reflect the values of a centrist Clinton administration or the principles of a deeply conservative Congress, whose two chambers were commanded by Republican majorities, following their 1994 midterm election victory.

President Clinton's 1996 budget was submitted to Congress on February 1, 1995—and was promptly ignored. Instead, in the sharply polarized partisan atmosphere that prevailed, Republicans in the House and the Senate developed and voted on their own budget, which diverged sharply from the president's and, according to journalist Elizabeth Drew, "redistributed the benefits from the less wealthy—especially the poor—to the better off."[41] It contained cuts in food stamps, school lunches, and Medicare at the same time it included tax cuts for the rich. However, as with ordinary legislation, the budget does not become binding until it is approved by the president (or passed over the president's veto by a two-thirds majority of both the House and the Senate). When President Clinton vetoed the budget, he asked Republican congressional leaders to send him a continuing resolution that did not carry conditions or policy changes while they negotiated over the

[40]The budgetary process is described in detail in Allen Schick, *The Federal Budget: Politics, Policy and Process* (Washington, D.C.: Brookings, 1995).

[41]Elizabeth Drew, *Showdown* (New York: Simon & Schuster, 1996), p. 326.

budget. A continuing resolution was necessary to fund the government and keep it running, since the previous budget had expired and a new one had not yet been passed. However, Republicans in Congress proceeded to use the need for a continuing resolution as a means to impose their own conservative policy changes. They attached to the resolution "riders" (provisions) that would have cut funds for education, limited the enforcement of environmental protection laws, and raised premiums for Medicare. President Clinton vetoed the continuing resolution, proclaiming, "I believe this budget debate is about two very different futures for America."[42] Without a budget or continuing resolution in effect, the government could not legally pay its workers, and many government offices and national parks were closed. The battle seesawed back and forth. Before it was over, the federal government had been shut for 26 days. With Republicans dropping in the polls and being blamed for closing down the government, Congress abandoned the fight and passed a continuing resolution—without the riders that Clinton had previously found so objectionable—that the president signed.

MONETARY POLICY

The second major pillar of government economic policy is monetary policy. Monetary policy attempts to fine-tune the economy by manipulating interest rates, the cost of money. High interest rates tend to slow down the economy by discouraging spending. Low interest rates, on the other hand, encourage borrowing and spending by making credit cheap and easy to obtain. Like fiscal policy, monetary policy is used to counteract tendencies toward economic instability. If the economy is tending toward inflation, or excessive demand relative to the available supply of goods and services, raising interest rates will tend to cool it down. Conversely, if demand is slack, reducing interest rates will make taking out loans more attractive for consumers who want to purchase new goods and for businesses that want to make new investments.

But manipulating interest rates is not simply about trying to counteract tendencies to inflation and recession. Like fiscal policy, monetary policy affects different groups in different ways. For example, the affluent generally benefit from higher interest rates, while the opposite is true for those without accumulated wealth. The affluent often have savings, and high interest rates—tight money—increase the value of these investments. On the other hand, middle- and lower-income groups are more likely to need to obtain loans. Lower interest rates mean that it is cheaper to repay these loans. Thus, whether to err on the side of setting interest rates high or low is not simply a technical matter of managing the economy, but a political one of rewarding some groups at the expense of others. A key question then is, Who decides, and on what basis, if the economy needs higher or lower interest rates?

---

[42]Ibid., p. 323.

The chair of the Federal Reserve Board (along with other members of the Open Market Committee of the Federal Reserve Board) determines the rate of interest that the Federal Reserve System charges American banks to borrow funds. And this decision, in turn, ripples through the economy, affecting the direction of the stock and bond market, the rate of interest that banks charge on mortgages, and the rate of interest that credit card companies charge on unpaid balances. But the ripples continue far beyond, affecting whether companies hire more employees or prune their payrolls, whether wages and salaries go up or down, and, most generally, whether the economy expands or contracts. The fact that so little is known about the operation of the Federal Reserve Board is an extraordinary feature of American politics.

According to journalist William Greider, the Fed is "the crucial anomaly at the very core of representative government, an uncomfortable contradiction with the civic mythology of self-government."[43] When the Fed was created in 1913, it was deliberately insulated from democratic pressures and the influence of elected politicians. The Fed enjoys more political independence from both Congress and the president than any other government agency. It enjoys this enviable position because, ostensibly, monetary policy, adjusting interest rates, is a technical matter beyond politics. But as we have seen, nothing could be further from the truth. The Fed was deliberately given substantial autonomy in order to insulate monetary policy from democratic control.

The president and Congress are not completely without power over the Fed. Congress now requires the chair of the Fed to testify biannually before the House and Senate Banking committees. The president can influence the Fed by appointing members to the Federal Reserve Board, subject to confirmation by the Senate. The president also appoints the chair of the Fed to a four-year term, and if the chair wishes to be reappointed, he or she must consider the president's priorities. While the Fed is anxious to appease the president, it is even more concerned with preserving its reputation for fiscal probity among bankers, who are its real constituency.

Banks and the financial community in general have inordinate influence over Fed policy. While the Fed is structured to insulate it from democratic influence, it tends to adopt the perspective of banks because banks are its primary constituency—over 2,000 banks are members of the Federal Reserve System; most Federal Reserve Board members either previously worked for banks or are economists trained in finance; and the Fed, after all, is a bank itself, the central bank of the United States. Moreover, representatives from the banking community participate and vote when the Fed deliberates over monetary policy. Interest rate targets are set by the Federal Open Market Committee (FOMC). The FOMC is comprised of the 7 members who form the Federal Reserve Board, in addition to the presidents of the 12 district

---

[43]Greider, *Secrets of the Temple,* p. 12.

Federal Reserve Banks. Commercial banks in each district select the president of each Federal Reserve Bank, five of whom have voting privileges on the FOMC. In 1993, Representative Henry B. Gonzalez, chair of the House Committee on Banking, wrote an open letter to President Clinton deploring the presence of bankers on the FOMC and the lack of influence the public has over its composition. Gonzalez wrote:

> In general, the Federal Reserve decision makers are bankers or friends of bankers. Decision makers representing the concerns of agriculture, small business, labor, and community groups are almost unheard of. . . . Last week, the Fed selected one of their [sic] own, William J. McDonough, as president of the New York Federal Reserve Bank. Mr. McDonough's qualifications and his views on monetary policy . . . will not be debated in public. His expertise in central bank monetary policy will not be questioned in Senate confirmation hearings. However, because he has been selected through the Fed's internal private mechanisms, he will manage our nation's money supply without ever going before the American people or their representatives.[44]

Banks influence the Fed in more subtle ways than the unusual practice described above of having representatives from the banking community actually participate and vote in policy-making discussions of the FOMC. The Fed tends to view the economy through the eyes of a bank because it adopts the financial markets as its frame of reference in setting policy. Nancy Teeter, a former Federal Reserve Board member, recalls how her own perspective changed once she began to serve on the Fed. She remembers telling Arthur Burns, the chair of the Federal Reserve Board who interviewed her for the position, "'Arthur, you don't want someone like me on the Board of Governors with my liberal background.' Arthur said, 'Don't worry, Nancy. Within six months, you will think just like a central banker.' Arthur was right. I think I'm very much like a central banker now."[45]

"Thinking like a central banker" means using monetary policy to fight inflation, to preserve the value of money. The Fed has driven up interest rates, inducing recession and unemployment, in order to preserve the value of money, which banks and the wealthy control. The Fed has favored the money economy over the real economy, which produces things and puts people to work. Protected by its insulation from democratic pressure and the forbidding language in which it explains itself, the Fed escapes close scrutiny by Congress, the press, and the public for its choices. Henry Ford, Sr., once observed, "It is well enough that the people of the nation do not understand our banking and monetary system for, if they did, I believe there would be a revolution before tomorrow morning."[46]

---

[44]Henry B. Gonzalez, "An Open Letter to the President," *Challenge*, September–October 1993, 30–31.

[45]Quoted in Greider, *Secrets of the Temple*, pp. 73–74.

[46]Quoted in ibid., p. 55.

THE END OF THE GOLDEN AGE OF CAPITALISM

Over the course of the 1970s, the economy began to experience stagflation, an unprecedented situation in which unemployment and inflation increased simultaneously. In the past, unemployment and inflation tended to move in opposite directions. Now they both rose together. The average rate of unemployment was 6.2 percent in the 1970s, compared to just 4.8 percent in the 1960s. In human terms, that translated into 2.3 million more unemployed *per year* in the 1970s. The inflation record was even worse. The average rate of inflation over the course of the 1970s—7.1 percent—was more than twice as high as it had been in the previous decade. The twin daggers of unemployment and inflation took their toll on economic growth, which sputtered in the 1970s compared to the previous decade.

Many factors combined to bring the postwar boom to an end. The exceptional conditions that made the golden age possible were replaced by conditions that no longer so clearly favored American firms. For example, European and Japanese industry, which was in ruins following World War II, had been rebuilt and could now compete with American manufacturers in world markets.

Second, the rate of productivity growth, which measures the output of goods and services the economy produces per hour of work, began to falter. Productivity increased an average of 3.2 percent from 1948 to 1966. From 1966 to 1973, productivity growth slowed to an average of 2.3 percent and then dropped to an average of only 1 percent yearly from 1973 until the 1990s, when it began to rise again.[47]

Slower productivity growth squeezed profits. Capitalists at first raised prices in order to stay ahead. But this threatened to price U.S. products out of their markets. Then capitalists tried to recover by engaging in corporate takeovers and mergers. Economic resources were frittered away in rearranging assets, rather than being invested in new plants and equipment that would maintain the competitiveness of American industry.[48] Other nonproductive, wasteful expenses included military spending, which diverted capital and talent that could have been used to strengthen the civilian economy, and multiple layers of management and supervision, which increased overhead.[49]

Finally, managers tried to restore productivity growth and relieve the profit squeeze by coercing employees to work harder for less money. Business threatened to close plants if unions did not agree to wage and work-rule

---

[47]Bureau of Labor Statistics Data, Major Sector Multifactor Producivity Index, series ID: MPU300003(B) from website: *http://146.142.4.24/cgi-bin/surveymost*.

[48]Ira C. Magaziner and Robert B. Reich, *Minding America's Business: The Decline and Rise of the American Economy* (New York: Vintage Books, 1982).

[49]Samuel Bowles , David M. Gordon, and Thomas E. Weisskopf, *Beyond the Wasteland: A Democratic Alternative to Economic Decline* (Garden City, N.Y.: Doubleday, 1982).

concessions in collective bargaining. Meanwhile, business engaged in old-fashioned union busting in order to reassert managerial control and intensify labor. In 1978, United Auto Workers President Douglas Fraser bitterly charged, "I believe leaders of the business community, with few exceptions, have chosen to wage a one-sided class war in this country—a war against working people, the unemployed, the poor, the minorities, the very young and the very old, even many in the middle class of our society. The leaders of industry, commerce and finance in the U.S. have broken and discarded the fragile, unwritten contract previously existing during a period of growth and progress."[50]

Conservative Keynesianism, which had provided the logic behind the golden age of capitalism, collapsed in the late 1970s, defeated by unemployment, inflation, and rising trade deficits. A new economic paradigm, articulated by a resurgent Republican Party, soon replaced discredited conservative Keynesianism. Much as Keynesianism had become widely accepted in the postwar period, the approach that we designate as Reaganomics became dominant in the 1980s.

REAGANOMICS

In 1980, American voters, battered by stagflation and polarized by race, turned to the Republican Party and elected Ronald Reagan president. Reagan was at the forefront of a new majority coalition that articulated a new economic philosophy, which departed from the exhausted Keynesian formula. Prosperity no longer depended on the welfare of workers whose wages propelled aggregate demand. Now, according to the new theory, prosperity depended on the welfare of the affluent, whose savings supplied the capital for investment.

Supply side economics (as the new approach was sometimes called) argued that the economy suffered from insufficient investment capital, not insufficient demand. In order to boost the supply of investment capital, Reagan proposed to cut taxes—most of all for the rich. Supply side economists forecast such powerful growth as the result of tax cuts that economic expansion would produce more tax revenue despite the cut in tax rates. But the opposite occurred. The Reagan tax cuts, combined with an enormous increase in military expenditures, produced the largest budget deficits in American history. Interest payments to cover this immense debt consumed 12.4 percent of all federal outlays in 1984, nearly twice their cost a decade earlier. Large deficits also shifted the burden of economic policy making among political

---

[50]Quoted in Taylor E. Dark, *The Unions and the Democrats: An Enduring Alliance* (Ithaca, N.Y.: Cornell University Press, 1999), p. 113.

President Ronald Reagan.

institutions. The fiscal wires were so overloaded with federal debt that they could not carry additional current. This left management of the economy increasingly to monetary policy and the Fed, which was removed from public accountability.

At the same time Reagan directed tax cuts to the rich, he directed spending cuts to the poor. Until an outraged public forced the decision to be reversed, the Reagan administration even tried to define ketchup as a vegetable so that it could reduce subsidies for the school lunch program! Aside from trying to balance the budget on the backs of the poor, Reagan slashed the budgets of federal agencies that regulated corporate behavior, such as the Environmental Protection Agency and the Occupational Safety and Health Administration. Without money and personnel, these agencies could not enforce the law and prevent corporate pollution or monitor unsafe workplaces. Denying federal agencies the money they needed to do their job was part of a broader strategy of deregulation his administration pursued. Reagan believed that business was hamstrung by costly government regulations. Only by reducing government, rolling back regulations that governed corporate behavior, and restoring business's right to manage could the free play of markets unleash prosperity.

Deregulation and supply side economics failed to revive the economy or spur economic growth. Instead, the economy contracted by 1.2 percent in 1982 and experienced its deepest recession since the 1930s. Ironically, when there was eventually a recovery, it was motored more by unfashionable Keynesian fiscal stimulation than by new supply side investment. *Business Week* commented, "In the short run at least, the combination of budget deficits and tax cuts has produced a recovery that looks less like a supply side miracle than an old fashioned super-Keynesian expansion."[51]

The Reagan administration, as well as the Bush administration that followed, failed to restore economic growth to postwar levels, deliver balanced budgets, prevent government outlays from growing, or improve productivity. Real wages stagnated amidst growing inequality. But Republican administrations were successful in shifting the terms of debate by placing government on the intellectual defensive and promoting the virtues of free markets. Unlike in the Keynesian era, when government intervention was regarded positively—when government regulation was regarded as useful in helping to reduce the inequality that markets produce, in policing corporate behavior so that the public interest was not sacrificed to profits, and in moderating the business cycle in order to prevent another depression—the burden of proof had shifted. Now markets and corporations were regarded as beneficent, and government was regarded as guilty until proven innocent. Although many of the specific policies associated with Reaganomics were diluted, never implemented, or reversed, the new paradigm succeeded on a deeper level by changing broad understandings of the appropriate relationship between markets and the state, between business and the government. The best evidence for this argument is that, when a Democrat won back control of the White House after 12 years of Republican administrations, he sponsored economic policies heavily influenced by Reaganomics.

CLINTONOMICS

The large sign in the "War Room" where Clinton's team plotted their campaign strategy, was a reminder of the issue they wanted to drive home with voters, one they believed would catapult their candidate into the White House in 1992. The sign was simple and direct: "It's the economy, stupid."

Bill Clinton repeatedly promised in his 1992 presidential campaign to revive the American economy with a quick stimulus package of tax breaks for business and the middle class and with new public investments to rebuild America's infrastructure. But journalist Bob Woodward reports that a critical turn occurred early in Clinton's first term. Clinton met with his advisers, who informed him that prosperity depended on low interest rates and that interest rates would come down only if the financial markets were convinced the president was serious about deficit reduction. Woodward writes, "At the president-elect's end of the table, Clinton's face turned red with anger and disbelief. 'You mean to tell me that the success of the program and my reelection hinges on the Federal Reserve and a bunch of [expletive

---

[51]*Business Week*, September 3, 1984, 75.

■ FIGURE 3-4

U.S. BUDGET DEFICIT/SURPLUS, 1960–1998

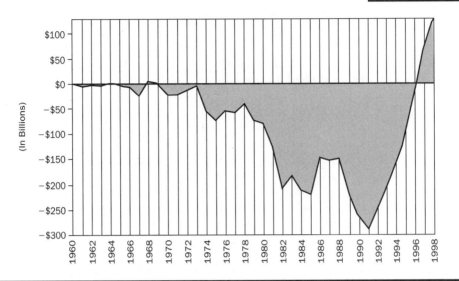

DATA SOURCE: Appendix F in the CBO publication *The Budget and Economic Outlook: Fiscal Years 2001–2010*, released electronically January 26, 2000, *http://www.cbo.gov/showdoc.cfm?index=1821& sequence=0&from=7*.

depleted] bond traders?'"[52] As a candidate, Clinton could gain election by promising new government programs and tax breaks for the middle class. But as president, he needed to win the confidence of the financial and business community. As a result, Clinton's promises of new public investments were scaled back and the economic stimulus package vastly reduced.[53] As Figure 3–4 demonstrates, the Clinton era marked the end of annual budget deficits stretching back to the 1970s.

Bill Clinton reversed some of the policies associated with Reaganomics. He sponsored tax increases that helped reduce enormous budget deficits, and he strengthened regulatory agencies that had been neutralized in the Reagan and Bush years. But the Clinton administration generally accepted the logic of markets driving economic activity. Nowhere was this more evident than in the Clinton administration's trade policy and approach to globalization, among the most important issues with which economic policy must grapple in the twenty-first century.

[52]Bob Woodward, *The Agenda: Inside the Clinton White House* (New York: Simon & Schuster, 1994), p. 84.
[53]Ibid., pp. 64–147.

THE GLOBAL MARKETPLACE

The Clinton administration is not responsible for the accelerated pace at which goods, capital, services, and labor now circulate around the world. But his administration is identified with globalization because of the eagerness with which Clinton embraced it. In 1994, Deputy Secretary of the Treasury Lawrence H. Summers acknowledged, "The Clinton Administration has consistently pursued a trade philosophy that can be labeled 'export activism.' This approach is based on the central idea that the United States and the rest of the world can best prosper through more exports and more trade, rather than through less trade. . . . In the international economic sphere, what we are for is clear enough—a more rapidly growing and more integrated world economy."[54]

In fact, Clinton's trade policy differed little from that of previous Republican administrations, which also promoted global free trade. But Clinton became identified with globalization because he had to defend it to an extent previous administrations did not. As the pace of globalization quickened and the U.S. economy became more integrated into the world market, citizens became more skeptical of its benefits. Globalization augments the power of capital, which is mobile, at the expense of labor, which is not. It also threatens to undermine the environmental and workplace protections that democratic governments and strong unions have created to regulate corporate behavior. Investors can direct capital flows to countries where business is not burdened with state regulations or high welfare and wage costs. Finally, globalization increases people's vulnerability because globalization promotes instability and competition among people throughout the world. This anxiety has created political opposition to trade agreements that promote globalization.

Conflict over globalization was displayed vividly in the struggle between Clinton and Congress over the North American Free Trade Agreement (NAFTA) and his request for fast-track authority. Both conflicts reveal that the pattern of state-economy relations in the context of globalization is far from settled.

NAFTA was originally negotiated and signed by President George H. W. Bush and Mexican President Carlos Salinas de Gorteri in 1992. The agreement promoted globalization by eliminating all tariffs on a broad spectrum of goods produced and sold in North America. The trade agreement's preamble acknowledged that the treaty's purpose was to "ensure a predictable commercial environment for business planning and investment."[55] The United States already had a trade agreement with Canada that lowered

---

[54]Lawrence H. Summers, "The Clinton Administration's International Economic Policy," *Challenge*, March–April 1994, 24–27.

[55]Quoted in Kim Moody, *Workers in a Lean World: Unions in the International Economy* (New York: Verso, 1997), p. 128.

barriers to trade. The issue that generated such passion over NAFTA was whether to extend those same terms to Mexico, where wages were much lower and environmental standards much weaker.

Clinton tried to finesse the issue during the 1992 presidential campaign by endorsing NAFTA, while at the same time he expressed misgivings about some of its details. As president, however, he endorsed NAFTA completely, despite opposition to it within his own party. Organized labor, for example, opposed NAFTA vociferously because unions claimed that NAFTA would cost jobs, not increase them as Clinton maintained. NAFTA, they argued, was an invitation to employers to close factories in the United States and reopen them in Mexico, where average hourly compensation costs in manufacturing were $1.51 compared to $17.20 in the United States. Environmentalists also opposed the treaty, charging that it would encourage industrial polluters to relocate in Mexico, where environmental standards were less stringent.

The core of opposition to NAFTA in Congress came not from Republicans, but from Democrats, members of Clinton's own party, who believed NAFTA would hurt their working-class constituents. Near the end of House debate on the measure, Democratic Majority Whip David Bonior urged lawmakers to defeat NAFTA, imploring, "If we don't stand up for working people in this country, who will?"[56]

In order to secure the congressional votes needed to assure approval of the NAFTA agreement, Clinton alienated friends, embraced enemies, and worked members of Congress "with all the attention and care typically found in a small town's sheriff's race."[57] A majority of Democrats voted to oppose the treaty in Congress. Only overwhelming support from Republican legislators secured its passage. On December 8, 1993, Clinton signed NAFTA into law. But as reports of job loss and plants relocating to Mexico accumulated and were confirmed by the Congressional Budget Office, opponents of globalization and NAFTA took a new tack. NAFTA had been considered by Congress under "fast-track" rules, which require Congress to vote yes or no, without amendment, on trade deals submitted to it by the president. Congress has voted fast-track authority to every president since Gerald Ford in 1974, on the grounds that the president would lose credibility in international trade negotiations if Congress altered an agreement he had made. When Clinton asked Congress to renew his fast-track authority in November 1997, he lobbied hard for it, business lent its support, and every prestige newspaper endorsed it. And it lost.

---

[56]David S. Cloud, "Decisive Vote Brings Down Trade Walls with Mexico," *Congressional Quarterly Weekly Report*, November 20, 1993, 3177.

[57]*New York Times*, November 19, 1993, quoted in C. Don Livingston and Kenneth A. Wink, "The Passage of the North American Free Trade Agreement in the House of Representatives: Presidential Leadership or Presidential Luck," *Presidential Studies Quarterly*, Winter 1997, 56.

Congress denied the president fast-track authority because of growing concerns about globalization from constituents. In July 1997, Clinton's own pollster, Penn Schoen, found that 51 percent of Americans believed that global economic integration "benefits multinational corporations at the expense of average working families."[58] Concerns about fast-track authority and globalization among congressional Democrats were expressed in economic terms: runaway plants and price competition from imports made by foreign workers who were paid one-tenth of what Americans in the same industry earned. Concerns about globalization among the Republican rank and file were expressed in political terms. Republican voters were anxious that globalization would undermine the sovereignty of the state—that is, that rules issued by such institutions as the World Trade Organization would supersede American law.[59]

The conflict over NAFTA and fast-track authority that occurred between Congress and the president is emblematic of a larger conflict between the imperatives of capitalism and the imperatives of democracy. On the one hand, global markets are emerging, which force the United States, in President Clinton's words, to "compete, not retreat."[60] NAFTA, Clinton believed, simply represented a way to compete better within global markets. On the other hand, people resist globalization because of the inequality and vulnerability it generates.

As we recounted in the previous chapter, Clinton's economic policies produced a flawed prosperity. Productivity went up, but most of these gains were captured by higher corporate profits, not by higher wages. The stock market went up, but rich people who own the most stock captured most of these gains. Half the public owns no stock whatsoever and derived no direct benefit from the rise in stock prices. In 1995, President Clinton sadly acknowledged the paradoxical economic record his administration had compiled: "I came to this job committed to restoring the middle class and I did everything I knew how to do. We lowered the deficit. We increased investment in education, in technology, in research and development. We expanded trade frontiers. We have seven million more jobs. We have a record number of millionaires. We have an all time high stock market. We have more new businesses than ever before. . . . And most people are still working harder for lower pay than they were making the day I was sworn in as president."[61]

---

[58]Quoted in Susan Ariel Aaronson, "Why Clinton Lost Fast Track," *International Economy*, November–December 1997, 5.

[59]Peter Beinart, "The Nationalist Revolt," *New Republic*, December 1, 1997, 20–26.

[60]Quoted from President Clinton's address on international economics delivered at The American University in Washington, D.C., February 26, 1993.

[61]Quoted in William Greider, *One World, Ready or Not: The Manic Logic of Global Capitalism* (New York: Simon & Schuster, 1997), p. 197.

CONCLUSION

In this chapter, we have described the relationship between the state and the capitalist economy at three levels. At the most general level, we have identified constant features that characterize the state and economy in all capitalist democracies. Far from markets growing at the expense of states, the two have grown together. At a second, more concrete level, we have focused on continuities in the relationship between the state and the economy in the United States. We have argued that the American state has fewer and less powerful levers with which to manage the economy than are available in other capitalist democracies. The American state commands few direct controls through public ownership of banks and industry to direct the flow of investment through the economy. In addition, deregulation prevents the state from setting political limits on corporate behavior. Finally, the American state lacks the institutional capacity to democratically manage the economy through the tools it does have. Authority over fiscal policy is divided between the president and Congress; monetary policy is run by the Fed, which is insulated from political control; and there is no mechanism to coordinate fiscal and monetary policy to ensure that each is pulling in the same direction. As a result, those who control capital govern the economy.

Finally, at a third, more detailed historical level, we have described several large-scale shifts in the last century between state and economy in the United States. The weak steering capacity of the American state is the result of political struggle. Groups have been successful at times, such as during the New Deal and the wave of social regulations in the 1970s, in using the government to manage the economy and control the behavior of corporations. But on the whole, business has been inordinately successful in shaping the extent, purpose, and institutions through which state intervention in the economy occurs, so that, even as state intervention grows, "it is consistent with the greatest possible preservation of private initiative and private-property ownership."[62]

The American model of letting markets rule has been embraced by both Democratic and Republican administrations. This model, as we described in Chapter 2, is comprised of deregulation, privatization, low taxes, labor flexibility, and a minimal welfare state. It is offered as a template today for other governments to follow if they want to compete successfully in the global marketplace. The Japanese have begun to take steps to deregulate their markets. European governments have cut welfare state benefits in order to reduce government spending, privatized industries that were once publicly owned, and ceded control of monetary policy to a European Central Bank, somewhat modeled on the Fed, which is insulated from political control.

---

[62]Sklar, *Corporate Reconstruction of America*, pp. 38–39.

Governments have adopted the American model, claiming There Is No Alternative (TINA).[63] Globalization, it is argued, has produced pressure for policy convergence toward the American model and has reduced the scope for policies that diverge from it. The removal of technical and political barriers to capital mobility has limited the burdens states can impose on corporations, which can now flee easily whenever domestic costs—in the form of wages, taxes, or regulations—become too high. TINA rules. It is argued There Is No Alternative other than to adopt the American model under the new terms of economic interdependence and free global markets.[64]

But there is evidence to support a very different picture of the future. If globalization is portrayed as an irresistible force in the view sketched above, democracy appears as the immovable object in this interpretation. Under pressure from below, governments have had to retreat from their attempts to play under the rules set by globalization. France was hit by an intense wave of strikes in late 1995, when the government tried to reduce spending by cutting welfare state benefits and freezing the pay of public-sector workers.[65] In 1999, American unions and environmentalist groups successfully disrupted a meeting of the World Trade Organization held in Seattle that was scheduled to set new ground rules for globalization. Calm was not restored until the National Guard was called out and a curfew was imposed on the city's central business district. Nor is there evidence that globalization has produced policy convergence around the least regulatory alternative. Welfare states remain stubbornly diverse in terms of eligibility criteria and benefit packages.[66] And under pressure from constituents, governments continue to protect domestic producers from imports even as they loudly proclaim the virtues of free markets.

The American economic model is currently the model *du jour*. This is ironic because the United States is *least* exposed to global markets. A larger proportion of our goods and services are produced and consumed internally and exports and imports comprise a smaller proportion of our GDP than is true of other industrialized countries. In addition, a larger proportion of our firms and workers are in the service sector, which is less exposed to international competition than is the case elsewhere.

The pendulum swings back and forth between the irresistible force of capitalism and the immovable object of democracy. But the temporary triumph of the current American model involves a quite extreme pendulum swing toward the capitalist side, with quite predictable results, at least in light of

---

[63]The slogan There Is No Alternative (TINA) was coined in the 1980s by British Prime Minister Margaret Thatcher, who shared President Reagan's fervent belief in the need to restore market forces.

[64]The best presentation of this view is Thomas L. Friedman, *The Lexus and the Olive Tree: Understanding Globalization* (New York: Farrar, Straus and Giroux, 1999).

[65]Raghu Krishnan, "The First Revolt Against Globalization," *Monthly Review,* May 1996, 1–23.

[66]Paul Pierson, "The New Politics of the Welfare State," *World Politics,* January 1996, 143–79.

the argument of this book. Ethan B. Kapstein, director of studies at the Council on Foreign Relations, an elite think tank, writes: "The global economy is leaving millions of disaffected workers in its train. Inequality, unemployment, and endemic poverty have become its handmaidens. Rapid technological change and heightening international competition are fraying the job markets of the major industrialized countries. At the same time systemic pressures are curtailing every government's ability to respond with new spending. Just when the working people most need the nation-state as a buffer from the world economy, it is abandoning them."[67]

History remains open, subject to sudden turns, depending on the outcome of political struggle. Political economies must succeed politically as well as economically. They must deliver the votes and deliver the goods. Whether the American model can meet these requirements is an open question: one that will be settled—as it has been in the past—on the picket lines, in the voting booth, and in the streets.

---

[67]Ethan B. Kapstein, "Workers and the World Economy," *Foreign Affairs*, May–June 1996, 16.

THE MANY FACES
OF POLITICAL PARTICIPATION

Moving from a Democracy of Friends
to a Democracy of Strangers

How is it possible for a democracy to function in a huge country with a large, diverse population? Two problems present themselves. The predicament of scale is the first of these. Direct democracy is possible in small groups in which participants are able to engage in face-to-face discussion and decision making. For many political theorists and activists this notion of all citizens freely debating among themselves and arriving at decisions provides a vibrant model for how democracy should be practiced in the United States. The leap from the small group to the society as a whole, however, is impossible to make. The United States is a sprawling, complex society. It simply is not possible for all citizens to participate directly in decision making.

The second dilemma concerns the immense variety of lifestyles, preferences, situations, and interests that characterizes the country's population. It is not easy to identify a single group, "the people," who actually can make decisions for the common good where deep basic inequalities exist—whether marked by race, class, gender, or some other basis of division—because of the absence of shared interests. Rather, "the people" are divided into groups that reflect an unequal distribution of power.

In these circumstances, some important theorists of democracy have argued in favor of a modest procedural approach that makes democracy a set of rules for choosing, by election, among competing political leaders. These theorists offer a more "realistic" standard for democracy that is rooted in a profound distrust of the governed. For example, the economist Joseph Schumpeter believed it is best that political elites, not the mass of the population, make decisions because the people are incompetent: "The typical citizen drops down to a lower level of mental performance as soon as he enters the political field. He argues and analyzes in a way which he would readily recognize as infantile within the sphere of his real interests. He becomes a primitive again."[1] The role of citizens in this conception resembles the role of consumers in a market economy. Much as consumers choose among competing products packaged by firms, so voters choose among competing candidates packaged by political parties.

Other theorists, rejecting this emasculated version of democracy, stress the importance of more active citizenship and robust political participation, and not only at election time. But in this respect, in addition to the problems of scale and diversity, there is the contrast between what is possible among friends and among strangers. Direct participatory democracy is based on principles of friendship, a relationship between equals. This is possible in very small groups of acquaintances. But what happens when friendship no longer serves as the basis of political participation because most citizens are strangers to each other and when these strangers often possess competing, even adversarial, perspectives and points of view?

This part takes up these puzzles. Chapter 4 discusses a type of political participation—the social movement—that brings together individuals who feel strongly about an issue or personal circumstances and who are willing to act outside the standard channels of political action to pursue their goals. This is one means by which democracy can be practiced and citizenship enlarged. Our primary example is the labor movement, which has sought, with mixed success, to counterbalance the advantages of business both in the workplace and in the sphere of public politics. Chapter 5 considers the main mechanisms of political participation in modern democratic states, political parties. The mass two-party system, which was invented in the United States in the early nineteenth century, when participation was limited to white men, is more than just a device to choose competing candidates. Parties and elections are also the main means by which democracies cluster ideas, interests, and supporters into competing institutions and introduce organized conflict into the country's politics of power.

---

[1]Joseph Schumpeter, *Capitalism, Socialism, and Democracy* (New York: Harper & Row, 1942), p. 262.

MOVEMENTS FOR CHANGE
Workers and Work

INTRODUCTION

At any particular moment in American history, the existing situation, the status quo, enjoys many advantages. The resources and political capacities of those who wish to keep things as they are, and preserve their privileges where possible, are considerably greater than the resources and capacities of those who wish to create change. Money, participation rates, access, prestige, and other political assets are unequally distributed. Each adult American may possess one vote, but not all Americans possess equal voice. The ability to lobby, contribute to campaigns, form an organization, influence public opinion, control policy groups, and deploy other means of influence—not to speak of the special position business occupies in the economy—is so unevenly distributed that those who challenge the status quo find the going difficult at best.

The most fundamental idea of democracy is that the preferences, interests, and needs of citizens deserve equal consideration, just as their abilities to influence political outcomes should be equal. The mechanism by which these goals are accomplished is political participation. Citizens participate by voting, supporting political parties, expressing opinions, forming interest groups, and engaging in social movements. Citizens use such strategies in order to encourage political decision makers to respond to their demands.

There are three broad types of situations in which political participation comes to be slanted. The most blatant is when groups of people are denied their rights to participate in politics. There are many such examples in American history, including the denial of the right to vote to the majority of African Americans before the passage of the Voting Rights Act of 1965. A second type of bias takes place when there is a systematic relationship between participation rates and group status. Every recent major study confirms that a pattern reported a half century ago in a study of interest group membership continues to hold. "The frequency of membership . . . increases from the lower to the upper reaches of the class structure," so that there is a "a specialization of organized interest groups along class lines and the atrophy or deficiency of such groups in the less privileged classes."[1] This pattern of skewed participation is characteristic of race and ethnicity as well as class.[2] The third aspect of uneven participation concerns the unequal distribution of politically relevant resources, including money, educational level, time, ability to read and write English, and rates of participation in nonpolitical organizations, like churches and voluntary associations, which offer networks and civic skills that potentially can be put to political use.

Despite these sources of inequality, there exists, nonetheless, a contested *politics* of power. Unlike dictatorial regimes, where political participation is actively repressed, in democracies all adult citizens can develop their political voice, especially when large numbers of people mobilize in organizations, at the polls, and in social movements. Political participation, which so often reinforces privilege, also can counteract advantages of wealth, income, color, ethnicity, and gender.

Political participation can take many forms. The most familiar is voting in elections where choices are organized by competing political parties (Chapter 5). Another is organizing interest groups, when people who share values, preferences, and attitudes join together to influence political parties and government by mobilizing pressure. A majority of interest groups are based on economic interests. Businesspeople, farmers, and workers join associations geared to advance their interests by shaping public opinion, lobbying politicians and bureaucratic agencies, and shaping the legislative process. Other interest groups promote moral or cultural concerns, such as groups opposed to excessive violence on television or gun control or abortion. Sometimes these forms of political participation are linked to social movements. Social movements are collective, mass campaigns in support of broad social goals. They differ from more familiar and more common political party and interest group forms of political participation in two ways. First, social movements are not as hierarchical or as well organized as political parties or interest groups. Second, social movements tend to be more disruptive, more spontaneous, than more conventional forms of political expression. As we shall see, participation in a social movement does not preclude other forms of political participation. Citizens who participate in social movements do not exclude other forms of participation. In fact, challenges to the status quo have the greatest chance of success when they combine social movement activity with electoral and interest group mobilization.

There have been a number of important instances in American history when the power of numbers and mobilization in social movements transformed the existing balance of capacities and power among groups and

---

[1]David B. Truman, *The Governmental Process: Political Interests and Public Opinion* (New York: Knopf, 1951), p. 522.

[2]Sidney Verba, Kay Lehman Schlozman, Henry Brady, and Norman H. Nie, "Race, Ethnicity, and Political Resources: Participation in the United States," *British Journal of Political Science* 23 (October 1993): 453–97.

thus altered the existing distribution of benefits and prerogatives. Such movements to end slavery and achieve civil equality for African Americans, to bring women into full and equal political participation, and to secure unions for working Americans have aimed to affect the scope, content, and meaning of citizenship. As large-scale cooperative efforts, they have used a variety of means to win attention, gain access to the political system, and change the environment within which politics operates, ranging from such conventional forms of political action as getting out the vote to such unconventional, even disruptive, activities as public protests that block the streets.

American history and politics have been marked by a wide range of movements of diverse ideological persuasions: for feminism and against nuclear weapons; for black rights and against abortion; for civil rights and against the use of American military force; and, in the nineteenth century, for the use of silver rather than gold to back the currency. Irrespective of their diversity, social movements share traits. They interrupt normal politics. They seek to alter existing social and political relations. They have to overcome the tendency for individuals to not participate and to let others do the job. They have a strong ideological current. They move citizen participation beyond the vote to a more active and demanding level.

The various forms of political participation are not neatly sealed off from each other. In the history of American labor, the main focus of this chapter, workers have secured influence and have sought to counter the special advantages of business by voting and participating in political parties, by carrying out interest-group lobbying activities, and by functioning as a social movement seeking change in the country's organizational balance of power. By attending to this story, we can also see how political participation does not always neatly fit into the "public" as opposed to the "private" sphere. The workplace straddles both. The familiar language we use to refer to the relations between workers and employers as the "private sector" masks how much law and regulation govern their relationship and how much the workplace constitutes a sphere of collective interaction. The effort to organize working people into unions is a public act, and the labor movement, which has sought to counterbalance business power in the workplace, is a public social movement whose vitality and capacities depend on its public role and effectiveness.

Organized labor has provided working people with the main counterweight to the power of business, both in the workplace itself and in the political arena. As a general rule, when unions have been most strong and capable, inequality has been reduced; at moments when they have grown weaker, income and wealth gaps in society have widened. Thus, the successes and failures of organized labor shape the resources that underpin other forms of political participation. Further, though their record is mixed in this respect, apart from the armed forces, organized labor has been the most racially integrated and egalitarian institution in American society for the past half century.

WORK TRANSFORMED: THE DECLINE OF THE INDEPENDENT MIDDLE CLASS

To understand the emergence and development of the labor movement and the challenges it has faced, we must begin with a fundamental human activity, productive work. Work is central to an individual's interests and identity. How people feel about their jobs, whether it be pride, boredom, exhilaration, or humiliation, defines to a great extent how they feel about themselves. Work shapes people's beliefs about whether and how their lives have meaning. So much of our time is spent preparing and learning skills for work, looking for work, actually working, and reflecting on the experience of work that its centrality in our lives should come as no surprise. Likewise, many political issues, activities, and social movements center on the rewards and shortcomings of employment and on the inequalities of these experiences in the lives of American citizens.

In the early years of the Republic, it appeared as if the United States was an exception to the general rule of sharply unequal chances with respect to work. It was common for travelers from Europe in the first half of the nineteenth century to remark on this astonishing feature of American life. Perhaps the most famous of these visitors was Alexis de Tocqueville, who arrived in the United States from France in 1831. Like other visitors to pre–Civil War America, when the country was mostly agrarian and the cities were unindustrialized, he was impressed most by the absence of class divisions. "Among the novel objects that attracted my attention during my stay in the United States," he wrote, "nothing struck me more forcibly than the general equality of condition among the people."[3] Similarly, on his trip to the United States in 1842, English novelist Charles Dickens discovered that, even in the newly established textile mills of New England, conditions contrasted sharply with those in factories in Great Britain. Describing factory life in Lowell, Massachusetts, where virtually all the employees were teenage farm girls, he wrote: "The girls, as I have said, were all well dressed; and that phrase necessarily includes extreme cleanliness. They had serviceable bonnets, good warm cloaks, and shawls; and were not above clogs and patterns. . . . They were healthy in appearance, many of them remarkably so, and had the manners and deportment of young women; not of degraded brutes of burden. . . . The rooms in which they worked were as well ordered as themselves. In the windows of some there were green plants, which were trained to shade the glass); in all, there was as much fresh air, cleanliness, and comfort as the nature of the occupation could possibly admit of."[4]

Dickens, like Tocqueville, devoted much of his account to a discussion of the consequences of relative economic and social equality. The analyses of both chroniclers (especially of Tocqueville) have been influential in shaping

---

[3]Alexis de Tocqueville, *Democracy in America* (1835; reprint, New York: Knopf, 1945), p. 3.
[4]Charles Dickens, *American Notes* (1842; reprint, London: Penguin, 1972), p. 115.

the popular view of America's social structure. But their accounts documented an era that was coming to a close. In the 1840s and 1850s, the country's social structure began to undergo fundamental change. The development of early industrial capitalism created new class divisions, which were soon to supplant the more egalitarian, individualistic democracy Tocqueville and Dickens observed.

By the late 1840s, the paternalism of the Lowell factories was a quaint memory. Had Dickens returned to Massachusetts in 1850, he would have had to confront a very different industrial reality. During the decade, the wages of the mill workers became severely depressed. According to historian Norman Ware: "In 1846 the wages of weavers in Newburyport were reduced 10 percent and in Lowell it was said that never since the beginning of the industry had the operatives received lower wages, though "they are compelled to do all of one-third more work and, in some cases, double." Whereas in 1840 weekly time wages were from 75 cents to $2 per week and board, in 1846 they ran from 55 cents to $1.50, making a 25 percent reduction in spite of the fact that they were doing 33 percent more work."[5]

There were sporadic strikes throughout the decade, in opposition both to more work at lower wages and to the length of the workday, which averaged 12 hours. Without exception, all the strikes, including one that lasted six months in the winter of 1850–51, were broken by the employers. When Dickens visited Lowell, it was possible "for the New England women who lived isolated lives in farming communities to feel, when they went to Lowell, as if they were going to boarding-school, in spite of the long hours." But, according to Ware, as the logic of profit replaced this genteel paternal tradition, "the older amenities had to go . . . the boarding-school dream faded. The girls were no longer able to relieve one another at their work, to snatch a rest of fifteen minutes, to read a book propped up on the frame. They ceased the cultivation of window flowers—in fact, they left the mills altogether and were replaced by new workers."[6] By the end of the 1840s, the deterioration of working conditions drove the women out. They were replaced by immigrants escaping the Irish famine of 1848.

Just after the American Revolution, four out of five workers (excluding slaves) had been farmers, artisans, merchants, doctors, traders, small businessmen, lawyers, and craftsmen; Tocqueville and Dickens visited an America of *independent* workers. Property was a liberating force. Because property, especially land, was distributed relatively equally, it provided a basis for a more substantive level of democracy than any country had known before. In this respect, the United States was truly a revolutionary society. Thomas Jefferson's dream of a dynamic agrarian democracy has been put into practice for white American men (excluding, however, a politically invisible majority of the population, made up of blacks, women, and Native Americans).

---

[5] Norman Ware, *The Industrial Worker, 1840–1860* (Chicago: Quadrangle, 1964), pp. 113–14.
[6] Ibid., pp. 120–21.

The basis for conflict between workers and industrialists developed rapidly. In community after community, the events that occurred in Lowell in the 1840s were replicated. By the end of the nineteenth century, as the western frontier closed, capitalist class divisions overtook an older America of self-employed merchants, artisans, farmers, professionals, and traders.

The impact of these changes on everyday life was overwhelming. In their study of Muncie, Indiana, between 1890 and 1924, sociologists Helen and Robert Lynd documented the massive shift in social relationships that resulted from the development of industrial capitalism. Traditional craft patterns broke down under the impact of machines and assembly-line techniques in the local factories; skilled labor was now unnecessary for most jobs. As self-employed craftsmen and local entrepreneurs were forced out of business, workers' traditional neighborhoods lost their cohesiveness and autonomy. The city as a whole lost its sense of autonomy as well, since most of the urban economic changes were the result of national forces outside the city's control. The businessman, not the independent craftsman, was now at the top of the town's wealth, status, and power hierarchies.[7] In short, the division between the capitalist class and the working class became more defined. Now people came to be divided by class not only at the workplace, but also in their daily lives in the community and in politics. New institutions, including unions and businessmen's associations, developed that became vehicles for the expression and containment of the new structural antagonisms of interest. Unlike regional or religious distinctions, class distinctions underpinned the experience of living in a total, inescapable way.

By 1900, however, the independent middle class had declined in size and was replaced by a growing percentage of Americans who did not own their tools of production but sold their labor for a wage. Whereas only 20 percent of the workforce was paid employees in 1780, 68 percent were wage earners in 1900; the independent middle class had shrunk to less than one-third of all workers. Thus, with the development of industrial capitalism, ownership of the tools of production has come to divide Americans rather than unite them. As a result of the dual trend of the decline of the independent middle class and the development of a working-class majority, almost all Americans, except those who own and control the means of production, work for a wage. Of course, their conditions of work, the size of their pay packets, and their life chances differ enormously. But their shared condition as wage earners makes them dependent on the opportunities made available to them in their local labor markets, and it makes the engineer as well as the dishwasher vulnerable to the threat and actuality of unemployment.

When individual workers confront their employers one by one, they do so in a state of dependency. They often need the job and have little ability to make effective demands about pay, working conditions, training, or possibil-

---

[7]Robert S. Lynd and Helen Merrell Lynd, *Middletown: A Study in American Culture* (New York: Harcourt, Brace, 1929).

ities for promotion. Likewise, when workers lack unions, their voice in national political affairs is attenuated, and the structural advantage business possesses can go largely unchallenged. Thus, much is at stake in creating an organized workforce. For just this reason, unions have tended to be constituted only as a key part of a larger movement to change the lives of working people for the better.

CREATING UNIONS

July 16, 1877, is a landmark date in American labor history. On that date, the Baltimore and Ohio Railroad cut wages by 10 percent. In protest of the move, the crew of a cattle train in Martinsburg, West Virginia, abandoned the train, and other trainmen refused to replace them. By the end of the month, the first mass strike in America had spread across the country. "Strikers stopped and seized the nation's most important industry, the railroads, and crowds defeated or won over first the police, then the state militias, and in some cases even the Federal troops" who were called out to deal with the class insurrection. In a dozen major cities, all industrial activity was stopped by general strikes. The strikes were eventually put down by employers with the help of police and military authorities, but the Great Upheaval, as the event came to be known, was profoundly important in two respects. First, it reflected the workers' sense of their new structural position in American society in the face of the decline of the independent middle class. ("There was no concert of action at the start," the *Labor Standard* wrote. "It spread because the workmen of Pittsburgh felt the same oppression that was felt by the workmen of West Virginia and so with the workmen of Chicago and St. Louis."[8]) Second, the strikes highlighted the need for workers to organize if they were to successfully resist the repression of workers' movements by employers and the government.[9]

By the mid-1880s, the Knights of Labor, the most important national union organization of the period, was growing at a phenomenal rate. In July 1884, it had just over 71,000 members; two years later it had over 729,000. The Knights sought to link all workers, skilled and unskilled, black and white, men and women. The Knights' leaders were ideologically quite radical. They denounced the wage system as exploitative and humiliating, robbing workers of their independence. But they were also quite conservative tactically, opposing strikes by workers in favor of creating a system of producer cooperatives. The Knights' opposition to strikes proved to be their undoing because strikes were the only weapon workers had to resist collectively the hardships inflicted by the developing factory economy. Hence by

---

[8]Quoted in Jeremy Brecher, *Strike!* (San Francisco: Straight Arrow Books, 1972), p. 46.
[9]Ibid., pp. 1–21.

the turn of the century, much strike action was spontaneously organized, outside of the formal structure of unions.

By World War I, two very different kinds of unions had emerged. The American Federation of Labor (AFL), which had been founded in 1881 and was led by Samuel Gompers, organized skilled craft workers, the most well paid of the new working class. The AFL was a conservative union force. It did not challenge the developing distribution of resources or the basic structure of industrial capitalism. Rather, the AFL sought to defend the relatively privileged position of the craftsmen it represented and limited its demands to higher wages and shorter working hours. By contrast, the Industrial Workers of the World (IWW), which was founded in 1905, appealed to the interests of all workers, especially those who were most exploited. By the end of World War I, the IWW had been smashed, and the AFL was gaining in strength. What accounts for the difference in their relative success?

The key factor was the response of management and government authorities to the two types of unions. Some employers tolerated the AFL because, by representing only skilled craft workers, it divided workers from one another. But the IWW, which sought to articulate the interests of all workers as a class and which posed socialist alternatives to prevailing economic arrangements, presented a far greater threat to both capitalist industry and the social order as a whole. Thus, between 1905 and the outbreak of World War I, IWW activities were systematically countered by government action:

> In Pennsylvania, the state police, which had been originally created by reformers "anxious to abolish the use of private police forces during industrial conflicts" constantly worked for the employers, not for the strikers. In San Diego, Washington State, and Arizona vigilante mobs . . . took direct repressive action against the IWW. Contacts between the mobs and leading state figures made such actions official government policy. . . . Vigilante action was frowned on, however, by some state officials who felt that there were "cleaner" ways to repress the organization. A public safety committee in Minnesota, a council of defense in Washington State, and a Commission on Immigration and Housing in California became official bodies seeking official solutions for the elimination of the IWW.[10]

Many of these local organizations urged President Woodrow Wilson to take federal action to repress the IWW. There followed a campaign of federal action that included the deportation of many IWW leaders who were aliens and the trial of hundreds of union activists on conspiracy charges (conspiracy against industrial production). In one instance, after deliberating less than an hour, a Chicago jury found more than one hundred defendants guilty of four counts of conspiracy each.

The demise of the IWW was also closely linked to the legitimization of the AFL. In particular, Gompers, Felix Frankfurter (who was later to become a justice of the Supreme Court), and Ralph Easley of the National

[10]Alan Wolfe, *The Seamy Side of Democracy: Repression in America* (New York: McKay, 1973), pp. 26–27.

Civic Federation campaigned actively for recognition of the AFL as a "safe" alternative to more threatening workers' organizations. One manufacturer urged that workers be granted the "shadow of industrial democracy without the substance" to keep them "contented and productive."[11]

The repression of the IWW was not the only response of capitalists and the government to the militancy of the new industrial working class. Ideological propaganda, the reliance on state militias to protect strikebreakers, and the fostering of anti-union violence were among the common techniques of the day. Also among these strategies were the manipulation of existing ethnic, racial, and sexual divisions in the workforce and the creation of new divisions between kinds of workers (clerical versus managerial, white-collar versus blue-collar). Indeed, these strategies were related, since the antagonisms based on personal characteristics were exacerbated in order to legitimize new divisions between levels of work in the firm. As two historians have noted: "Within the shop immigrants and Negroes did almost all unskilled and some semiskilled work, whereas the skilled jobs and minor administrative positions were reserved for native white Americans. 'That job is not a hunky's job, and you can't have it,' was the answer given to intelligent foreigners who aspired to rise above the ranks of common labor. Thus a wedge of racial discrimination was driven into the labor force."[12] And as white-collar work increased, discrimination against women was used to solidify emerging lines of division within the office between jobs with and without managerial career potential. Jobs came to be identified with particular groups in plants and in offices, and they were associated with the hierarchies of prestige and power that elevated whites above blacks, men above women, and earlier groups of immigrants above new arrivals.

Until the coming of industrial unions during the New Deal era, the workers who packed the meat and produced the cars, steel, electrical goods, rubber, and other commodities at the heart of the country's economy worked very long hours for little pay under difficult working conditions. At the start of the 1920s, the typical work week was 54 hours for automobile workers and over 60 hours for steelworkers. Even automobile workers, who were the country's best-paid factory employees, earned just enough to decently support their families, while unskilled steel workers earned less than was required for basic subsistence. When factory workers, the vast majority of whom were either immigrants from southern and eastern Europe or African Americans who had moved from the South, were laid off during recessions or could not work because they were sick or injured, they faced dire circumstances. There was no safety net.

Until the 1930s, as a result of the divisions in the workforce and in the union movement and the massive resistance to unions by employers, often

---

[11]Ibid., p. 29.

[12]Thomas Cochran and William Miller, *The Age of Enterprise: A Social History of Industrial America* (New York: Harper, 1961), pp. 230–31.

backed by the police powers of local, state, and federal governments, the vast majority of American workers were without union protection or representation. When the Depression hit, their situation badly worsened as millions of Americans lost their jobs, including half of all automobile workers between 1929 and 1933. Soon, however, three sets of changes vastly altered the ability of workers to unionize to protect their jobs, improve their pay, and enhance their working conditions. First, the New Deal changed the rules. In 1933, clause 7(A) of the National Industrial Recovery Act, then the pillar of the Roosevelt administration's strategy to jump-start the dormant economy, gave workers the right to organize unions. Then, in 1935, the National Labor Relations Act (also known as the Wagner Act, after its chief sponsor, New York's Senator Robert Wagner) established a durable national framework for recognizing unions under the auspices of the National Labor Relations Board. This legislation announced that it was now a national goal for workers to join unions to protect their collective interests.

Second, between the start of the Depression in 1929 and the period when the legislation establishing this national context for labor organizing was passed, workers displayed a great deal of militancy. Especially in the Midwest, many unemployed workers formed councils of the unemployed. Textile and mine workers went on strike throughout the South and in West Virginia and Pennsylvania. Across the country, a mass of increasingly angry and militant workers was on the move.

Third, workers' insurgent energies were captured and advanced by a group of union leaders who, in 1935, formed the Congress of Industrial Organizations (CIO) to organize in unions those workers in mass industries left outside the AFL craft unions. Unlike AFL unions, which organized members by craft, the CIO organized workers on an industrial basis, recruiting all the workers in an industry regardless of whether they were unskilled assembly-line workers or skilled machinists. As a result of the emergence of the CIO, the number of unionized workers more than doubled from 3.1 million to 7 million in the 1930s. In that decade, CIO unions succeeded in organizing the most important mass-production industries in the country, including meatpacking, rubber, steel, and automobiles and in becoming a major force to be reckoned with in American political life. By 1945, another doubling had occurred, with union membership exceeding 14 million (6 million in the CIO), or more than one in three of the country's workers.

This success was the product of bitter, often protracted struggles. Class antagonisms were raw and palpable. In 1936 and 1937, a massive wave of sit-down strikes, starting in the rubber industry, swept the country. Some 400,000 workers refused to leave their factories unless their unions were recognized.[13] "Four men were killed and eighty-four persons went to hospitals with gunshot wounds, cracked heads, broken limbs or other injuries re-

---

[13]On the rise of the CIO, see Robert H. Zieger, *The CIO: 1935–1955* (Chapel Hill: University of North Carolina Press, 1995).

ceived in a battle late this afternoon between police and steel strikers at the gates of the Republic Steel Corporation plant in South Chicago" as the United Steel Workers of America successfully sought recognition, the *New York Times* reported in May 1937.[14] In January 1936, automobile workers demanding recognition of the United Automobile Workers (UAW) staged sit-ins and took control of General Motors (GM) automobile plants in Flint, Michigan; Atlanta, Georgia; Anderson, Indiana; Norwood, Ohio; and Kansas City, Missouri. On the 44th day of the sit-in and strike at Flint, GM gave in and recognized the UAW, but only after massive police violence and cooperative attempts between the governor and the company had failed to dislodge the workers. It took longer, until 1941, to fully organize the steel industry, and only after the Democratic governors of Ohio and Pennsylvania had called out the National Guard to curb the union effort.

Thus, between 1935 and the early 1940s, workers, through union-led mass actions, moved rapidly to achieve a significant amount of substantive representation and fundamental structural change. What genuinely could be called a labor *movement*, mobilizing hundreds of thousands, then millions, of workers in all the regions of the country in a wide array of jobs, transformed the balance of capacities between business and labor. In this period, labor also became the most important organized element in the Democratic Party, making demands for participation in the decision-making bodies of the federal government and in support of augmented social welfare programs, including national health insurance, improvements to unemployment insurance and Social Security, national housing programs, fairer taxation, and,

Autoworkers occupy factory in 1937 sit-down strike in Flint, Michigan.

---

[14]Melvyn Dubofsky, ed., *American Labor Since the New Deal* (Chicago: Quadrangle, 1971), p. 113.

above all, full employment.[15] The CIO also advanced a program for racial equality, opposing discrimination at work and the disfranchisement of blacks in the South. Unions further demanded a share in managerial authority in the workplace and access to information about profits and plans in big firms. By the close of World War II, the labor movement had transformed the terrain of the country's politics of power and had redefined the content of citizenship for many millions of ordinary Americans.

THE GROWTH AND DECLINE OF UNIONS

For a period, union growth continued, reaching a peak of some 15 million members in the private sector in 1954 and another 3 million who worked for the government. Then, for the next 20 years, the actual number of private sector workers in unions continued to increase, but more slowly than the number of jobs added to the economy, so that the proportion of unionized employees began to drop. Since 1974, the actual number of union members in the private economy has been cut in half, and the proportion of such workers has dropped to under 10 percent. (See Table 4–1.)

When union membership was at its peak in the mid-1950s, the proportion of workers in some industries was very high: 42 percent in manufacturing, 65 percent in mining, 80 percent in transportation, and 84 percent in construction. But even during this heyday, key developments put these gains at risk. In retrospect, we can see how the capacity of the labor movement was blunted, if not broken, in the late 1940s. Four aspects of the situation of labor unions were particularly decisive in bringing their expansion to a halt and then causing their membership to begin a long and steady decline, which only very recently may have begun to be arrested.

The first was the failure of both the AFL and the CIO to extend their reach into the South. During the era of Jim Crow, southern business and political leaders were especially resistant to unions, for they feared that labor organizing had the potential to overturn the region's racial order by promoting interracial unions and by making it more difficult to exploit a poor black, and white, labor supply. Though hundreds of organizers took part and millions of dollars were spent in the effort, successful local resistance blunted the campaigns and forced the unions to withdraw from the scene of battle. The AFL effort lasted just one year; the CIO stayed in the fray officially until 1953, but had really given up five years earlier. In effect, by falling far short of their goals

---

[15]The leading discussion of the political role of the union movement in this period remains J. David Greenstone, *Labor in American Politics* (New York: Knopf, 1969). See also Alan Draper, *A Rope of Sand: The AFL–CIO Committee on Political Education, 1955–1968* (New York: Praeger, 1989), and Taylor E. Dark, *The Unions and the Democrats: An Enduring Alliance* (Ithaca, N.Y.: Cornell University Press, 1999).

■ TABLE 4–1

U.S. PRIVATE SECTOR TRADE UNION MEMBERSHIP:
FROM 1900

Year	Union Members (000)	Market Share
1900	917	6.5%
1905	1,923	11.1%
1910	2,109	10.5%
1915	2,508	12.2%
1920	4,664	19.2%
1925	3,495	13.2%
1930	3,482	13.3%
1935	3,337	14.2%
1940	6,848	24.3%
1945	11,674	33.9%
1950	13,550	34.6%
1955	15,341	35.1%
1960	16,907	37.0%
1965	16,906	33.5%
1970	18,295	31.0%
1975	18,210	28.5%
1980	15,273	20.6%
1985	11,226	14.6%
1990	10,247	12.1%
1991	9,898	11.9%
1992	9,703	11.5%
1993	9,554	11.2%
1994	9,620	10.9%
1995	9,400	10.4%
1996	9,385	10.2%
1997	9,363	9.8%
1998	9,306	9.5%
1999	9,419	9.4%

SOURCES: U.S. Department of Labor Bureau of Labor Statistics; Leo Troy and Neil Sheflin, *U.S. Union Sourcebook: Membership, Finances, Structure, Directory*. West Orange, N.J.: IRDIS, 1985.

and by failing in their effort to organize southern workers, the major labor federations conceded that they never would become a genuinely national force.[16]

Second, the passage in 1947 of the Taft-Hartley bill, which amended the National Industrial Relations Act, placed obstacles in the way of union organization by restricting strike activities and by legalizing state-level "right-to-work" laws, which allow the individual worker to choose whether to join a union even after a majority in the plant or firm votes to be represented by a union. The effect of such legislation is an increase in free riding, in which nonmembers of unions gain benefits of union organization without having to join. In practice, where such laws prevail, unions find it difficult, if not impossible, to organize. Since most of the country's right-to-work laws were in force in the South, Taft-Hartley made union activity in that region even more difficult.

The third was the manner in which Cold War battles between Communists and anti-Communists were reproduced inside the labor movement. During the 1930s and 1940s, some of the most militant members of key CIO unions were Communists. When the country was aligned with the Soviet Union during World War II, most anti-Communist union leaders downplayed these differences lest the union movement come to be divided. But tensions mounted in the second half of the 1940s, with the Communist takeover in Czechoslovakia and the Berlin blockade. As it became increasingly clear that the Soviet Union would rule eastern Europe with an iron fist and as the Red Scare campaign against Communists at home gained force, the labor movement split on the issue of Communism. At its 1949 convention, the CIO expelled 11 unions, with more than 1 million members, for being led or strongly influenced by Communists. This schism gained wider acceptance for the labor movement because it no longer could be tarred as sympathetic to communism, but cost it some of its most effective unions.

Fourth, once it was clear that the labor movement had to contract its attention to its strongholds in the Midwest, Northeast, and Far West, it also made sense for the labor movement to cease demanding major changes to social welfare policy, such as public health insurance, on a national scale and, instead, to secure for its own workers an employer-funded welfare state as part of collective bargaining agreements. The attention of unions thus turned from politics and policy in Washington to the gains that could be secured from their workers' firms. Private health benefits, pensions, and other fringe benefits were achieved for unionized workers; those outside unions were left out. In this way, important gains were won for workers, but these were restricted. Although unions continued to fight for broader extensions of the

---

[16]F. Ray Marshall, *Labor in the South* (Cambridge: Harvard University Press, 1969); Michael Honey and Solomon Barkin, "Operation Dixie: Two Views," *Labor History* 31 (Summer 1990): 373–86; Barbara S. Griffith, *The Crisis of American Labor: Operation Dixie and the Defeat of the CIO* (Philadelphia: Temple University Press, 1988); and Michael Goldfield, "The Failure of Operation Dixie," in *Race, Class and Community in Southern Labor History,* ed. Gary M. Fink and Merl E. Reed (Tuscaloosa: University of Alabama Press, 1994).

welfare state, their members had less of a stake in it, as their pensions and health insurance would now come from the private welfare state their unions were able to win through collective bargaining.

In this context, the union movement—shut out of the South, confronted with a harsher legal climate, internally torn, and focused on private wage and fringe benefits deals—became increasingly tame and bureaucratic. Writing in 1973, 36 years after the Flint sit-in, *Business Week* editorialized: "[T]he unions have become an established institution, well financed and run by highly professional managers. These officers are paid on much the same basis as businessmen. . . . And they deal with many of the same problems—budgets, investments, taxes, even bargaining with staff and office worker unions."[17] The editorial also noted that the unions were "acting responsibly" and that strike figures had reached "the lowest level in years." In the same year, the steelworkers (led by a president who earned an annual salary of $70,000) signed a contract that pledged the union to fight wildcat strikes by its members. They also agreed—in advance of a wage settlement—not to strike, but to settle all wage disputes by arbitration. A major study of the UAW concluded that "the relationship between the General Motors corporation and the United Automobile Workers has altered— they are not enemies, nor, in any large sense, adversaries. It is true . . . that the two, General Motors and the UAW, have *a greater community of interest than of conflict*."[18] What had happened to produce the shift in less than four decades from militant class organization and confrontation to "responsible" routinized cooperation?

The development of a relatively conservative AFL–CIO (the two labor federations merged in 1955), which became more a force for stability than for change in the country's economy, was made possible by the growing divisions between the corporate and small-capital sectors of the American economy. Unlike small-capital-sector industries, whose major costs are wages and who have to absorb wage increases at the expense of profits, the corporate-sector industries are largely able to pass along wage increases in the form of higher prices. In the corporate sector, wages, prices, and profits are not determined by the operation of a traditional competitive market, but are planned by the corporations and government. Hence corporate-sector companies, whose major expenses relate to technology, not men and women, were able to accept the emergence of mass industrial unionism as one more element among many to be planned for in advance. Indeed, corporate-sector firms gain tangible benefits from the existence of a unionized workforce because the unions guarantee that, outside of strike periods, the companies will have a predictably available workforce at predictable wages.

---

[17]*Business Week*, August 18, 1973, 88.

[18]William Serrin, *The Company and the Union* (New York: Knopf, 1972), pp. 305–6. Emphasis in original.

By the end of World War II, most industrial unions had entered into permanent collective bargaining agreements with the largest corporations in the corporate sector. The unions succeeded in obtaining higher wages for their members, but not without relinquishing much in return. In addition to agreeing to increase productivity, union leaders began to collaborate with company managements to introduce technologically advanced production methods, which usually are resisted by the rank and file. Overall, from the standpoint of those who own and control corporate capital, "the main function of unions was (and is) to inhibit disruptive spontaneous rank and file activity (e.g., wildcat strikes and slowdowns) and to maintain labor discipline in general. In other words, *unions were (and are) the guarantors of managerial prerogatives.*"[19]

By the mid-1950s, the union movement had reached something of an equilibrium relationship with employers, especially with big firms. The pattern of collective bargaining that unions had secured as the result of major mass struggles now settled into a mutually acceptable and beneficial pattern. The number of strikes went down, and strikes, when they occurred, tended to be short. Contracts with employers included pledges not to strike during the duration of the contract. The right of management to define the character, pace, and specifications of jobs was exchanged for a high degree of job security that prevented workers from being fired without cause, as well as relatively high wages and good fringe benefits. This "accord" between business and labor represented, two scholars of the labor movement have observed, "a program for orderly industrial government and for avoiding class confrontations. Moderate Republicans, mainstream Democrats, and many of the most important corporate leaders supported reliance on collective bargaining, 'responsible' unionism, and the integration of the union movement into the legitimized institutional structure of American society as a means for achieving industrial and class peace." The result was an effective "program for managing American capitalism."[20]

From the perspective of organized labor, this equilibrium did not remain stable for very long. Soon a steep decline set in as a result of job losses to international competition and a growing disinclination of many workers, especially in white-collar jobs, to join unions. In 1955, the United Steel Workers had 980,000 members; in 1995, 403,000. In the same period, the membership rolls of the International Ladies Garment Workers Union declined from 383,000 to 123,000 and the United Automobile Workers from 1,260,000 to 751,000. In 1955, more than one in three private-sector workers belonged to a union; in 2000, just under one in ten belonged. At the start of the twenty-first century, some 14 percent of American workers were in

[19]James O'Connor, *The Fiscal Crisis of the State* (New York: St. Martin's Press, 1973), p. 18. Emphasis added.

[20]Richard Edwards and Michael Podgursky, "The Unraveling Accord: American Unions in Crisis," in *Unions in Crisis and Beyond: Perspectives from Six Countries*, ed. Richard Edwards, Paolo Garonna, and Franz Todtling (Dover, Mass.: Auburn House, 1986), p. 27.

unions, a figure bolstered by the remarkable growth of unionism in the public sector, where some 38 percent of federal, state, and municipal employees
are union members. If not for this large increase in government workers in
the union movement, the decline would have been even more steep. In the
private sector, union organizing had declined precipitously. In 1980, three
times as many union certification elections were held to determine whether
workers wanted a union than in 1996. And whereas unions for many
decades won well over half of such elections, by the mid-1990s they prevailed only just over 40 percent of the time, and the majority of new plants
come into operation without unions.[21]

Unions also strike for higher wages and better working conditions less
often. In 1970, there were nearly 400 work stoppages involving over 1,000
people, but in the 1990s, there were fewer than 40 each year, and the level of
strike activity is now lower than at any time since the 1930s.

What accounts for the accelerating decline of the labor movement in numbers and in militancy? Three factors stand out: changes to the character and
location of workers and employment; an increasingly hard-line, anti-union
stance by employers, often with governmental support; and organized
labor's own failure to maintain and expand its membership by successful
organizing. Let us consider each of these factors in turn.

There has been a huge shift in the country's labor force away from manufacturing, where unionization traditionally has been high, to service work.
In 1970, manufacturing and services employed an equal number of Americans. Since then, the number of manufacturing workers has not increased at
all, but service workers have nearly tripled in number. In this period, health
care workers have doubled in number, from 6 to 12 million, and the number of providers of business services has increased from just over 1 million
to 9 million.

The term *services* applies to a number of distinct kinds of employment, all
of which are expanding. Service work is a very heterogeneous category, en-
compassing vastly different levels of skill, earnings, and authority. In high-
technology industries—particularly in electronics—scientists, technicians,
and engineers comprise the majority of employees. Indeed, two very different fields of white-collar jobs have developed since World War II: clerical
jobs (two-thirds of which are held by women) and technical and professional
jobs (about two-thirds held by men). The increase in both types of white-
collar employment is linked to the shift in the economy from manufacturing
to service occupations. As sociologist Daniel Bell notes, "[I]n the very development of industry there is a necessary expansion of transportation and of
public utilities as auxiliary services in the movement of goods and the increasing use of energy, and an increase in the non-manufacturing but still

[21]Glenn Perusek, "The Politics of Organized Labor in the United States," in *Postwar Trends in
the Evolution of French and American Industrial Societies,* ed. Monique Borrel (Berkeley:
University of California, International and Area Studies, forthcoming).

blue collar force."[22] Thus, the first kind of service employment is an integral part of the industrial process. This is not a new service sector.

With the growth of the population and mass consumption of goods, more and more people are involved in the distribution of goods and in the fields of insurance, real estate, and finance. This cluster of activities provides the supportive services needed to keep goods circulating and to provide capital for industrial expansion. Personal services have also expanded numerically, but their organization has changed. Chains of restaurants, hotels, and automobile garages as well as the entertainment and sports industries carry out functions that were once fulfilled by independent entrepreneurs. Today the production and distribution of personal services are increasingly in impersonal corporate hands.

Another major area of services is those provided by government, including education, health care, and welfare. Government service employment grew more rapidly than any other sector between 1945 and 1980; in the 1980s and 1990s, in a climate of austerity, the rate of government employment growth slowed, but did not stop. More generally, the shift from manufacturing to services continued to accelerate, vastly enhanced by the remarkable technological revolution in computers and information. Each of these shifts has made union organizing more difficult by changing the composition of the workforce to include areas that traditionally have been harder to unionize. So, too, did the development, especially in the country's big cities, of a large and growing "underground" economy, accounting for about 15 percent of the gross national product. This term refers both to illegal activities like drug traffic and to various cash transactions not reported to tax authorities, as well as to low-wage manufacturing, often employing illegal immigrants who provide cheap labor for employers.

These various changes to the character of work, which affected the ability of unions to bring workers into their fold, were magnified by the basic regional rearrangement to the economy. During the 1980s, much of the East and Midwest "deindustrialized." Manufacturing plants closed down in large numbers, some moving to the South and West, where there were fewer unions and lower wage rates. This trend was reinforced by an oil boom in Texas, Oklahoma, and Louisiana and by the massive increases in military spending in the first Reagan term, whose impact was felt disproportionately in the Sun Belt. During the 1990s, this internal shift in the geography of production and employment was overlaid by another geographical redistribution of work to overseas plants, where labor costs were much lower and unions rarely challenged business management.

Especially in the South and West, the second major factor affecting union success and failure, the concerted effort business firms have made to undermine the power of organized labor, has been most pronounced. A number of recent studies have estimated that up to half of the recent union decline has

---

[22]Daniel Bell, *The Coming of Post-industrial Society* (New York: Basic Books, 1973), p. 127.

been the result of a stiffening resistance by employers to the organization of unions and to their effective campaigns to persuade workers to vote against union representation. And where unions have long existed, businesses are demanding that workers make wage concessions and agree to changes in work rules in order to keep plants open and competitive. At the extreme margin, employers increasingly use openly illegal tactics, such as discharging union activists and blacklisting union organizers.[23]

If unions were performing important activities that helped secure the stability of the American economy, why did so many employers turn against them? In a thoughtful analysis, Glenn Perusek argues that the Civil Rights movement and the call for black power helped reinvigorate militancy in otherwise quite static unions in the late 1960s and early 1970s. By the end of the 1960s, about one in six union members was African American. They tended to be younger than other workers. Forced to confront continuing job discrimination, they turned their attention to securing more of a role in their unions and, in some cases, to mounting radical demands, at times outside official unior structures, for more power in the workplace. Concurrently, many white workers were emboldened by the example of the Civil Rights and Black Power movements. Suddenly workers became much more assertive. The number of strikes, both official and unofficial, climbed. An increasing number of workers voted to reject contracts negotiated by their union leaders. With boom economic conditions during the late 1960s and workers feeling secure in their jobs, this pattern of militancy spread.[24] Soon employers were acting vigorously to stem this pattern. By the time Ronald Reagan was elected in 1980, it was clear they were succeeding, as strike levels were declining and union membership resumed an increasingly steady fall.

Some aspects of government policy have also made it harder for unions to organize workers. A key turning point came in 1981, when President Reagan fired the 14,000 air traffic controllers who had rejected a contract negotiated by their union, PATCO, and had gone on strike. Reagan issued an ultimatum: Work or lose your jobs. When the strike continued, he followed up, replacing the strikers with supervisors, members of the military, and replacements brought in from outside. The union was busted, and a powerful indication of the costs of militancy was given. Soon unions found themselves on the defensive, offering wage and productivity concessions in order to keep threatened jobs. The Reagan administration pursued other policies that added to labor's woes. It made fighting unemployment a lower priority than fighting inflation, thus creating something of a surplus of labor. Moreover, Reagan's appointments to the National Labor Relations Board (NLRB) were

---

[23]Michael Goldfield, *The Decline of Organized Labor in the United States* (Chicago: University of Chicago Press, 1987); Rob Wrenn, "The Decline of American Labor," *Socialist Review* no. 82/83 (July–October 1985): 89–119.

[24]Perusek, "Politics of Organized Labor"; see also Glenn Perusek and Kent Worcester, eds., *Trade Union Politics: American Unions and Economic Change, 1960s–1990s* (Atlantic Highlands, N.J.: Humanities Press, 1995).

very conservative, creating a tilt against the union movement. When President Bill Clinton's NLRB appointees tried to change the pro-employer bias of labor law, they were harassed and threatened by Republicans in Congress for doing so.

Unions themselves are not free from responsibility for their difficulties. Until the second half of the 1990s, labor's response to the various developments affecting its capacity to organize was very defensive. In part, this defensiveness was the result of union success, which had turned a vulnerable working class into a fairly well off population that increasingly thought of itself as part of the middle class. Labor in these circumstances often worked harder to protect its traditional terrain than to organize new workers. In the 1940s and 1950s, unions spent 40 percent of their budgets on efforts to expand their membership. By 1995, this spending had fallen to just 3 percent. The unions turned again to the Democratic Party, becoming its most important source of funds, in the hope of winning political allies to stem the tide of decline. Increasingly, unions also adopted policy views favoring protectionism in trade as a means to appeal to workers threatened by the loss of their jobs overseas and thus as a fix for their organizational infirmity. Many unions had grown comfortable as partners to corporate capitalism and now had trouble readjusting to a more difficult environment. With good cause, union leaders tended to blame their hard times on the anti-union assault by business and government and on the growth of conservatism, but they rarely confronted their own decision to spend a declining share of their budgets on efforts to bring new workers into the fold, thus depleting their most basic asset: union members. In all, unions came to be less and less part of an assertive social movement and more and more part of the political and industrial establishment. When other movements came to the fore in the 1960s and 1970s—most notably, the Civil Rights and feminist movements—insisting, among other demands, on an end to workplace discrimination, they did not generally turn to unions, which were seen as exclusionary and self-satisfied. In part as a result of the internal decision to focus AFL–CIO budgets more on lobbying in Washington than on grassroots efforts, the union movement by the late 1990s had become weaker than at any time since World War II. For at least a quarter century, labor has seemed paralyzed.

Labor's weakness is uneven. Union membership is higher among men (16 percent) than women (11 percent) and higher among blacks (17 percent) than whites (13 percent) or Latinos (12 percent). Middle-aged workers, between 35 and 64, are more likely to be in unions than are younger employees. Some industries—notably, transportation and public utilities—are relatively unionized (26 percent), while others, including finance, insurance, and real estate, have virtually no union members (2 percent). There also is a good deal of regional imbalance, as shown in Figure 4–1. One in 4 workers belongs to a union in New York and Hawaii; 1 in 5 in Michigan, Ohio, and New Jersey; and 1 in 6 in California and Pennsylvania; but only 1 in 16 in Arizona, Arkansas, Florida, Idaho, Mississippi, North Carolina, South Carolina,

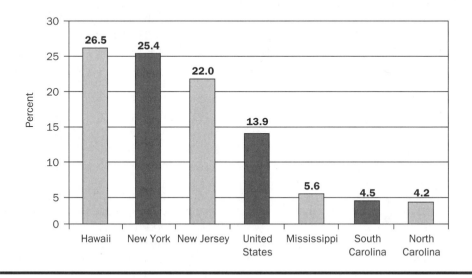

■ FIGURE 4–1

VARIATION IN UNION MEMBERSHIP BY STATE:
UNION MEMBERSHIP IN U.S. AND SELECTED STATES, AS
A PERCENT OF NONAGRICULTURAL WAGE-AND-SALARY
WORKERS, 1998

Texas, Utah, and Virginia.[25] The organizational failures of more than a half century ago continue to affect the capacities of organized labor today.

There has been a major shift in the efforts of the AFL–CIO, though its effects are not yet clear. With the election of John Sweeney as president of the labor federation in 1995, a decision was taken to make labor organizing the top priority, with oversight by a new Organizing Department. Since then, a set of well-funded strategic organizing campaigns targeted at low-wage workers, minorities, and underunionized occupations and geographic areas has been initiated. With the financial support and encouragement of AFL–CIO headquarters in Washington, D.C., unions have hired and trained new organizers and have stepped up their efforts to secure new members. There have been notable, even surprising, gains. In Los Angeles, for example, some 75,000 low-wage home health care workers, mostly Latino and African American, were brought into the union fold in 1999. The same year 5,000 textile workers at Fieldcrest Cannon in North Carolina were organized after failures to unionize these workers that go back to the 1930s. And nearly 15,000 doctors have joined the National Doctors Alliance, a group affiliated with the Service Employees International Union (SEIU). Overall, in 1998,

[25]U.S. Department of Labor, *Bureau of Labor Statistics News,* January 27, 2000; U.S. Department of Labor, *Monthly Labor Review OnLine* 122 (June 1999) at *stats.bls.gov/opub/mlr/mlrhome.htm.*

union membership increased by 112,000 and in 1999 by more than 265,000, the largest annual growth in two decades and an increase large enough to hold the percentage of workers overall even in a period of robust job growth. Now unions were again winning a majority of contested certification elections.[26] "After years of decline," the *New York Times* concluded, "labor has once again become a powerful political force."[27]

In 1994, when Republicans gained control of the House and the Senate, the AFL–CIO seemed politically inert. Two years later, stunned by the conservative shift, labor spent $35 million, including $15 million on issue ads, to mobilize voters in support of their favored candidates, most of whom were Democrats. The results were mixed, as Republicans maintained control of Congress, but President Clinton, labor's choice, was reelected. In 1998, labor switched strategies, spending the great bulk of its $28 million investment on phone banks, direct mail, and other basic tools to get union members to turn out to vote. As a result, Democrats made some gains, the result of a higher than usual turnout among union voters. In Wisconsin, for example, Senator Russell Feingold was narrowly reelected, with 67 percent of union members voting for him, as compared to 44 percent of other Wisconsin voters. In California, labor activism helped elect a Democratic governor and secure a majority in the state's legislature, where it also helped defeat Proposition 226, a ballot initiative aimed at prohibiting labor unions from spending their dues money on political activities unless members specifically approved.

Still the labor movement is vastly less powerful and more insecure than during its peak years. It faces a difficult battle to secure its future. Because so many jobs were created by a prosperous economy in the 1990s, unions have to run faster and faster even to maintain their organized percentage of the workforce. Moreover, as labor shows new signs of life, its critics are renewing efforts to make organizing more difficult by lobbying to weaken existing labor laws.

FUTURE LABOR PROSPECTS

Today, despite the new energy being poured into organizational efforts by the AFL–CIO, the factors that make it difficult for unions to expand their reach and influence seem greater than those on the other side. But, we might recall, unions have faced such troubles before. In December 1932, George Barnett, one of the country's leading labor economists, observed to the American Economic Association that, with membership of the AFL having dropped by some 40 percent in the 1920s, "the decline in the power of American trade unionism is due to occupational changes and technological

---

[26]U.S. Department of Labor, Bureau of Labor Statistics, *Monthly Labor Review,* January 28, 2000.
[27]*New York Times,* June 28, 2000.

advances likely to continue in the same direction. I see no reason to believe," he predicted, "that American trade unionism could so revolutionize itself within a short period as to become, in the next decade, a more potent social influence than it has been in the past decade."[28] Of course, as we have seen, he could not have been more wrong.

Labor currently is weak. Only one in ten American workers carries a union card today compared to one in three a half century ago. Many Americans think unions are archaic, the product of a labor movement from times past. They believe that the shift from manufacturing to services and the growth of a working middle class have made the gradual disappearance of the labor movement more likely and not to be regretted. Organized labor, in this view shared by many business leaders and conservative intellectuals, is no longer relevant. In a globalized, high-technology, flexible economy, unions are seen as rigid forces impeding change.

A key part of this orientation is the view that traditional class differences between capital and labor have been superseded by a much more complex, stratified occupational order in which there are numerous gradings of material rewards, status, and power. A related proposition is that the shift in employment from the production of goods to the production of services has fundamentally transformed American capitalism. From this perspective, we have entered a new age, in which the basic antagonism is not between capitalists and workers in the context of the factory, but between the white-collar professionals and technical experts and the rest of the population. These views are partial truths at best. Perhaps most important, they overstate the distinctiveness of white-collar and service occupations.

In 1870, there were only 82,200 clerical workers in the whole country (less than 1 percent of the workforce). These bookkeepers, secretaries, bank tellers, payroll and postal clerks, and stenographers more often than not had the status of craftsmen and were very well paid. In 1900, economist Harry Braverman noted, "[C]lerical employees of steam railroads and in manufacturing had average annual earnings of $1,011; in the same year the average annual earnings of [blue-collar] workers in these industries was $435 for manufacturing and $548 for steam railroads."[29] The division between the large mass of blue-collar workers and the tiny number of white-collar workers was great. If this gap had continued, the rapid expansion of white-collar clerical work would have been significant indeed.

But the very process of clerical expansion made office work more and more like blue-collar work. Indeed, according to the Bureau of Labor Statistics, weekly clerical wages today are lower than those for every type of blue-collar work, including unskilled labor. Moreover, clerical work has become increasingly depersonalized. It has been stripped of its craft status, routinized, and

[28]Quoted in Julie Kosterlitz, "Searching for New Labor," *National Journal*, September 4, 1999, 2470–71.

[29]Harry Braverman, "Labor and Monopoly Capital," *Monthly Review* 26 (July–August 1974): 51.

systematized. The tasks of most clerical workers have come to resemble those of shopfloor workers of some decades ago. Common office tasks were precisely quantified so that corporate offices may be run as large, efficient machines. The Systems and Procedures Association of America, for example, has published a guide based on information provided by General Electric, General Tire and Rubber Company, and other enterprises that presents a standard for office performance: "File drawer, open and close; no selection, .04 minutes; . . . desk drawer, open side drawer of standard desk, .014 minutes"; and so on.[30] As sociologist C. Wright Mills concluded a half century ago in his classic study of office work, except for hard physical labor, there are few characteristics of blue-collar work that are not also found in at least some white-collar work. "For here, too, the human traits of the individual, from his physique to his psychic disposition, become units in the functionally rational calculations of managers."[31]

Even skilled and professional white-collar work has changed. Engineers, scientists, and technicians have lost much of their traditional independent craft status. Like traditional manual laborers, they work for others who control the aims and conditions of their labor. Even lawyers and doctors, the best-paid and most respected white-collar workers, have lost a significant amount of their traditional independence. Year after year, a diminishing proportion of lawyers engages in their own practices, as a larger number work for big law firms or are employed directly by government or corporations on a salary basis. Similarly, an increasing proportion of doctors work for a salary in large health maintenance organizations, urban research centers, clinics, and hospitals.

Undeniably, the rapid growth in the production and distribution of services has changed American capitalism. But it has not eliminated or transformed the most fundamental distinction between capital and labor. Although the content of production has changed, its class character has not. Like factory workers, service workers (both blue- and white-collar) remain wage earners without control over the means of production or the work process. In light of these developments, it should not come as a surprise that the fastest-growing sectors of the unionized workforce in the 1990s were the white-collar and professional segments of the private sector, and especially of government.

Indeed, in just those high-technology areas of the economy where many think unions are unnecessary, workers often are more insecure, more in need of group-based assistance, and more likely to be faced with new kinds of exploitation than more traditional employees. Moreover, so long as basic class divisions characterize the work experience, unions have good chances to recruit workers, build their membership, regain political influence, and

[30]Ibid., p. 74.
[31]C. Wright Mills, *White Collar* (New York: Oxford University Press, 1954), pp. 226–27.

perhaps rediscover their energy as a social movement. There is good reason to believe that unions make a tangible difference in the income and quality of life for their members. In 1997, the median weekly earnings of full-time workers over the age of 16 was $503; for union members, it was $640.[32] Perhaps even more important are the other contributions unions make to working-class well-being. These include the placement of limits on the authority of managers in the workplace, the possibility of a degree of partic- ipation in workplace decision making, and a positive impact on the life chances of workers via the provision of health insurance, decent pensions, and greater job security.[33]

The combination of the vulnerability of all kinds of workers and the bene- fits unions offer holds out the promise that the labor movement may well have bottomed out. Its long-term impact on the politics of power—both as an important interest group lobbying to reduce inequality and extend the welfare state, among other issues, and as a movement capable of extending the character of American citizenship—remains uncertain. The various fac- tors that caused the decline of unions are mainly intact. And yet the new vigor demonstrated recently by the labor movement is grounded in signifi- cant opportunities.

In some cases, these are quite traditional. The two states with the lowest proportion of workers in unions, North Carolina and South Carolina, have become major industrial centers. With the exception of California, more man- ufacturing now takes place in the Carolinas than anywhere else in the coun- try. As the South more generally has become more like the rest of the country in its jobs, economy, and social structure, there clearly are major opportuni- ties for unions to try, once again, to become a genuinely national movement. In other cases, the chances to organize are quite new. We know that, in the past two decades, women and racial minorities have been joining unions at a significantly faster rate than white men. And these groups now make up a growing proportion of the labor force. In 1950, adult women overwhelm- ingly did not work outside the home. Today nearly half the people with jobs are women. If we include undocumented immigrants, at least one in four workers today is nonwhite.

The future, of course, is hard to know. What is clear is that not just the labor movement, but also various movements for change, from conservatism to feminism to civil rights, have transformed the character of citizenship and the meaning of politics in American life. Like political parties, to which we turn in the next chapter, they are key instruments for exerting popular influ- ence and for shaping the country's politics of power.

---

[32]U.S. Department of Labor, *Bureau of Labor Statistics News,* January 27, 2000.

[33]Daniel B. Cornfield, "The US Labor Movement: Its Development and Impact on Social Inequality and Politics," *Annual Review of Sociology* 17 (1999): 27–49.

SOCIAL MOVEMENTS AND DEMOCRATIC CITIZENSHIP

The checkered history of the labor movement is a reminder that particular goals can be pursued in more than one way. Organized labor has lobbied as an interest group, has engaged in elections, has bargained for better wages and working conditions with business within a framework established by law, and, at times, has mobilized millions of workers in a mass social movement.

Though all these forms of political participation contain the potential to challenge the existing distribution of powers and capacities in American life, the most basic instances of change have always been bound up with a social movement. Because of their often irregular, even disruptive, character, movements are often viewed with suspicion; in some cases—think of Europe's fascist mass movements in the 1920s and 1930s—they can undercut, even destroy, democracy. Yet it is important to understand that social movements are not abnormal parts of the democratic political process.

Though movements tend to be less durable and long-lasting than such other forms of organization as political parties and business associations, at any historical moment a number of substantial social movements usually are active. Often, of course, the boundary between a movement and political organizations and lobby groups is not crisp. As we have seen, we can speak of the labor movement, labor unions, and the major labor federation, the AFL–CIO, in one breath. So, too, with today's conservative movement, the Christian Coalition, and a host of right-wing think tanks and foundations. Moreover, both major political parties have privileged relations with different movements and movement-related organizations. Organized labor is much closer to the Democratic Party than the Republican Party; quite the reverse is true for conservative movements and movement-connected organizations. Yet social movements can still be understood as a distinctive form of collective action by citizens. Though social movements often engage in activity that is outside conventional institutional channels and, at times, is disruptive, they are important parts of the routine political scene. Many active participants invest their hopes for large-scale transformation and emancipation in social movements. Most often they are best thought of as instruments to subvert existing arrangements in order to reshape society and American democracy in ways that party politics and other more common forms of activity are unlikely to achieve, but are then able to adapt to. Today's "normal" party politics is the result of such struggles in all parts of the political spectrum.

Consider two further examples: the Civil Rights and women's movements. Today both major political parties, though they disagree about such controversial public policies as affirmative action and abortion, announce themselves as beacons of inclusiveness. A kind of egalitarian social minimum (albeit an uneven one, marked by many exceptions and a great deal of inequality) regarding black rights and gender equality underpins American political life today. Social and political change has overwhelmed candidates who would wish to support racial segregation or keep office-holding as a white preserve or confine women to the home, each of which was a common political position at the close of World War II.

These changes were the products of social movements. The mass Civil Rights movement of the late 1950s and 1960s mainly used nonviolent mass protest to make the continuation of Jim Crow segregation in the South unsustainable. African Americans were first promised fundamental rights as citizens after the Civil War, when the Thirteenth, Fourteenth, and Fifteenth Amendments guaranteeing racial equality were added to the Constitution between 1865 and 1870, and when Congress passed the Civil Rights Act of 1875, requiring equal accommodations for blacks with whites in public facilities apart from schools. After this legislation was voided by the Supreme Court in 1883 and segregation in "separate but equal" facilities was upheld by the Court in 1896 in *Plessy v. Ferguson,* all the South's states made Jim Crow lawful.

When the Court overturned *Plessy* in *Brown v. Board of Education* in 1954, declaring that segregated education was inherently unequal and thus a violation of the Constitution, southern white resistance helped trigger a mass movement by African Americans and white allies. A key moment came in 1955 in Montgomery, Alabama, when a 43-year-old black seamstress, Rosa Parks, refused to give up a seat in the front (white) part of a public bus. To protest her arrest, the city's blacks staged a one-day boycott of the bus system, which then grew into a protracted struggle that ended eight months later when the Supreme Court ruled against bus segregation. The strategy of picketing and boycotting spread to other cities and towns, but continued to meet determined opposition. In 1957, President Dwight Eisenhower had to dispatch 1,000 federal troops and mobilize 10,000 members of the Arkansas National Guard to carry out a court order to desegregate Little Rock's Central High School in the face of white resistance.

In 1960, the Civil Rights movement picked up steam when all-black and integrated groups held sit-ins, demanding service at southern lunch counters. Fanning out from Greensboro, North Carolina, this protest strategy spread quickly to force the desegregation of supermarkets, movie theaters, libraries, and department stores. In 1961, the sit-ins were complemented by freedom rides, where blacks and whites traveling together challenged segregation in interstate bus and train transportation. There were more than 70,000 freedom riders in 20 states and 100 cities. In August 1963, the Civil Rights movement brought more than 200,000 protesters to a March on Washington, to which the Reverend Martin Luther King, Jr., a Baptist minister, delivered his famous "I Have a Dream" oration in favor of racial justice. After the assassination of President John Kennedy in November 1963, the new president, Lyndon Baines Johnson of Texas, led a successful effort to pass the Civil Rights Act of 1964, outlawing segregation in public places and prohibiting workplace discrimination. A year later, after a clash between police and demonstrators in Selma, Alabama, on "bloody Sunday" and a mass march two days later, Johnson spearheaded the passage of the Voting Rights Act of 1965, which removed such instruments as the poll tax and literacy tests southern states had used to prevent blacks from voting and holding

Dr. Martin Luther King delivers his "I Have a Dream" speech in Washington, D.C.

public office. The landmarks of the Civil Rights movement are summarized in Figure 4–2.

If an end to segregation was inconceivable without a mass social movement, so, too, the transformation in the situation of women has been the result of the feminist movement, which itself was inspired by nineteenth- and early-twentieth-century struggles by women to win the vote and by the example of the Civil Rights movement (Figure 4–3).

In the 1960s, a movement of women began to use social criticism and mass agitation as instruments to bring about gender equality. A key development came in 1966 with the creation of the National Organization for Women (NOW), which, together with other women's organizations, mobilized women to fight to overturn workplace discrimination, the enforcement of male patriarchal dominance in gender-based contract and property rights, and restrictions on contraception and abortion. The movement also sought to enhance the participation of women in politics.

Social movements like these are recurring features of political life despite the odds, at any time, against getting them going. Social movements speak directly to people at two levels. They mobilize supporters on the basis of such material interests as how much money they can earn and the kind of work they can do. Not just the labor movement, but also the feminist and Civil Rights movements aimed to transform the class-connected situations of their members. But what also distinguishes such social movements is their capacity to activate commitments by defining people's identities as members of this or that group—as women or as workers or as blacks or as conservatives of faith. Social movements tend to be most potent when they appeal

CIVIL RIGHTS MOVEMENT TIMELINE

Date	Event	Development
1861–1865	Civil War	Slavery abolished
1910	NAACP founded	Black-led, multiracial civil rights group
1948	Military desegregated	President Truman orders end to segregation by executive order
1954	*Brown v. Board of Education*	Supreme Court declares school segregation to be unconstitutional
1955	Montgomery School boycott	Rosa Parks refused to move to back of bus; successful protests followed
1957	Little Rock integration	Federal troops ensure compliance with court order to integrate high school
1960	Sit-in movement	Four black college students begin sit-ins in Greensboro, North Carolina
1961	Freedom rides	Multiracial protests to integrate bus and train lines
1962	University of Mississippi integration	Enrollment by James Meredith enforced by federal troops
1963	March on Washington	Martin Luther King proclaims, "I have a dream"
1964	Civil Rights Act	Declares segregation and racial discrimination illegal
1965	Voting rights protests	March from Selina to Montgomery, Alabama
1965	Voting Rights Act	Protected right to vote by all Americans, irrespective of race

simultaneously to the satisfaction of interests and the recognition of identities. Social movements tend to be concerned with what people need and want and who they are at the same time. This powerful combination usually is overlaid with more appeals to such contested values as social equality and fidelity to God's will that often serve to elicit the participation of large numbers of people, even many who otherwise have scant political experience. Movement politics thus is charged politics.

Social movements also are marked by their challenges to the bias of existing institutions. When New Deal liberalism was ascendant, conservatives felt themselves to be, and, in fact, were, on the outside of much of political life. They fought to change that situation. Now they are insiders. Before the New Deal, working-class people largely found it impossible to organize unions. The labor movement they fashioned knocked down these walls and offered working people many new avenues for influence and access. The

WOMEN'S VOTING MOVEMENT TIMELINE

Date	Event	Development
1790, 1807	New Jersey voting rights	Women first gain, then lose, right to vote
1833	Oberlin College	First co-educational college in the United States
1837	National Female Anti-Slavery Society	81 delegates from 12 states meeting in New York
1848	Seneca Falls	First women's rights convention
1850	National Women's Rights Convention	Speakers included Sojourner Truth and Frederick Douglass
1866	Equal Rights Association	Elizabeth Cady Stanton and Susan B. Anthony promote universal suffrage
1869	Women's movement divides	Stanton and Anthony form National Women's Suffrage Association; Lucy Stone leads the more moderate American Women Suffrage Association
1872	Votes refused	Susan B. Anthony arrested for trying to vote; Sojourner Truth turned away at polls
1878	Amendment introduced	Women's suffrage amendment introduced in Congress
1890	Women's movement unites	National American Woman Suffrage Association formed
1893	Colorado rights	First state to pass an amendment enfranchising women
1913–1919	Mass protests	Massive campaign conducted on behalf of voting rights for women
1920	Nineteenth Amendment	The Constitution is amended to grant women the right to vote

same was true of the Civil Rights and feminist movements. Located outside the leading legal and political institutions of society, they fought against closure and exclusion to make their way into the political process. Irrespective of how we evaluate the substance of the demands of each movement, it is clear that social movements are key instruments for widening and extending democratic participation and the content of political life. They are critical counterweights to privilege and key sites of political conflict.

CONCLUSION

Social movements are always mixed in their effects. When they succeed, they disrupt, overcome, even destroy conventional practices. The system of Jim Crow was overturned in the South largely by the Civil Rights movement.

Today almost no American would fail to recognize the immense gains to democracy achieved by the end of segregation. But at the time, large numbers of white southerners, perhaps a significant majority, believed these changes to be so negative that massive resistance was called for. Because they change definitions of citizenship, break down traditional barriers to political participation and the circulation of ideas, and alter the field of possibility, social movements always are controversial. By mobilizing and shaping particular social and political identities, they challenge other valued forms of identification. When women demand equality in the workplace, for example, many others believe the traditional male-headed family is brought into question. When movements challenge the political boundaries that keep their participants out of the center of political life, they inevitably challenge the position of others. And by establishing new boundaries, they invite those others to make a stand. Thus, when labor unions won many battles in the 1930s and 1940s, business organizations fought back and succeeded in changing labor laws to make it more difficult for unions to organize. Often, then, social movements are the repositories of great hopes and great fears. Much of the heat in American politics comes from the existence and activities of social movements.

Because it is not easy to motivate and mobilize large groups of people, especially those with few resources, movements tend to use exaggerated, at times extreme, language about their situation and their adversaries. Movement politics rarely is civil. Movement members believe, often correctly, that an enormous amount is at stake in their words and actions. Resentment at losing often is strong. Thus, for example, evangelical Christians struggle mightily against the teaching of evolution in the schools, and the fight for gains by one ethnic group risks taking the form of hostile expression about others. When morality, identity, and interest intertwine, particularly outspoken, often uncompromising, forms of politics ensue.

Despite these features, social movements are key instruments of any decent democratic politics. By disrupting normal routines and practices, they invite new participants into politics, challenge present arrangements, and provide scope for genuine, often deep, debate about such core issues as who is a citizen, what citizenship means, and to what extent privileges outside the political sphere should be allowed to shape political life and policy outcomes. In the West generally, and in the United States in particular, the meaning and scope of citizenship would be much narrower without the contributions to civil, political, and social rights made by social movements.

5

Political Parties, Elections, and Movements

Chads—pregnant chads, hanging chads, and dimpled chads[1]—electors, votomatics, and butterfly ballots. Citizens who had never heard any of these terms prior to the election on November 7, 2000, were all too familiar with them by the time the election was over, a month and a half later. Viewers who watched the returns on television were treated to a dazzling light show, which they had not anticipated. First, Florida turned blue, indicating the networks were calling Al Gore the winner there. And then Florida turned red, meaning the networks had reversed themselves and were now calling George W. Bush the winner of the Seminole State. And then Florida turned gray, meaning that the networks had reversed themselves yet again and that they now believed the race for Florida's 25 electoral votes was too close to call. More than a month later, it was finally determined that George W. Bush had won Florida by a margin of 537 votes out of more than 6 million cast statewide, amidst charges of voting irregularities and a recount of thousands of contested votes that was cut short by order of the U.S. Supreme Court, following a controversial 5–4 decision. By the time Al Gore conceded, 36 days after the election was held, it was not clear that he had so much lost a close election among voters in Florida due to all the ballots that were not counted as he had lost by one vote on the Supreme Court.

What happened in the 2000 presidential election was extraordinary, if not unprecedented. There were concessions and retractions, lawsuits and appeals, and evidence of ballot tampering and disputed votes. Election night does not usually extend over 36 days. The Supreme Court does not usually intervene in such a way as to determine the winner of a presidential election. And votes do not usually go uncounted and unrecorded. Elections are supposed to confer democratic legitimacy on a government. As a result of the turmoil in Florida, President George W. Bush enjoyed little of it

---

[1]A chad, we now know, is a piece of paper that is supposed to fall from the ballot when voters cast their votes. Unfortunately, many chads did not fall when voters marked their ballots, putting their votes in dispute.

All the different headlines the *Chicago Sun-Times* newspaper produced as the 2000 presidential election results unfolded.

when he was sworn into office as the 43rd president of the United States on January 20, 2001.

Though victorious, Republicans could take little solace in the results. Their majority in the House of Representatives was reduced almost in half, they lost their majority in the Senate, their presidential candidate lost the popular vote by 550,000, and exit polls revealed the public preferred Al Gore's positions on Social Security, education, and health care to George W. Bush's.

While the conflict to determine who actually won the presidential election transfixed the country, the fact is that only a bare majority of eligible citizens chose to participate in it. Only 51 percent of all eligible voters cast ballots on November 7, 2000. Turnout is lower in the United States than in any major democracy, yet Americans are far from politically apathetic. Political participation increasingly occurs outside the electoral process. Citizens are abandoning the voting booth to express their demands through other forms of political participation, such as interest groups, social movements, community activism, and court challenges. As political participation overflows electoral and party limits, the contrast is striking between the overfull and chaotic nature of American politics outside of electoral politics and the desiccated state of elections and parties within it.

This chapter takes a deeper look at the issues just identified by examining the development of the American party system, the structure of political parties, voting patterns within the electorate, the role of the media in election campaigns, the impact of money on elections and campaigns, and, finally, forms of political participation outside the party system.

THE DISAPPEARING AMERICAN VOTER

According to political scientist E. E. Schattschneider, "The political parties created modern democracy and modern democracy is unthinkable save in terms of the parties."[2] Political parties are the agency that organizes and transmits the will of the majority to the government. They are the heart of any democracy because they pump the blood of electoral consent that informs and flows through political institutions. Political parties mobilize and educate voters, recruit and nominate candidates for office, offer voters a choice of political programs, and then carry out these programs if given an electoral mandate by the people.

If, as Schattschneider claims, political parties are the measure of democracy's health, then American democracy is very ill and in need of powerful drugs. American political parties are suffering from a case of severe political anemia, reflected in alarmingly low voter turnout. The United States ranks 35th in turnout out of 37 democracies, finishing ahead of only Poland and Switzerland! In the 1996 elections, less than half the electorate bothered to vote. Turnout was the lowest it had been since 1924. In 2000, as we have already seen, turnout increased slightly to 51 percent. Turnout is even lower in years when there is no presidential race (in what are called off-year elections). In the 1998 congressional elections, only 36 percent of the electorate went to the polls, the lowest turnout in a midterm election since 1942—when citizens, at least, had the excuse of a world war to divert them from voting.

Nations are rightly held up to scorn when only a single political party is permitted to run candidates or there is sloppiness or fraud in counting ballots. There is no better example than the 2000 presidential election, when undercounted votes, ballots that were tampered with, and recounts that yielded different results led many to question whether the winner actually received the most votes. But in an even more general way, American democracy is of dubious quality when more people watch the Super Bowl each year than bother to vote for president. Political scientist V. O. Key, Jr. once observed, "[A] government founded on democratic doctrines becomes some other sort of regime when large proportions of its citizens refrain from voting."[3] Nonvoting on such a massive scale is indicative of a dysfunctional democracy.

The dilemma voters face was portrayed on the Halloween episode of *The Simpsons*, aired just before the November 1996 elections. Homer Simpson

---

[2] E. E. Schattschneider, *Party Government* (New York: Holt, Rinehart & Winston, 1942), p. 1.

[3] V. O. Key, Jr., *Southern Politics in State and Nation* (New York: Knopf, 1949), p. 508.

discovers that aliens have abducted incumbent Democrat Bill Clinton and Republican challenger Bob Dole and are posing as these presidential candidates in disguise. Homer thwarts the aliens' plans by attending a presidential debate where he leaps on stage and tears off their masks. The audience at the debate is horrified and disgusted when the true identities of the choices offered are revealed to them. One of the aliens turns to the audience and says, "It's true, we are aliens. But what are you going to do about it? It's a two-party system. You have to vote for one of us."

Although third parties exist, they are not often competitive. The more typical way voters express their disappointment with what the Democrats and Republicans offer is by not voting at all. Since parties are in the business of electing their candidates to office, one would expect that they would be on the lookout for issues, such as national health insurance, that attract wide support. But party competition does not ensure that these demands are articulated because they may challenge the interests and values of party elites. Party elites may be reluctant to raise issues that would attract nonvoters because doing so might upset the power that elites currently exercise within the party.

The same logic applies to candidates. They may be more responsive to wealthy donors and current voters than to nonvoters. Parties and candidates concentrate their scarce resources on a smaller and smaller universe of voters who tend to have strong partisan feelings and are likely to vote. Candidates and parties may be quite content with the low level of turnout and for good reason have little interest in changing it. Party competition, in short, does not ensure responsiveness to citizens' demands.[4]

Nonvoting is also a symptom of and contributes to widespread popular cynicism directed at politicians from both parties. "Us" versus "them" no longer refers to the partisan division of the electorate between Democrats and Republicans. It now describes skeptical citizens on one side and the governing class on the other side. Citizens are sullen and suspicious of political elites from both parties, who are perceived as simply out for themselves. Citizens express their disgust by withdrawing from a process that they regard as corrupt and unresponsive to their interests. Ironically, the result is a self-fulfilling prophecy. That is, believing that the system cannot be improved discourages participation in it; the result is to further discredit politics and the public sphere.

Finally, the narrow range of alternatives offered voters in the United States also depresses voter turnout. Turnout is typically far higher in Europe, where parties have traditionally represented a wide range of policy choices. However, as European party systems look more like the American model, in

---

[4] Richard F. Hamilton, *Class and Politics in the United States* (New York: Wiley, 1972), pp. 1–22. See also Paul Frymer and John David Skrentny, "Coalition Building and the Politics of Electoral Capture During the Nixon Administration: African Americans, Labor and Latinos," *Studies in American Political Development,* Spring 1998, 131–61. Frymer and Skrentny write, "Instead of competitive parties being uniquely suited to aid the incorporation of group interests into the political system, we argue that party competition can at times hinder such efforts" (p. 161).

which parties of the left and the right all support the demands of global cap-italism for free markets, deregulation, lower taxes, and fewer state services, European voters have begun to express their dissatisfaction by abstaining, just as American voters do.

Although the Democratic and Republican parties may disagree on spe-cific and occasionally even broad policies, they agree on the fundamental purpose of the political economy: to preserve and perfect corporate capital-ism. This tendency is reinforced by political contributions from business and wealthy individuals, who are the largest contributors to both Democra-tic and Republican candidates, and by the mobilization of bias we described in Chapter 2. As a result, blue-collar workers are twice as likely as profes-sionals to believe party distinctions are meaningless. Not perceiving a dif-ference between the parties, workers are more likely to drop out of the electorate. The greatest difference between the rich and the poor is not for whom they vote for but whether or not they vote. According to political sci-entist Walter Dean Burnham, there is a hole in the American electorate where the working class should be.[5] Lower-class citizens in the United States vote at roughly 60 percent of the rate of upper-class citizens, a much greater difference in voting participation between classes than one finds in other Western nations.[6] For example, as Table 5–1 shows, only 38.7 percent of those in the bottom fifth of the income scale voted in the 1996 presidential election compared to 72.6 percent in the top quintile. Moreover, the voting gap between the rich and the poor is increasing. According to the Index of Political Inequality, the bottom fifth in income voted at roughly two-thirds of the rate of the top fifth in income in 1960. In 1996, they voted at little more than half the rate of those in the top income brackets. This disparity means that the electoral influence of those at the bottom of the income hierarchy is declining relative to that of those at the top.[7]

The failure of parties and candidates to articulate the demands of lower-class voters confirms Schattschneider's profound insight: "*The definition of the alternatives is the supreme instrument of power.*"[8] By and large, parties set the agenda of government, and have done so in a way that effectively disfran-chises the lower classes by failing to articulate their demands. The result has been massive nonvoting by the underprivileged and a bias of the electoral process—and of the benefits that can be derived from government through elections—toward those who are more fortunate. Party competition does not

---

[5] Walter Dean Burnham, "The 1980 Earthquake: Realignment, Reaction or What," in *The Hidden Election: Politics and Economics in the 1980 Presidential Campaign,* ed. Thomas Ferguson and Joel Rogers (New York: Pantheon, 1981), pp. 126–27.

[6] Jan E. Leighley and Jonathon Nagler, "Socioeconomic Class Bias in Turnout, 1964–1988," *American Political Science Review* 86 (1992): 725–36.

[7] Tom DeLuca, "Joe the Bookie and the Class Gap in Voting," *American Demographics,* November 1998, 26–29.

[8] E. E. Schattschneider, *The Semi-Sovereign People: A Realist's View of American Democracy* (Hinsdale, Ill.: Dryden Press, 1975), p. xxvi (emphasis in original).

■ TABLE 5-1

INDEX OF POLITICAL INEQUALITY

Year	Overall Turnout	Income		Inequality Index
		Bottom 5th	Top 5th	
1996	49.0	38.7	72.6	.533
1992	55.2	42.0	78.0	.538
1988	50.1	42.2	73.7	.573
1984	53.1	44.7	74.7	.598
1980	52.6	45.7	76.2	.600
1976	53.5	46.7	74.1	.630
1972	55.2	49.2	79.7	.621
1968	60.9	54.5	81.3	.670
1964	61.9	54.1	84.0	.644
1960	62.8	NA	NA	

SOURCE: Tom DeLuca, "Joe the Bookie and the Class Gap in Voting," *American Demographics* (November 1998), p. 27.

correct this bias by giving the losing party an incentive to mobilize nonvoters. Instead, it serves to legitimize the results as fair and democratic even though the alternatives offered are unrepresentative and truncated. Elections obscure citizens' lack of representation with the fig leaf of party competition.

PARTY SYSTEMS

The Constitution made no provision for political parties; they have no official status in our political system. Indeed, the authors of the Constitution viewed political parties with contempt and believed they were a threat to liberty. The Founding Fathers, according to historian Richard Hofstadter, "hoped to create not a system of party government under a constitution, but rather a constitutional government that would check and control parties."[9] However, the very design of government included in the Constitution, with its checks and balances and separation of powers among the different branches of government, indirectly contributed to the development of political parties. Parties arose to give some cohesion to government, whose authority was fragmented among separate and independent institutions. In

[9]Richard Hofstadter, *The Idea of a Party System: The Rise of Legitimate Opposition in the United States, 1780–1840* (Berkeley: University of California Press, 1969), p. 53.

addition, party formation arose from the conflict of interests among the different groups in society.

Even as the framers of the Constitution condemned parties in theory, they helped create them in practice. Both Thomas Jefferson and James Madison, who cofounded the Republican Party (the forerunner of today's Democratic Party), and Alexander Hamilton and John Adams, who led the Federalist Party, viewed political parties, at best, as necessary evils. It is ironic, Hofstadter notes, that the "the creators of the first American party system on both sides, Federalists and Republicans, were men who looked upon parties as sores on the body politic."[10]

From the start, parties proved to be a democratizing force in the United States. They expanded political participation, mobilized eligible voters, and broke down a deferential system of politics in which only the socially privileged and wealthy could participate. This point, however, must be qualified because blacks and women were excluded from the electorate. The United States did not become a fully realized democracy with universal suffrage until the 1960s, when southern blacks were finally as free to vote as other Americans.

While not forgetting or neglecting this uncomfortable fact, the United States was in an important respect the first popular government in the world. Citizen interest in elections ran high, with turnout in the nineteenth century sometimes reaching 75 percent of the eligible voters, far above current turnout rates.[11] The current design of two parties that reached into the grass roots to organize voters first reached maturity under President Andrew Jackson (1829–37).[12] By the Jacksonian period, political parties had institutionalized the idea of a legitimate opposition to the government and had become the accepted means by which citizens organize and transmit their demands to government.

A TWO-PARTY SYSTEM

In the United States, whoever gets the most votes wins the general election. These electoral rules create a powerful bias toward a two-party system. Voters fear wasting their votes on small parties that cannot win and so tend

---

[10] Ibid., p. 2.

[11] See Table 2.3, Transformations at the National Level: Turnout, 1824–1968, in Walter Dean Burnham, *Critical Elections and the Mainsprings of American Politics* (New York: Norton, 1970), p. 21. It should be noted that the French Revolution of 1789 ushered in universal manhood suffrage earlier than in the United States. But Napoleon's coup d'état ended France's brief democratic experiment.

[12] Richard P. McCormick, "Political Development and the Second Party System," in *The American Party Systems: Stages of Political Development*, ed. William Nesbitt Chambers and Walter Dean Burnham (New York: Oxford University Press, 1977), p. 102.

GABLE
THE GLOBE AND MAIL
Toronto
CANADA

to coalesce around two major parties that can gain the most votes and attain power. Third parties have a difficult time competing because voters know there are no rewards for finishing second under our rules. Under different electoral rules, such as proportional representation, where legislative seats are allotted to parties based on their percentages of the vote, multiparty systems flourish. Losers are rewarded with legislative seats, something to show for their efforts. Voters can now vote their conscience without fear they are throwing their vote away, as would be the case under our winner-take-all rules—and thus avoid the situation depicted in the cartoon in Figure 5–1.

Our presidential form of government further strengthens the bias toward a two-party system. Groups need to form broad coalitions in order to create majorities that can win the ultimate prize in American politics. Presidential elections create strong incentives for voters to coalesce around two blocs that compete to win this office, the most powerful in the entire government.

In addition, the two major parties collude to restrict competition. Democratic and Republican legislators have used their influence to ensure that state governments, which control access to the ballot, put obstacles in the way of third-party candidates. States can require that third parties present filing petitions signed by a certain proportion of eligible voters in order to appear on the ballot. Obtaining signatures for filing petitions is expensive and labor-intensive. While the two major parties concentrate on attracting votes, third parties must expend scarce resources simply to get on the ballot. Third parties must also contend with a strong media bias. Because the media decide that only the two major parties are worthy of coverage and generally ignore third-party candidates, most voters have little sense that other parties compete in elections.

Although the factors reviewed above have made it difficult for third parties to break the two-party mold, it has been done. The Republican Party emerged in the 1850s as a third party and successfully replaced the Whigs. In addition, third parties can take advantage of American federalism and establish themselves at state and local levels. There are many examples of third parties electing mayors and other local officials. Although there are countless "third parties"—actually, then, third, fourth, and fifth parties—on the ballot in virtually every election, the two major parties tend to monopolize voter choice.

CRITICAL ELECTIONS

The two-party system limits the choices available to voters and creates parties that consist of broad coalitions composed of diverse and sometimes conflicting groups. For example, at one time, the Democratic Party included both blacks who supported integration and southerners who opposed it. American political parties try to contain such conflicts by being evasive on issues. They do not offer the kind of clear, ideologically distinctive programs that voters are offered in multiparty systems. American political parties believe that to stake out clear positions on issues might antagonize groups and thus jeopardize their chance of winning elections. Consequently, parties are unresponsive to emerging groups and their demands. The parties blur issues, ignore new demands, and fail to adapt to new conditions. The result is that such demands build up, pressure in the system increases, and dissatisfaction with the lack of alternatives offered by the parties grows. The party system fails to reflect changes that are occurring in the broader society. At first, citizens seek answers outside the existing party system, in the form of protests and social movements. But dissent eventually is expressed through the electoral system in what political scientists refer to as a *critical* or *realigning election*. Such elections are characterized by unusually high turnout and more intense ideological conflict between the parties. The issues that divide the parties change, and party conflict is organized around a new set of issues. Voters are realigned and party coalitions shift. Some groups defect, shifting their loyalty from one party to another. Or groups that were unattached to one of the parties or did not participate in elections previously now join one of the political parties. The result of these changes in voting patterns may give rise to a new party to replace one of the established parties, as occurred when the Republicans replaced the Whigs in the 1850s. Or the minority party prior to the critical election may become the new majority party, as happened to the Democrats in the 1930s. Or the majority party may capitalize on the dramatic changes to maintain its position on the basis of a new coalition and a new set of issues, as happened to the Republican Party in 1896.

Party systems have life cycles. A new party system is inaugurated by a critical election in which party coalitions are formed and party conflict is organized around a particular set of issues. But as new groups with new demands emerge, the parties do not respond or address their concerns. Demands build until another critical election occurs, ushering in a new party system—new party coalitions organized around a new set of issues—at which point the process begins again.[13]

PARTY DECAY

American political parties were not always weak and unable to mobilize voters. In the late nineteenth century, parties were powerful organizations that, according to Steven Skowronek, lent "order, predictability and continuity to governmental activity."[14] They were complex, well-staffed organizational structures that reached down into the grass roots, communicated to voters through a partisan popular press, and controlled the nomination of candidates and the platform on which they ran.[15] Turnout was high, and there was little of the class bias so evident in turnout patterns today. Still one should avoid idealizing the political parties of this period, often considered the high point of American political party development. While parties were able to turn out the vote, they mostly depended on patronage and spoils to motivate activists and voters. Urban political machines integrated workers as voters, but in a way that insulated business from democratic challenge.[16] High voter turnout, especially among the working class, does not guarantee that party competition will be organized around class issues or that economic elites will be challenged. But it is hard to imagine class issues emerging or business being challenged politically in the absence of high levels of working-class turnout.[17]

---

[13] The classic account of the theory of critical elections is Walter Dean Burnham, *Critical Elections*.

[14] Stephen Skowronek, *Building a New American State: The Expansion of National Administrative Capacities, 1877–1920* (New York: Cambridge University Press, 1982), pp. 24, 25.

[15] See Burnham, *Critical Elections*, pp. 71–73.

[16] Ira Katznelson, "The Crisis of the Capitalist City: Urban Politics and Social Control," in Willis D. Hawley and Michael Lipsky, eds., *Theoretical Perspectives on Urban Politics* (Englewood Cliffs, N.J.: Prentice-Hall, 1976), pp. 224–25. Also see Ira Katznelson, *City Trenches: Urban Politics and the Patterning of Class in the United States* (New York: Pantheon, 1981).

[17] Francis Fox Piven and Richard Cloward, *Why Americans Don't Vote* (New York: Pantheon, 1988), pp. 28–41.

Party decline set in following the critical election of 1896. Turnout in presidential elections declined from 79 percent in 1896 to 49 percent in 1924, with nonvoters concentrated among the working class and minorities. This demobilization was due to many factors. First, party competition declined dramatically following the 1896 election. Both the South and the North became one-party regions, with the Democrats enjoying a political monopoly in the South, where they made themselves the vehicle for the defense of white racism, while the Republicans dominated elsewhere. Noncompetitive, one-party systems permit party leaders to ignore the demands of voters and cater to elites, confident that their party will triumph at the polls anyway. Both Republicans and Democrats were content with their monopolies of voters in different regions of the country and were under little pressure to offer clear alternatives or maximize votes. As a result, voters lost interest and turnout fell.

Second, following the 1896 critical election, business groups and middle-class reformers made a vigorous and effective effort to weaken parties. They became impatient with the expense and corruption of urban political machines and feared that working-class politics might take an even more ominous, more radical turn. As a result, business progressives tried to weaken political parties as organizations by cutting off the flow of incentives parties could offer voters. Civil service rules limited party control of patronage. Direct primaries prevented parties from controlling the nominating process, and nonpartisan elections for local office reduced the salience of parties to voters. These reforms weakened parties as organizations, depriving them of resources to recruit and mobilize voters.

Finally, turnout was depressed by new legal barriers to voting. Nowhere was the effort to put obstacles in the way of voting pursued with more vigor and ingenuity than in the South. Southern states, which traditionally relied on fraud and violence to keep blacks from the polls, now institutionalized racial—as well as class—repression through such devices as poll taxes (which required paying a hefty fee to vote), literacy tests, and tests of "good character." Three-quarters of all citizens in the South, especially blacks and poor, uneducated whites, lost the right to vote through these stratagems. Turnout in the South in presidential elections declined from 57 percent in 1896 to a mere 19 percent of eligible voters by 1924.[18]

Northern elites pursued the same goal as their southern counterparts, but with less spectacular results. Complicated voter registration systems discouraged voting by imposing residency requirements, setting early closing deadlines to register to vote, and opening the voter registration office only for short and inconvenient periods. While the formal right to vote remained, helping to legitimize the United States as a democracy, the introduction of these procedural obstacles prevented millions of citizens from exercising that right.[19]

---

[18] J. Morgan Kousser, *The Shaping of Southern Politics: Suffrage Restrictions and the Establishment of the One-Party South* (New Haven, Conn.: Yale University Press, 1974).

[19] Piven and Cloward, *Why Americans Don't Vote.*

THE DECLINE OF PARTY ORGANIZATION

The 1896 critical election set in motion a process of party decay that has continued, with twists and turns, through the present. For example, in an exhaustive survey of party organizations in all 50 states, political scientist David R. Mayhew found that "local [party] organizations . . . sloped downward between 1950 and the late 1960s and have fallen precipitously since."[20] Party organizations decayed as the resources they depended on slipped from their grasp. Civil service reforms meant that government jobs were filled on the basis of competitive examination, not party loyalty, which cut off the supply of patronage that parties controlled to attract and reward supporters. In addition, the spread of the direct primary, in which the party's nominee is selected by an election among party members, not a caucus of party activists and officials, hastened the decline of party organization. The party organization no longer controlled who received the party's nomination to run for office; instead, rank-and-file party members had the decisive say.

Finally, party organizations have become much less important players in the game that is presumably the reason why they exist in the first place: to contest elections. In the heyday of mass parties, in the late nineteenth century and for some decades thereafter, candidates depended on parties to provide them with the financial resources and campaign workers they needed to wage election campaigns. Nowadays candidates no longer depend on the party apparatus for support. The functions that party organizations previously performed during campaigns have lost their value as modern campaigns depend increasingly on money and technology, not labor and organization, which parties could offer. An era of candidate-centered politics has developed, and parties must run to catch up with the action. Candidates now raise their own money through computer-generated direct mail and fund-raisers with affluent supporters. They hire polling organizations and political consultants to conduct focus groups and market research to advise them how to fine-tune their message, and they reach voters through television advertising and telephone appeals conducted by political consultants who hire out their services.

Some political scientists suggest that American parties are experiencing a revival. While local party organizations may be hollow, state party organizations now have full-time staffs, ample budgets, and services they can offer to candidates and supporters.[21] Party organization is even more robust at the level of each party's national committee. The Republican National Committee

[20] David R. Mayhew, *Placing Parties in American Politics* (Princeton, N.J.: Princeton University Press, 1986), pp. 220, 225.

[21] Cornelius P. Cotter, James L. Gibson, John F. Bibby, and Robert J. Huckshorn, *Party Organizations in America* (New York: Praeger, 1984), pp. 13–41. See also John F. Bibby, "State Party Organizations: Coping and Adapting," in *The Parties Respond,* 2nd ed., ed. L. Sandy Maisel (Boulder, Colo.: Westview Press, 1994), pp. 21–45.

(RNC) was the first to modernize its operations in the 1980s by hiring pollsters and political consultants. It also began to use direct mail to raise soft money—that is, money that private donors contribute to a political party for supposedly educational purposes, such as get-out-the-vote drives, voter registration, and party building. Soft money, as opposed to hard money, is not subject to federal regulations on contributions, and parties and candidates can raise unlimited amounts of it. The RNC's success in raising soft money and offering low-cost services to Republican candidates and state organizations compelled the Democratic National Committee (DNC) to upgrade its operations. According to political scientist Paul S. Herrnson, "[N]ational parties are now stronger, more stable and more influential in their relations with state and local party committees and candidates than ever before."[22]

But the party renewal thesis confuses increased levels of activity by party organizations with party strength. Party organizations have, in essence, become large political consulting firms at the service of candidates. The party renewal thesis is valid only if we dilute our measure of party strength. British political scientist Alan Ware observed: "A strong party organization is one, which, at the very least, can determine who will be the party's candidate, can decide (broadly) the issues on which campaigns will be fought by its candidates, contributes the 'lion's share' of resources to the candidate's election campaign, and has influence over appointments made by public officials."[23]

Judged by these reasonable and traditional standards, party organization in the United States remains feeble. Primaries have undermined party control of nominations, candidates raise their own money and define the issues in a campaign, and personal loyalty counts more than party loyalty when elected officials make appointments. The parties may be more active, provide more services, and raise more money, but they are doing so in a context in which they play a more subordinate role to candidates.[24]

PARTY STRUCTURE AND ORIENTATION

American political parties have always been decentralized; they just have not always been weak. Party organization reflects the federal structure of government, with Democratic and Republican organizations located at the

[22]Paul S. Herrnson, "The Revitalization of National Party Organizations," in *The Parties Respond*, p. 67.

[23]Quoted in John J. Coleman, "Resurgent or Just Busy? Party Organizations in Contemporary America," in *The State of the Parties: The Changing Role of Contemporary American Parties*, 2nd ed., ed. John C. Green and Daniel M. Shea (Lanham, Md.: Rowman & Littlefield, 1996), p. 377.

[24]Ibid., p. 382.

national, state, and local levels. But relationships among the different levels of the party are not hierarchical, with the DNC or RNC issuing instructions to the party's lower levels. To the contrary, the different levels of the party are relatively independent of each other, with state and local parties putting forth their own slate of candidates and programs without direction from above. Candidates and state and local parties are free to define for themselves what it means to be a Democrat or Republican. For example, the RNC (but not the Louisiana Republican Party) censured neo-Nazi David Duke, but could not prevent him from running under the party label for the Senate and for governor, and even winning a seat as a Republican in the Louisiana state legislature. The loose, disorderly party structure that characterizes both the Democratic and Republican parties once led Will Rogers to quip, "I don't belong to an organized political party. I'm a Democrat."[25]

The Republican and Democratic national party conventions possess formal authority over the parties. The parties call conventions every four years to nominate the party's presidential and vice presidential candidates, adopt a party platform, select party officers, and review party rules. Party conventions were once significant because competition among contending candidates for the party's presidential nomination meant that convention delegates had a real choice over their party's nominee. An extreme example of this occurred when delegates to the 1924 Democratic Party convention cast 103 ballots before finally settling on John W. Davis as their presidential candidate. Today, however, the parties' nominating conventions have declined in significance because the parties' presidential nominees are now effectively chosen in the primaries, which are held in most states in the winter and spring of the presidential election year, months before the conventions. National party conventions simply crown the candidate who has amassed the requisite number of votes from convention delegates during primary season. Indeed, the last time when either the Democratic or the Republican Party convention needed more than one ballot to select a presidential nominee was in 1952. Presidential primaries have so reduced the drama and spectacle of the party conventions that the television networks devote little coverage to them anymore.[26]

Today the real drama in choosing the party's nominee occurs in the primaries. Primaries appear to broaden the choice of the party nomination, since party members who care enough to turn out to vote in the primary make the choice. However, the matter is not so simple. Because turnout in

---

[25] Quoted in Frank J. Sorauf and Paul Allen Beck, *Party Politics in America* (Glenview, Ill.: Scott Foresman, 1988), p. 101.

[26] After the 1984 Democratic convention, Daniel Patrick Moynihan, senator from New York, observed, "The convention does not decide and it does not debate. . . . [T]he nomination is settled before the convention begins. . . . We have to make up our arguments to have on the floor so that television has something to cover." Quoted in Theodore J. Lowi, *The Personal President: Power Invested, Promise Unfulfilled* (Ithaca: Cornell University Press, 1985), p. 111.

the primaries is terribly low, candidates with money and close ties to interest groups that can provide resources and mobilize their members to vote in the primary can "steal" the election. When the primary electorate is so small, the difference in resources among candidates looms larger.

Candidates in primary elections must walk a fine line to gain the nomination. Candidates in primaries must appeal to the party's most zealous, most ideological supporters because they are the party members most likely to vote in primary elections. Republican candidates thus find themselves appealing to the most right-wing members of their party in primary elections, while Democratic candidates appeal to their party's most left-wing members. However, once the candidate gains the party's nomination, a different strategy is necessary to win the general election in November. Now the candidate must appeal to broadly centrist opinion within the general electorate, which involves loosening earlier ties to the more committed groups. The dilemma was well illustrated by a journalist's report of Al Gore's strategic challenge as the 2000 primary season wound down: "Having locked up the Democratic nomination with considerable help from organized labor, Vice President Al Gore now faces the tricky problem of showing his gratitude to the nation's trade unions, while convincing voters that he is not in labor's pocket."[27]

Republican presidential candidate George W. Bush faced an even more difficult task than Gore in moving toward the center as a result of his drift to the right during the 2000 Republican presidential primaries. He appealed to conservative religious fundamentalists within the party during the Republican primaries in order to turn back a surprisingly effective challenge by Senator John McCain. In the general election, he carefully tacked back to the middle, talking about increasing federal aid to education and prescription plans for the elderly, to attract more centrist voters in the general election in November.

The dynamics of election campaigns usually drive the candidates from the two major parties to the ideological middle. The consequence of this logical strategy is that candidates alternate between appealing to the bland middle of the spectrum and highlighting the relatively minor differences that divide them. At the same time that George W. Bush and Al Gore were emphasizing that their positions in the 2000 presidential race were fundamentally different, a journalist characterized them as "J. Crew vs. Banana Republic."[28]

The two parties have converged to a large degree on economic policy in the current era. They share a commitment to maintaining tight fiscal discipline, restricting social spending, and supporting market forces. Where they differ more sharply is over such social issues as gay rights, gun control, and

[27] *New York Times*, March 18, 2000.
[28] *New York Times*, March 11, 2000.

abortion. Within both parties, there is a struggle for control between moderates and groups toward the fringe of the party. Within the Republican Party, the New Christian Right has sought, with some success, to make the party a vehicle for using government to restore conservative values in the area of sexuality and gender relations. The struggle within the Democratic Party is the mirror image, where the battle pits moderate party leaders against pro-choice and gay rights groups.

MONEY AND ELECTIONS

Candidates need more than votes to succeed; they also need money—and lots of it. The comment by Mark Hanna, a key Republican strategist in the early 1900s, remains as pertinent today as a century ago: "There are two things that are important in politics. The first is money, and I can't remember the second."[29] Money pays for political ads and media time, pollsters and political consultants, research and advance work, and travel costs and overhead expenses. A record $5 billion was spent on the 2000 elections at all levels, 20 percent more than the previous spending record set in 1996. Paradoxically, ever more money is being spent at the same time that a dwindling proportion of the electorate votes. The result is that more money is being spent per voter than ever before.

Fund-raising is at the core of politicians' activity, whether they are campaigning or legislating. Political scientist Thomas E. Mann found, "The money chase . . . structures how elected officials allocate their time, where they travel, who they speak with, and how they deploy their legislative energies."[30]

Business and wealthy individuals provide the bulk of political contributions to candidates and political parties. Candidates appeal to these groups for contributions for the same reason that Willie Sutton said he robbed banks: because that's where the money is. One study found that families with incomes over $75,000 were ten times more likely to contribute money to political campaigns than poor families that earned less than $15,000 and that they were overrepresented in comparison to middle-income citizens as well.[31]

The gap between labor and business campaign contributions is also glaring. The difference between labor and business spending on candidates and parties nearly doubled, from $307 million in 1994 to $606 million in 1998. In

---

[29] Quoted in the *New York Times*, April 1, 2001.

[30] Quoted in Task Force on Campaign Reform, *Campaign Reform: Insights and Evidence* (Princeton, N.J.: Woodrow Wilson School of Public and International Affairs, 1998), p. 34.

[31] Sidney Verba, Kay Lehman Schlozman, and Henry E. Brady, *Voice and Equality: Civic Voluntarism in American Politics* (Cambridge: Harvard University Press, 1995), p. 189.

1998, only 20 members of the House of Representatives received more campaign funds from labor than they did from business, and only 6 House candidates received more than half their total funds from labor interests. The most any winning candidate for the House received from labor in 1998 was $448,000. In contrast, 15 winning House members received $1 million or more from business interests, and another 126 representatives received $500,000 or more.[32]

The arena of political parties and elections is supposed to provide the most important means by which citizens can participate, convey demands to their representatives, and hold these representatives accountable. But this comforting view ignores the substantial difference in class location and political values between the general population and those citizens who provide the resources on which parties and candidates depend. Rather than the party system acting as an engine of democracy, it helps skew the political system to reflect the interests and preferences of affluent Americans. The increasing demand for campaign contributions, and dependence on the rich for them, simply reproduces the inequalities of the private economic system within the public electoral sphere and corrupts genuine democratic government.

American political campaigns last longer, cost more, are less regulated, and are financed by a higher proportion of private (as opposed to public) funds than in any other Western democracy. Public outcry over campaign finance abuses periodically results in the passage of reform legislation, but the power of money has time after time proven stronger than efforts to control it. In 1971, Congress passed the Federal Election Campaign Act (FECA), and amended it in 1974, in order to limit political contributions, control spending, and require public disclosure of all receipts and disbursements. But the power of money trumps the FECA. According to political scientist Anthony Corrado, "In 1996 this regulatory system, already riddled with loopholes, finally collapsed. Candidates and party organizations spent more money than ever before, including hundreds of millions of dollars from sources supposed to be banned from contributing in federal elections."[33]

One factor that has stymied effective campaign finance reform is the Supreme Court's 1976 *Buckley v. Valeo* decision, which struck down limits on spending by candidates from their own funds. The Supreme Court ruled that restricting candidates from spending their own funds interfered with free speech.[34] The *Buckley* decision helped contribute to the rise of self-financed millionaire candidates, who need not rely on contributions from individuals that are limited to $1,000, but can bankroll their campaign from their own personal fortune.

[32]Ellen S. Miller and Micah L. Sifry, "Labor's Loss," *American Prospect,* August 14, 2000, 8.

[33]Anthony Corrado, "Financing the 1996 Elections," in Gerald M. Pomper, ed., *The Election of 1996* (Chatham, N.J.: Chatham House, 1997), p. 164.

[34]Jamin B. Raskin and John Bonifaz, *The Wealth Primary: Campaign Fundraising and the Constitution* (Washington, D.C.: Center for Responsive Politics, 1994), pp. 58–63.

The most vivid example of the self-financed millionaire candidate is billionaire Ross Perot. With assets over $3.3 billion, Perot did not need to sponsor many fund-raisers to come up with $60 million of his own money in his third-party quest for the presidency in 1992. Steve Forbes followed in Perot's shadow. Forbes's personal fortune of $250 million gave him the means to spend $25 million of his own funds in 1992, $37 million in 1996, and $28 million in 2000 in pursuit of the Republican Party presidential nomination. Both Perot and Forbes lacked any previous political experience. The only quality that made them viable, credible candidates was the vast wealth at their disposal. Apparently, all you need to run for president these days is a hundred million dollars and a dream.

In 2000, the field of presidential candidates was as full of millionaires as in years past. Both contenders for the Democratic nomination, former New Jersey Senator Bill Bradley and Vice President Al Gore, were millionaires. On the Republican side, Steve Forbes, Governor George W. Bush, Senator John McCain, and Elizabeth Dole all reported assets of more than $1 million.

The rise of self-financed, wealthy candidates is not restricted to presidential elections. The 106th Congress (1999–2000) included 39 senators who were millionaires. The undisputed champion among self-financed candidates for Congress was John Corzine from New Jersey. Corzine, formerly the head of a large Wall Street brokerage house, spent $60 million from his personal fortune to win a Senate seat in 2000.

Another major source of unregulated funds is soft money, which, as noted above, is money that campaign laws authorize for so-called educational and party-building purposes. Soft money is not subject to federal limits on contributions. The only restriction is that it supposedly cannot be used in coordination with a candidate's campaign. Once parties began to realize how easy it is to evade restrictions on the use of soft money, they began to pursue it with gusto. As Figure 5–2 demonstrates, the big breakthrough occurred in 1996, when parties raised more than double the amount of soft money they had raised during the 1992 campaign. In 2000, soft money accounted for 35 percent of the $700 million raised by the Republican Party and nearly half of the $500 million raised by the Democrats. Thus, the total in soft money raised by both political parties approached $500 million during the 2000 election cycle. The largest contributors of soft money were corporations. Many firms hedged their bets and gave money to both political parties so that no matter which party won, firms were assured access and influence (as depicted in the cartoon in Figure 5–3). In 1996, for example, Philip Morris Corporation divided $2 million in contributions between the Democratic and Republican parties, the Atlantic Richfield Oil Company contributed more than $1 million to both parties, and AT&T distributed $84,000 to both parties.[35]

Public disgust has increased as particularly unsavory instances of parties selling themselves to the highest bidder have come to light. For example,

---

[35] Corrado, "Financing the 1996 Elections," p. 155.

■ FIGURE 5-2

GROWTH IN SOFT MONEY, 1984–1998

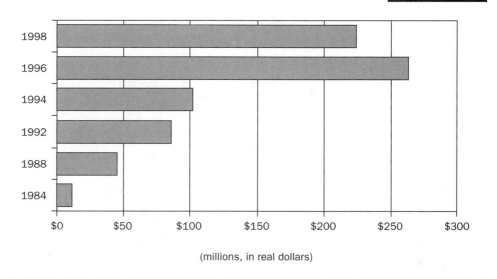

(millions, in real dollars)

Note that 1998 was an off year, in which no presidential election was held.

SOURCE: Common Cause web site, *http://commoncause.org/publications/campaign_finance_stats_facts.html.*

during President Clinton's administration, individual donors who contributed $100,000 to the DNC were invited to have coffee with President Clinton, attend White House receptions where they could discuss issues with administration officials, and spend the night in the Lincoln Bedroom in the White House. Several officials in the Clinton-Gore campaign organization were convicted of accepting illegal contributions during the 1996 election.

Like the credit card companies with their silver, gold, and platinum cardholders, the Republicans had different tiers of donors with different benefits attached to them. The highest tier of donors to the Republican Party in 2000 was a group of 139 people and corporations called the Regents, each of whom contributed over $250,000 in soft money to the party. In return for their generosity, the Regents were invited to attend gilded receptions at the 2000 Republican national convention, play golf with Republican officials, and meet privately with George W. Bush and his family.[36] But a Regent's contribution of $250,000 was only half of what it would take to join the most elite group of platinum cardholders among the Democrats. It took $500,000

---

[36] *New York Times*, August 2, 2000.

to join the Chairman's Circle, the highest tier of donors to the Democratic Party, which also produced the greatest benefits. Members of this select group of donors were rewarded with invitations to dine with Bill Clinton and Al Gore and attend receptions with other Democratic officeholders in return for their contributions.

In order to understand why wealthy donors and corporations contribute to political campaigns, it is useful to regard contributions as investments rather than donations. Jerome Kohlberg, a founding partner of the Kohlberg, Kravis Roberts & Co. investment firm, commented, "Even what we think of as large soft-money contributions are a small price for big corporations to pay to gain political influence. . . . [C]orporations give for one reason: self-interest. They can easily justify their expenditures because they get an outstanding return on their investment."[37]

Donors receive access and influence over government appointments, tax policy, antitrust enforcement, and regulatory decisions in return for their campaign contributions. Representative Michael G. Oxley of Ohio acknowledged, "It would be unrealistic to ask people to contribute and not

[37] *New York Times*, July 8, 1998.

let them have a voice, not let us know their opinion."[38] Four of the ten largest contributors to the RNC in 2000—Philip Morris, Enron Corporation, National Rifle Association, and Microsoft—all faced legal, regulatory, and legislative problems in Washington at the time they made their donations. An outright exchange of cash for a presidential decision or favorable vote in Congress is illegal; the contribution process is typically more indirect and therefore fully legal. Campaign contributions can motivate legislators to support a bill more energetically, to intervene with federal bureaucrats on behalf of a contributor, to recommend certain amendments to a bill, and to reduce the intensity of a policy-maker's opposition. Justin Dart, founder of Dart Industries and a large contributor to and fund-raiser for the Republican Party, expressed it well when he observed that dialogue with politicians "is a fine thing, but with a little money they hear you better."[39]

Money does not guarantee success at the polls. The candidate who spends the most does not always win. But money surely increases the odds. In 1996, candidates who outspent their opponents won 92 percent of House races and 86 percent of Senate races. In 1998, money spoke even louder: better-financed candidates won 95 percent of the House races and 94 percent of the Senate races.[40] While it is true that money does not guarantee victory in politics or happiness in life, it is also true that winning in politics or being happy in life is much harder without it.

THE PAC PHENOMENON

Campaign finance was revolutionized by the emergence of political action committees (PACs) in the 1970s. PACs were formed to evade campaign finance reforms, such as the prohibition on business firms or labor unions contributing money directly to political campaigns. PACs solicit money from individuals, which is then contributed to election campaigns, usually congressional races. In 1974, 608 PACs registered with the Federal Election Commission (FEC), and they contributed a total of $34.1 million to political campaigns. Since then, the number of PACs and their resources have skyrocketed. In 1996, there were over 4,000 PACs registered with the FEC, and they spent over $200 million, more than a fivefold increase.

Business PACs account for much of the growth in PAC activity. The number of corporate PACs has grown from 433 in 1976 to 2,480 only 20 years later—more than half of all registered PACs in 1996. As Figure 5–4 shows, since the 1990s, business and trade association PACs spend double that of

---

[38] *Washington Post National Weekly Edition*, April 17, 2000, 13.

[39] Quoted in Elizabeth Drew, *Politics and Money: The New Road to Corruption* (New York: Macmillan, 1983), p. 78.

[40] *New York Times*, November 6, 1998.

■ FIGURE 5-4

COMPARATIVE CORPORATE AND LABOR PAC
CONTRIBUTION GROWTH, 1978-1998

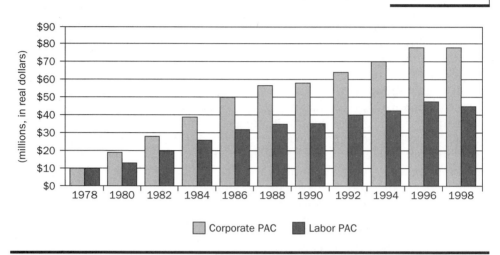

SOURCE: *The Almanac of Federal PACS: 2000–2001*, Edward Zuckerman, Amward Publications, 2000.

labor unions, the second largest contributors.[41] Two scholars warn that the predominance of business PACs over labor PACs creates "an imbalance in this kind of access-influence mechanism between these two types of interests. . . ." Furthermore, they note, "[o]ther types of interests—those less affluent—are not represented [at all] through money-based mechanisms of representation such as PACs."[42]

Corporate PACs emerged as part of a larger political and economic counteroffensive by business in the 1970s. Social movements and public interest groups succeeded in getting Congress to pass social regulations that protected the environment, safeguarded consumers, and outlawed discrimination in the workplace. Corporations regarded such legislation as an unwarranted intrusion on their operations and managerial authority. They fought back by

---

[41] These figures are drawn from document 5.3, Number of PACs Registered with the FEC, 1974–96, and document 5.4, Total PAC Contributions to Congressional Candidates, 1978–96, in Anthony Corrado, et al., *Campaign Finance Reform: A Sourcebook* (Washington, D.C.: Brookings Institution Publications, 1997), pp. 140–41. We combined corporate and trade-membership-health PACs, composed mostly of business interests, to calculate the totals for business PACs and business PAC spending. See Thomas Byrne Edsall, *The New Politics of Inequality* (New York: Norton, 1984), p. 131. References to corporate or business PACs in the text combine the categories of corporate and trade-membership-health PACs, which the FEC uses.

[42] M. Margaret Conway and Joanne Connor Green, "Political Action Committees and Campaign Finance," in *Interest Group Politics*, 5th ed., ed. Allen J. Cigler and Burdett A. Loomis (Washington, D.C.: Congressional Quarterly Press, 1998), p. 209.

forming PACs, which enabled corporations to evade limits on political contributions.[43]

Money follows power. Incumbents received two-thirds of all PAC money
in 1996 and a whopping 84 percent of all PAC money in 1998. The imbalance
in PAC contributions led Fred Wertheimer, president of Democracy 21, an
organization supporting campaign finance reform, to comment, "Today, we
don't have a Democratic or Republican Party, we have an incumbency party.
If you are an incumbent, whether a Democrat or a Republican, you will get
the bulk of the money in the race."[44]

But the party that incumbents come from has changed. Prior to the 1994
congressional elections, when the Republicans took control of both houses of
Congress, House Democrats enjoyed a two-to-one advantage in PAC money,
while Senate Democrats ran even with their Republican counterparts.
Democrats owed their fund-raising advantage to the fact that they received
more business PAC money than their Republican opponents. As the majority
party in Congress, the Democrats shaped legislation, and it was, therefore,
pragmatic for business to contribute to their campaigns. That all changed
with the 1994 congressional election results. When Republicans became the
majority party in Congress, business interests could be both pragmatic and
principled by helping the Republican Party. In 1996, corporate PACs gave
70 percent of their money to Republicans, a 20 percent increase over 1994,
with an equal decline recorded for the Democrats.

One of the most corrosive effects of parties' and politicians' dependence on
large private sources of campaign funds is that it feeds public cynicism about
politics. Because every politician is forced to hold out the begging bowl, this
conveys the impression that politicians are for sale to the highest bidder. Of
course, there are enough examples of money being exchanged for political
favors that this impression is not entirely without foundation. But politicians
are probably not more unethical than corporate executives, salespeople, car-
penters, or college professors. Yet the system of private campaign finance—
above all, politicians' need to raise ever larger campaign chests—taints the
entire political sphere. During the 1997 Senate hearings into campaign finance
reform, Senator Richard Durbin of Illinois acknowledged that legislators
vote on issues with an eye on how it might affect their fund-raising, that the
flow of money has increased the voters' skepticism, and that "if the system
isn't corrupt, it's corrupting. It forces you into compromising yourself."[45]

---

[43] Edsall, *New Politics of Inequality*, pp. 107–41. See also David Vogel, *Fluctuating Fortunes* (New
York: Basic Books, 1989), pp. 148–240.

[44] *New York Times*, November 1, 1998. The growth in campaign spending is nearly entirely
accounted for by incumbents. As a result, the spending gap between incumbents and
challengers has been widening for decades. Indeed, a significant amount of contributions
pour into the coffers of the winning candidate after the election. See *Congressional Quarterly
Weekly Reports*, April 15, 1995, 1055.

[45] Elizabeth Drew, *The Corruption of American Politics: What Went Wrong and Why* (Woodstock,
N.Y.: Overlook Press, 2000), p. 24.

An alternative to the exaggerated influence of money on elections in the United States exists in Europe. No country is perfect—as illustrated by examples of campaign finance scandals in France, Germany, Italy, Sweden, and other European countries in recent years. But the differences between European and American political finance are significant, and it is hard to see how the American system can be defended as preferable. In Europe, parties receive a large proportion of their funds from public finance. In addition, European governments prohibit political ads on television and mandate that all political parties above a certain threshold receive free and abundant television and radio time to air their messages. These messages help level the playing field and reduce the cost of campaigning.

MEDIA AND ELECTIONS

Money is essential to politicians because it permits them to use the media, especially television, to reach voters. In the past, candidates depended on party workers to distribute literature door to door and organize rallies on their behalf; they now rely on television to deliver their message. The efficiency of television—a candidate now appears in thousands or millions of living rooms simultaneously—and the fact that citizens rely on television for information have made it the major link, replacing political parties as the primary means of communicating with voters.

Not only are candidates sending more messages through the media, but also their messages are having a more powerful influence on the voters who receive them. Because party identification is so weak nowadays and a larger percentage of the vote is up for grabs in each election, the campaign swings more votes than in the past. When citizens voted according to party, the media were less consequential. According to Marvin Kalb, former head of Harvard's Center for the Press, Politics and Public Policy, "With the demise of political parties, the press has moved into a commanding position as arbiter of American presidential politics—a position for which it is not prepared emotionally, professionally or constitutionally."[46] Although the media perform the same function of communicating to voters as parties once did, they do so with very different effects. When the relationship between voters and candidates was mediated or filtered through political parties, information about the candidates was presented in the context of a larger set of values that the parties represented. This set of values was fairly stable and provided a relatively good guide as to how politicians would govern, that is, what voters could expect if their candidate was elected.

Journalists, however, work from a different set of principles. Parties are concerned about winning elections and governing; reporters are interested in getting a good story and selling newspapers. Consequently, the ways in

---

[46]Quoted in Thomas E. Patterson, *Out of Order* (New York: Knopf, 1993), p. 26.

which election campaigns are presented by the two are very different. According to political scientist Thomas E. Patterson, the media present elections as a strategic game in which politicians compete for personal advantage, money, and power. In this game, the players' motives are suspect, strategy is more important than substance, controversy is valued over context, the sensational trumps the routine, and manipulation by candidates is taken for granted. Journalists impose the schema of a strategic game or sports contest on political campaigns in order to keep the audience interested and to provide fresh material every day. They are driven by the demands of their profession to project elections in this way.

When campaigns are presented as a game, unfavorable reporting increases and skepticism of the candidates is encouraged. Bad news drives out good news, and election coverage concentrates on strategy, not substance. Voters are offered a cynical projection of the electoral process through the media, and the information that voters need is often missing. Voters are interested in finding out how the candidates intend to solve the problems that concern them, that is, what consequences the election will have for how the country will be governed. Instead, they are offered reporting about candidates' tactics. The result is that voters become disinterested and begin to perceive the electoral process through the cynical lens the media offer. Voters turn off and tune out.[47]

In order to avoid the skeptical probes of reporters, presidential candidates have increasingly turned to softer, less adversarial venues to reach voters. They have bypassed the traditional news shows in favor of appearing on programs devoted to entertainment. Bill Clinton played the saxophone on *The Arsenio Hall Show*, a variety show, and appeared on *MTV*. In the course of the 2000 presidential primary and election campaigns, Bill Bradley, George W. Bush, Al Gore, and John McCain all made appearances on either *The Late Show with David Letterman* or *The Tonight Show*, hosted by Jay Leno. Nowhere, however, has the line between politics and entertainment become hazier than on talk radio. The exaggerated political combat one hears on talk radio is the sound of the war for ratings, not a clash of principles. Talk radio is the equivalent of televised wrestling: Hard blows are landed, no one really gets hurt, and, if all goes well (from the advertisers' point of view), the audience returns tomorrow for more entertainment.

Ownership of the key media outlets is becoming more concentrated. A handful of giant corporations, including AOL Time Warner, Disney, Westinghouse, General Electric, Sony, and Gannett, largely determine what Americans see and hear through newspapers, radio, television, magazines, movies, and books.[48] The Telecommunications Act of 1996 scrapped most limits on corporate concentration of the media and set off a wave of corporate mergers and shared ownership arrangements.

[47]Ibid., pp. 21–22.

[48]Ben Bagdikian, *The Media Monopoly*, 5th ed. (Boston: Beacon Press, 1997), p. xiii.

Corporate concentration of the media tends to reduce the press to a vehicle for purveying commercial values. It is becoming increasingly difficult to tell where the news ends and entertainment begins. Media concentration has driven up profit expectations as newspaper chains and corporations try to justify the price of their new acquisitions. To improve the bottom line, news budgets are cut, hard news is replaced by lifestyle stories, and publishers and television executives are reluctant to run stories that might offend advertisers who account for most of their revenue.[49] An even more ominous development resulting from the merger of media companies with megacorporations is a form of self-censorship where broadcasters refrain from presenting their parent company in an unfavorable light.[50]

The media have not sold their souls to corporations. They *are* corporations. The media tend to respond to the same commercial imperatives as any other business. Applying business principles might be acceptable when making widgets, but it is quite another thing when those same principles are applied to the media. Modern democracies rely on the media to inform the public. When the news is trivialized, miniaturized, standardized, and screened politically in order to improve the corporate bottom line, the quality of democracy, which depends on an informed, engaged public, suffers.

POLITICAL CONSULTANTS

Along with the media, political consultants, who package and market candidates, make politics more trivial, less about substance and more about style. According to political scientist Samuel J. Eldersveld, political consulting firms "apply the basic principles of merchandising to political campaigns. They are selling a product (a candidate) and they therefore will use whatever many persuasion techniques of a manipulative nature to do the job."[51] Marketing the candidate involves testing positions on issues with focus groups to gauge their reaction, conducting continuous polls to track how well the candidate is selling, coaching the candidate on how to appear on camera, reducing messages to 30-second (or shorter) sound bites, and having spin doctors (press handlers) waiting in the wings to interpret the candidate's remarks.

---

[49] Neil Hickey and Joseph S. Coyle, "Money Lust," *Columbia Journalism Review,* July/August 1998, 28–44. In the past, media executives stressed the importance of maintaining firewalls separating the editorial, news, and advertising departments. Those firewalls have long since been breached in an attempt to boost corporate profits. For example, when the *Los Angeles Times*, one of the most distinguished newspapers in the country, was sold, its new publisher ruled that news stories about companies advertising in the *Times* had to be routinely submitted to advertisers before publication so they could alter the content.

[50] Neil J. Mitchell, *The Conspicuous Corporation: Business, Public Policy, and Representative Democracy* (Ann Arbor: University of Michigan Press, 1997), p. 53.

[51] Samuel J. Eldersveld, *Political Parties in American Society* (New York: Basic Books, 1982), p. 286.

Campaign consulting has grown in size and significance as the influence of parties declines. The less attached voters are to parties, the more clever campaigning can affect their decisions. Joseph Napolitan, a media consultant, once described his task as "communicating a candidate's message directly to voters without filtering it through the party organization."[52] Few candidates now enter congressional races without the aid of professional consultants to advise them on their campaign. Political consultants have also become a regular presence in races for lesser offices, such as state legislative contests. A few decades ago the party-centered campaign was replaced by the candidate-centered campaign. The candidate-centered campaign is now threatened with being replaced by one that is consultant-centered.[53] After being elected president in 1976, Jimmy Carter sent his political consultant, Gerald Rafshoon, a message that humorously sums it up: "I'll always be grateful that I was able to contribute in a small way to the victory of the Rafshoon agency."[54]

A recent poll of political consultants suggests the depth of their cynicism. Forty percent of the consultants acknowledged helping to elect candidates whom they were sorry to see serve in office, and 48 percent rated the congressional candidates for whom they worked as fair or poor. A large majority of consultants had no qualms about negative campaigning, and many were confident that with enough money they could persuade voters to elect the weaker candidate.[55]

Political consultants have contributed to the problem of declining turnout, with which we began this chapter. They have pitched their appeal to small market segments without concern for how this may restrict the size of the overall marketplace. Consultants have also undermined the legitimacy of the electoral process by offering symbols and empty images in place of substance. The marketing of candidates in this manner has left voters unmoved and unmotivated. More than half of the voters are not buying what the consultants are selling. But this does not trouble the consultants. All they care about is whom the voters select regardless of how few voters there are.[56]

We have focused until now in this chapter on the institutional mechanisms that organize citizens' electoral choices. We now turn to analyzing the social base of different parties and candidates. The social bases of governing or dominant coalitions and the broad programs that they have supported provide important clues to the kinds of policies that governments will enact. We begin our analysis with the rise of the New Deal coalition, which propelled Franklin Delano Roosevelt to the presidency in 1932 and which dominated American political life for several decades.

---

[52] Quoted in Richard M. Pious, *The American Presidency* (New York: Basic Books, 1979), p. 90.

[53] Daniel M. Shea, *Campaign Craft* (New York: Praeger, 1996), pp. 12–13.

[54] Quoted in Pious, *American Presidency*, pp. 89–90.

[55] *New York Times*, June 22, 1998.

[56] Lance W. Bennett, *The Governing Crisis: Media, Money and Marketing in American Elections* (New York: St. Martin's Press, 1996), p. 104.

THE RISE AND FALL OF THE NEW DEAL COALITION

Participants in the critical election of 1932 voted Franklin Delano Roosevelt into office, ushering in a long period of Democratic Party dominance. The New Deal coalition that Roosevelt forged over four consecutive presidential terms (1933–45) included blacks, who received some benefits from New Deal programs targeted for the poor and unemployed; southerners, whose Democratic sympathies dated back to the Civil War; immigrant Jewish and Catholic workers from southern and eastern Europe, who appreciated Roosevelt's efforts to end the Depression; Irish supporters of big city machines; and some renegade financiers and corporate executives, who believed the New Deal would be good for business. Each group was attached to the Democratic Party for the benefits it could derive from the federal government, whose growth the party supported. But that was where the consensus that bound them together ended. The New Deal coalition was a marriage of convenience, in which the partners were content to lead separate lives and use their union to enlarge the federal government and extract benefits from it.

The Democratic Party leadership was relatively successful in maintaining the support of the various elements in its coalition in the 1940s and 1950s. But this became increasingly difficult as the initial impetus of the Depression receded and the needs of the various coalition members began to conflict. The most profound and destabilizing issue to upset the New Deal coalition was race.

Racial conflict deeply divided the southern and northern wings of the Democratic Party. Southern Democrats demanded as the price for their loyalty that party leaders not interfere with the region's laws enforcing racial segregation. But as the Civil Rights movement of the 1960s gained momentum, the Democratic Party responded to black demands. Presidents John F. Kennedy and Lyndon B. Johnson sponsored civil rights legislation that threw the weight of the federal government behind the attempt to outlaw racial discrimination. Feeling betrayed, southerners began to abandon the Democratic Party. Native white southern identification with the Democratic Party dropped from 74 percent in 1956 to half that level by 1984.[57] At first, this change in party loyalty among white southerners was evident only in presidential voting. But then it began to trickle down and appear in voting for state and local offices as well.[58] By 1994, for the first time in the twentieth century, Republicans comprised a majority of the southern delegation to both the Senate and the House, and they occupied a majority of Dixie's gubernatorial offices. Southern realignment is the most important factor

---

[57]Earl Black and Merle Black, *Politics and Society in the South* (Cambridge: Harvard University Press, 1987), p. 241.

[58]See ibid.

behind the success of the Republican Party and the diminishing gap now separating the number of people who identify themselves as Democrats and those who identify themselves as Republicans.[59]

Not only did the New Deal coalition lose its southern flank to racial conflict, but its base in the North was badly damaged by it as well. Beginning in the 1960s, race began to drive out class as the line that divided Democrats from Republicans in the minds of voters.[60] White working-class support for the Democratic Party began to erode. Some white workers defected from the Democratic Party because they were racists. But many defected because of anger that the burden of racial change legislated by Democrats fell unfairly on them. Their children were more likely to attend schools that fell under busing orders, their jobs were more likely to be subject to affirmative action reviews, and their communities adjoining black neighborhoods were more likely to be integrated. White workers resented that the Democrats permitted upper-class whites to avoid the racial changes that white workers were experiencing.[61]

The New Deal coalition was also eroded by the emergence of new issues that created political and cultural conflict within the Democratic Party. The Vietnam War was fought within the Democratic Party, as students who thought of themselves as liberal Democrats challenged Democratic Party leaders who prosecuted the war. Feminism, gay rights, abortion, and crime also divided Democrat from Democrat and further fragmented the New Deal coalition. The party was torn increasingly between two wings. One was comprised of traditional working-class voters that were economically liberal, but socially conservative. They supported federal regulation of markets and welfare state programs, but opposed policies such as gay and abortion rights that offended this group's traditional values. The other wing was composed of wealthier, more educated, and more recent supporters. They were economically conservative, but socially liberal. These Democrats saw the party as a vehicle for challenging gender hierarchies and sexual stereotypes, but they were opposed to programs that threatened to redistribute wealth. Reconciling the two wings of the party was a difficult balancing act.

The New Deal coalition was further wounded by the decline of labor unions. Union membership peaked in 1953, when one-third of all nonagricultural workers were union members. Union density—the proportion of the workforce that is organized—has declined steadily from that point (as

---

[59] John Petrocik, "Realignment: New Party Coalitions and the Nationalization of the South," *Journal of Politics* 49 (May 1987): 347–75.

[60] R. Robert Huckfeldt and Carol Weitzel Kohfeld, *Race and the Decline of Class in American Politics* (Urbana: University of Illinois Press, 1989).

[61] These points are made by Thomas Byrne Edsall and Mary D. Edsall, *Chain Reaction: The Impact of Race and Taxes on American Politics* (New York: Norton, 1991); Jonathon Reider, *Canarsie: The Jews and Italians of Brooklyn Against Liberalism* (Cambridge: Harvard University Press, 1985); and Anthony Lukas, *Common Ground* (New York: Knopf, 1985).

we reviewed in Chapter 4). Union decline has cost the Democratic Party a dependable core of voters because union members are more reliable Democratic Party voters than their nonunion counterparts.

Finally, the New Deal coalition became prisoner to a weakened political economy and the inability of the Democratic Party to devise an alternative to it. The New Deal political economy was based on the formula of conservative Keynesianism, which offered economic growth without redistribution, and fiscal fine-tuning in place of structural economic change. (See Chapter 3 for a fuller description of conservative Keynesianism.) The inadequacy of this formula became apparent in the 1970s, when economic growth faltered and both inflation and unemployment accelerated. Conservative Keynesianism could no longer deliver the economic growth that the New Deal coalition needed to satisfy the demands of its various constituents. Nor could the Democrats develop a new economic formula around which to revive their faltering coalition.

A NEW REPUBLICAN PARTY

As the Democratic majority faltered, the Republicans gathered steam and changed direction. The Republican Party's political and geographic transformation can be traced through the evolution of a political dynasty—the Bush family. The Bush family odyssey in politics began with Prescott Bush, father of the 41st president George H. W. Bush (1989–1993), and grandfather of the 43rd president, George W. Bush (2001–). Prescott Bush was a Wall Street banker before being elected to the Senate from Connecticut in 1952. He was a moderate, Eisenhower Republican who had a good civil rights record, voted in favor of new federal programs, and accepted the legitimacy of the New Deal. He was a compassionate conservative.

His son, George H. W. Bush, was a transitional figure, connecting the Republican Party of the past, represented by his father, to the Republican Party of today, represented by his son, George W. Bush. George H. W. Bush, like Prescott Bush, was a member of the Eastern Establishment and reflected its politics of moderate conservatism. When he ran in the 1980 Republican presidential primary, he disdainfully condemned Ronald Reagan's conservative proposals for cutting taxes and balancing the budget as "voodoo economics."

When Reagan won the Republican nomination, he chose Bush as his running mate. For the next eight years, George H. W. Bush served as a loyal vice president within a Reagan administration that chipped away at the New Deal his father had accepted. When Bush himself was elected president in 1989, he presided over a government that was consistent with the new Republican orientation of smaller government, a reduced welfare state, and relaxed government regulation of business.

In 2000, Prescott Bush's grandson and George H. W. Bush's son, Governor George W. Bush of Texas, ran as the Republican candidate for president against the type of government his grandfather had helped to consolidate. While Prescott Bush made his reluctant peace with the New Deal, his grandson hoped to repeal it. While Prescott Bush was a member of the Eastern Establishment, his grandson made his home in the South. While Prescott Bush made his money on Wall Street, his grandson made his fortune in oil and ownership of the Texas Rangers baseball team.

The postwar history of the Republican Party is reflected in the history of the Bush family as it moved right politically and to the South and West geographically. The Bush family pulled up its stakes in the Eastern Establishment to find a new home in the more conservative Republican Party of the Sun Belt. But it is also a history of party revival. During Prescott Bush's time in the 1950s, the Republican Party was the minority party, trailing the Democrats electorally and politically. Now, two Bush generations later, the Republican Party is competitive with the Democrats. Its resurgence is due to three factors. First, white males became more Republican in their voting patterns, especially when Republican candidates could play to their fears about the dismantling of racial and gender hierarchies. Second, the party found an enthusiastic base among religious fundamentalists. The Christian Right mobilized through the Republican Party in order to challenge the moral decay they saw around them. Third, the business community gave the party a boost by infusing it with money and by funding think tanks to develop conservative policies. The party added to its traditional business base among northeastern financiers and midwestern industrialists a new breed of maverick multimillionaire entrepreneurs from the Sun Belt, who were fiercely opposed to government regulation.

The result of these forces was to recenter the party politically and geographically.[62] The key moment in this transformation was the party's nomination of Senator Barry Goldwater from Arizona for president in 1964. Goldwater's nomination signaled that power had shifted from the Eastern Establishment, which grudgingly accepted certain aspects of the New Deal, to hard conservatives from the South and the West, who were militantly anti-government, anti-taxes, anti-union, and anti-communist. It is no accident that the two leading contenders for the Republican presidential nomination in 2000, George W. Bush from Texas and Senator John McCain from Arizona, both came from the Sun Belt.

Although Goldwater lost the 1964 election by the largest margin in American history, the conservative Sun Belt forces that engineered his nomination eventually triumphed. After years of patiently funding PACs, conservative think tanks, and grassroots groups, these forces were victorious in 1980, when their standard bearer, Ronald Reagan, was elected president. Acknowledging the similarities between Goldwater and Reagan—each came from the West, each was militantly anti-communist, each wanted to

---

[62]Nicol C. Rae, *The Decline and Fall of the Liberal Republicans from 1952 to the Present* (New York: Oxford University Press, 1989), p. 198.

downsize government and increase military spending—one historian wrote, "If there had been no Barry Goldwater, there would have been no Ronald Reagan."[63]

Today the Republican Party no longer orbits the Democratic Party, as it did in Prescott Bush's time. Today the party is electorally competitive, intellectually vibrant, and financially prosperous and has a base in the South and the West, which are the fastest growing parts of the country. It sealed its ascendancy in the 2000 elections, although the contested election returns represented a bittersweet victory for the party's standard bearer.

A MAGICAL MYSTERY TOUR: THE 2000 PRESIDENTIAL ELECTION

There are few events in American politics as dramatic as elections. Although this book emphasizes the importance of structural factors—notably, the political economy and political institutions—election contests make an important difference. First, although candidates from the major parties may generally agree on the fundamental features of the American political and economic system, they often differ on specific aspects. Who wins will affect how the country is governed. Second, elections confer democratic legitimacy on the government. Even though the options offered to voters may be limited and narrow, elections promote the belief that the political system is democratic.

No election contest is more meaningful in shaping how the country will be governed and whether the government is regarded as legitimate than the presidential contest held every four years. For these reasons, however, when presidential elections fail to produce a universally recognized winner, the result potentially threatens the very foundations of the American political system. And this was precisely what occurred in the 2000 presidential election.

The 2000 presidential contest shaped up as a close race for months before the election, as first George W. Bush and then Al Gore took the lead in polls. But no one predicted the extraordinary outcome of the election—or what followed. By the end of election night, it was clear that Al Gore had won the popular vote by a margin of 550,000 more votes nationwide than his opponent, George W. Bush. But presidential elections in the United States are not decided according to which candidate receives the most votes. Instead, presidents must win a majority vote among electors who vote in the electoral college. Electors are selected by states, and each state has as many electors or votes in the electoral college as it has senators and representatives in Congress. It is the custom or law in almost all states that each state's electors will cast their votes as a bloc in the electoral college for whichever candidate

---

[63]Mary C. Brennan, *Turning Right in the Sixties: The Conservative Capture of the GOP* (Chapel Hill: University of North Carolina Press, 1995), p. 141.

George W. Bush's inauguration following the disputed 2000 election.

receives the most votes statewide. In other words, a candidate who wins by 1 percent of the vote in a state will still receive 100 percent of that state's votes in the electoral college. Figure 5–5 humorously depicts this system. (The electoral college is discussed more fully in Chapter 6.)

As election night proceeded, it became increasingly clear that Al Gore would receive more votes than his major opponent, George W. Bush. But it was not clear whether he would win a majority of votes in the electoral college, which, after all, selects the president. When the dust settled on election night, Gore had 267 electoral votes, and Bush had 246. Neither had the magic number of 270, which constituted a majority in the electoral college. The outcome of the election hinged on who would win the incredibly close race in Florida and thereby capture the state's 25 electoral votes.

But Florida played coy. At first, the networks assigned Florida to Gore; then the networks reversed themselves and called Florida for Bush. Gore called Bush to concede, but then retracted his concession after the networks admitted the race in Florida was too close to call. Several hundred votes separated the candidates out of more than 6 million cast statewide in Florida. Three days after the election, a mandatory machine recount of the votes reduced Bush's lead to just 327 votes. Democrats then demanded a manual recount of votes in four Florida counties where thousands of ballots were in dispute. A number of voting irregularities put Florida's election results in doubt. The design of the ballot in one county confused many voters and produced utterly illogical results; voting machines failed to register the votes of thousands of partially punched ballots; voters were wrongly classified as

ineligible and disqualified from voting; in a black precinct, a police road-block deterred many citizens from voting; and in still another county, Republican Party officials altered ballots in order to correct errors on applications for absentee ballots.

Given the large number of voting irregularities and the fact that the election was virtually a dead heat, Gore sued to have Florida ballots recounted manually. The Bush campaign sued to stop the recounts.

As both candidates took their case to court, the dispute became increasingly partisan. The Florida secretary of state, who would certify Florida's vote, was a Republican who also served as cochair of George W. Bush's election campaign in Florida. Even more dramatic, the governor of Florida, who served as the other cochair of Bush's Florida campaign, was none other than Jeb Bush, George W.'s younger brother!

The Bush campaign organization had time on its side, and it vigorously pursued judicial challenges to slow the clock. If it could prevent vote recounts and the tabulation of uncounted ballots, time would eventually run out. The reason was that Florida law provided that the state's electors who cast Florida's votes in the electoral college had to be chosen by December 12 so that the slate of electors could be certified to Congress by December 18, when the electoral college convened.

■ FIGURE 5–6

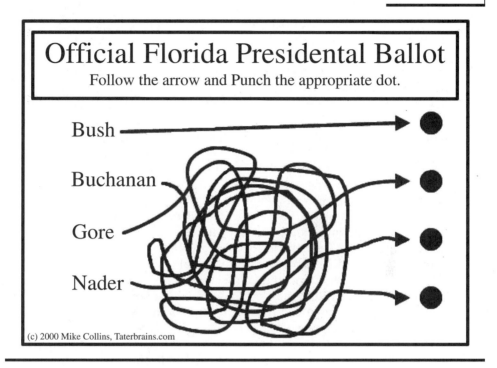

Official Florida Presidental Ballot

Follow the arrow and Punch the appropriate dot.

Bush

Buchanan

Gore

Nader

(c) 2000 Mike Collins, Taterbrains.com

Incredibly, the controversy lasted from election day (November 7) to the fatal deadline of December 12—and even beyond. It appeared that the Gore forces might succeed in assuring a hand count of 45,000 uncounted ballots, thanks to a ruling by the Florida State Supreme Court. But as December 12 approached, two key developments assured a Bush victory in Florida—and thereby in the electoral college as a whole. First, the Republican-dominated Florida state legislature met in special session for the purpose of choosing a slate of electors that would cast their electoral college votes for Bush regardless of what the recount showed.

Second, the Bush campaign appealed the Florida Supreme Court ruling, which had mandated a manual recount of votes, to the U.S. Supreme Court. With the recount in process, the Supreme Court voted 5–4 to stop the counting of disputed ballots even before it heard Bush's appeal. The Court ruled that the recount might "cast a cloud upon what [Bush] claims to be the legitimacy of his election." In other words, five justices on the Court moved to suppress the fact that the recount might show that Gore received more votes in Florida than Bush. Following arguments by both the Gore and the Bush camps, the Court voted, again by a 5–4 margin, to overrule the Florida Supreme Court. Previously, the Court had merely stopped the recount temporarily until it heard arguments from both sides. Now, upon hearing those arguments, the Court ruled that there would be no further official counting of Florida's disputed presidential votes.

The manner in which the Court issued its ruling and the ruling itself led many people to view the Court's intervention as tainted by partisanship. The majority opinion was unsigned, was released to the press at night instead of being read by the Court in public session as is the usual custom, and was issued as a *per curiam* brief, which is usually reserved for unanimous, uncontroversial decisions—which this surely was not. The Court vacated the Florida Supreme Court ruling, claiming that the ballots could not be counted by December 12, and that counting ballots in the absence of a uniform standard violated the Equal Protection Clause of the Constitution. Regarding the Court's first point, critics charged that it was based on expedience and not on law, and that the disputed ballots could be counted by December 18, when the electoral college was scheduled to vote. Moreover, critics charged that many states, including Texas, where George W. Bush was governor, permitted hand counts and failed to provide a uniform standard![64] As the *New York Times* declared in an editorial the day after the decision, "This will long be remembered as an election decided by a conservative Supreme Court in favor of a conservative candidate while the ballots that could have brought a different outcome went uncounted in Florida."[65]

The day after the Supreme Court issued its opinion, Gore conceded. For the fourth time in American history, the candidate who became president failed to receive the most votes.

The 2000 presidential election thus did not deliver what presidential elections usually produce: a closure to political debate and a fresh legitimacy to American political institutions and the next administration. George W. Bush received 550,000 fewer votes than Al Gore; Florida's electoral votes were cast before all the votes in that crucial state were counted; the results from Florida were plagued with voting irregularities; and every institution that was involved, from county election supervisors to the Supreme Court, was infected with partisanship. Instead of providing a clear result, the election provided a magical mystery tour that left doubt in the minds of many citizens about the sanctity, fairness, and efficiency of the electoral process.

CONTEMPORARY PARTY COALITIONS

Although each election is distinctive, turning on specific events, personalities, and strategies that affect voters' decisions, voting patterns from one election to the next are relatively stable. Both the Democratic and Republican

---

[64] Bruce Ackerman, "Anatomy of a Constitutional Coup," *London Review of Books*, February 8, 2001, 2–6.

[65] *New York Times*, December 13, 2000.

parties tend to attract different groups of voters, which helps to explain the parties' different policy orientations. Analyzing the 2000 presidential election results provides insight into contemporary party coalitions.

Even a casual inspection of Table 5–2, based on nationwide exit polls among voters who had just cast their ballots, reveals that the two major parties' presidential candidates in 2000 received very different levels of support from different groups in the electorate. The table also reveals that different groups are quite stable in their voting preferences, so that similar electoral patterns stretch back through many presidential elections.

No group is more united behind the Democratic Party than blacks. Support for the Democratic Party among blacks persists at extraordinarily high levels of 80 percent or more. Black voting is bloc voting. From Washington, D.C., to Washington State, from professors to postal clerks, blacks have voted as one to reward the Democratic Party for its support of welfare state programs and civil rights legislation.

Hispanics are a diverse group composed of Spanish-speaking citizens. Some emigrated from the Caribbean, some from Mexico, and still others from South and Central America. They came from various cultures and did not necessarily share a common experience once they arrived here, as blacks did. While turnout among Hispanics is notoriously low, and there is great diversity within this group, Hispanics have settled in the Democratic Party. In 2000, Al Gore received almost two out of every three votes from Hispanics.

Another reliable group of voters within the Democratic Party coalition is union members. As union membership has declined steadily since the 1950s, so has this base of support that the Democratic Party could depend on. Union members are not only more likely to vote Democratic than their nonunion counterparts, but are also more likely to vote. Union membership helps overcome the class bias in turnout that we discussed at the beginning of this chapter.

Other social differences also influence partisanship. Religion influences how one votes. White Protestants are staunchly Republican, and Jews are strongly Democratic, while Catholics, who once identified with the Democratic Party, are now relatively unattached. Catholics have become swing voters, and in 2000, they pretty evenly divided their vote between the two parties. Region influences how one votes. The Northeast and the West Coast tend to be Democratic havens, while the South, the West, and the Plains states are Republican. Town size influences how one votes. Voters from rural areas and small towns tend to be Republican, while urban voters, who are predominantly minorities, tend to be Democratic.

Class and gender also influence the vote. As one goes up the income ladder, the Republican vote increases. The 2000 election also revealed a striking gender gap in voting between men and women. Men were more likely to vote for Bush, while women were more likely to vote for Gore. Interestingly, gender trumped class among upper-income women, who tended to vote for Gore despite their class position. At the same time, gender also trumped class among low-income white males, who tended to vote for Bush despite their class position.

Pct. of 2000 Total Vote		1976		1980			1984	
		Carter	Ford	Reagan	Carter	Anderson	Reagan	Mondale
	Total vote	50	48	51	41	7	59	40
82	White	47	52	56	36	7	64	35
10	Black	83	16	11	85	3	9	90
4	Hispanic	76	24	33	59	6	37	62
48	Men	50	48	55	36	7	62	37
52	Women	50	48	47	45	7	56	44
65	Married	—	—	—	—	—	62	38
35	Unmarried	—	—	—	—	—	52	47
Family Income Is:								
7	Under $15,000	58	40	43	49	7	45	55
16	$15,000–$29,999	55	43	53	39	7	57	42
24	$30,000–$49,999	48	50	59	32	8	59	40
53	Over $50,000	36	63	64	26	10	69	30
28	Over $75,000	—	—	—	—	—	—	—
15	Over $100,000	—	—	—	—	—	—	—
20	Liberals	71	26	25	60	11	28	70
50	Moderates	51	48	49	42	8	53	47
30	Conservatives	29	70	73	23	4	82	17
26	Union household	59	39	44	49	6	46	53
Size of Place:								
9	Population over 500,000	—	—	—	—	—	—	—
20	Population 50,000 to 500,000	—	—	—	—	—	—	—
43	Suburbs	—	—	55	35	9	61	38
5	Population 10,000 to 50,000	—	—	—	—	—	—	—
23	Rural areas	—	—	55	39	5	67	32
23	From the East	51	47	47	42	9	53	47
26	From the Midwest	48	50	51	41	7	58	41
31	From the South	54	45	52	44	3	64	38
21	From the West	46	51	53	34	10	61	38
47	White Protestant	41	58	63	31	6	72	27
26	Catholic	54	44	50	42	7	54	45
4	Jewish	54	34	39	5	15	31	67
17	18–29 years old	51	47	43	44	11	59	40
33	30–44 years old	49	49	55	36	8	57	42
28	45–59 years old	47	52	55	39	5	60	40
22	60 and older	47	52	54	41	4	60	39
39	White men	47	51	59	32	7	67	32
43	White women	46	52	52	39	8	62	38
4	Black men	80	19	14	82	3	12	85
6	Black women	86	14	9	88	3	7	93

SOURCE: *New York Times,* November 12, 2000. Based on Voters News Service and other exit polls.

1988		1992			1996			2000		
Bush	**Dukakis**	**Clinton**	**Bush**	**Perot**	**Clinton**	**Dole**	**Perot**	**Gore**	**Bush**	**Nader**
53	45	43	38	19	49	41	8	48	48	2
59	40	39	40	20	43	46	9	42	54	3
12	86	83	10	7	84	12	4	90	8	1
30	69	61	25	14	72	21	6	67	31	2
57	41	41	38	21	43	44	10	42	53	3
50	49	45	37	17	54	38	7	54	43	2
57	42	40	41	20	44	46	9	44	53	2
46	53	51	30	19	57	31	9	57	38	4
37	62	58	23	19	59	28	11	57	37	4
49	50	45	35	20	53	36	9	54	41	3
56	43	41	38	21	48	40	10	49	48	2
62	37	39	44	17	44	48	7	45	52	2
—	—	36	48	16	41	51	7	44	53	2
65	32	—	—	—	38	54	6	43	54	2
18	81	68	14	18	78	11	7	80	13	6
49	50	47	31	21	57	33	9	52	44	2
80	19	18	64	18	20	71	8	17	81	1
42	57	55	24	21	59	30	9	59	37	3
37	62	58	28	13	68	25	6	71	26	3
47	52	50	33	16	50	39	8	57	40	2
57	42	41	39	21	47	42	8	47	49	3
61	38	39	42	20	48	41	9	38	59	2
55	44	39	40	20	44	46	10	37	59	2
50	49	47	35	18	55	34	9	56	39	3
52	47	42	37	21	48	41	10	48	49	2
58	41	41	43	16	46	46	7	43	55	1
52	46	43	34	23	48	40	8	48	46	4
66	33	33	47	21	36	53	10	34	63	2
52	47	44	35	20	53	37	9	49	47	2
35	64	80	11	9	78	16	3	79	19	1
52	47	43	34	22	53	34	10	48	46	5
54	45	41	38	21	48	41	9	48	49	2
57	42	41	40	19	48	41	9	48	49	2
50	49	50	38	12	48	44	7	51	47	2
63	36	37	40	22	38	49	11	36	60	3
56	43	41	41	19	48	43	8	48	49	2
15	81	78	13	9	78	15	5	85	12	1
9	90	87	8	5	89	8	2	94	6	0

An inspection of Table 5–2 reveals that George W. Bush gained much stronger support among most groups in 2000 compared to Republican presidential candidates in the previous two elections. This result is surprising in light of the fact that the economy was widely regarded as flourishing throughout the eight years that Al Gore was vice president. The same exit poll results reveal that, among voters who reported that their family situation was better off than in 1996, 61 percent voted for Gore compared to 36 percent for Bush. The proportions were nearly reversed among those who reported being worse off in 2000. It may be especially significant in this regard that 60 percent of voters who reported that their financial situation had not changed voted for Bush compared to only 35 percent for Gore. Indeed, prosperity may have created the worst of both worlds for Gore. He never really received credit with voters for prosperity, and the lack of economic issues in the campaign as a result of prosperity brought other issues to the fore, such as gun control, that hurt him with working-class male voters who normally vote Democratic.

The outcome of the 2000 race may have been substantially influenced by the personal attributes of the candidates. Many voters regarded Gore as untrustworthy and arrogant, while Bush inspired confidence and appeared more able to unify the country. For many voters, these qualities mattered more than Gore's intelligence and experience, compared to Bush's apparent lack of experience and competence. Finally, the race may have been influenced by the "sleaze factor," including reports of campaign finance violations by Clinton and Gore, as well as Clinton's affair with Monica Lewinsky. Although a large majority of Americans opposed Clinton's impeachment, many voters were receptive to Bush's argument that he would restore honor and dignity to the presidency.

A POSTELECTORAL ERA?

Political scientists Benjamin Ginsberg and Martin Shefter argue that America has entered a postelectoral era, in which elections are no longer as decisive as they once were for resolving political conflicts and constituting governments. The decline of parties and voting has reduced the significance of elections for how the country will be governed and has made their results more subject to challenge.[66] Conflict and mobilization have shifted to arenas other than elections and to forms of political participation other than voting. This is hardly surprising in light of parties' inability to produce results that people want. The close and disputed outcome of the 2000 election will only accelerate tendencies in the direction of the postelectoral era, where elections fail to settle and resolve political issues.

---

[66]Benjamin Ginsberg and Martin Shefter, *Politics by Other Means: The Declining Implications of Elections in American Politics* (New York: Basic Books, 1990).

In the postelectoral era, declining turnout at the polls is not the result of growing political apathy. Indeed, other forms of political participation, such as contacting public officials, contributing to political campaigns, and participating in interest group activity, show no signs of erosion similar to that which afflicts voting. Yet the fact that voting turnout has declined while other forms of political participation have not only serves to magnify the political voice of the rich. Voting is the most egalitarian form of political participation. Although those who are affluent are more likely to vote than those who are not, the participatory gap between the rich and the poor for other forms of political participation is even greater than it is for voting.

In principle, anyone can vote, write his or her representative in Congress, or contribute to political campaigns. But some citizens are in a better position to take advantage of these opportunities than others. Political participation may be open, but it is not free. It is greatly facilitated by class-related factors, including adequate time, money, and civic skills; the ability to communicate well; a feeling of empowerment; and connections. Political scientists Sidney Verba, Kay Lehman Schlozman, and Henry E. Brady conclude from a massive survey of political participation that, "[o]ver and over, our data showed that participatory input is tilted in the direction of the more advantaged groups in society—especially in terms of economic and education position, but in terms of race and ethnicity as well. The voices of the well-educated and the well-heeled—and, therefore of those with other politically relevant characteristics that are associated with economic and educational privilege—sound more loudly."[67]

In the postelectoral era, there has been an increase in extraparty forms of mobilization, such as interest groups, social movements, civic activism, and litigation. For example, the number of interest groups surged in the 1960s and 1970s as parties declined and government regulation increased.[68] Interest group formation moderated in the 1990s only because the market became saturated; that is, organized lobbies now covered virtually all the policy bases.[69] Political participation beyond parties and elections is also evident in the emergence of such social movements as the feminist movement, the gay rights movement, and the environmentalist movement (as we discussed in Chapter 4). Social movements mobilize citizens politically in less formal, more spontaneous ways than political parties do. Finally, groups that find themselves locked out of the electoral arena now bring their case to court and litigate what they cannot win at the ballot box.

The postelectoral era is characterized by more political participation that flows outside electoral channels. Political participation takes different paths

---

[67] Sidney Verba, Kay Lehman Schlozman, and Henry E. Brady, *Voice and Equality* (Cambridge: Harvard University Press, 1995), p. 512.

[68] Jack L. Walker, Jr., "The Origins and Maintenance of Interest Groups in America," *American Political Science Review* 77 (June 1983): 390–406; Kay Lehman Schlozman and John T. Tierney, *Organized Interests and American Democracy* (New York: Harper & Row, 1986), pp. 75–76.

[69] Jeffrey Berry, *The Interest Group Society*, 3rd ed. (New York: Longman, 1997), p. 24.

because political parties do not provide groups with what they consider to be adequate representation. Indeed, the postelectoral era has created a paradox. Given the different forms that political participation takes, government appears besieged. It is the target of more organized and unorganized pleading than ever before. At the same time, given the decline of parties and voting, government appears more insulated and removed from democratic accountability than ever before. The decline of parties means that it becomes harder to organize cohesive majority opinion. The paradox of the postelectoral era is that both appearances may be true, meaning government is simultaneously more besieged and more insulated from demands.

CONCLUSION

American democracy depends on a revival of the party system—one that can inform and mobilize the electorate—and is inconceivable without it. Without high turnout, the link between the public and the government is frayed, and this can produce both unresponsiveness and undirected anger. Disaffected groups that renounce democracy, like the citizens militias, can flourish under these circumstances.

While the fact that citizens participate in politics through other means suggests that the postelectoral era is not simply one of apathy, the lack of a vibrant party system impairs the quality of American democracy. There is even more class bias in who participates in extraparty forms of political activity than there is in who votes. The costs and demands of other forms of participation, such as social movements and civic activism, are simply too great and too difficult to sustain over the long run to act as a substitute for voting.[70]

Revival of the American party system is a daunting challenge. It depends on making elections relevant again to those lower- and middle-class voters who have given up on them out of disgust, cynicism, boredom, and distress with the choices they are offered. First, getting these citizens engaged and to the polls requires campaign finance reform that can loosen the grip of the wealthy and corporations on candidates and parties. The role of money in elections makes a mockery of American democracy and violates the principle of political equality. The corrupting influence of money on elections raises a perennial question that Edward G. Ryan, who would later become chief justice of the Wisconsin Supreme Court, asked way back in 1873: "The question will arise . . . which shall rule—wealth or man; which shall lead—money or intellect; who shall fill the public station—educated and patriotic free men, or the feudal serfs of corporate capital?"[71]

---

[70] Mark Kesselman, "Poor People's Movements: Must Organizations Corrupt?" *Insurgent Sociologist,* Winter 1979, 62–69.

[71] Quoted in Paul S. Herrnson, "The Money Maze: Financing Congressional Elections," in *Congress Reconsidered,* 7th ed., ed. Laurence C. Dodd and Bruce I. Oppenheimer (Washington, D.C.: Congressional Quarterly Press, 2001), p. 120.

Second, in order to make elections meaningful, programs must speak to the needs of disengaged voters, giving them a reason to participate. Finally, the disengaged must mobilize to promote such a program. Until these changes occur, the American party system—and thus American democracy—will continue to overrepresent the haves at the expense of the have-nots.

POLITICAL INSTITUTIONS

A Brilliant and Mischievous Design

The Constitution lays out the architecture of government. By architecture, we mean the design of political institutions—notably, the three branches of the federal government: the executive, legislature, and judiciary. The Constitution also specifies how political authority is distributed among these different institutions, as well as between the federal and state governments. With over 88,000 governmental units of all types nationwide—from familiar state legislatures to obscure special district authorities—the design is complicated, with much overlap and jurisdictional conflict among different government bodies. The design of the American political system is quite distinctive because of the degree to which the Constitution disperses authority widely among a variety of political institutions. Authority is divided in two ways. First, the United States is a federal system, which means that authority is divided between national and state governments. The Tenth Amendment to the Constitution specifies that all power not expressly delegated to the national government by the Constitution is reserved to the states. For much of American history, state governments exercised the bulk of governmental power. In comparison, the national or federal government was lean and mean, primarily engaged in maintaining law, arbitrating conflicts, issuing a common currency, and maintaining a defense establishment for use abroad and against native American populations. Today political power is more concentrated at the federal than at the state level, although state governments continue to formulate, implement, and finance programs in vitally important domains like education, transportation, and property rights.

Despite the fact that the Constitution created a federal system, with power distributed between national and state governments, one cannot neatly distinguish which level of government is responsible for which function. Sometimes there is a near-complete separation of functions: The national government alone decides whether to commit troops abroad; state governments are solely responsible for regulating marriage and divorce. But the typical situation is more complicated, with federal and state governments operating more or less cooperatively in the same policy areas. Political scientist Morton Grodzins suggested that American federalism resembles a marble cake, in which governmental functions are interwoven and shared among the different levels of government, as opposed to a layer cake, in which the national and state governments are neatly separated from each other and performing different functions.[1]

The Constitution fragments governing authority in a second way. Political power is divided not only vertically between different levels of government, but also horizontally between different branches of government. Rather than uniting power within a single powerful agency, as in the famed "Westminster model" of British parliamentary government, power is divided among the legislative, executive, and judicial branches of the federal government. The term *separation of powers* is often used to describe this dispersion of power among the different branches of government. But like the layer cake image of federalism, the concept of the separation of powers can be misleading if taken to mean that each branch of government has exclusive authority in certain domains. In fact, the opposite is the case. A better term to describe how power is distributed within the federal government would be *shared* or *overlapping powers*, as opposed to separation of powers. For example, both the Congress and the president share power in the realm of foreign policy. The president can make treaties with foreign governments, but these must be ratified by a two-thirds vote in the Senate. The president can command the military, but Congress appropriates the necessary funds for military operations. Similarly, all three branches share power when it comes to legislation. Congress can pass a law, but the president is authorized to approve or veto it. Congress can then override a presidential veto with a two-thirds vote in both the Senate and the House. Finally, the Supreme Court, by exercising the power of judicial review, can nullify the law by declaring it unconstitutional.

It is this architecture of shared or overlapping powers that creates a system of "checks and balances." Each branch of government has the power to check the actions of the other branches and must depend on their cooperation to achieve its goals. We do not mean to imply by checks and balances that the three branches have equal power, only that government is designed in such a way that many policies and activities require the tacit or explicit support of all three institutions. Unlike a parliamentary system, where the executive and legislative branches are fused and there may be no judicial review by the courts, the system of divided, yet shared, powers ensures that each branch possesses autonomous power and has a say in governing.

Legislation must run a difficult gauntlet in a political system where each branch of government can check the other and success depends on the cooperation of all of them. Chances of completing this obstacle course are made even smaller by having each elected branch of government represent different constituencies. The president is elected nationally, senators are elected from each state, and members of the House of Representatives are elected from districts within states. In effect, our constitutional design

---

[1]Morton Grodzins,*The American System: A New View of Government in the United States,* ed. Daniel J. Elazar (Chicago: Rand McNally, 1966).

requires legislation to win three different types of majorities—nationally, by state, and by district. That is, shared powers require groups to build overlapping, simultaneous majorities at the level of the presidency, the Senate, and the House. Legislation must run the equivalent of a triathlon (neglecting the courts for the moment), a series of three different athletic events requiring three different kinds of skills: running, cycling, and swimming—but with one important difference. In a triathlon, a contestant can lose an event, but still be declared the winner so long as he or she has the highest combined score at the end of the contest. This would be insufficient under our system of government. The Constitution requires contestants to win all three events *outright*. Groups who desire political change must win at every step of the process, while groups that want to defend the status quo have to win just once to block a bill. Unless proposed legislation passes the House and the Senate and is then signed by the president (excluding the difficult task of overriding a presidential veto), it will fall short of passage.

The design of government in the Constitution, with its system of shared powers among independent institutions representing different constituencies, has conservative implications that were intended by the Founders who created it. On the one hand, the designers of the Constitution embarked on a remarkable political experiment in 1787. They proposed to create the first republic in which political authority would be located in the hands of the people instead of a king. The architects of the Constitution were intent on protecting the government against tyranny, which they had just fought a revolution to defeat. On the other hand, the Founders were frightened by the audacity of their own democratic inclinations. They believed that democracy, if left to its own devices, posed a threat to the natural hierarchy in society. Political scientist Robert Dahl observes that the Founders were "alarmed by the prospect that democracy, political equality, and even political liberty itself would endanger the rights of property owners to preserve their property and use it as they please."[2] They thus devised checks and balances as a way to protect the unequal social order without taking away any of the majority's democratic rights. Checks and balances, they believed, would protect the rich by requiring workers and farmers to build concurrent majorities at every level of government. Majorities would have to be built in the House of Representatives by districts based on population, in the Senate according to states, and in the presidency across the entire country. The Founders anticipated the result would be deadlock and government paralysis, as majorities would find it difficult to win at every level required of them.

The Founders sought to create a government powerful enough to promote market-based economic development, but not so powerful that it could be used as an instrument of popular forces to restrict the rights of property. They succeeded brilliantly at this task of constitutional engineering. In the

---

[2]Robert Dahl, *A Preface to Economic Theory* (Berkeley: University of California Press, 1985), p. 2.

several centuries since the Constitution was drafted, it has been effective in achieving the positive goal of capitalist economic development and in thwarting groups who tried to use government to alter the status quo. When public power is unable to rule because it is gripped by deadlock, private power rules in its place.

The next three chapters, covering the presidency, Congress, and the courts, respectively, examine the institutional structure of government and how power is distributed within and among the three branches. The structure of government, the relationships among the different institutions of government, and the formal and informal rules that govern how they work internally have important consequences for policy. In other words, institutions count. Policy is not simply a reflection of economic and social forces; rather, these social forces are refracted through institutions whose rules and relationships affect the outcome of their struggle. Some groups win and some groups lose depending on the structure of government.

But the structure of government, the relationship among institutions, and their formal and informal rules are not set in stone and are themselves subject to political conflict. The Constitution may have created the architecture of government more than 200 years ago, but the design is constantly being remodeled. The executive branch does not look like it did 50 years ago, nor is its relationship to Congress the same as it was 50 years ago. Groups struggle over not only who will occupy the government, but also what it will look like. The result is that the institutional form of government changes as a result of political conflict. Political institutions—through their relationships to each other and their internal procedures—reflect the larger distribution of power in society at the same time they help to shape it.

The focal point of the federal government, and therefore the place we begin our study of political institutions, is the presidency.

6

The Presidency:
Imperial or Imperiled?

Delegates to the Constitutional Convention arrived in Philadelphia in 1787 with many complaints about their form of government. One of their objections to the Articles of Confederation, which established the first American government that emerged from the Revolutionary War in 1776, was that it did not provide for a single official responsible for directing the executive branch who would be independent of Congress. The Founders believed that a new government required an autonomous and energetic presidential office, as opposed to the weak executive that labored under the Articles. But the Founders disagreed over the powers that should be invested in this new presidential office. Alexander Hamilton, a brilliant 30-year-old delegate from New York, shocked the gathering by praising the British monarchy—against whom the colonies had revolted a mere decade before—as a suitable model to emulate. Recognizing that hereditary monarchy would never be accepted in America, Hamilton suggested that the new federal government be directed by an elected monarch who would hold office for life.

Hamilton's view was an extreme one among the delegates in Philadelphia. But it made the arguments of those who supported a stronger executive independent of the legislature appear moderate in comparison. A strong executive was needed, advocates argued, because elected assemblies succumbed too easily to the forces of democracy and would be too ready to bend in the winds of popular demands. The constitutional architects specifically designed the office of the president as independent of Congress in order to check what they perceived as the latter's democratic excesses.

The creation of a single executive independent of Congress was one of the innovations that distinguished the new form of government under the Constitution from that under the Articles—and, indeed, from any other government in the world at that time. The creation of the presidential office is one of the key institutional innovations of the American Constitution. While the delegates to the Constitutional Convention could agree that a more powerful and independent executive was necessary, they could only settle the question of specifying the president's powers by leaving them undefined, ambiguous, and incomplete. The president's powers are described in Article II of the

The White House.

Constitution: "The executive Power shall be vested in a President of the United States of America." As political scientist Richard Pious comments, "The phrase 'executive power' was a general term, sufficiently ambiguous so that no one could say precisely what it meant."[1]

Aside from being unsure what powers to invest in the president's office, delegates to the Constitutional Convention also disagreed over how presidents should be chosen. James Wilson of Pennsylvania proposed that the executive be elected by the people. But the delegates rejected this proposal because it would make the president responsive to the very democratic spirit the delegates had come to Philadelphia to tame. After creating an executive independent of Congress, delegates were not about to propose selecting the president through direct election, which would reflect the same popular opinion they saw lurking in legislatures. Instead, the convention delegates devised a plan by which a majority of members of the newly created electoral college would elect the president.

The electoral college system was created because the Founding Fathers feared direct democracy and the southern slaveholding interests thought this would help protect them from the demands of more populated northern states. The Constitution specifies that states have as many votes in the electoral college as they have members of Congress. That is, each state is

---

[1]Richard M. Pious, *The American Presidency* (New York: Basic Books, 1979), p. 29.

given a number of electoral votes equal to the total number of senators and representatives in Congress from that state. As a result, the electoral college tends to overrepresent small states. For example, Wyoming, with 3 electoral votes, has one electoral vote for every 166,000 citizens in the state, while California, with 54 electoral votes, has one electoral vote for every 500,000 citizens.

Over time, a pattern developed in which the presidential candidate who receives the most votes in a state receives all of that state's votes in the electoral college. This is known as the unit rule.[2] If no presidential candidate wins an absolute majority of votes in the electoral college (presently 270 votes), the House of Representatives selects the president by majority vote.

The electoral college distorts the popular vote because the electors or delegates from each state generally follow the unit rule. The unit rule permits presidential candidates who win the most votes in a particular state to get all of that state's votes in the electoral college even though the difference separating the two candidates in the actual election may be just a few votes out of millions that were cast. For example, in 2000, the presidential election hinged on several hundred votes separating Al Gore and George W. Bush in Florida. The winner would receive all of Florida's 25 electoral votes. After recounts and charges of voting irregularities, all of Florida's electoral votes were awarded to Bush, when he barely carried the state: according to the official tabulation, Bush received 2,912,790 votes to 2,912,253 votes for Gore. This razor-thin margin resulted in 100 percent of Florida's 25 electoral votes being awarded to Bush, giving him just enough electoral votes to win the presidency. If it were not for the unit rule, the conflict over Florida's vote, which delayed a declaration of the winner of the 2000 presidential election for over 36 days, would have mattered far less, for only 1 or 2 electors, rather than the entire Florida slate of 25 electoral votes, would have been affected. By the same token, Al Gore benefited from the unit rule when he won all of the electoral votes from Iowa (7), New Mexico (5), Oregon (7), and Wisconsin (11), even though he carried each of those states by less than 1 percent of the popular vote.

The unit rule, by which all of a state's electoral votes go to the statewide winner, regardless of how narrow the margin of that victory, so distorts the popular vote that it is even possible for a presidential candidate to win the popular vote nationwide and to lose in the electoral college. This is precisely what happened in 2000. Al Gore received over 550,000 more votes than George W. Bush in the popular election, but lost 271–267 in the electoral college. The democratic legitimacy of presidents such as George W. Bush is suspect when they lose the popular vote, but win in the electoral college.

---

[2] There are exceptions. For example, delegates elected on a slate pledged to support one presidential candidate occasionally bolt and vote for an opposing presidential candidate in the electoral college. Further, although most states have enacted the unit rule, either by state law or custom, there are exceptions. For example, Nebraska allocates two electoral votes to the candidate who has received a plurality of votes at the state level, but divides its remaining votes in the electoral college on the basis of who wins pluralities at the level of congressional districts.

They are "accidental presidents" who owe their victory to the distortions built into the way the electoral college operates.

The last time before 2000 that the popular and electoral college votes diverged was in 1888, when Republican presidential candidate Benjamin Harrison received 100,000 fewer votes than his opponent, Grover Cleveland, but nonetheless became the 23rd president when he won the electoral college 233 to 168. Most of the time, however, the effect of the unit rule within the electoral college is not to reverse the result of the popular vote, but to exaggerate it. For example, in 1996, Bill Clinton received 49 percent of the popular vote, but received 70 percent of the votes in the electoral college. In 1992, Ross Perot finished third in the presidential election with 19 million votes, but he received *no electoral votes* because he did not finish first in any state.

Presidential candidates campaign with the strategic goal of winning the 270 electoral college votes that assure victory. Because most states follow the unit rule in the electoral college, presidential candidates tend to lavish particular attention on states where the outcome is uncertain, on the reasonable assumption that this is the most efficient way to allocate scarce resources of time and money. Thus, in the 2000 presidential campaign, George W. Bush ignored California, with the most electoral votes of any state, because polls showed him to be hopelessly behind in the Golden State. Al Gore, on the other hand, made only a perfunctory effort to campaign in Texas, which has the third highest total of electoral votes, because Bush already had the state sewn up. Both presidential candidates instead concentrated on states like Michigan and Florida, which were up for grabs.

Some political scientists argue that Republican presidential candidates have an advantage in the electoral college.[3] Republicans have won at least two-thirds of the South's 146 electoral votes in every election since 1972, with the exception of 1976. In addition, they can count on winning votes from the Mountain and Plains states, which have also gone Republican in election after election.[4] That is, Republicans start the presidential race with about 169 votes in their pocket from the South and the Mountain and Plains states—about 62 percent of the electoral votes needed to win.[5] Democrats, on the other hand, begin the campaign assured of only 13 electoral votes from the reliable Democratic enclaves of Minnesota and the District of

---

[3]Earl Black and Merle Black, *The Vital South: How Presidents Are Elected* (Cambridge: Harvard University Press, 1992).

[4]By the South, we mean the 11 states that comprised the old Confederacy. The Mountain and Plains states include Arizona, Colorado, Idaho, Kansas, Nebraska, Nevada, North Dakota, Oklahoma, South Dakota, Utah, and Wyoming.

[5]We derive the figure of 169 electoral votes by taking two-thirds of the South's electoral votes and the electoral votes of every state that voted Republican in every presidential election but one from 1968 to 1996. This group of states includes the Plains states of North Dakota, South Dakota, Nebraska, Kansas, and Oklahoma and the Mountain states of Idaho, Montana, Wyoming, Colorado, Utah, and Arizona. The other consistently Republican states in presidential elections are Indiana and Alaska.

Columbia. They must win 72 percent of the electoral votes from the states that are competitive in order to win, whereas their Republican opponent needs to win only 28 percent of the remaining electoral votes.

However, in the 1992 and 1996 presidential elections, the Republican presidential candidates' base of strength in the South and the Mountain and Plains states turned into a ghetto when the party's candidates were unable to attract sufficient support outside these regions. These heavily Republican states tend to be more agricultural, more religious, more culturally conservative, and whiter than the rest of the country. These factors, which gave the Republicans a virtual lock on the South and the Mountain and Plains states before the campaign actually began, prevented the party from extending its appeal to other regions and social groups during the campaign itself. What made the Republicans so attractive to their loyal following in the South and the Mountain and Plains states made the Republicans harder to sell outside of them.

In 2000, George W. Bush was able to escape the limits of the Republican ghetto that had contributed to the defeat of his two predecessors. But only barely. He won the Border states of Missouri, Kentucky, and West Virginia, which had gone Democratic in 1992 and 1996. Inasmuch as these states reflect their southern neighbors in many ways, this is really a case not of breaking out of the box, but of extending it a bit. But Bush also won New Hampshire and Ohio, which is evidence that he was able to pick up electoral votes outside Republican strongholds.

But the real secret of George W. Bush's success was not how well he performed outside of Republican citadels in the South and the West, but how well he performed within them. His predecessors ran well in these rock-ribbed Republican areas—as one would expect—but both George H. W. Bush (George W. Bush's father) in 1992 and Bob Dole in 1996 experienced some defections from their base of support within these regions. Clinton picked up 39 electoral votes from the South in 1992 and 51 electoral votes in 1996. In 2000, Al Gore won no votes at all from this region. Clinton picked up 20 electoral votes from the West in 1992 and 17 electoral votes in 1996. In 2000, Al Gore received just five electoral votes from this region, when he carried New Mexico. Bush's electoral college victory in 2000 owed more to his intensive harvesting of Republican strongholds in the South and the West than it did to his extending the Republican appeal beyond them. Bush defended Republican states spectacularly well, preventing almost any defections from the party's base in the South and West, and won just enough electoral college votes outside of them to sneak through.

THE HISTORICAL PRESIDENCY

In the debates over the Constitution in Philadelphia, Alexander Hamilton defended the office of the president as one that would give "energy" to the government. He believed that a strong executive was necessary to provide leadership and decisiveness to a government that could otherwise drift and be stalemated in a system of checks and balances. According to political scientist Stephen Skowronek, the "energy" that Hamilton sought to invest in the office has made the president a powerful source of political change. Far from being defenders of the status quo, presidents regularly upset it. More than other government officials, presidents routinely "disrupt systems [and] reshape political landscapes."[6] Regardless of whether they are liberal or conservative, all presidents, according to Skowronek, are agents of change. They set the wheels of government in motion in order to remake it in their own image.

Today the president remains the energy center of the government, just as Hamilton envisioned it, in part by default. Congress is often too decentralized and fragmented to compete for leadership with the president. But there are no constitutional or political guarantees that the president will be successful in wielding power. Presidential power must be constructed; it cannot be taken for granted. The contingent nature of presidential power is evident in how long it took the office to play a commanding role within the government—a position it must struggle continually to defend. Indeed, throughout much of American history, the president was at most first among equals—and not always that. Prior to the Civil War, most presidents exercised relatively few powers because the responsibilities of the national government itself were quite limited. The president was regarded a bit derisively as the nation's "chief clerk." Bold innovators like Andrew Jackson and Abraham Lincoln were isolated exceptions, not the rule.

As late as the end of the nineteenth century, the presidency was viewed as a relatively weak office. In 1885, a young Princeton professor published an influential study of American politics entitled *Congressional Government,* in which he asserted that Congress was the foremost policy-making institution of American government. The president, this scholar argued, was powerful in the legislative domain only to the extent that he exercised veto power over bills passed by Congress. Twenty-three years later the author changed his mind and, in *Constitutional Government in the United States,* developed a far more expansive view of the presidency. Soon after, by his actions as president, Woodrow Wilson, the former Princeton professor, contributed even more directly to the creation of a powerful presidency.

Through much of the nineteenth and twentieth centuries, there were swings between strong and weak presidents, between presidential and congressional supremacy. But as corporate capitalism developed, the federal government grew in both size and power, and the presidency as an institution expanded along with it. First, the regulatory role of the federal government increased because corporations had outgrown the police power of mere states. Only federal law could regulate the behavior of firms that now operated nationally. Second, the federal government became responsible for economic management, as both business and workers looked to the federal

[6]Stephen Skowronek, *The Politics Presidents Make: Leadership from John Adams to George Bush* (Cambridge: Harvard University Press, 1993), p. 6.

government to protect them from the boom-and-bust swings of the business cycle. Third, the federal government took on new social responsibilities, creating a welfare state that would tend to the victims of capitalist production. Finally, the federal government grew in response to the global character of corporate capitalism. The United States became a world power and was drawn deeper into world affairs by the global spread of American corporations. As the focal point of the federal government, the presidency was positioned to take advantage of the federal government's growing responsibilities. The growth of big government, the growth of corporate capitalism, and the growth of presidential power occurred together in a mutually supportive relationship.

Since Franklin D. Roosevelt, who served as president from 1933 to 1945, the balance of power among the three branches of government has tilted clearly toward the president, although this does not mean, as we shall see, that presidents are able to achieve their goals easily. FDR gave birth to the modern presidency; as a result, the office is now looked upon as "the preeminent source of moral leadership, legislative guidance, and public policy."[7] Roosevelt led people, first, to expect the federal government to respond to problems and, second, to expect the president to provide leadership when it did so.[8] The executive branch under Roosevelt grew dramatically as the federal government took on more responsibilities domestically and internationally. Joseph Cooper writes, "The New Deal and World War II permanently established the president as the single most powerful figure in both the legislative and administrative processes of government, as well as the elected official charged, in the eyes of the public, with primary responsibility for initiating and securing policies in the public interest."[9] As the presidency accumulated power, the executive branch expanded around it. Federal employment increased from 605,000 employees in 1932 to 2,696,000 federal workers by 1946.

Ironically, Congress was the midwife to this expansion of the federal government and the growth of presidential power within it. It legislated new federal agencies into existence, funded them, and delegated power to them.[10] Often Congress simply identified a problem and left it to agencies in the executive branch, managed by the president, to decide the best way of

---

[7]Sidney M. Milkis and Michael Nelson, *The American Presidency: Origins and Development, 1776–1990* (Washington, D.C.: Congressional Quarterly Press, 1990), p. 260.

[8]Theodore Roosevelt, not FDR, first used the media in a systematic way. He was the first president to have a press secretary, a press office, and frequent meetings with reporters. In his famous phrase, he used the presidency as "a bully pulpit." However, FDR's presidency coincided with the diffusion of radio, which enabled him to establish direct contact with vast audiences.

[9]Joseph Cooper, "The Twentieth-Century Congress," in *Congress Reconsidered*, 7th ed., ed. Lawrence C. Dodd and Bruce I. Oppenheimer (Washington, D.C.: Congressional Quarterly Press, 2001), p. 335.

[10]Theodore J. Lowi, *The End of Liberalism: Ideology, Policy and the Crisis of Public Authority* (New York: Norton, 1969).

■ FIGURE 6-1

THE RELATIONSHIP BETWEEN THE
PRESIDENT AND CONGRESS

Spheres of Presidential Control

Congressional Organization
(Committees)

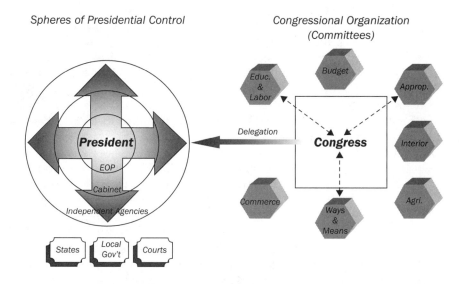

SOURCE: David Epstein and Sharyn O'Halloran, "The Institutional Face of Presidential Power: Congressional Delegation of Authority to the President," in Robert Y. Shapiro, Martha Joynt Kumar, and Lawrence R. Jacobs, eds., *Presidential Power: Forging the Presidency for the Twenty-First Century* (New York: Columbia University Press, 2000), p. 314.

fixing it. By issuing broad delegations of power to agencies in the executive branch and beholden to the president, Congress abdicated power to its rival. We shall see later in the chapter that, as the political and partisan interests of the president and Congress have diverged in recent decades, Congress has regained some of the power over the federal bureaucracy it previously ceded to the president. Figure 6–1 provides a simplified model of the relationship between the president and Congress.

THE IMPERIAL PRESIDENT?

The symbolism and substance of presidential power are so vast that the president might best be seen as towering over the other parts of the government, a veritable Gulliver standing over the Lilliputians. The perquisites attached to the office are enormous. The president draws an annual salary of $400,000, and another $150,000 is available for expenses. It gets better from here. A staff of more than 500 assistants, a fleet of limousines, helicopters, and a small fleet of planes are available to help the president with the work of the office. The presidential family resides at the most exclusive address in the world—1600 Pennsylvania Avenue—in the 123-room White House. A staff of about 100 attends to the First Family's personal needs at a cost of about $8 million per year. For privacy and relaxation, the president can go to Camp David, a 180-acre retreat in the mountains of Maryland. To ease the transition from office, each ex-president receives a special grant of $1 million to cover expenses for the return to private life, a generous lifetime pension, and year-round Secret Service protection.

While presidents are well compensated, few get rich from the job. Indeed, presidents of medium-sized corporations take home more than presidents of the United States earn, and corporate executives can match presidents limousine for limousine. The relatively modest remuneration of presidents—in comparison to their peers in the private sector—reflects a populist vigilance over what politicians can pay themselves. But it also reflects the low evaluation of public affairs in the United States. That the private sector is more significant than the public sector in the United States is symbolized by the greater compensation given to corporate presidents and even college presidents than to the presidents of the United States.

The president has substantial power and authority, but the nature and extent of that power vary considerably and are based on quite diverse sources. The president's authority is based only in part on the powers enumerated in the Constitution. Article II of the Constitution, which addresses the power of the presidency, has been referred to as "the most loosely drawn chapter of the Constitution."[11] As we have seen, drafters of the Constitution were reluctant to enumerate the president's powers and preferred to ascribe a general grant of powers to the office. The president was authorized to veto legislation passed by Congress, act as commander in chief of the armed forces, execute the laws, pardon criminals, make treaties, call Congress into special session, appoint government officials, and recognize foreign governments. This list provides a base for presidential power, which presidents expand on by using the ambiguity, silences, and incompleteness of the Constitution to claim even broader powers for themselves. Presidents claim authority to act from what is in the Constitution, and if not explicitly proscribed, what is not mentioned in the Constitution is claimed equally by presidents as giving them the authority to act.

Presidential power lies not only in the explicit constitutional grants of authority, but also in the use presidents make of them and in the claims presidents have successfully staked out over the centuries. Presidential power is based on elements that are as real as the powers enumerated in the Constitution and as subtle as the president's reputation among powerful members of Congress and ordinary citizens. It is based on the inescapable authority attached to the office and on fickle impressions of the president's professionalism and popularity. It is based on both legal and political grounds.

---

[11]E. S. Corwin, *The President: Office and Powers,* 3rd ed. (New York: New York University Press, 1957), p. 2.

The president's greatest political resource is the position of chief executive of the government, the person who defines and articulates the national interest. No one else can make a legitimate claim that he or she represents the national interest, as no one else was elected on a national basis. The president embodies the nation, with all the emotional and patriotic symbols attached to it. The identification of the president with the nation was never more clear than when President Lyndon Johnson declared, in a television interview, "The office of the Presidency is the only office in this land of all the people. . . . At no time and in no way and for no reason can a President allow the integrity or the responsibility or the freedom of the office ever to be compromised or diluted or destroyed, because when you destroy it, you destroy yourselves."[12]

As chief executive, presidents command media attention through which to deliver their message. The office is a powerful bully pulpit that permits presidents to appeal directly to the people for support of presidential initiatives. By attracting the media, political scientist Bruce Miroff writes, "the president gains an unparalleled advantage in defining political reality for most Americans. . . . Press or partisan criticism may challenge a president . . . but the outline of reality that he has sketched is usually left intact."[13] Realizing the usefulness of the media in molding public opinion, presidents have made increasing use of them. The number of presidential appearances and addresses has increased over time.[14] In addition, constant daily reporting about the president tends to reinforce the image of the presidency as an essential institution at the center of political life. The extent of coverage devoted to the president is as helpful in promoting a favorable image of the office as is the deferential reporting it generally receives.

In addition, presidents manage the federal bureaucracy, which includes over 2.7 million employees and a budget of over $1.6 trillion. Through management of the executive branch, presidents influence how federal policy is interpreted and implemented. They influence federal agencies by staffing them with their appointees, subjecting the agencies' policies to their review, and proposing changes to the agencies' budgets. While presidents' power over the bureaucracy is contested, as we shall see, they can also issue executive orders requiring or authorizing federal agencies to take some action. For example, President Harry Truman ordered the racial integration of the armed forces by executive order. Through executive orders and other forms of executive lawmaking, presidents can "establish policy, reorganize executive branch agencies, alter administrative and regulatory processes, [and]

---

[12]Robert S. Hirschfeld, ed. *The Power of the Presidency: Concepts and Controversies,* 2nd ed. (Chicago: Aldine, 1973), p. 150.

[13]Bruce Miroff, "Monopolizing the Public Space: The President as a Problem for Democratic Politics," in *Rethinking the Presidency,* ed. Thomas E. Cronin (Boston: Little, Brown, 1982), p. 220.

[14]Jeffrey K. Tulis, *The Rhetorical Presidency* (Princeton, N.J.: Princeton University Press, 1987).

affect how legislation is interpreted and implemented," according to political scientist Kenneth R. Mayer.[15]

When presidents cannot obtain cooperation from federal agencies, they can appeal to the extensive bureaucracy in the Executive Office of the President (EOP), which is more subject to their direct control. Almost 1,600 people work in the specialized offices within the EOP, such as the Council of Economic Advisors, the Office of Management and Budget, and the National Security Council. These units provide presidents with expertise, perform management tasks on their behalf, and are a dependable resource to which they can turn for help.

One of the key ways in which presidential power has grown in the past century is through the ability of the president to set the agenda of government. It requires extraordinary unity and discipline in the majority party in Congress to usurp this power. Republicans temporarily were able to do it following their success in the 1994 congressional elections, but such occurrences are rare. And, when they occur, they do not last very long—in the case of the congressional Republicans in 1994, less than two years! Presidents' command of the media, their ability to focus their message, their direction of the federal bureaucracy, and their claim to speak for the entire nation permit the president to define the issues the government will address. Of course, setting the terms of the national debate does not ensure winning that debate. But the power to define what needs attention means that the president is at the very center of the nation's business.

Presidents also have rewards they can dispense in order to obtain compliance with their policies. For example, they have patronage, including judgeships and ambassadorships, and benefits, such as invitations to the White House, with which to repay loyal supporters and persuade recalcitrants who may need more convincing. They can strike bargains by offering inducements to members of Congress in return for votes, as we saw Clinton do with members of Congress from agricultural and textile districts that feared the North American Free Trade Agreement might hurt local producers. President Ronald Reagan's budget director, David Stockman, was unusually candid when he described what it took to get Congress to approve Reagan's proposed tax cut: "[T]he last 10 or 20 percent of the votes needed for a majority of both houses had to be bought, period."[16]

Presidents have sticks to punish opponents as well as carrots to obtain support. They can exclude opponents from White House social events, deny access to the president, and use their office to orchestrate pressure on reluctant members of Congress. Take a relatively "small" example— although not so small to those involved! When Senator Richard Shelby from

---

[15] Kenneth R. Mayer, "Executive Orders and Presidential Power," *Journal of Politics* 61 (May 1999): 445.

[16] David Stockman, *The Triumph of Politics: Why the Reagan Revolution Failed* (New York: Harper & Row, 1986), p. 257.

Alabama opposed Clinton's 1993 budget package, he was given only one ticket to the White House ceremony honoring the University of Alabama national championship football team. In contrast, Howell Heflin, Alabama's other senator, who supported the president's budget, received more than 25 tickets.[17]

Presidents are also party leaders and can appeal for loyalty from members of their party in Congress and elsewhere. In return, they can lend the aura of their office to party members by making appearances on their behalf, raising money for them, or supporting their pet projects.

Finally, presidents have benefited more than any other political institution from the rise of the United States as a global power. As the United States has become the dominant actor on the world stage, presidents are in a privileged position to write the script because they are uniquely situated to speak for the national interest. As the world becomes smaller, as foreign policy decisions touch people's lives in more intimate ways, from economic globalization to global warming, presidents become bigger. The more foreign policy matters, the more presidents matter. The power of the office has grown with the economic and military power of the United States and its influence throughout the world.

The rapid growth in size and power of the presidency can be illustrated by a single statistic. When Herbert Hoover served as president from 1929 to 1933, a personal secretary and two assistants aided him. Today the White House staff alone includes over 500 people to assist the president, to say nothing of the more than 1,000 others who work in the EOP. The bold innovations of one president to extend the powers of the office have come to be accepted as a normal feature of presidential power by the next. "In instance after instance," Richard E. Neustadt, the most influential scholar on the modern presidency, has observed, "the exceptional behavior of our earlier 'strong' Presidents has now been set by statute as a regular requirement."[18] Expressions of presidential powers that were once thought to be extraordinary have become routine.[19]

The modern presidency (which, as we will describe, extends far beyond the president) commands the most powerful military in the world, manages a vast bureaucracy, sets the agenda of government, defines the national interest, monopolizes the media, provides party leadership, and has a vast supply of benefits with which to reward supporters. If this were the whole story, the president would be a modern Leviathan. Yet, because it is not, some scholars describe not an imperial, but an imperiled president.

---

[17] James P. Pfiffner, *The Modern Presidency*, 2nd ed. (New York: St. Martin's Press, 1998), p. 145.

[18] Richard E. Neustadt, *Presidential Power: The Politics of Leadership* (New York: Free Press, 1963), p. 5.

[19] Richard S. Gilmour, "The Institutionalized Presidency: A Conceptual Clarification," in *The Presidency in Contemporary Context*, ed. Norman C. Thomas (New York: Dodd, Mead, 1975), p. 155.

THE IMPERILED PRESIDENT

In *Gulliver's Travels,* Jonathan Swift's satire on the modern condition, Gulliver not only found himself standing over the Lilliputians, towering above them, but also, at times, tethered by them. Presidential impotence is conveyed in the famous remark President Harry Truman made as he imagined what would happen when his newly elected successor, popular World War II hero General Dwight Eisenhower, took office. Truman predicted, "He'll sit here and he'll say, 'Do this! Do that!' *And nothing will happen.* Poor Ike—it won't be a bit like the Army. He'll find it very frustrating."[20] A sense of the president's weakness is reflected in the plea for help that the President's Committee on Administrative Management issued in 1937. The report's opening sentence, "The President needs help," has been reaffirmed many times by subsequent reports since then.[21]

Beginning in the 1970s, political scientists began to reassess the presidency and to characterize it as a weak and ineffective institution. The debacle in Vietnam under President Johnson, the criminality involved in Watergate under President Richard Nixon, the duplicity of the arms-for-hostages deal under President Reagan, and the sleaziness of the Monica Lewinsky scandal under President Clinton all contributed to a shift in public attitudes toward the president. A history of failure, corruption, and deceit has weakened the office of the president, removing the awe and veneration previously attached to it. With the aura surrounding the president tarnished, the media and Congress are now more ready and more willing to resist presidential leadership.

The end of the golden age of capitalism in the 1970s also weakened the presidency. Since at least the New Deal, the president's fortunes have been closely tied to the fate of the economy. The power and prestige of the president (as well as that of the entire government) have prospered when corporate capitalism has prospered; and when the economy stagnates, the president's popular and professional standing falls. The decline in presidential favor corresponds to the heightened economic fears and insecurities people feel as inequality increases, globalization proceeds, and the economy gyrates between periods of boom and bust.

Recent presidents have also been confronted by a resurgent Congress, often led by the opposing party. In the 1950s and 1960s, Congress was willing to follow the president's lead because it agreed with the president's policies. For example, during the Cold War, Congress often deferred to the president because it shared the president's goal of containing Communism. But when Congress and the president began to disagree over substantive issues of domestic and foreign policy beginning in the 1970s, Congress acted to recover

---

[20] Quoted in Neustadt, *Presidential Power,* p. 9 (emphasis in original).

[21] This point is taken from Theodore J. Lowi, *The Personal President: Power Invested, Promise Unfulfilled* (Ithaca, New York: Cornell University Press, 1985), pp. 1–7.

■ FIGURE 6-2

PROBABILITY OF DIVIDED GOVERNMENT

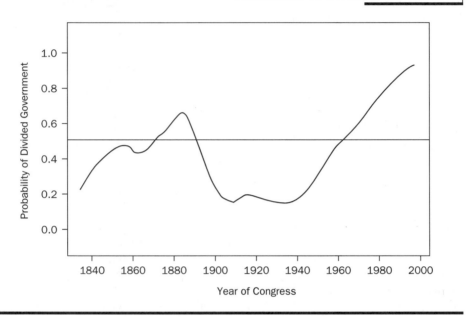

0.0 represents unified government; 1.0 represents divided government.

SOURCE: Charles M. Cameron, "Bargaining and Presidential Power," in Robert Y. Shapiro, Martha Joynt Kumar, and Lawrence R. Jacobs, eds., *Presidential Power: Forging the Presidency for the Twenty-First Century* (New York: Columbia University Press, 2000), p. 54.

its lost prerogatives. For example, Congress tried to legislate limits on presidential powers in the War Powers Act of 1973. It also sought to create its own expertise to match that available to the president when it created the Congressional Budget Office in 1974.

The reassertion of Congress was, in part, driven by the almost routine appearance of divided government beginning in the 1970s, in which different parties controlled Congress and the presidency. (Figure 6–2 charts the trend.) Democrats held majorities in Congress throughout much of the Republican presidencies of Richard Nixon, Ronald Reagan, and George Bush, just as the Republicans held majorities in Congress through six of Bill Clinton's eight years in the White House. Divided government gives Congress an incentive to challenge, not cooperate with, the president.

Moreover, presidents have been weakened by the decline of the party system and the emergence of what we described in the last chapter as the "post-electoral era." Today presidents do not broker coalitions among interest groups as they did in the past; they appeal directly to voters through the media. They do not rely on political parties, but create their own campaign apparatus and build their own personal coalitions. But personal appeals are based on inflated promises, raising expectations that cannot be met. Theodore J. Lowi describes the irony that presidents inevitably fail when judged according to the inflated expectations that they themselves create by making extravagant promises.[22]

Finally, the vacuum left by the decline of the party system has been filled by a proliferation of interest groups. This, too, poses a dilemma for presidents. The institutional universe of political action that presidents face today has, according to Skowronek, "gotten thicker all around." Skowronek argues that, for presidents, "there are more organizations and authorities to contend with, and they are all more firmly entrenched and independent."[23] Going over the heads of interest groups to build their own personal coalitions may free presidents of obligations to other political actors. But the flip side of this is that interest groups are similarly less obliged to remain loyal members of the president's team, making it difficult for presidents to govern once they are elected.

In conclusion, presidential power sometimes appears imperial and sometimes appears imperiled. It depends on particular circumstances and the ability of presidents to take advantage of them. Some presidents, as we shall argue, are more fortunate than others. They encounter a less resistant environment when they take office, one in which the opposition is in disarray and their party commands a working majority in Congress. Other presidents are not so lucky. And some presidents are simply more skillful than others at using the political resources available to them.

While there is much contingency, and even luck, regarding presidential power (think of the contrast between the roaring stock market during Clinton's tenure in office and the American hostages held in Iran during Jimmy Carter's presidency), there is also much continuity. Presidential power is exercised most decisively and effectively when the president opposes some action. The Constitution authorizes the president to veto bills passed by Congress. Vetoing a bill does not require the cooperation of any other political actor—just a pen that works. The veto is very effective because the House and the Senate are often unable to assemble the two-thirds majority in each chamber to override it.

But presidents get elected and make their mark not by preventing action but by promoting it. It is thus ironic that presidents find their power magnified and most effective when they thwart change and find their power diminished and most constrained when they try to enact change. The independence of Congress, the inflexibility of the federal bureaucracy, and the influence of special interest groups are daunting obstacles for the president to overcome. And yet, as we argued at the beginning of this chapter, presidents are agents of change in our political system despite these obstacles, if only by default. No other office in our political system can muster comparable initiative and coherence to assemble its resources on behalf of a concerted course

---

[22] Lowi, *The Personal President.*

[23] Skowronek, *Politics Presidents Make,* p. 55.

of action. That presidents may not succeed when they do so says less about the weakness of a given president and more about the power of the obstacles that that president must overcome.

PRESIDENTIAL STYLES

While all presidents reach office by promising to sponsor change, presidents construe their role in quite different ways. Presidential styles are, in part, a function of personality. John F. Kennedy was supremely confident to the point of arrogance, Lyndon Johnson was beset by profound insecurity, and Richard Nixon was suspicious by nature. In more recent times, Bill Clinton wanted to please so badly that he was called "slick Willie" because of his tendency to tell people what they wanted to hear, while George W. Bush projected an affable ignorance that left people wondering whether he was fit for the job.

Presidential style is also a function of the unique skills and aptitudes presidents bring to office with them. Ronald Reagan had little patience for the details of policy, but was brilliantly effective at communicating their broad themes to the public. Jimmy Carter was just the opposite. He brought his training as an engineer to the presidency and was intensely interested in the details of policy. (Some idea of the enormous range of issues with which Carter dealt—and his grueling schedule—can be gleaned from Figure 6–3.) Richard Nixon and George H. W. Bush each came to office with an interest in foreign policy, while Bill Clinton preferred domestic policy and, like Carter, would participate in detailed policy discussions within his administration.

Presidents shape the office in their own image. This is reflected in how the White House is organized and run. Some presidents are hands-on managers, while others prefer to delegate authority. Some are comfortable with a rigid chain of command, while others prefer to improvise. Journalist Elizabeth Drew writes that the Clinton White House was so unstructured during his first term that one White House aide described it as an "adhocracy."[24] Because of his temperament and training (including an MBA from the Harvard Business School), George W. Bush decided the broad orientation of his policies but delegated to Vice President Richard Cheney detailed management and implementation. Each president puts a personal stamp on the office, but it is hard to draw a straight line from personality to policy. The institutional and political configuration that presidents face is far more important than their personality in explaining presidential decisions and determining their success. Of course, their innermost demons can affect their presidency profoundly. Nixon's suspiciousness led him to order a cover-up of crimes committed by his aides against the Democratic Party (the Watergate affair), and it cost him his presidency. And Clinton would not have been

---

[24] Elizabeth Drew, *On the Edge: The Clinton Presidency* (New York: Simon & Schuster, 1994), p. 231.

■ **FIGURE 6–3**

From	To	Activity
5:00		The President received a wake up call from the White House signal board operator
5:36		The President went to the Oval Office
7:15	7:20	The President met with his Assistant for National Security Affairs, Zbigniew Brzezinski
7:32	7:38	The President talked with Senator Russell B. Long (D–LA)
7:45	7:55	The President met with his Assistant for Congressional Liaison, Frank B. Moore
8:00	9:00	The President hosted a breakfast meeting for Democratic Congressional leaders
9:20	9:25	The President met with his assistant, Hamilton Jordan
9:30	9:48	The President telephoned the Chief of Government of the Republic of Panama, Brig. Gen. Omar Torrijos Herrera
9:33	9:46	The President met with: Warren M. Christopher, Deputy Secretary of State Stephanie R. van Reigersberg, Dept. of State interpreter Mr. Lordan
9:46	10:00	The President met with: Rex L. Granum, Deputy Press Secretary Jerrold L. Schecter, Associate Press Secretary, NSC
10:30	10:45	The President participated in an arrival ceremony in honor of the Prime Minister of Israel, Menachem Begin
10:48	1:00	The President participated in a meeting with U.S. and Israeli officials
1:00	1:04	The President met with Mr. Brzezinski
1:04	1:30	The President met with Vice President Walter F. Mondale
1:30	1:53	The President met to discuss urban policy with: Richard G. Hatcher, Mayor (D–Gary, IN) Lee A. Alexander, Mayor (D–Syracuse, NY) Henry W. Maier, Mayor (D–Milwaukee, WI) Stuart E. Eizenstat, Assistant for Domestic Affairs and Policy Jack H. Watson, Jr. Assistant for Intergovernmental Affairs Bruce Kirschenbaum, Associate for Intergovernmental Affairs
2:15	2:27	The President participated in a ceremony to present the National Teacher of the Year Award to Mrs. Henry (Elaine) Barbour of Montrose, Colorado

SOURCE: Michael W. Link, "The Presidential Kaleidoscope: Advisory Networks in Action," in Robert Y. Shapiro, Martha Joynt Kumar, and Lawrence R. Jacobs, eds., *Presidential Power: Forging the Presidency for the Twenty-First Century* (New York: Columbia University Press, 2000), p. 237.

ensnared in the Lewinsky scandal and impeached if he had not displayed moral weakness. But, in general, presidential success depends far more on the circumstances presidents encounter than on their character.

According to Skowronek, only presidents elected in the wake of an electoral realignment, with the opposition in disarray, can impose their will on the nation. During most periods, institutional checks are too powerful for presidents to carry out their programs successfully. Great presidents come to office following electoral upheavals, when "government has been most thoroughly discredited, and when political resistance to the presidency is weakest."[25] Presidents who come to office facing a Congress that is dominated by the opposition party (Richard Nixon) or whose presidency rested on the laurels of others (George H. W. Bush) or whose presidency reflected the last gasp of a dying order (Herbert Hoover) were not any less fit for office than more successful presidents, such as Andrew Jackson, Abraham Lincoln, and Franklin Delano Roosevelt. Less successful presidents simply take office under conditions that permit them less freedom to maneuver—witness Bill Clinton, who had to contend with a Republican Congress for much of his two terms, as well as an independent and highly organized interest group environment, at the same time that he had only a slim electoral base—never a majority—from which to govern.

BILL CLINTON AS PRESIDENT

The sign reading "It's the economy, stupid" was prominently displayed in the room where Clinton's team plotted campaign strategy, reminding them of the issue that determines the fate of presidential contenders. Throughout the campaign, Clinton single-mindedly focused on the economic failures of the Bush administration at the same time that he distanced himself from the exhausted political themes and failed economic formulas of the New Deal. Clinton portrayed himself as a "New Democrat," one who was willing to stand up to labor and minorities, was going to be tough on crime, and was in favor of putting people in welfare-to-work programs. He tried to blend Republican appeals for tax cuts with Democratic demands for new investments, Republican appeals for law and order with Democratic demands for tolerating differences, and Republican faith in markets with Democratic demands for government regulation. While some perceived his program as nothing more than opportunism, others regarded it as an attempt to recenter the Democratic Party. Clinton was praised or blamed (depending on one's point of view) for trying to steer the party away from its traditional New Deal base, the lower classes, and toward the "New Democrats"—educated, middle-class, suburban voters who had the "knowledge skills" to prosper in

---

[25] Skowronek, *Politics Presidents Make,* p. 37.

a global service economy. He also displayed an uncanny knack for championing issues on which the Republicans had formerly won votes from the Democrats, such as welfare, crime, and spending.[26]

The result was not spectacular, but sufficient. In 1992, Clinton received only 43 percent of the vote and failed to receive a majority from any state other than his home state of Arkansas. But this was enough to win in a three-way race against incumbent president George H. W. Bush and Reform Party candidate Ross Perot. Not only did the election label Clinton a minority president, unable to claim a mandate by the people, but also his appeal was so limited that the Democrats actually lost ten seats in the House and made no gains in the Senate to go along with his victory in 1992.

The Clinton administration's honeymoon with the public was remarkably brief. Outcries from the military and their supporters in Congress forced Clinton to retreat from his promise to protect homosexuals who served in the armed forces. Instead of stimulating the economy as he promised, Clinton concentrated instead on deficit reduction. And his major legislative initiative on health care never even reached the stage of a vote in Congress.

The Clinton administration stumbled through its first two years. After that, things got worse. Republicans won control of both houses in Congress in the 1994 elections and proceeded to challenge the president's mastery of the nation's political agenda. The Republican forces that dominated Congress were unified and disciplined in support of their own program as laid out in their bible, the Contract with America. Pundits began to ask whether the president was still "relevant." But the Republican leadership overreached by refusing to pass spending bills and closing down the government (as we recounted in Chapter 3). Clinton took back the initiative by standing firm and casting himself as the defender of Medicare, Medicaid, education, and the environment against Republican threats to harm them.

While Clinton successfully defeated attempts by Republicans in Congress to impose their program, he worked within the conservative criteria of less government they had staked out. Clinton shied away from addressing big issues, such as economic inequality and environmental decay. Instead, he proposed small programs that conveyed a symbolic message, such as school uniforms, v-chips, and the right of mothers to an extra day in maternity wards after childbirth—all of which polled well and did not cost much. As Michael Nelson argues, Clinton was able to walk successfully a fine line, defending particular government programs without seeming to defend government as a proposition.[27]

Clinton articulated a modest program because he was content to rely on low unemployment and a soaring stock market. The strategy succeeded, and Clinton was reelected in 1996, permitting him to claim that voters had given

---

[26] For a fine account, see Elizabeth Drew, *Whatever It Takes: The Real Struggle for Political Power in America* (New York: Viking, 1997).

[27] Michael Nelson, "Chins Up, Liberals," *American Prospect*, February 26, 2001, 43.

his presidency a vote of confidence. But the election reflected voters' lack of interest, not enthusiasm. Turnout in the 1996 election was the lowest it had been since 1924.

Clinton began his second term with renewed political capital from the 1996 returns. But if a defiant Congress hamstrung his first term, his second term suffered from self-inflicted wounds. In 1994, Special Prosecutor Kenneth Starr was appointed to look into a complicated land deal that involved the president and First Lady Hillary Rodham Clinton while Clinton was governor of Arkansas. (The deal informally became known as Whitewater.) However, the focus of the investigation eventually shifted to an affair the president had with Monica Lewinsky, a White House intern. In 1998, the special prosecutor issued his report, charging Clinton with perjury, obstructing justice, and tampering with witnesses in an attempt to cover up the affair. Faced with incontrovertible evidence, the president was forced to retract his denial of having a sexual relationship with Lewinsky. The strongly partisan Republican-controlled Judiciary Committee in the House of Representatives voted to recommend that Clinton be impeached for committing perjury and obstructing justice. In a vote that went almost completely along party lines, the full House of Representatives decided to impeach Clinton. The Senate then met to decide whether to convict Clinton of the impeachment charges and remove him from office. But in a Senate vote that also went almost completely along party lines, supporters of impeachment failed to obtain the constitutionally required two-thirds vote needed to remove Clinton from office, and the president served out the remainder of his second term.

Clinton's lying and tawdry behavior undermined the power of his presidency. Yet the authority invested in the president by the Constitution remains real. The same week that Clinton became the first president in American history to testify before a grand jury, he demonstrated the power of the president as commander in chief by ordering a military strike against what he claimed were terrorist outposts in Afghanistan and the Sudan. At the very moment the House Judiciary Committee was debating whether to proceed with his impeachment in the Capitol, President Clinton was just two miles away meeting with international financial leaders about how to cope with the collapse of financial markets throughout the world. His power may have been stripped away by the sordid details of his affair, but the legal authority invested in the office of the president by the Constitution and his ability to command the political stage as the leader of the world's most powerful nation remained considerable.

THE EXERCISE OF PRESIDENTIAL POWER

Given how central the president's position is within American government and how poorly that position is defined in the Constitution, scholars have devoted enormous effort trying to understand the bases of presidential power. For many years, the most influential treatment was offered by political scientist Clinton Rossiter, who identified the president's various "hats" or roles. Rossiter designated them as chief of state, chief executive, commander in chief of the armed forces, chief diplomat, chief legislator, chief of the party, voice of the people, protector of the peace, manager of prosperity, and world leader.[28] Political scientist Thomas E. Cronin reduced Rossiter's extensive list to just four spheres or subpresidencies: foreign policy, economic management, domestic policy, and symbolic or moral leadership.[29] Aaron Wildavsky, a specialist in public policy, suggested a still simpler classification by distinguishing two presidencies, one for foreign affairs and the other for domestic affairs.[30]

Using these classifications as a point of departure, we suggest three broad purposes on behalf of which contemporary presidents exercise power: to defend corporate capitalism and American power abroad, to foster economic growth and assist the system of corporate capitalism at home, and to maintain social control.

DEFENDING CORPORATE CAPITALISM ABROAD

The growth in the power of the presidency is inseparable from the rise of the United States as a superpower. Presidential power has thrived on foreign involvement, crisis, and war.

The Constitution gives the president authority to negotiate treaties, receive ambassadors from foreign countries (which implies the right to recognize or refuse to recognize the government of a particular country), and, above all, command the armed forces. The framers of the Constitution intended the president's power as commander in chief to be confined to the limited authority of a military leader once hostilities begin. The Constitution granted Congress, not the president, the power to declare war and appropriate funds for military expenditures.

Presidents, however, have expanded the power of the presidency by interpreting broadly their authority as commander in chief. Supreme Court Justice Robert Jackson once warned that, as commander in chief, the president essentially has the power "to do anything, anywhere that can be done with an army or navy."[31] Presidents have used the open-ended authority vested in them as commander in chief to deploy American troops in pursuit of their foreign policy objectives. For example, President James K. Polk provoked war with Mexico in 1846 by sending American troops into

[28]Clinton Rossiter, *The American Presidency*, rev. ed. (New York: Harcourt, Brace, 1960), ch. 1.

[29]Thomas E. Cronin, "Presidents as Chief Executives," in *The Presidency Reappraised*, ed. Rexford G. Tugwell and Thomas E. Cronin (New York: Praeger, 1974), p. 235.

[30]Aaron Wildavsky, "The Two Presidencies," *Trans-action*, December 1966, 7–14.

[31]Quoted in Byron W. Daynes, Dennis L. Soden, and Raymond Tatalovich, *To Govern a Nation* (New York: St. Martin's Press, 1997), p. 265.

disputed land between Texas and Mexico. When Mexican forces fired on the troops, Polk quickly extracted from Congress a declaration of war. Polk's actions brought forth an angry reaction from a young Illinois congressman: "Allow the president to invade a neighboring nation, whenever *he* shall deem it necessary to repel an invasion . . . and you allow him to make war at his pleasure. Study to see if you can fix *any limit* to his power in this respect."[32]

The words of the young congressman, Abraham Lincoln, proved prescient. Indeed, when Lincoln himself became president, he vigorously used presidential war powers during the Civil War to expand the power of his office. He refused to call Congress into special session in the first months of the war and sponsored numerous unauthorized measures in its absence: blockading southern ports, expanding the armed forces beyond their congressionally prescribed size, and spending money for purposes not approved by Congress.

Contemporary presidents, like their predecessors, have often deployed troops first and asked for congressional approval later, if they bothered to seek approval at all. President Carter informed Congress only after he had sent troops on an ill-fated mission to rescue American hostages held in Iran. In 1983, President Reagan ordered U.S. troops to invade the tiny Caribbean nation of Granada and overthrow its government without seeking authorization from Congress. After Saddam Hussein of Iraq invaded Kuwait in 1991, President Bush sent 200,000 troops to neighboring Saudi Arabia to protect its oil fields, in which American corporations had interests. Bush did not ask Congress to approve of his actions until he doubled the number of American troops in the area. Two political scientists contend that, when Congress considered the issue, it "had little choice except to grant the president the authority he requested" because a number of military and diplomatic actions had already been taken by the Bush administration. They write, "As most legislators were doubtless aware, withholding such approval would mean that the United States stood in real danger of incurring a serious diplomatic and military defeat in the Middle East. This was an outcome for which few legislators were willing to take responsibility."[33]

President Clinton acted as other presidents did before him. In 1993, he dispatched American troops to Haiti without congressional authorization or appropriations to pay for their deployment. After Clinton announced that he was dispatching troops, Senator Ted Stevens (R–Alaska) declared, "I oppose this deployment but . . . it is [not] our prerogative to debate . . . with the president. . . . The president has ordered deployment and we have no way to prevent that." Political scientists William C. Banks and Jeffrey Straussman correctly note that Senator Stevens had it completely backwards.

---

[32] Quoted in Arthur M. Schlesinger, Jr., *The Imperial Presidency* (Boston: Houghton Mifflin, 1973), p. 42 (emphasis in original).

[33] Cecil V. Crabb and Kevin V. Mulcahy, "George Bush's Management Style and Desert Storm," *Presidential Studies Quarterly* 25 (Spring 1995): 262.

The Constitution authorizes Congress, not the president, to declare war, and Congress's constitutional power to appropriate funds gives it the power to prevent military actions it does not authorize.[34]

Presidents frequently defend their actions on the basis of their unique access to secret information. "If you knew what I know," Lyndon Johnson once asserted, "then you would be acting in the same way."[35] Yet backstage glimpses of the workings of the presidency, such as those provided by the Pentagon Papers (high-level administration conversations about the Vietnam War leaked by a Pentagon insider) and the transcription of White House conversations secretly tape-recorded during the Watergate affair, reveal the limited role of superior information. Moreover, Johnson's argument has a suspiciously self-serving ring. Presidents do their utmost to withhold information in order to prevent citizens from knowing what presidents know. Presidents frequently invoke "executive privilege" to prevent sharing their information with Congress and the wider public.

Presidents also try to monopolize the flow of information by classifying it for security purposes and thereby restricting access to it. More and more information is restricted to classified use for reasons that have less and less to do with national security. As one reporter observed, "Most of what is concealed through classification is anything whose revelation might be politically embarrassing to the Administration in power, or to individual officials, in terms of the enemy at home, the opposition party, the Congress, the press, and thereby the wider voting public."[36] Finally, the quality of this inside information is often of dubious value. Charles Frankel, an assistant secretary of state under President Johnson, was surprised by the poor quality of information that was classified and restricted. He recalled, "I used to imagine when the government took actions I found inexplicable that it had information I didn't have. But after I served in the government for some months, I found that the information was often false."[37]

National security may also be invoked for reasons having more to do with presidential interests than with the survival of the United States. President Nixon mentioned national security 31 times during a speech he gave trying to escape responsibility during the Watergate affair.[38] In 1998, President Clinton ordered an air attack on Iraq the day before the House of Representatives was scheduled to vote on his impeachment. The president's actions placed Republicans in the uncomfortable position of having to impeach the

[34] Quoted in William C. Banks and Jeffrey D. Straussman, "A New Imperial Presidency? Insights from U.S. Involvement in Bosnia," *Political Science Quarterly* 114, no. 2 (1999): 196.

[35] Robert T. Nakamura, "Congress Confronts the Presidency," in *1984 Revisited: Prospects for American Politics*, ed. Robert Paul Wolff (New York: Knopf, 1973), p. 82.

[36] Quoted in Daynes, Tatalovich, and Soden, *To Govern a Nation*, p. 283.

[37] Charles Frankel, *High on Foggy Bottom* (New York: Harper & Row, 1969), p. 78.

[38] Charles M. Hardin, *Presidential Power and Accountability: Toward a New Constitution* (Chicago: University of Chicago Press, 1974), p. 24.

commander in chief while the country was engaged in armed hostilities with a foreign nation. James Oliver, a student of presidential foreign policy making, observes, "Authoritarian and totalitarian governments are often accused of trying to divert the attention of their populations from domestic difficulties by means of wars or fabricated international crisis. It seems, however, that American presidents faced with their own domestic pressures are no less susceptible to [this temptation]."[39]

Following World War II, presidents had a relatively free hand in foreign policy. Through the 1940s and 1950s, Congress and the public followed presidential leadership in conducting the Cold War and containing Communism. According to Aaron Wildavsky, presidents have enjoyed more success in foreign policy than they have in domestic policy because checks and balances are simply not as effective in foreign policy as they are in domestic policy, as we saw with regard to the critical issue of committing American troops abroad. In addition, Wildavsky claimed that presidents have more expertise available to them within the area of foreign policy, encounter less interest group opposition, and can respond to foreign crises more quickly and decisively than Congress.

But according to political scientists George C. Edwards III and Stephen J. Wayne, at the very moment when Wildavsky presented his thesis on the two presidencies in 1964, conditions were changing. Protests against the Vietnam War were gathering momentum, upsetting the Cold War consensus and challenging the authority of the president to make foreign policy. Wildavsky also presented his interpretation before globalization opened the United States to economic forces beyond its borders. American workers, firms, and consumers are no longer isolated from the global economy. They now connect foreign policy to their pocketbooks and expect the president to do something about it, as we have already seen in the escalating conflict over foreign trade treaties described in Chapter 3. Finally, in the years since Wildavsky presented his claim about presidents' greater success in foreign policy, the environmental movement has made people aware of the global effects of pollution, and the media now bring visceral images from around the world into people's living rooms. The distinction between domestic and foreign policies, which Wildavsky wanted to highlight, was collapsing at the very moment he published his essay. As the world got smaller, and impinged on citizens' lives more directly, the latitude presidents enjoyed in foreign policy began to contract.

In the 1970s, Congress began to reclaim the prerogatives it had ceded to the president during the Cold War. Given impetus by the Vietnam War protests, Congress tried to restore its constitutional authority when it passed the War Powers Act in 1973 over President Nixon's veto. The law required that the president gain congressional approval after deploying American

---

[39]James K. Oliver, "Presidents as National Security Policymakers," *in Rethinking the Presidency,* ed. Thomas E. Cronin (Boston: Little, Brown, 1982), p. 397.

troops abroad. Congress also began to scrutinize presidential foreign policy more closely. We reviewed in Chapter 3 how Congress defeated President Clinton's appeal for fast-track authority to negotiate international trade agreements. In 1998, Congress mandated a reorganization of the State Department and rejected some of President Clinton's ambassadorial appointments. While presidents remain more successful in the realm of foreign policy than domestic policy, Congress is now more likely to modify their proposals than in the past.[40]

Congress also has been spurred to play a more independent role in foreign policy by the changing interest group environment around these issues. Organized interest-group pressure in foreign affairs used to be dominated by groups representing business, such as trade associations interested in trade policy and the corporate-dominated Council on Foreign Relations. Today these groups compete in a more crowded and diverse interest group environment that includes ethnic groups interested in policies affecting their countries of origin, human rights groups, and environmentalists. Presidents find they must satisfy or at least neutralize more groups to build support for their foreign policies than they did in the past. Finally, divided government has led Congress to become more assertive and less likely to follow the presidents' lead in foreign policy.

This congressional and popular resistance to presidential direction of foreign policy has had an impact. Yet the presidency retains immense power and initiative in foreign affairs. First, presidents still enjoy the authority granted them by the Constitution, such as their position as commander in chief of the armed forces, which presidents have successfully expanded on. Second, presidents can use crises, even manufacture them, to focus attention on the president and put Congress in a position where it would not dare raise opposition. Third, presidents retain the initiative in foreign affairs and control the flow of information regarding it. Fourth, presidents have the staff resources of the entire defense establishment at their disposal and enjoy unique access to the media to defend their actions. Fifth, while Congress is more assertive than it has been in the past, there is still substantial agreement between the two branches over the goals of foreign policy: to protect and promote the interests of American corporate capitalism.

DEFENDING CORPORATE CAPITALISM AT HOME: CONGRESS, THE BUREAUCRACY, AND THE EXECUTIVE PLANNING PROCESS

The presidency operates as the central planning agency for an American political economy that is highly concentrated and interdependent. There is no institution comparable to the presidency that can present a coherent

---

[40]These paragraphs on the "two presidencies" draw on the analysis in George C. Edwards III and Stephen J. Wayne, *Presidential Leadership: Politics and Policy Making*, 4th ed. (New York: St. Martin's Press, 1997), pp. 460–64.

program, mobilize public support for it, and implement policies to stabilize and strengthen capitalist democracy. Presidential planning is an essential feature of modern capitalism, no less under a laissez-faire ideologue like Ronald Reagan than under a "New Democrat" like Bill Clinton or a "compassionate conservative" like George W. Bush. It is the nerve center of corporate capitalism.

But presidents have a hard time getting the different parts of the executive branch that they manage—to say nothing about Congress—to cooperate. Getting the federal bureaucracy to implement presidents' wishes does not occur automatically. In fact, presidents find this difficult to achieve. The enormous size, diversity, and fragmentation of the federal bureaucracy means that it is a lumbering giant. Commands issuing from the top have a curious way of being distorted or ignored at the bottom. (Recall President Truman's rueful observation that his successor, Dwight Eisenhower, would say "do this, do that" and nothing would happen.) For example, one study of the Carter presidency (and the findings are doubtless valid for earlier and later periods as well) found that, two years after Carter issued an order on a topic that required 75 administrative agencies to issue their own implementing regulations, only 15 had done so.[41]

The bureaucracy has been aptly described as the "fourth branch of government" because of the discretion it has to interpret the vague legislative instructions it receives from Congress. The impact that laws passed by Congress have depends on how bureaucrats use their broad discretion to interpret and implement them. For this reason, presidents have sought to influence the bureaucracy so that laws are implemented in a manner that reflects the administration's values and political agenda. But presidents' efforts are often resisted by Congress, bureaucrats, and privately organized interests. While presidents may manage federal agencies, Congress creates them, provides their legislative mandates, and controls their purse strings. Bureaucrats also possess powerful resources to resist presidents' efforts to control them. They can withhold information from presidents' appointees and leak information to the press in order to stymie presidents. Presidents may be located at the top of the bureaucratic chart, but they are a world away from where the real administrative action takes place. It is impossible for presidents to keep close tabs on hundreds of federal agencies and over 2.7 million federal employees.

Finally, presidents must contend with powerful private groups that have a stake in what federal agencies do. These groups form mutually supportive relationships with agencies and can appeal to Congress when they oppose the way presidents direct these agencies to interpret and implement federal law. In short, presidents must compete with other political actors for influence over the federal bureaucracy. Although presidents enjoy powerful

---

[41]Ron Duhl, "Carter Issues an Order, But Is Anybody Listening," *National Journal*, July 14, 1979, 1156–58.

resources they can use to obtain bureaucratic compliance, presidential direction of the federal bureaucracy is an aspiration, not a guarantee.

THE EXECUTIVE.   Presidents seek to influence the bureaucracy through the specialized agencies located within the Executive Office of the President (EOP). The EOP has grown in size over the years, befitting the growing demands on presidents to manage corporate capitalism. About 1,600 people are employed in the different units within the EOP. Most are political appointees who were likely to have had a close association with the president prior to their appointment. For example, different FOBs, or "Friends of Bill," were distributed throughout the Executive Office under the Clinton administration. Members of the EOP, especially the White House staff, are personally loyal to the president, owe their position to the president, and share the president's goals.

The EOP includes the National Security Council, the Council of Economic Advisors, the Office of the Vice President, and the White House Office (which includes the president's personal staff and advisers). But the largest office within the EOP and the one presidents depend on most to ensure that federal agencies reflect their values is the Office of Management and Budget (OMB).[42] OMB prepares the presidents' budgets. Agencies that reflect an administration's agenda are likely to be rewarded with fatter budgets, while those that engage in activities to which the president is opposed have to hope for favorable action when Congress considers the president's proposed budget. In addition, OMB reviews legislative requests from federal agencies to ensure they are in accord with the president's program. Even regulations—how an agency intends to implement the law—must clear OMB before they are issued.

The EOP is the first in a series of concentric circles surrounding the presidential center (see Figure 6–4). It is the part of the executive branch most responsive to the president, orbiting closest to the president, absorbing and reflecting its heat most intensely. The next ring out from the president is the "permanent government," comprised of the 14 departments in the executive branch, including the Department of Defense, the Department of Commerce, and the Treasury Department. Departments are umbrella organizations into which most of the agencies and bureaus that comprise the federal bureaucracy are placed. For example, the Department of Commerce includes over 25 different offices and agencies, with responsibilities as diverse as those of the Bureau of the Census, the Patent and Trademark Office, and the National Oceanic and Atmospheric Administration within it. About three-quarters of all federal workers work for 1 of the 14 executive branch departments, and the departments spend two-thirds of all federal money.

---

[42] A complete description of the different agencies within the EOP is available in Bradley H. Patterson, Jr., *The Ring of Power: The White House Staff and Its Expanding Role in Government* (New York: Basic Books, 1988).

■ **FIGURE 6-4**

EXECUTIVE BRANCH

Executive Office of the President (EOP)
includes
Council of Economic Advisors
National Economic Council
National Security Council
Office of Management and Budget

Cabinet Departments
Agriculture
Commerce
Defense
Education
Energy
Health and Human Services
Housing and Urban Development
Interior
Justice
Labor
State
Transportation
Treasury
Veteran's Affairs

Independent Regulatory Commissions
includes
Federal Reserve Board
National Labor Relations Board

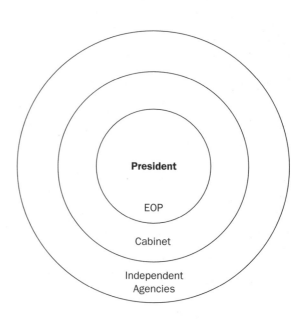

The president appoints a secretary to lead each department, and the 14 department secretaries compose the president's cabinet. The cabinet does not play an important role in presidential decision making. Presidents come to office promising to consult frequently with their cabinet, but none ever do so. For example, President Clinton met with his cabinet only 18 times over the course of his first term and had even fewer cabinet meetings in his second. The classic story about presidents' relations with their cabinet involves Lincoln's announcement when he disagreed with his entire cabinet: "Eight votes for and one against; the nays have it."

Along with OMB and the other offices in the EOP, presidents exert influence over the federal bureaucracy through their power of appointment. Presidents appoint political allies to direct the departments and to staff other key government positions. Regardless of whether the president is a Republican or a Democrat, political appointees are drawn overwhelmingly from the ranks of Washington insiders and the corporate elite, with financiers and corporate lawyers predominating. Each administration comes to Washington promising to bring new people with it, but they somehow all arrive from the same revolving corporate door. President Clinton came to office promising to appoint a cabinet that "looked like America." While he appointed more minorities and women to his cabinet than any previous president, many Clinton appointees—including the minorities and women—had the same corporate connections as their predecessors. For example, Warren Christopher, his first secretary of state, was a corporate lawyer who served on three corporate boards of directors, and his longest-serving treasury secretary was Richard Rubin, a director of the Wall Street investment banking firm Goldman, Sachs. More than two-thirds of Clinton's original cabinet consisted of lawyers, most attended elite colleges, and almost all grew up in privileged homes. If Clinton's cabinet looked more like America in terms of its gender and racial composition, that was as far as the resemblance went.[43] Key positions were still staffed with wealthy lawyers and managers—whatever their gender or color—temporarily on sabbatical from their corporate posts.

The third ring out from the president, enjoying more autonomy from the president than do the departments, is the independent regulatory commissions, such as the National Labor Relations Board (NLRB) and the Federal Reserve Board, which we described in Chapter 3. While presidents appoint members to the independent regulatory commissions, subject to confirmation by Congress, these appointees—unlike secretaries of departments—serve for a fixed term and cannot be fired by the president. The terms of independent regulatory commission appointees often straddle administrations, and new presidents must wait for members to resign or for their terms to expire before appointing new members.

CONFLICT OVER THE FEDERAL BUREAUCRACY.   As this description of the federal bureaucracy makes clear, the federal government is not organized hierarchically, but rather in concentric circles that surround the president. The federal bureaucracy is like a solar system, in which some planets orbit closer to the presidential sun, reflecting its heat and light more than others. Even though presidents head the executive branch, getting the agencies under them to conform to their programs cannot be taken for granted. Presidents can utilize their powers of appointment, OMB review of agency activities, and budgetary requests that they submit to Congress to obtain bureaucratic compliance. But federal agencies are under the magnetic pull of another sun in the galaxy that threatens to draw them away from presidents' directions. The system of shared powers endows Congress with influence over federal agencies, exerting a gravitational pull on the agencies that competes with the force of the president. Federal agencies depend on Congress for appropriations, and they get their legislative mandate—their job description—from Congress, which performs oversight to ensure they comply with it.

For example, from its inception in 1937, the NLRB was a battleground fought over by the president and Congress, as each institution tried to impose its will on the agency. At stake was how labor laws would be interpreted and

---

[43] Burt Solomon, "Clinton's Gang," *National Journal*, January 16, 1993, 116–20.

enforced. Roosevelt initially appointed pro-union members to the NLRB, which antagonized conservatives in Congress. Congress subsequently passed legislation reorganizing the NLRB, held hearings designed to intimidate the agency, and cut its budget. When the roles were reversed and Republican presidents threatened the agency, pro-union supporters in Congress rushed to defend it.[44] This swordplay between Congress and presidents over the NLRB has continued into the present. In the 1990s, President Clinton appointed people to the NLRB who proceeded to interpret labor laws in a way that was sympathetic to unions. This antagonized Republicans in Congress, who tried to penalize the NLRB for its decisions by cutting its budget, holding up presidential appointments to fill NLRB vacancies, calling oversight hearings with the intent of embarrassing the agency, and trying to intimidate NLRB members to decide cases in certain ways. The interpretation and implementation of labor policy continue to be a source of conflict between the president and Congress, as each tries to impose its vision on the NLRB.[45]

Not only do presidents have to worry about Congress imposing its will on federal agencies, but also bureaucrats have their own sources of power to defy presidential direction. They have knowledge of the files and expertise that they can make available to or withhold from presidents' appointees. Presidential appointees often find themselves dependent on the knowledge bureaucrats possess and have to become advocates of the agency in order to obtain it. Consequently, presidents often complain that their appointees abandon them, "go native" on them. Rather than acting as the president's agent, ensuring that the agency complies with the president's program, the appointee is "turned" and becomes a double agent, representing the agency's interests to the president.[46]

Finally, presidential command of the bureaucracy is challenged by private groups that develop mutually supportive, friendly—sometimes called clientelistic—relationships with federal agencies. In exchange for tax breaks, subsidies, and favorable rulings, special interests give the agencies political support in bureaucratic struggles over "turf" (jurisdiction), OMB budgeting, and congressional appropriations. Presidential management of the bureaucracy is thwarted when private groups are powerful enough to capture a government agency. The agency has legal authority in a policy area

[44] A rich history of presidential and congressional conflict over the NLRB is available in James Gross's trilogy. See James A. Gross, *The Making of the NLRB* (Albany: State University of New York Press, 1974); *The Reshaping of the NLRB* (Albany: State University of New York Press, 1981); and *Broken Promise: The Subversion of U.S. Labor Relations Policy, 1947–1994* (Philadelphia: Temple University Press, 1995). See also Seymour Scher, "Regulatory Agency Control Through Appointment: The Case of the Eisenhower Administration," *Journal of Politics* 23 (November 1961): 667–88.

[45] Matthew M. Bodah, "Congress's Influence on Administrative Outcomes: 'Extra-statutory' Challenges to U.S. Labor Policy, 1995–1998" (unpublished paper).

[46] Hugh Heclo, *A Government of Strangers: Executive Politics in Washington* (Washington, D.C.: Brookings, 1977).

that special interests "rent" for their benefit. Clientelism works best when these rental agreements are exclusive—that is, when other rival agencies and private groups can be excluded from participating in the agency's domain.

THE PRESIDENT'S RESPONSE: END-RUNNING THE BUREAUCRACY

When their appointment, budgetary, and OMB review powers are not suffi-cient to defeat congressional, bureaucratic, and special interest challenges to their management of the executive branch, presidents circumvent the bu-reaucracy altogether. As one White House staff person explained, "Every-body believes in democracy until he gets to the White House and then you begin to believe in dictatorship because it's so hard to get things done."[47] Presidents increasingly draw inward and bring policy making inside the EOP, concentrated among people whom they know, whom they trust, and who are personally loyal to them. This was particularly true during the Reagan administration. According to presidency scholars Sidney M. Milkis and Michael Nelson, policy making in the Reagan administration "was con-centrated in the White House Office and the Executive Office of the Presi-dent." The Reagan administration, they continue, "resumed the long term trend toward concentrating power in the White House that had been briefly suspended in the aftermath of Vietnam and Watergate."[48]

But the Reagan administration overreached in its zealousness to avoid po-litical challenges from bureaucrats and Congress in the Iran-Contra affair. Both the State Department and the Defense Department were out of the loop in the plan to trade arms for hostages with Iran and then divert profits from the arms sales to Contra opponents of the leftist government in Nicaragua. All of this was carried out within the National Security Council and the Cen-tral Intelligence Agency, which operate out of the EOP and report directly to the president, and violated an act of Congress prohibiting the United States from giving military aid to the Contras in Nicaragua.

While not all presidents go so far as Reagan did by violating an act of Congress in the Iran-Contra affair, they all submit to the same temptation of concentrating policy making within the isolated and insulated confines of the White House. The Clinton presidency was no different. James F. Pfiffner, a scholar of the presidency, reports that "the main policy initiatives of the Clinton Administration were run out of the White House, not in the depart-ments or in the cabinet policy groups set up by the president."[49] Pfiffner cites the example of Clinton utilizing special task forces organized by the White House to draft his economic plan and health care proposals as evidence of how insulated and White House–centered the policy process has become.

---

[47] Quoted in Thomas E. Cronin, *The State of the Presidency* (Boston: Little, Brown, 1980), p. 223.

[48] Sidney M. Milkis and Michael Nelson, *American Presidency*, pp. 342–43.

[49] Pfiffner, *Modern Presidency*, p. 110.

Former presidents gather at the dedication ceremonies for the Ronald Reagan Presidential Library in Simi Valley, California.

The presidency is the institutional site where the conflicting demands in society are sifted in a way that promotes the general interest of capitalism. Only the presidency is in a position to coordinate the different parts of the government behind a coherent program that promotes the interests of capital *as a whole*. But presidential management of the government is not a sure thing. Other political actors, including Congress, bureaucrats, and private interests, influence what federal agencies do and bend them away from presidential direction. Presidents respond by moving the policy process inside the White House, insulated from broader social forces.

SOCIAL CONTROL

Capitalist production systematically generates dislocations, inequalities, and discontent. This provides the structural context for the third arena of presidential activity, containing the conflicts generated by the collision of democratic politics and capitalist production. Thomas E. Cronin suggests that " calibration and management of conflict is the core of presidential leadership."[50] Presidents are concerned with keeping conflict from threatening

---

[50] Thomas E. Cronin, "'Everybody Believes in Democracy Until He Gets to the White House. . . .': An Examination of White House–Department Relations," *Law and Contemporary Problems* 35 (Summer 1970): 575.

the stability of the capitalist system, most often among wage earners and minorities.

The legitimacy of American corporate capitalism depends on the periodic ratification of existing arrangements by electoral majorities and on popular acceptance of presidential policies. When discontented groups express grievances, presidents often take to the media to mollify them. Sympathetic symbolic gestures are made on behalf of the aggrieved group. For example, President Clinton was known for his ability to empathize. For example, during the 1992 campaign, he assured an AIDS activist, "I feel your pain."[51] Sometimes presidents try to defuse an issue by forming commissions to study it. "These commissions," according to one skeptic, "study the situation and, in due course, issue a report, which after a flurry of publicity, is filed away, its recommendations unimplemented and forgotten."[52] For example, in 1997, President Clinton formed the Commission on Race, directed by John Hope Franklin, a distinguished African-American historian, to advise the president on the topic and stimulate a national conversation. After one year and many public meetings, the commission's report was ignored and quickly forgotten, like countless presidential commissions preceding it.

Presidents can also wrap themselves in the flag and appeal to patriotic sentiments as a tool of social control. Presidents try to project themselves as indistinguishable from the nation and the American people. Presidents also can draw on the salience and pomp of the presidential office to characterize those who disagree with them as unpatriotic and beyond the pale. Patriotism operates as a functional substitute for a state religion in the United States, with the president acting as the high priest.[53]

Social control also occurs through presidential manipulation of the media. No other person in the world enjoys as much access to the media, and presidents spare no effort in managing how they are presented through it. Almost one-third of the president's White House staff is devoted to packaging the president for media consumption. Speechwriters, press secretaries, pollsters, and media consultants strive to present the presidents and their policies in a favorable light. No group was more successful at managing the news than the media handlers around Ronald Reagan. His presidency was a meticulously crafted nonstop media event. According to the *New York Times* White House correspondent, "To an unprecedented extent, Mr. Reagan and his staff have made television a major organizing principle of his Presidency. His day is planned around opportunities for TV coverage. Every effort is made to assure a constant flow of positive visual images and symbols from the White

---

[51] Quoted in James L. Nolan, Jr., *The Therapeutic State* (New York: New York University Press, 1998), p. 236.

[52] Derrick Bell, quoted in *New York Times,* June 14, 1997.

[53] Henry Fairlie develops this point in *The Kennedy Promise: The Politics of Expectation* (Garden City, N.Y.: Doubleday, 1973).

House."[54] President Clinton was no less aggressive in his use of the media to package his presidency, although the periodic scandals that erupted around him demonstrate that presidential control of the media is far from assured. When the Starr report provided details of Clinton's affair with a White House intern, Clinton took pains to appear presidential, appearing in public at the United Nations and beside world leaders who enjoyed moral standing, such as South African leader Nelson Mandela and Czech President Vaclav Havel. His administration was known for its rapid media response to stories critical of the president and for its style of governing, which was indistinguishable from campaigning. Political consultants participated more in policy discussions within his administration than under any previous president. George C. Edwards described the Clinton administration as "the ultimate example of the public presidency—a presidency based on a perpetual campaign to obtain the public's support and fed by public opinion polls, focus groups, and public relations memos."[55] Clinton's comment that "[t]he role of the President of the United States is message" was confirmed by his actions.[56] Clinton traveled throughout the country giving more speeches that promoted his administration's work than any previous president. Campaigning and policy making blended into each other under Clinton. President George W. Bush picked up where Clinton left off, making speeches in twenty-six states in his administration's first 100 days, a record for the start of a presidency.

Today the public face of the presidency is highly managed and contrived. Reporters covering presidents work in a controlled environment. The news is managed with regard to what the administration chooses to reveal and when it chooses to reveal it. Presidential addresses and public appearances that can be scripted and managed for maximum impact have increased in number, while the number of presidential press conferences, in which reporters raise questions without advance notice, has declined.

Of course, sometimes presidents wish that some things they have done would escape the media's spotlight, and they cannot control the spin the media give to a story. While the media can turn ugly, exposing presidents in a less than flattering light, it is really the presidents' game to win or lose.

BEHIND THE VELVET GLOVE

Sometimes presidents find that symbolism and style are not enough to achieve social control. Presidential expressions of concern, blue ribbon commissions, and other symbolic gestures may not suffice. At these times, if the

---

[54] *New York Times,* April 29, 1984.

[55] George C. Edwards, "Bill Clinton and His Crisis of Governance," *Presidential Studies Quarterly* 28 (Fall 1998): 755.

[56] Quoted in ibid., p. 755.

challenge to the existing order is sufficiently great, presidents may propose new policies or expand existing programs to satisfy aggrieved groups. Francis Fox Piven and Richard Cloward found that welfare funding expanded "during the occasional outbreaks of civil disorder produced by mass unemployment" and then contracted when political stability was restored. For example, labor unrest in the 1930s and black militancy in the 1960s provoked concessions by the government in the form of new and more generous welfare programs. Such programs were designed to pacify the protesters and were then cut back when the political challenge subsided.[57] Presidents may also use force along with concessions in an attempt to restore order in times of crisis. They have called out the National Guard, mobilized the armed forces, engaged federal marshals, and used the FBI to maintain political order. The police power under the presidents' command is the iron fist cloaked by the velvet glove of presidential symbolism, media glorification, and policy concessions. Presidents have resorted to repression most often to break strikes by workers and to quell urban protests by minorities. Presidents usually claim they are defending the rule of law by using the government's police powers—but the rule of law is not neutral: The law and order being defended involve protecting the status quo and, above all, the existing system of corporate capitalism.

CONCLUSION

Political power is centralized in the executive branch, and within the executive branch, political power is concentrated in the Executive Office of the President. The presidency is at the apex of the government and oversees the stability and growth of corporate capitalism. It enjoys this exalted position by virtue of the constitutional power vested in it and as a result of its unique position as the only office elected on a national basis. The fact that only presidents are elected by a national constituency is a powerful political asset, permitting presidents—and only presidents—to claim that they speak for the nation as a whole and represent the national interest. But presidential power is highly contingent. Powers shared among the legislative, executive, and judicial branches create a system of checks and balances. Congress and the courts are independent of the president. Presidential success requires obtaining their cooperation, which may or may not be forthcoming. Even federal agencies in the executive branch, which are supposed to be under the president's management, are subject to various influences that pull them away from presidential direction. In such circumstances, presidents tend to move policy making inside the EOP, where staff are more loyal and

---

[57]Francis Fox Piven and Richard Cloward, *Regulating the Poor: The Functions of Public Welfare* (New York: Vintage, 1971), p. xiii.

subject to their direct control. They tend to depend more on executive orders, recess appointments, and executive agreements; make more claims of executive privilege; and exert more political control over appointments, the budget, and rule making in order to avoid congressional impasses and minimize bureaucratic obstructions.[58]

But presidents are elected to make change, not prevent it. Presidents themselves encourage the impression that they are supposed to provide leadership and initiative to the government. Ironically, presidents find their power is most compromised by the system of checks and balances when they attempt to do just that! Presidential power is most effective when it is least important (when preventing change) and least effective when it is most important (when creating change). Even with all the political resources at their disposal, presidents find it very difficult to overcome interest group opposition, congressional resistance, adverse court rulings, and bureaucratic obstruction. In these circumstances, presidential power looks more imperiled than imperial. Yet, for all the obstacles presidents might encounter from other political institutions, they are in a better position than any other part of the federal government to provide energy and direction to it. Presidents are at the center of government and attempt, not always successfully, to motor and direct it as well. Presidents attempt to provide initiative and coherence to the federal government as it pursues and protects the interests of corporate capitalism abroad, defines and promotes capital's interests at home, and engages in social control to cope with the dislocations that its policies in the first two arenas produce.

---

[58] Joseph Cooper, "The Twentieth Century Congress," in Lawrence C. Dodd and Bruce I. Oppenheimer, eds., *Congress Reconsidered*, 7th ed. (Washington, D.C.: Congressional Quarterly Press, 2001), p. 356.

7

Congress

Writing in 1885, twenty-eight years before he became the president of the United States, Woodrow Wilson analyzed "the essential machinery of power" in America. He believed "that, unquestionably, the predominant and controlling force, the center and source of all motive and regulative power, is Congress."[1] Wilson held that power would devolve to Congress as the federal government grew in stature because "the President and his Cabinet must wait upon the will of Congress." Rather than applaud this situation, Wilson was suspicious of congressional power. Congress, he concluded, was too unwieldy, too unpredictable, and too interested in patronage and spending to produce good government.

Wilson's argument that Congress is central to American government, but unfocused and irresponsible, reflects the misgivings that many Americans have had regarding this institution. Disaffection with Congress was a regular feature of popular understanding before Wilson's contribution, and skepticism about Congress in the wider culture has a vibrant life even today. For example, the Broadway musical *1776* begins with an actor playing John Adams, a delegate to the Continental Congress from Massachusetts who would later become the second president of the United States, taking the stage alone to address the audience. With the spotlight on him and the curtains still drawn, Adams dispenses this clever bit of wisdom: "I have come to the conclusion that one useless man is called a disgrace, that two are called a law firm, and that three or more become a Congress." At that point, the curtain opens, the play begins, and the audience is treated to the chaotic, quarrelsome process by which the Continental Congress went about drafting the Declaration of Independence.[2]

The public's impression of Congress has not improved much since Adams offered the views of his contemporaries more than 200 years ago. Americans consistently express less confidence in Congress than in either

---

[1]Woodrow Wilson, *Congressional Government: A Study in American Politics* (New York: Meridian Books, 1958), p. 25.
[2]Peter Stone, *1776* (New York: Viking, 1970), p. 1.

The U.S. Capitol.

the presidency or the Supreme Court. While confidence in all political institutions has declined, none is as low in public esteem as Congress.

Political scientists John Hibbing and Elizabeth Theiss-Morse argue that the public's suspicions of Congress are not so much rooted in policy or disappointment with legislative results as derived from the procedures Congress uses to arrive at those results. Congress is perceived as inefficient, "loaded with staffers, committees and perquisites" that may serve the selfish needs of members of Congress, but do little to meet the needs of the country.

But people also perceive procedures that are unfair, not simply inefficient, at work in Congress. Hibbing and Theiss-Morse write, "[T]he people believe they see processes that are not just, processes that are not equitable. A minority—the extremists, the special interests—are seen as having more access and influence than 'the people.' Lobbyists are in and ordinary people are out, so there is a clear injustice present."[3] Public respect for and confidence in Congress are modest because it is perceived as captured by

---

[3]John R. Hibbing and Elizabeth Theiss-Morse, "What the Public Dislikes About Congress," in *Congress Reconsidered,* 6th ed., ed. Lawrence C. Dodd and Bruce I. Oppenheimer (Washington, D.C.: Congressional Quarterly Press, 1997), p. 77.

special interests who contribute to congressional campaigns, employ lobby-ists to influence legislation, and enjoy special access to members of Con-gress. In essence, when people condemn Congress for being unfair, they are condemning it for reflecting all too well the inequalities that exist in Ameri-can society.

A paradox is at work. Precisely because Congress is the most open and ac-cessible of the three branches of the federal government—not only to voters, but also to interest groups—the advantages that social inequalities confer are exaggerated within it. The wealthy, who are more likely to vote, contact their senator or representative, and contribute to their campaigns, will enjoy more influence in Congress than other citizens, just as big business, which is more organized, employs more lobbyists, and contributes more money, will have more influence than other special interests. "The flaw in the pluralist heaven," political scientist E. E. Schattschneider once wrote, "is that the heavenly chorus sings with an upper-class accent."[4] Congress tends to hear the upper-class members of the chorus better because their money, their votes, and their organization tend to amplify their accented voices.

While both the presidency and Congress are more responsive to groups, like business, that have wealth and power, a division of labor exists between the legislative and executive branches as to how they respond to them. Congress, according to the Founders, was supposed to represent local constituencies, while the president, in Thomas Jefferson's words, was "the only national officer who commanded a view of the whole ground."[5] Where the purview of Congress tends to be local and regional, reflecting the size of the constituencies its members represent, the purview of the presi-dent tends to be national and international, reflecting the constituency from which the president is elected and the foreign policy leadership the presi-dent is expected to provide. Whereas Congress represents powerful local business interests, the president, in the words of Elizabeth Sanders, tilts to-ward the interests of "advanced, internationally competitive enterprises and finance capital," which share the same national and global perspectives as the president.[6]

Congress's perspective is parochial in the type of demands and issues it addresses. Congress engages particularistic, specific demands of local groups within the confines of committees and subcommittees with narrow jurisdictions that discourage dissent. The president, on the other hand, as we argued in Chapter 6, tries to condense these specific demands, examine them

---

[4]E. E. Schattschneider, *The Semi-sovereign People* (New York: Holt, Rinehart & Winston, 1960), p. 35.

[5]Quoted in Jeffrey Tulis, "The Two Constitutional Presidencies," in *The Presidency and the Political System*, ed. Michael Nelson (Washington, D.C.: Congressional Quarterly Press, 1984), p. 68.

[6]Elizabeth Sanders, *Roots of Reform: Farmers, Workers, and the Administrative State, 1877–1917* (Chicago: University of Chicago Press, 1999), p. 395.

in relation to each other, and modify them into a coherent program that promotes the interests of corporate capitalism as a whole.

It would, however, be inaccurate to present Congress as merely a handmaiden of local business interests. Groups other than business, including organized labor, also find their particular interests well represented within Congress. Business may have more political resources at its disposal to influence Congress, but it is not active on all issues, it is often divided internally, and popular pressure on an issue, such as raising the minimum wage, at times is sufficient to overcome business preferences. According to Sanders, Congress is often responsive to pressures from less privileged groups because its members are "bound to local constituencies," making them "exquisitely sensitive to the economic pain and moral outrage of their electorates."[7] Moreover, the decentralized structure of Congress, with its committees specializing in different policy areas (see Figures 7–1 and 7–2), attracts a wide variety of organized interests to influence policy. Congress is fragmented enough that many groups, from environmentalists to minorities, can cultivate different committees and subcommittees as their advocates within Congress.

Finally, what happens inside Congress is not simply a function of outside forces brought to bear on it in the form of lobbying, campaign contributions, and election results. Senators and representatives come to office with their own preferences and ideological orientations. They are not blank pads on which outside interests simply inscribe their views. Moreover, policy is a product of Congress's own structure, rules, and procedures. The most important aspect of Congress's structure is its division into two parts, the Senate and the House of Representatives. Each chamber of Congress represents different kinds of constituencies. The Senate represents states, with each state electing two members to the Senate, while the House of Representatives represents districts within states based on population. Senators and representatives serve for different terms: six years for senators and two years for representatives. Each chamber is governed by its own formal and informal rules, which affect how they consider laws, certify appointments, conduct investigations, and remove officials from office.

This chapter will review the origins of Congress, the changing fortunes of congressional power, the legislative process, the different cultures of both the Senate and the House, and their relationship to the wider society.

THE ORIGINS OF CONGRESS

James Madison put the matter bluntly to the delegates at the Constitutional Convention in Philadelphia in 1787. The problem confronting them was to devise a political formula that would guard against the "inconveniences of

---

[7]Ibid., p. 396.

■ FIGURE 7-1

**U.S. HOUSE OF REPRESENTATIVES COMMITTEES
AND SUBCOMMITTEES**

Agriculture
- Department Ops, Oversight, Nutrition, & Forestry
- General Farm Commodities, Resource Conservation, and Credit
- Livestock and Horticulture
- Risk Management, Research and Specialty Crops

Appropriations
- Agriculture
- Commerce, Justice, State, and Judiciary
- Defense
- District of Columbia
- Energy and Water Development
- Foreign Operations, Export Financing and Related Programs
- Interior
- Labor, Health and Human Services, and Education
- Legislative
- Military Construction
- Transportation
- Treasury, Postal Service, and General Government
- VA, HUD and Independent Agencies

Armed Services
- Armed Services Special Oversight Panel on Morale, Welfare & Recreation
- Armed Services Special Oversight Panel on the Merchant Marine
- Military Installations
- Military Personnel
- Military Procurement
- Military Readiness
- Military Research and Development

Banking and Financial Services
- Capital Markets, Securities & Government Sponsored Enterprises
- Domestic and International Monetary Policy
- Financial Institutions and Consumer Credit
- General Oversight and Investigations
- Housing and Community Opportunity

Budget

Commerce
- Energy and Power
- Finance and Hazardous Materials
- Health and the Environment
- Oversight and Investigations
- Telecommunications, Trade, and Consumer Protection

Education and the Workforce
- Early Childhood, Youth and Families
- Employer-Employee Relations

continued

- Oversight and Investigations
- Postsecondary Education, Training & LifeLong Learning
- Workforce Protections

Government Reform and Oversight
- Census
- Civil Service
- District of Columbia
- Government Management, Information and Technology
- Human Resources
- National Economic Growth, Natural Resources & Regulatory Affairs
- National Security, International Affairs & Criminal Justice
- Postal Service

House Administration Committee

International Relations
- Int'l Economic Policy and Trade
- Int'l Operations and Human Rights
- Africa
- Asia and the Pacific
- Western Hemisphere

Judiciary
- Commercial and Administrative Law
- Constitution
- Courts and Intellectual Property
- Crime
- Immigration and Claims

Permanent Select Committee on Intelligence
- Human Intelligence Analysis & Counterintelligence
- Technical and Tactical Intelligence

Resources
- Energy and Mineral Resources
- Fisheries Conservation, Wildlife and Oceans
- Forests & Forest Health
- National Parks and Public Lands
- Water & Power Resources

Rules
- Legislative and Budget Process
- Rules and Organization of the House

Science
- Basic Research
- Energy and Environment
- Space and Aeronautics
- Technology

continued

■ **FIGURE 7–1**

CONTINUED

Small Business
- Empowerment
- Government Programs and Oversight
- Regulatory Reform and Paperwork Reduction
- Tax, Finance, and Exports

Standards of Official Conduct

Transportation and Infrastructure
- Aviation
- Coast Guard and Maritime Transportation
- Public Buildings and Economic Development
- Railroads
- Surface Transportation
- Water Resources and Environment

Veterans' Affairs
- Benefits
- Health
- Oversight and Investigations

Ways and Means
- Health
- Human Resources
- Oversight
- Social Security
- Trade

JOINT COMMITTEES
- Joint Committee on Printing
- Joint Committee on Taxation
- Joint Committee on the Library of Congress
- Joint Economic

democracy" in a manner that was still "consistent with the democratic form of government."[8] The Founders, who believed in sovereignty by the people, also were concerned that democracy would threaten the social order. They conceived their task as one of "preserving the spirit and form of popular government," while avoiding what experience under the Articles of Confederation had taught them was its consequence: that the majority would use their democratic rights to pursue their economic interests through the government—what many Founders condemned as "the leveling spirit."

---

[8]Quoted in Merrill Jensen, *The Making of the American Constitution* (Malibar, Fla.: Krieger, 1979) , p. 47.

Agriculture, Nutrition, and Forestry
- Forestry, Conservation, and Rural Revitalization
- Marketing, Inspection, and Product Promotion
- Production and Price Competitiveness
- Research, Nutrition, and General Legislation

Appropriations
- Agriculture & Rural Dev & Related Agencies
- Commerce, Justice, State, and Judiciary
- Defense
- District of Columbia
- Energy and Water Development
- Foreign Operations
- Interior
- Labor, Health & Human Services, Education
- Legislative Branch
- Military Construction
- Transportation
- Treasury and General Government
- VA, HUD, & Independent Agencies

Armed Services
- Acquisition and Technology
- Airland Forces
- Personnel
- Readiness
- Seapower
- Strategic Forces

Banking
- Economic Policy
- Financial Institutions
- Housing and Transportation
- International Trade and Finance
- Securities

Budget

Commerce, Science and Transportation
- Aviation
- Communications
- Consumer Affairs, Foreign Commerce and Tourism
- Manufacturing and Competitiveness
- Oceans and Fisheries
- Science, Technology and Space
- Surface Transportation and Merchant Marine

Energy and Natural Resources
- Energy Research, Development, Production and Regulation
- Forests and Public Land Management
- National Parks, Historic Preservation, and Recreation
- Water and Power

Environment and Public Works
- Clean Air, Wetlands, Pvt Property & Nuclear Safety
- Drinking Water, Fisheries and Wildlife
- Superfund, Waste Control, and Risk Assessment
- Transportation and Infrastructure

continued

Finance
- Health Care
- International Trade
- Long-Term Growth, Debt and Deficit Reduction
- Social Security and Family Policy
- Taxation and IRS Oversight

Foreign Relations
- African Affairs
- East Asian and Pacific Affairs
- European Affairs
- Int'l Econ Policy Export & Trade Promotion
- International Operations
- Near Eastern and South Asian Affairs
- Western Hemisphere and Peace Corps Affairs

Governmental Affairs
- Int'l Security, Proliferation and Fed. Srvs
- Oversight of Gov't Management & DC
- Permanent Subcommittee On Investigations

Health, Education, Labor and Pension
- Aging
- Children and Families
- Employment and Training
- Public Health and Safety

Indian Affairs

Judiciary
- Administrative Oversight and the Courts
- Antitrust, Business Rights, and Competition
- Constitution, Federalism, and Property Rights
- Immigration
- Technology, Terrorism, and Government Information
- Youth Violence

Rules and Administration

Select Committee on Ethics

Select Committee on Intelligence

Small Business

Special Committee on Aging

Special Committee on the Year 2000 Technology Problem

Veterans' Affairs

JOINT COMMITTEES
- Joint Committee on Printing
- Joint Committee on Taxation
- Joint Committee on the Library of Congress
- Joint Economic

In order to protect the government against what the Founders perceived as the excesses of democracy, they created the presidency, as we saw in Chapter 6. But they did not stop there. The Founders also sought to check too strong a popular voice in the government by creating a bicameral legislature, with a House of Representatives, whose members would be elected by popular vote, and a Senate, whose members would be chosen by the various state legislatures.[9]

It was widely assumed at the convention, political scientist Robert Dahl has written, that a popularly elected House of Representatives with small districts and frequent elections "would be the driving force in the system; that the people's representatives would be turbulent and insistent; that they would represent majorities and would be indifferent to the rights of [elite] minorities; that the people would be the winds driving the ship of state and their representatives would be the sails, swelling with every gust."[10] The House of Representatives would be the institutional expression of democracy and reflect the will of the majority.

But the Founders believed the will of the majority, this popular force, needed to be modified and checked by a Senate, which, according to Madison, "ought to be constituted as to protect the minority of the opulent against the majority."[11] The Senate was modeled on the British House of Lords as much as the convention delegates dared.[12] While the House of Lords was composed of a hereditary aristocracy, the Senate was to be composed of society's natural aristocracy, its wealthy, educated, cultivated elites. Senators were not to be elected directly, but were to be appointed by state legislatures, presumed to be more favorable to mercantile, financial, and business interests than the electorate as a whole. The Founders sought to further ensure the autonomy of senators by permitting them to serve for a term three times longer than that of members of the directly elected House of Representatives. The independence, character, and virtue of senators, the Founders believed, would stand as a bulwark against what they feared would be the irresponsible democratic tendencies of representatives. The Senate, in the words of George Washington, would be "[t]he cooling saucer into which the hot coffee from the cup of the House should be poured."[13]

---

[9]Senators were not popularly elected until the passage of the Seventeenth Amendment to the Constitution in 1912.

[10]Robert Dahl, *Democracy in the United States: Promise and Performance*, 2nd ed. (Chicago: Rand McNally, 1973), p. 151.

[11]Quoted in Jensen, *Making of the American Constitution*, p. 58.

[12]Elaine K. Swift, *The Making of an American Senate: Reconstitutive Change in Congress, 1787–1841* (Ann Arbor: University of Michigan Press, 1996).

[13]Quoted by Newt Gingrich in William F. Connelly, Jr., and John J. Pitney, Jr., "The House Republicans: Lessons for Political Science," in *New Majority or Old Minority: The Impact of Republicans on Congress*, ed. Nicol C. Rae and Colton C. Campbell (Lanham, Md.: Rowman & Littlefield, 1999), p. 186.

THE ORIGINS OF CONGRESS

But the most enduring protection against democratic excess the Founders designed into the Senate was how Senate seats were to be apportioned. Each state, regardless of whether it was large and populous or barely inhabited, was entitled to the same two members in the Senate. This deliberate mal-apportionment, in which voters in small states are more represented within the Senate than voters in large states, violates democratic principles of political equality. When the Senate is measured by the one person, one vote standard, political scientist Arend Lijphart found it was the most malapportioned legislative body in the world. Forty percent of all U.S. senators come from the smallest states in terms of population, together comprising just 10 percent of the population; more than 80 percent of all senators come from states that together account for just one-half of all Americans.[14] Not only is unequal representation greater in the Senate than in any other legislature, but also its effects are more meaningful in the United States than elsewhere. In other countries with two separate legislative houses, the chamber not based on population, such as the House of Lords in Britain and the Senate in France and Canada, is always the weaker of the two. By contrast, the U.S. Senate is never less than equal in power to the House of Representatives, and even possesses powers not granted to the House, such as approving presidential appointments and foreign treaties.[15]

The degree to which Senate malapportionment contradicts principles of political equality is evident in a comparison of Wyoming and California. The 480,000 people in Wyoming, our least populous state, receive the same two votes in the Senate as the 32 million people who live in California, our most populous state. Such malapportionment makes it possible for small states representing a small minority of the country to block legislation supported by a large majority of citizens. (Senate malapportionment has a greater political effect on blocking bills as opposed to passing them because the House of Representatives, which is based on population, would almost certainly defeat legislation that depended on malapportionment to pass the Senate.)[16]

The inequalities between large and small states reflected in the Senate are not innocent.[17] Senate malapportionment helps and hurts different groups.

---

[14]Arend Lijphart, *Patterns of Democracy: Government Forms and Performance in Thirty-Six Countries* (New Haven, Conn.: Yale University Press, 1999), p. 208.

[15]Malapportionment and its consequences are examined thoroughly in Frances E. Lee and Bruce I. Oppenheimer, *Sizing Up the Senate: The Unequal Consequences of Equal Representation* (Chicago: University of Chicago Press, 1999), p. 2. It is noteworthy also that, while many state governments under the Articles of Confederation had two legislative chambers, the lower house, based on population, was often stronger than the upper house. Thus, the creation of a Senate, of an upper house, with powers even greater than those of the lower House was a departure from the more democratic legislatures of the states under the Articles of Confederation.

[16]Tom Geoghagen, "The Infernal Senate," *New Republic*, November 21, 1994, 17–23.

[17]Gary C. Jacobson, *The Politics of Congressional Elections*, 4th ed. (Washington, D.C.: Congressional Quarterly Press, 1997), p. 11.

For example, urban states are disadvantaged compared to rural, agricultural states. In addition, the fact that minorities are concentrated in the most populous states, such as California and New York, means that they are most disfranchised by the equal number of votes given to both large and small states in the Senate. On the other hand, whites, which comprise the overwhelming majority in racially homogenous small states like Wyoming and North Dakota, are given more weighted votes.[18]

THE HISTORICAL CONGRESS

The Constitution gives the House and the Senate substantial responsibilities. Article I, section 8 enumerates Congress's powers to levy taxes, borrow and spend money, regulate interstate and foreign commerce, declare war, support the armed forces, create courts inferior to the Supreme Court, and, more generally, "make all laws which shall be necessary and proper for carrying into execution the foregoing powers, and all other powers vested by this Constitution in the government of the United States, or any department or officer thereof." In addition, the House of Representatives was given the power to impeach—that is, bring charges against—members of the executive and judiciary branches. The Senate then acts as a trial court for all impeachments, requiring a two-thirds majority of those voting in order to convict.

In the early nineteenth century, the Constitutional Convention's conception of the House as the driving force of the government was borne out. Under the leadership of Henry Clay, the House of Representatives dominated the federal government, although, as we explained in Chapter 3, the federal government had a much-reduced role compared to its current significance.

The House of Representatives reached the height of its powers in the early years of the twentieth century. The secret of its success lay in its structure, which was highly centralized, with power concentrated in the Speaker, who led the majority party in the House. Joe Cannon, the Speaker of the House from 1903 to 1911, was considered by many to be even more powerful than the president. A form of party government existed in which the Speaker acted much like a British prime minister, organizing party members in the House behind a common program. The Speaker led his party's caucus, which adopted a formal legislative agenda, which was then passed by disciplined party majorities.

The House of Representatives thrived during this period of party government. But the centralization of power in the Speaker and his ability to provide effective leadership to the majority party in the House came at the expense of

[18]On the advantages of small states in the Senate and the benefits whites derive from this at the expense of minorities, see Francis E. Lee and Bruce I. Oppenheimer, *Sizing Up the Senate*, pp. 21–23.

individual representatives, who were reduced to near impotence. The House of Representatives as an institution may have been powerful, but individual members outside the majority party leadership enjoyed little of it. By 1910, the rank and file of the House rebelled and stripped Cannon of much of his power. Ironically, the big winner from this revolution inside the House of Representatives was the presidency. Party unity imposed by the Speaker, which once brought representatives together, now gave way to the tug of diverse local interests, which pulled them apart. With power now decentralized and the majority party unable to act in a disciplined fashion in support of a common program, it was now easier for the president to seize the initiative and exercise legislative authority. Once the era of party government came to an end in the House of Representatives, the presidency assumed legislative leadership.

This shift in the congressional-presidential balance of power first began to unfold during Woodrow Wilson's administration (1913–21), altering the relationship between Congress and the president. Whereas strong Speakers like Joe Cannon had once been able to command disciplined party majorities in support of their party's program, it was now the president who assumed the role of party leader and legislative initiator. Neil McNeil writes: "Wilson laid out to Congress a fully formulated legislative program and then used the full powers of his office to induce Congress to enact it. He signaled this major political alteration of the President's role in American politics by dramatically going before Congress in person to address the members. It was the first such appearance of a president before Congress since Jefferson gave up the practice in 1801."[19]

The shift in power from the legislative to the executive branch that began with Woodrow Wilson accelerated under Franklin Delano Roosevelt's presidency. Elected in 1932 during the Depression, Roosevelt presented a presidential program to address the crisis in his first 100 days. He virtually ran over Congress, as the Senate and the House passed legislation they barely had time to read. Rather than offering their own programs, the leaders of both houses of Congress became the president's men on Capitol Hill. And when Congress balked at presidential direction, Roosevelt went over its head and appealed directly to the public through press conferences and radio "fireside chats."

Congress did reject some legislation that Roosevelt proposed, but the shift to the president as the initiator of policy, with the expectation that the executive branch and not Congress would now set the agenda of government, went unchallenged. Only a brief renewal of party government in 1994, when House Republicans tried to seize the legislative initiative with their Contract with America, interrupted this trend, though Congress already had begun to be more assertive in the 1970s.

---

[19]Neil McNeil, *Forge of Democracy: The House of Representatives* (New York: McKay, 1963), p. 32.

During the golden age of capitalism, from 1945 to 1973, Congress played a subordinate role to the presidency. Congress was content to let the president provide leadership and even encroach on congressional powers because it largely agreed with the president's policies. An uneasy consensus on domestic and foreign policy prevailed that promoted cooperation between the two branches of government. Congress left the broad design of policy to the president, to which it would then respond. In 1965, political scientist Samuel P. Huntington confirmed the general drift of power to the executive branch, with Congress only responding defensively to presidential initiatives. Congress's role in legislation, Huntington offered, "has largely been reduced to delay and amendment."[20]

But the uneasy consensus on foreign and domestic policy that had existed in the 1950s began to collapse in the 1960s. Racial issues, which had been kept off the domestic agenda, permitting the appearance of a satisfied consensus, exploded in the streets of Birmingham, on the roads of Mississippi, and in the slums of Detroit, Newark, and Los Angeles. At the same time racial turmoil emerged to upset the consensus on domestic policy, college campuses erupted in protest to the war in Vietnam, shattering the consensus on foreign policy. Policy disagreements between the presidency and Congress that began to emerge soon were reflected in institutional combat between the two branches. Congress appropriated funds for domestic programs that President Richard Nixon refused to spend, and Nixon pursued a covert war in Cambodia despite congressional action proscribing it. Moreover, divided government, in which different parties are in control of the presidency and one or both houses of Congress, became the norm. When government is divided between the parties—as it has been for all but six years since 1968—congressional leaders have more incentive to pursue agendas independent of the president.

Congress began to reassert itself in the 1970s and reclaim the authority it had ceded to the president. Congress tried to restrict the president's encroachment on Congress's war-making powers through the War Powers Resolution of 1973, match the president's budgetary powers by revamping its own budgetary procedures, challenge claims of presidential prerogatives, increase Congress's resources to equal those available to the president, scrutinize presidential appointments more carefully, and alter the president's legislative proposals. As the policy differences separating the legislative and executive branches of government increased, so did their battles over "turf" and conflict over institutional prerogatives.

The resurgence of Congress reached its peak in 1994, when a majority of Republicans were elected to both the Senate and the House. Rather than run on local issues specific to each district, as is customary in midterm congressional elections, the Republicans "nationalized" the 1994 election. They

[20]Samuel P. Huntington, "Congressional Responses to the Twentieth Century," in *The Congress and America's Future,* ed. David B. Truman (Englewood Cliffs, N.J.: Prentice-Hall, 1965), p. 23.

offered a focused, integrated alternative to the Democrats in the form of their Contract with America, which 330 Republican congressional candidates pledged to enact if elected. Republicans gained control of the House of Representatives for the first time since 1952, picking up 52 seats in the largest partisan election swing since 1948. The new Republican Speaker of the House, Newt Gingrich, claimed the election was a mandate to enact the Republican agenda as laid out in the Contract with America, even though polls revealed that a majority of voters had never even heard of it. The large, unified, disciplined Republican majority under Speaker Gingrich's direction acted swiftly to seize the legislative agenda and pass all but one of the planks in their Contract with America in the session's first hundred days.[21] (Of course, bills passed by the House still require the approval of the Senate and the president before they become law.) After a hiatus of 85 years going back to Speaker Joe Cannon, party government had returned to the House of Representatives. Pundits wondered whether the president was still "relevant." Patrick Griffin, the assistant to President Clinton for legislative affairs, acknowledged that "[w]e're not setting the day-to-day agenda."[22]

But this moment of party government was brief. As we recounted in Chapter 3, the Republicans engaged in a game of "fiscal chicken" with President Clinton regarding the 1996 budget. House Republicans were willing to risk shutting down the government in order to impose their agenda. President Clinton was uncharacteristically firm and presented himself as the defender of Medicare, Medicaid, and other social programs that the Republican budget proposed to slash. He successfully portrayed the House Republicans and their leadership as extremists who were willing to hold the government hostage if he did not capitulate to their radical demands. The 1995 government shutdowns in November and again in December turned the public against the Republican House leadership, forcing it to capitulate on the budget.

The budget defeat broke the momentum generated by the Republicans' remarkable victory in the 1994 elections. Gingrich came under fire from the public for being too inflexible, while members of the Republican caucus in the House criticized him for being too compromising. As party government crumbled under the burden of the budget fiasco and internal dissension among House Republicans, the legislative initiative passed to the president once again. The brief moment of congressional agenda setting had ended, but not before House Republicans made one last effort to dominate the country's agenda by impeaching President Bill Clinton. This strategy was a

---

[21]The only part of the contract that did not pass the House was the constitutional amendment requiring term limits. This received a majority of votes in the House, but failed to get the two-thirds majority required of constitutional amendments.

[22]Quoted in Norman C. Thomas and Joseph A. Pika, *The Politics of the Presidency,* 4th ed. (Washington, D.C.: Congressional Quarterly Press, 1996), p. 213.

costly one, as the public rebuked Congress for pursuing impeachment instead of legislating solutions to the country's problems.

It would be inaccurate to view conflicts between the president and Congress as a zero sum game, in which one institution grows in power at the expense of the other. Congress retains formidable power rooted in the Constitution, which requires the presidents to obtain the approval of an independent Congress for their programs to succeed. The authority Congress derives from the Constitution makes it more powerful and more capable of independent action than any legislature in the world. Moreover, as government has grown, so has Congress's power. As more and more legislation is proposed by the president, more and more legislation must be disposed of by Congress. Its ability to say "no," to oppose presidential measures, to amend legislation, to deny presidential appointments, to ignore the president's budget requests, and to challenge the president's management of federal agencies has become more consequential as the agenda and work of government have grown. The decline of Congress is thus not absolute, but rather a decline relative to the powers of the presidency, which have grown even more.

CONGRESS AS A CAREER

Senators and representatives have desirable jobs. They are treated with respect, they have a chance to influence policy, they meet interesting people, and their work is varied and stimulating. Their salary was raised in 1997 to $141,300. Members of the House and Senate receive generous pensions (if they last at least five years in office), inexpensive life insurance, tax breaks (if they own two homes), allowances for their offices, almost unlimited mailing privileges, nearly free medical care, free parking, frequent trips abroad at government expense, and a large staff. Congress also provides many services as amenities for its members. The Senate alone has swimming pools, a health club, a barbershop, and a variety of restaurants for use by its members. The total package of salary, benefits, and perquisites members of Congress receive is worth almost $200,000. But such benefits are available also to high-priced lawyers and corporate managers in the private sector. What being a member of Congress provides that cannot be found in the private sector is the deference accorded to members of this exclusive club. "The most seductive part of it," a congressman from the Midwest acknowledged, "is the deference. My God, its amazing how many people can never seem to be able to do enough for you, here or when you go home. . . . Maybe I could and maybe I couldn't make more money in private business, but I do know this: I'd never have my ego fed half so grandly."[23] Or as former Senator Larry Pressler from South Dakota commented in 1998 regarding his return to private life after 22 years in Congress: "I feel like Cinderella after the ball. Poof! . . . Overnight my staff dropped from more than 100 down to one.

---

[23]*New York Times*, May 30, 1978.

My personal assistants disappeared into thin air. . . . Christmas season is an eye opener. The traditional flood of holiday cards has dwindled to about one-fourth of the senatorial level. And speaking of cards, I now hand out business cards. United States Senators don't do business cards. Everyone knows who they are."[24]

While some members of Congress have retired recently, complaining that the job is not as rewarding as it used to be, there is no lack of applicants to replace them. Congress continues to be filled with professional politicians, who view their job in Congress as their career. Even those members elected to Congress promising to leave after serving for a certain number of terms find the rewards of office so enticing they want to extend their stay beyond what they said would be their limit. Indeed, political scientist David R. Mayhew argues that most of the behavior of representatives and senators follows from their principal goal of getting reelected. In pursuit of this goal, members of Congress will try to generate favorable publicity that will impress voters back home, claim credit for benefits that they bring back to their district, respond to interest groups that can supply them with money for their campaigns, and avoid controversial issues that might offend voters.[25]

Political scientist Morris Fiorina found that the electoral connection between voters and Congress is based more on solving problems that constituents have with federal agencies, such as replacing a lost Social Security check, than on taking coherent and consistent positions on political issues. More and more members of Congress, according to Fiorina, prefer "to be reelected as an errand boy than not be reelected at all."[26] One House member told Richard F. Fenno, Jr., who studied what representatives did back in their local districts, "This is a business, and like any other business you have to make time and motion studies" as to what activities are most electorally rewarding.[27] Since the first order of business is to stay in business by getting elected, representatives develop what Fenno called a "home style," calculated to make members identify with voters in their district.

MONEY AND CONGRESSIONAL ELECTIONS

But all of this—developing a home style, getting and keeping your name before the voters, satisfying various constituencies back in your district—costs money . . . lots of money. Congressional candidates have to raise their own

[24]*New York Times,* August 17, 1998.

[25]David R. Mayhew, *Congress: The Electoral Connection* (New Haven, Conn.: Yale University Press, 1979).

[26]Morris Fiorina, *Congress: Keystone of the Washington Establishment* (New Haven, Conn.: Yale University Press, 1977), pp. 36–37.

[27]Richard F. Fenno, Jr., *Home Style: House Members in Their Districts* (Boston: Little, Brown, 1978).

money and organize their own campaigns. Their success depends in no small part on how effective they are at these tasks. In order to be a credible candidate, as opposed to one who can be dismissed, a candidate for the House needs about $600,000 to wage a plausible campaign, while a candidate for a Senate seat needs $2 million to be taken seriously. In comparison, when Abraham Lincoln ran for Congress in 1846, he had only one campaign expense—a barrel of cider. Candidates need to raise so much money not because they want to, but because they are afraid not to. Campaign fundraising follows the same logic as the arms race: Incumbents and challengers alike try to build up their arsenals and raise more money in order to prevent their opponent from gaining a financial advantage. Fear ratchets up the cost of campaigns to higher and higher levels. Most of these funds are spent for television advertisements in order to enhance name recognition and image rather than discuss substantive issues.

The sheer cost of running for office has many consequences. Members of Congress and their staff devote a great deal of time to raising money. Congressional candidates are on the circuit continuously asking for money, attending fund-raisers, and appealing to lobbyists. It does not matter whether a member of Congress has a safe seat and faces only token opposition, or won by a narrow margin in the last election and can expect another close contest. Either way the member will be out raising money relentlessly. While members from competitive seats are out raising money to hold off capable rivals, members from safe seats are building up war chests in order to discourage opponents and those who would invest in them. In 1998, about 100 incumbents in the House either ran uncontested or faced only token opposition. This did not stop these easy winners from raising $400,000 on average to defeat their phantom opponents.[28]

Funds are targeted to members on key committees. Journalist Elizabeth Drew has observed that "serving on some congressional committees is more lucrative—the term is actually used on Capitol Hill—than it is on others, the most lucrative being the House Ways and Means and the Senate Finance Committees, which have jurisdiction over tax legislation, and the House Energy and Commerce Committee and the Senate Committee on Commerce, Science and Transportation. The Commerce Committees have jurisdiction over, among other things, regulatory policy affecting business."[29]

The list of congressional donors is very long, and it reflects local as well as national interests. Money often flows into a representative's or senator's campaign coffers from beyond the district or state he or she represents. Interest groups contribute money to Congress members who sit on committees with jurisdiction over issues that affect them. Thus, members of the House Energy and Commerce Committee receive donations from the milk industry;

[28]*New York Times*, November 1, 1998.

[29]Elizabeth Drew, "Politics and Money," *New Yorker*, December 6, 1982, 123.

commodity exchanges; poultry and livestock producers; the automobile, chemical, and computer industries; real estate and construction; hospitals; gun groups; hotel industries; and unions—among others. The committee system, in which committees have jurisdiction over specific policy areas, makes it easy for groups to target their contributions to legislators who sit on committees and subcommittees that have jurisdiction over issues of concern to them. Most of these sources of funds are invisible to the average voter; and most buy access to the Congress member on behalf of issues that are of narrow concern to a particular group.

The high cost of running for office affects not only how members spend their time and which groups they respond to, but who is elected to Congress. Money follows power. Contributors want a return on their investment. Since incumbents win nine out of ten House races and three out of four Senate races, they receive most of the money contributed to congressional candidates. The gap in campaign contributions between incumbents and challengers is wide and getting wider with each new election. In 1998, the gap in fund-raising increased to about four dollars for incumbents to every one dollar a challenger took in, while on the Senate side incumbents raised twice as much as their opponents. Money is so critical to making a race involving an incumbent competitive that political scientists have found a direct relationship between the amount of money challengers raise and their odds of winning. Money permits challengers to escape obscurity, to get known and be recognized by voters—something incumbents already enjoy from years of service in their district. The problem is that so few challengers can raise enough money to be a serious threat.[30] The fund-raising advantage incumbents enjoy explains, in part, why such a large proportion of them win and why most congressional elections are not really competitive.[31]

SAFE SEATS AND TURNOVER

Elections are mechanisms designed to hold Congress accountable to the voters, to ensure its representativeness. In 1787, George Washington endorsed the two-year term for members of the House of Representatives, expecting the House would turn over rapidly in membership. Power, he wrote, "is entrusted for certain defined purposes, and for a certain limited period . . . and, whenever it is executed contrary to [the public] interest, or not agreeable to their wishes, their servants can and undoubtedly will be recalled." Washington's expectation has not been borne out. In the nineteenth century, congressional turnover was very high; in 1870, more than half of

---

[30]Jacobson, *Politics of Congressional Elections*, pp. 39–42.

[31]Gary Jacobson, *Money in Congressional Elections* (New Haven, Conn.: Yale University Press, 1980).

the representatives sent to the House were newly elected. By 1900, new members comprised less than one-third; by 1940, less than one-quarter; and by 1988, less than one-tenth. Congress has become a career in which representatives and senators expect to serve long tenures.

The immutable nature of Congress—that is, its unchanging membership composed of recurrent Democratic majorities—elicited demands from Republicans in the 1990s for a constitutional amendment that would limit the number of terms a member of Congress could serve. Republicans argued that term limits would make Congress more responsive by bringing new blood into it.[32] Yet even as Republicans were demanding term limits, elections were imposing their own form of term limits, creating turnover in Congress and making a constitutional amendment unnecessary. Less than one-third of the House members and less than one-half of the Senate who were in the 101st Congress, which opened in 1989, were still in office when the 106th Congress convened in 1999.

Surprisingly, the arrival of so many new faces in Congress did not come at the expense of incumbents. Congressional freshmen were much more likely to arrive by winning open seats in which the incumbent was not running than they were by defeating a member seeking reelection. Incumbents have not become more vulnerable. Instead, retirements have increased the supply of open seats for new members to fill. Retirements prompted by the relentless demands of fund-raising, redistricting that assigned incumbents to new districts, a growing incivility in Congress, and premonitions of defeat in the next election temporarily created an unusually large supply of open seats. For example, in the 1994 elections, which saw Republicans win a majority in the House for the first time in 40 years, 84 percent of all incumbent House Democrats were reelected. Much of the Republicans' success in that election can be attributed to their winning 39 of the 52 open-seat House contests in that election—a success rate of 75 percent.

In 1998, only 34 seats were open, indicating that the cycle of turnover that began in 1992 may have run its course. Ninety-eight percent of all House incumbents won in 1998—one of the highest reelection rates ever recorded—with 100 of them either running unopposed or facing no major party opposition. The 1998 congressional campaign, the most expensive in history, resulted in very few changes to either chamber. The 2000 election results were no different. There were only 35 open-seat races, and 98 percent of all House incumbents were victorious. Only 6 out of 400 incumbents lost their seats. Incumbency remains a powerful electoral asset because incumbents enjoy an enormous financial advantage over their opponents, they have access to perquisites such as mailing privileges and staff with which to contact and serve voters back home, and they come from districts that are disposed already to vote for members of their party. With the decline in the number of

[32]In 1995, House Republicans voted for a constitutional amendment imposing term limits, but the bill died in the Senate. As it turned out, the Supreme Court ruled in *U.S. Term Limits v. Thornton* (1995) that term limits are unconstitutional.

retirements and the continuing power of incumbency, the cycle of turnover in Congress that began in 1992 may have ended already.

Not only do incumbents continue to win, but also they continue to win big. The number of marginal seats, where the winner received less than 55 percent of the votes, has declined. For example, in the 2000 elections, the margin of victory was 6 percent or less in only 24 out of 435 House races, or about 5 percent of all House elections. Conversely, the number of safe seats, those that are not very competitive, remains high. The electorally volatile 1990s, which saw Democratic majorities in the House and Senate replaced by new Republican majorities, have been no different. Close to two-thirds of all House incumbents won with 60 percent of the vote or more in 1992 and 1994, while almost three-quarters won by that safe margin in 1996 and 1998. Senate elections tend to be more competitive and the incumbency advantage less powerful than in the House. Senate incumbents face more experienced, better-financed opponents, and their statewide constituencies are large enough that one party does not dominate them so clearly, as is often true in smaller House districts.

Regardless of how large the margin of victory was in the last election, no district is ever completely safe. Roughly one out of every three House members is eventually thrown out of office by voters either in a primary or in a general election.[33] In addition, Gary C. Jacobson found that the interelection vote swing for incumbents has been increasing. Congressional voting has become more volatile. Incumbents who win easily in one election can no longer feel secure given the larger swing in the vote from one election to the next. The 17 House incumbents who lost in 1992 found little protection in the fact that they won by an average of 64.1 percent of the vote in 1990.[34]

Still the advantages of incumbency continue to hold. Nine out of ten House members and three out of four senators will be reelected to office. The number of truly competitive congressional contests remains low. Safe seats continue to predominate, even if those occupying the seats are less assured they will remain safe for long. Elections do an imperfect job of translating political and social change into the composition of Congress, which, in the absence of retirement, remains slow to turn over. Who are these members of Congress that generally enjoy long tenures and become, using Morris Fiorina's term, "keystones" of the Washington Establishment?

MEMBERS OF CONGRESS

The ideal representative body mirrors the population as a whole. According to Nye Bevan, a leading British politician in the 1940s, "Election is only one part of representation. It becomes full representation only if the elected

[33]Robert S. Erikson, "Is There Such a Thing As a Safe Seat," *Polity* 8 (Summer 1976): 623.

[34]Jacobson's findings are discussed in John R. Wright, *Interest Groups and Congress: Lobbying, Contributions and Influence* (Boston: Allyn & Bacon, 1996), p. 84.

person speaks with the authentic accents of those who have elected him."[35] No legislature in the world has the exact demographic profile of the citizens who vote for its members. Moreover, not only is perfect symmetry between representatives and the represented unlikely, but also the interests of the population as a whole can still be represented without it. Fair enough—but a disproportionately unrepresentative legislature is likely to leave many members of the population without representatives who even minimally comprehend their life situations and needs, while others who are overrepresented are likely to have their views taken into account as a matter of course, sometimes without the representatives even being aware of their own predispositions.

Whether representatives should reflect the demographic profile of the people they represent is not simply a philosophical or theoretical issue. Since the Civil Rights movement, it is an issue that has drawn the attention of state legislatures and the Supreme Court. Following the Voting Rights Act of 1965, the black electorate in the South increased significantly, but few blacks actually won elections in that region. Racially polarized voting and the drawing of district lines so as to dilute the black vote created a conspicuous gap between the large size of the black electorate and the small number of elected black officials in the South. For example, in 1972, blacks comprised about 25 percent of the electorate in Mississippi. Yet Mississippi had no black representatives in Congress, only 1 black representative in its 174-member state legislature, and only 8 black county supervisors out of a total of 410 county supervisory positions in the state.[36] As a result, civil rights lawyers filed suit, claiming that Mississippi's discriminatory districting plans made black votes ineffective and that such plans violated the Voting Rights Act. The courts and the Justice Department agreed with the black plaintiffs who had brought suit and promoted the creation of districts in which minorities would comprise the majority. They expected these districts to elect black officials, which would help bring the number of black elected officials more into line with the proportion of black voters in Mississippi. By 1979, the number of blacks in the Mississippi state legislature had grown to 15, and there were now 27 black county supervisors.[37] (For a list of minorities who have served in the U.S. Senate, see Figure 7–3.)

Once the courts approved racial gerrymandering—that is, drawing district lines with the intent of creating districts where blacks comprised the majority—the number of elected black officials increased.[38] The most

---

[35]Quoted in Percy Allum, *State and Society in Western Europe* (Malden, Mass.: Blackwell, 1995), p. 325.

[36]Frank R. Parker, *Black Votes Count: Political Empowerment in Mississippi in 1965* (Chapel Hill: University of North Carolina Press, 1990), p. 31.

[37]Ibid., p. 127.

[38]Racial gerrymandering in the South, concentrating blacks in districts that would increase the chances of electing black officials, actually gave Republican candidates in the South a terrific boost. Concentrating reliable Democratic black voters in one district reduced the number of votes for Democrats in surrounding districts, leading to Republican victories.

■ FIGURE 7-3

MINORITIES IN THE SENATE

African-Americans
Hiram R. Revels (R–Mississippi), 1870–1871
Blanche K. Bruce (R–Mississippi), 1875–1881
Edward W. Brooke (R–Massachusetts), 1967–1979
Carol Moseley-Braun (D–Illinois), 1993–1999

Asian-Americans
Daniel K. Akaka (D–Hawaii), 1990–
Hiram L. Fong (R–Hawaii), 1959–1977
Samuel I. Hayakawa (R–California), 1977–1983
Daniel K. Inouye (D–Hawaii), 1963–
Spark M. Matsunaga (D–Hawaii), 1977–1990

Hispanic-Americans
Dennis Chavez (D–New Mexico), 1935–1962
Octaviano Larrazolo (R–New Mexico), 1928–1929

Native-American Indian
Charles Curtis (R–Kansas), 1907–1913; 1915–1929 (Kaw)
Robert Owen (D–Oklahoma), 1907–1925 (Cherokee)
Ben Nighthorse Campbell (R–Colorado), 1993– (Northern Cheyenne)

obvious example of racial gerrymandering occurred in North Carolina when the 12th Congressional District used Interstate 85—the northbound lane in some counties and the southbound lane in others—to put black communities in Durham, Winston-Salem, and Charlotte, which were 150 miles apart, into one congressional district. But the Supreme Court has since drawn back from its earlier view and handed down decisions in 1995 and 1996 that rejected using race "as a predominant factor" in drawing congressional districts—even though race was used by whites previously to reduce the number of black elected officials. The Court is no longer willing to approve obvious racial gerrymandering and confirm redistricting plans that would help blacks receive representation roughly proportional to their statewide population.

It is emphatically *not* the case that, just because someone comes from a certain social background, they will necessarily promote the interests of that group: that former car dealers in Congress will promote the interests of car dealers or that wealthy members of Congress will automatically defend the interests of the rich. For example, Senators Jay Rockefeller and Ted Kennedy come from very wealthy families and are among the leading advocates of social programs for the poor. Similarly, a white member of Congress can do a very good job representing a black-majority district, as Lindy Boggs did for a number of years (1972–89), and a black member of Congress can do a very good job representing a district where whites significantly outnumber blacks, as Ron Dellums did for a number of years (1971–98). The effects of social background on congressional decision making are more subtle than that. The social background of members of Congress is important because they bring assumptions to their work based on their life experiences. Inasmuch as some life experiences are more likely to be found in Congress than others, members of Congress are more likely to be sensitive to, to be intuitively aware of, some issues more than others. Consequently, it matters whether the social backgrounds of members of Congress are roughly similar to those of the people they ostensibly represent. It is certainly true that members of Congress, like all of us, are able to appreciate and understand issues that go beyond their own limited experience. But social background makes a difference in whether Congress members will have to make that extra effort or will gravitate naturally to the responses and issues they are familiar with based on their life experiences.

John Adams, the second president of the United States, once said that the legislature should be "an exact portrait in miniature, of the people at large."[39] It is ironic that Congress, our most democratic institution, is so far from this ideal and so demographically unrepresentative of the people its members are supposed to represent. Congress contains a much higher proportion of white, male, educated, rich, professional and businesspeople than the population as a whole. While Congress is less male and less white than it used to be, the average social background of members of Congress still differs strikingly from that of the rest of the population. For example, blacks comprise 12 percent of the electorate. Following the 2000 elections, they occupied 9 percent of the seats in the House and no seats in the Senate. Hispanics are 8 percent of the electorate, and they occupied 4 percent of the seats in the House and, like blacks, no seats in the Senate. Women make up 52 percent of all eligible voters, and they held about 14 percent of the seats in the House and about the same percentage in the Senate. (See Figure 7–4 for a list of women senators.)

A great gap between Congress members and the people they represent lies in class status. In 1998, one out of every four members of Congress was a millionaire. The vast majority of members of Congress are lawyers, bankers, or businesspeople. Very few people from working-class occupations are ever seated. Only when electoral realignments occur, when new groups break through the party system, has the virtual monopoly that upper-class people have on seats in Congress been disrupted. Only during such turbulent periods have legislators from the lower class replaced the wealthy in winning congressional seats.[40]

---

[39]Quoted in Robert B. Kuttner, *Everything for Sale* (New York: Knopf, 1996), p. 349.

[40]Lester G. Seligman and Michael R. King, "Political Realignments and Recruitment to the U.S. Congress, 1870–1970," in *Realignment in American Politics: Toward a Theory,* ed. Bruce A. Campbell and Richard J. Trilling (Austin: University of Texas Press, 1980), pp. 157–75.

■ FIGURE 7–4

Rebecca Latimer Felton (D–Georgia), 1922

Hattie Wyatt Caraway (D–Arkansas), 1931–1945

Rose McConnell Long (D–Louisiana), 1936–1937

Dixie Bibb Graves (D–Alabama), 1937–1938

Gladys Pyle (R–South Dakota), 1938–1939

Vera Cahalan Bushfield (R–South Dakota), 1948

Margaret Chase Smith (R–Maine), 1949–1973

Eva Kelley Bowring (R–Nebraska), 1954

Hazel Hempel Abel (R–Nebraska), 1954

Maurine Brown Neuberger (D–Oregon), 1960–1967

Elaine S. Edwards (D–Louisiana), 1972

Muriel Humphrey (D–Minnesota), 1978

Maryon Allen (D–Alabama), 1978

Nancy Landon Kassebaum (R–Kansas), 1978–1997

Paula Hawkins (R–Florida), 1981–1987

Barbara Mikulski (D–Maryland), 1987–

Jocelyn Burdick (D–North Dakota), 1992

Dianne Feinstein (D–California), 1993–

Barbara Boxer (D–California), 1993–

Carol Moseley-Braun (D–Illinois), 1993–1999

Patty Murray (D–Washington), 1993–

Kay Bailey Hutchison (R–Texas), 1993–

Olympia Jean Snowe (R–Maine), 1995–

Sheila Frahm (R–Kansas), 1996

Mary Landrieu (D–Louisiana), 1997–

Susan Collins (R–Maine), 1997–

Blanche Lincoln (D–Arkansas), 1999–

Maria Cantwell (D–Washington), 2001–

Jean Carnahan (D–Missouri), 2001–

Hillary Rodham Clinton (D–New York), 2001–

Debbie Stabenow (D–Michigan), 2001–

Congress, in short, does not look like America. As a result, underrepresented groups risk having their concerns misunderstood or left out entirely.[41]

THE LEGISLATIVE PROCESS

While the social background of Congress members influences what they do, more critical in our view for the shaping of legislation are the ways in which Congress is organized and the formal and informal rules that govern its decision making. Seemingly archaic and technical procedural rules, such as the terms under which the Senate and House consider a bill, can determine the fate of legislation. Representative John Dingell of Michigan reportedly said, "If you let me write the procedure and I let you write the substance, I'll [beat] you every time."[42] For example, the key roll call vote on President Reagan's economic program in 1981 was a procedural vote in the House. At issue was whether the president's budget would be considered in a single up-or-down vote on the entire package or in a series of separate votes. Liberals, who proposed a series of separate votes, knew that, if legislators were required to vote explicitly to cut specific programs, they would not do so. The president's supporters also knew that putting all the cuts into a single package offered legislators protection because it would prevent specific reductions from being traced to a legislator's specific vote. "Once the conservatives prevailed on the procedural point (by four votes)," Douglas Arnold writes, "the substantive battle was over."[43]

Although each member of Congress has only one vote, some members are more powerful than others. The internal distribution of power among members is influenced by the structures and procedures of Congress. Legislators have different amounts of power depending on which committee they sit on, whether they are a committee or subcommittee chair, whether they are a member of the majority party, and whether they are a party leader. The

---

[41]Sometimes a legislator's personal experience shapes his or her behavior in not so subtle ways. John Dingell (D.–Mich.), chair of the House Commerce Committee's Subcommittee on Energy and Power in the 1970s and a proponent of price controls on oil, explained how his personal experience led him to switch positions to favor decontrol of oil prices. Dingell discovered from his own experience how higher energy prices could lead to greater effort at energy conservation. Dingell explained his conversion to decontrol of oil prices thusly: "I moved into a little town house and it costs me $70 a month to heat it. Then I insulated and caulked to beat hell and double glazed the windows, and all of a sudden it's costing me $40. Quoted in R. Douglas Arnold, *The Logic of Congressional Action* (New Haven: Yale University Press, 1990), pp. 236–37.

[42]Quoted in C. Lawrence Evans and Walter J. Oleszek, "Congressional Tsunami? The Politics of Congressional Reform," in *Congress Reconsidered*, 6th ed., ed. Lawrence C. Dodd and Bruce I. Oppenheimer (Washington, D.C.: Congressional Quarterly Press, 1997), p. 193.

[43]Douglas Arnold, *The Logic of Congressional Action* (New Haven, Conn.: Yale University Press, 1990), p. 105.

procedures and rules of the House and the Senate determine the powers invested in these positions and are never neutral. Some groups win and some groups lose depending on how the rules distribute power within Congress. The structure, procedures, and rules of Congress, or what we might call the rules of the game, "give different interests differential chances of attaining favorable policy outcomes."[44] For this reason, the legislative process is constantly in flux as groups seek to adjust the rules, procedures, and organization of the House and the Senate in order to advance their interests. For example, liberals eager to curb the power of the conservative committee chairs who thwarted their policy goals precipitated a wave of internal reforms to Congress in the 1970s. Similarly, the first day of business when Republicans became the majority in 1995 was devoted to changing the rules of the House that had been set by the Democrats. After the new 104th Congress was gaveled to order on January 4, 1995, Republicans, as the new majority party, proceeded to reduce congressional staff; impose term limits on committee chairs, subcommittee chairs, and the Speaker; make Congress subject to federal labor and civil rights laws; eliminate some committees; and change the names and jurisdictions of still other committees. And they did not stop until two o'clock the next morning! Political struggle over the legislative process occurs, introducing change into the way Congress is organized and operates, because this affects legislative outcomes. Congress always is reforming itself, as groups seek to change the process by which legislation is made in order to change the results.

HOW A BILL BECOMES LAW

The legislative process begins with the submission of a bill to Congress. The identical bill is introduced in both the House and the Senate for consideration by both chambers. Most bills are introduced without any expectation of success. More than 6,000 pieces of legislation are introduced into Congress each year, with fewer than 400 actually having a chance of passage. Only members of the Senate and the House may submit bills. When legislators introduce a bill in Congress, they often are acting on behalf of constituents or interest groups or a federal agency or the president, or they may even be acting out of their own personal convictions.

The bills that have the greatest chance of success and that generally define the agenda of Congress are those submitted by legislators on behalf of the president. The Office of Management and Budget (OMB), together with the congressional liaison staff in the Executive Office, coordinates the executive's legislative efforts. OMB acts as a clearinghouse, reviewing legislative requests from federal agencies and departments to ensure they conform to

---

[44]Ellen M. Immergut, *Health Politics: Interests and Institutions in Western Europe* (New York: Cambridge University Press, 1992), p. 29.

the president's program, while the legislative affairs officers in the White House coordinate presidential lobbying of Congress.

Once a bill is introduced in the House and the Senate, it is referred to a committee for consideration. There bills proposed by the president are almost always modified substantially. Committee referrals made by the House Speaker and Senate majority leader are generally routine. Farm bills go to the House Agriculture Committee and the Senate Agriculture Committee, tax bills go to the House Ways and Means Committee and the Senate Finance Committee, and so on.[45] But in the House, the Speaker now enjoys more discretion than in the past on where to assign a bill. Part of this is the result of more issues, such as energy and environmental policy, that cut across existing committee lines in Congress. In addition, the Speaker was granted more discretion to assign bills to one or multiple committees as a way to augment the powers of that office. Bill referral is important because a legislative proposal might receive a warmer reception in one committee than it would receive in another.

Congress at work, Woodrow Wilson once said, is Congress in committees. Committees are legislative gatekeepers, "little legislatures," that perform the bulk of the legislative work in Congress. They collect information through hearings and investigations, they draft legislation in what are called markup sessions, and they report legislation to the floor of their respective chambers.[46] While it is unusual for the House or the Senate to review legislation that has not been reported to them from one of their committees, it is less unusual than in the past.

Once a committee receives a bill, it is assigned to the appropriate subcommittee for consideration. According to congressional scholars Christopher J. Deering and Steven S. Smith, "[S]subcommittees assume the initial responsibility for discussing and designing legislation, thereby setting the agenda for subsequent stages in the legislative process."[47] Subcommittees conduct hearings to educate legislators about the issue covered by a bill and to give them a sense of public reactions to it. At hearings, subcommittee members listen to testimony from policy experts, interest groups that would be affected by the bill, members of the general public with an interest in the issue, and other members of Congress and administration officials with a position on the bill. The process of holding hearings and taking testimony is not as disinterested and impartial as it sounds. Committees and subcommittees generally use hearings to "garner support for the views they already hold" through the witnesses they choose to invite to give testimony.[48]

---

[45]Congressional Quarterly, *How Congress Works,* 1st ed. (Washington, D.C.: Congressional Quarterly Press, 1998), p. 61.

[46]Christopher J. Deering and Steven S. Smith, *Committees in Congress,* 3rd ed. (Washington, D.C.: Congressional Quarterly Press, 1997), pp. 11–20.

[47]Ibid., p. 156.

[48]Bryan Jones, Frank Baumgartner, and Jeffrey Talbot, "The Destruction of Issue Monopolies in Congress," *American Political Science Review* 87 (September 1993): 657–71.

Following hearings, the subcommittee members will mark up the bill, amending it according to their judgment on what to retain from the original bill. Presuming the subcommittee still finds merit in the measure, the subcommittee reports its marked-up version of the bill to the full committee. The full committee may then repeat the process of hearings and markup that took place in subcommittee, or it may ratify the bill that the subcommittee marked up, or, as happens with over 90 percent of the bills it receives, it may decide not to act, effectively killing the measure. If the full committee decides to act, it will frequently engage in some markup itself, amending the subcommittee's proposal so that it now satisfies a majority of the members on the committee.[49]

The bill is then placed on the House and Senate calendars, but bills do not come to the floor of each chamber in the order in which they were received. Some never come to the House or Senate floor at all. In the House, the Rules Committee determines which bills will come to the House floor, when they will be scheduled, and under what conditions they will be debated. In the past, the Rules Committee used its power to control the flow of legislation from committees to the House floor in order to kill bills it opposed, even those supported by the majority party. But House reforms in the 1970s made the Rules Committee an arm of the party leadership by giving the Speaker the right to appoint members of the majority party to the committee.

The rules under which the House considered legislation began to change in the 1970s. Previously, legislation often came to the House floor under open rules from the Rules Committee, with no restrictions on germane amendments. But as the House became more partisan and divided in the 1980s and 1990s, the Rules Committee attached more restrictive rules to more legislation. Restrictive rules limited the time for debate and the amendments that could be offered on the floor of the House. House Republicans, who were in the minority, complained that such restrictive rules stifled debate and prevented them from amending legislation that came out of Democratic-controlled committees. But when Republicans became the majority in 1994, they used the Rules Committee in the same partisan way the Democrats had to prevent the opposing party from delaying and amending the majority party's program on the House floor. Bills came out of the Rules Committee under the Republicans with the same restrictive rules that they had complained about so vehemently when they were in the minority.

The Senate has no equivalent committee to schedule and set the terms of debate on the Senate floor. Scheduling is largely the work of the Senate majority leader, but he or she requires unanimous consent to bring a bill up for Senate consideration. Individual senators who want to prevent passage of a bill can filibuster—that is, hold the Senate floor and not give it up until the offending bill is removed from consideration. Nor does the Senate limit and set the terms of debate on the Senate floor, as the Rules Committee does for

---

[49]The process is a bit different in the Senate, where few subcommittees engage in markup. In the Senate, subcommittees generally hold hearings, leaving markup to the full committee.

legislation considered by the House. The rules of the Senate are much more freewheeling than those for the House.

Whereas the versions of a bill introduced in both the Senate and the House are the same, they may look very different after they come out of the committee process in both chambers. House and Senate committees mark up a bill without reference to each other. House and Senate committees follow their own majorities when making changes to the bill, and amendments to it on the floor of the House and the Senate proceed independently. The result is that the version of the bill passed by the House will not look the same as the one passed by the Senate. The president can sign only bills that have been passed in identical form by both houses of Congress. Differences between the House and Senate versions of the bill are resolved in conference committees. Conference committees, composed of House and Senate members selected by the Speaker and the Senate majority leader, respectively, meet to reconcile differences in the versions of a bill passed by the House and the Senate.

If conference can resolve the differences between the House and Senate versions of the bill, the new, reconciled version of the legislation is then sent back to the House and the Senate to be voted up or down, without amendment. If both houses vote to accept the conference report—that is, to accept identical versions of the bill—the final bill is then sent to the president for signature. The bill becomes law when the president signs it, or it becomes law without the president's signature ten days after the president receives it, provided Congress is still in session. The president may also veto the bill, which can be overridden by two-thirds votes in both the House and the Senate.

The legislative process sketched above is noteworthy for the number of choke points, opportunities to block legislation, it contains. "It is very easy to defeat a bill in Congress," President John F. Kennedy once observed. "It is much more difficult to pass one."[50] A bill can be waylaid at the subcommittee and committee levels, it may never be scheduled for consideration on the floor of the Senate or the House, it may fail to pass either the Senate or the House, conference may not be able to reconcile differences between the Senate and House versions of the bill, the Senate or House may find the conference bill objectionable, the president may veto the legislation, and the Senate and House may be unable to marshal the two-thirds majority necessary to overturn a presidential veto. And all of these potential veto points must be successfully negotiated within the two-year life span of a single Congress, or else the measure has to be introduced and the whole procedure repeated again when a new Congress is seated.

The legislative process we have just outlined is so daunting that Congress deviates from it quite often to avoid its tendency toward gridlock. According to congressional scholar Barbara Sinclair, unorthodox lawmaking has become routine as Congress increasingly circumvents its own procedures.

---

[50]Quoted in Congressional Quarterly, *How Congress Works*, p. 51.

Committees are bypassed more frequently, bills are now more likely to be re-worked after they emerge from committee, the content of legislation is more likely to be worked out in summits among executive and legislative leaders, and omnibus legislation, in which disparate bills are offered together in one legislative package, is now more common. Sinclair argues that it is no longer accurate to speak of one legislative process; rather, there are now many.[51] The legislative process has become a maze in which bills may now take many different paths through Congress on the way to enactment. The growth of unorthodox lawmaking has mitigated to some extent the tendency toward blockage and gridlock in Congress. But the legislative process as a whole still remains a challenging obstacle course for those who try to run it.

A legislative process loaded with so many points where new legislative proposals can be stopped is not politically neutral, but serves to protect the status quo. The legislative process puts these roadblocks in the way of those who seek to use the government to bring about change. Groups that are sys-tematically disadvantaged or that depend on political power and public pol-icy to offset the economic power of corporations and other dominant actors often find themselves stymied by a legislative process that creates so many opportunities for blockage and defeat. They must build winning coalitions within both the House and the Senate at the subcommittee level, at the com-mittee level, on the floor of each chamber, within the conference committee, and within the executive branch. Opponents, on the other hand, need to win only once at any level to defeat the bill. A legislative process that creates so many opportunities for obstruction, that promotes failure rather than suc-cess, makes it difficult for the disadvantaged to enlist public power against corporate private power.

Below we examine the legislative process in more detail as it operates within the separate chambers of the Senate and the House of Representatives.

THE SENATE

The fate of the congressional Republicans' Contract with America reveals much about the different rules and culture of the House and the Senate. In 1994, Republicans in the House of Representatives acted swiftly to seize the legislative initiative and pass the ten points in the Contract with America. But the Republican juggernaut stumbled in the Senate before the president could even consider the legislation. The enthusiasm and kinetic energy of the House collided with the deliberative, obstructionist ways of the Senate. Even though Republicans took control of the Senate for the first time in eight

---

[51]Barbara Sinclair, *Unorthodox Lawmaking: New Legislative Processes in the U.S. Congress* (Washington, D.C.: Congressional Quarterly Press, 1997), p. 7.

years in 1994, the less centralized, more individualistic nature of the Senate prevented Senate Republicans from capitalizing on their new majority status as effectively as House Republicans did. When one freshman Republican senator was asked what it was like to be part of the revolution in Washington that the 1994 class of new Republican legislators was associated with, he answered: "I don't know. I'm in the Senate!"[52]

The Republican victory in 1994 did not mean the same thing in the Senate as it did in the House because dramatic electoral shifts are moderated in the Senate by the fact that only one-third of its seats are up for grabs each election. While the entire House must stand for election every two years and is thus exposed as a body to electoral swings, two-thirds of the Senate is not up for reelection and is insulated from a vengeful electorate. The six-year terms for senators are staggered so that only one-third of all senators face election every two years. Electoral forces thus wind their way through the Senate more slowly than they do the House. In addition, the fact that senators represent large, diverse constituencies moderates the politics of senators. Senators have to reach out and satisfy broader electorates, which tends to push them more to the political center than House members are. In these ways, the unique political and institutional characteristics of the Senate contributed to the irony that it was the Republican-controlled Senate, not a Democratic president, that stopped the Contract with America dead in its tracks.[53]

With only 100 members—compared to the House, which has 435—the Senate is a more intimate chamber, providing more latitude for action by individual members. In the past, the Senate's intimacy caused it to resemble a private, exclusive men's club where an elaborate set of formal and informal rules regulated the behavior of club members. In December 1956, newly elected Joseph Clark of Pennsylvania had lunch with an old friend, Senator Hubert Humphrey. Clark reports that he said to Humphrey, "Tell me how to behave when I get to the Senate." "He did—for an hour and a half. I left the luncheon I hope a wiser man, as well briefed as a neophyte seeking admission to a new order can be. In essence he said, 'Keep your mouth shut and your eyes open. It's a friendly, courteous place. You will have no trouble getting along. . . . You will clash on the filibuster rule with Dick Russell and the Southerners as soon as you take the oath of office. Don't let your ideology embitter your personal relationships. It won't if you behave with maturity. . . . And above all keep your mouth shut for awhile.'"[54]

Humphrey advised Clark to abide by the Senate's unwritten rules: Members should work at their legislative tasks, becoming workhorses, not show

[52]Nicol C. Rae, *Conservative Reformers: The Republican Freshmen and the Lessons of the 104th Congress* (New York: Sharpe, 1998), p. 131.

[53]Norman J. Ornstein, Robert L. Peabody, and David W. Rohde, "The U.S. Senate: Toward the Twenty-First Century," in *Congress Reconsidered*, 6th ed., ed. Lawrence C. Dodd and Bruce I. Oppenheimer (Washington, D.C.: Congressional Quarterly Press, 1997), pp. 1–2.

[54]Joseph Clark, Congress: *The Sapless Branch* (New York: Harper & Row, 1964), p. 2.

horses; they should specialize in matters connected to their committee assignment and of direct interest to their state; they should be courteous to other senators and avoid personal conflicts; they should help colleagues when possible and keep bargains; and they should expect to serve a period of apprenticeship, during which they learn the Senate's customs.[55] Senators were expected to defer to senior members, be restrained in their use of power so as not to obstruct the work of the Senate, and be loyal to the institution. The Senate was "like a small town," according to accounts of those who served in it in the 1950s. Power in the town was distributed unequally, in that it was reserved for committee chairs with seniority. The committee chair set the committee's agenda, called committee meetings, appointed subcommittee chairs, and controlled the committee staff. Residents, who were all equal according to the Constitution, accepted this inequality because they expected to accumulate seniority and become a committee chair themselves someday. In the meantime, they were supposed to bide their time, concentrate on their own business, take pride in the Senate, and be courteous to their colleagues.

Today senators are more rude and less familiar with each other, more equal in power and less restrained in using it, more individualistic and less willing to cooperate, more willing to poach on each other's business and less willing to work hard at their own, and more interested in drawing attention to themselves than in the past. The customs and norms that governed behavior within the chamber have changed dramatically in the last 40 years.

The apprenticeship norm was one of the first Senate norms to go. According to three congressional scholars, "[N]ot only do junior members not want or feel the need for an apprenticeship, but also the senior members do not expect them to do so."[56] A mark of the decline of the apprenticeship norm is that freshmen are now more likely than in the past to sponsor amendments to legislation on the floor of the Senate.[57] In 1994, the 11 new Republican senators made their presence felt immediately. They organized their own group, "The Freshman Focus," to make their concerns known within the Republican Senate caucus, and they sponsored a "variety of legislative initiatives, including constitutional amendments to impose term limits and require a balanced budget."[58]

Another Senate norm that has disappeared is courtesy. As ideological differences among senators have increased, so has the level of incivility among

[55]Donald R. Mathews, *U.S. Senators and Their World* (New York: Random House, 1960).

[56]Norman J. Ornstein, Robert L. Peabody, and David Rohde, "The Changing Senate: From the 1950s to the 1970s," in *Congress Reconsidered*, ed. Lawrence C. Dodd and Bruce I. Oppenheimer (New York: Praeger, 1977), p. 8.

[57]Barbara Sinclair, *The Transformation of the U.S. Senate* (Baltimore: Johns Hopkins University Press, 1989), p. 83.

[58]Ornstein, Peabody, and Rohde, "The U.S. Senate," p. 9.

them. Senator Joseph Biden of Delaware complained in 1982, "There's much less civility than when I got here 10 years ago. . . . Ten years ago you didn't have people calling each other [expletive deleted] and vowing to get each other."[59] Some senators have cited the decline of comity and civility as their reason for retiring from the Senate. The specialization norm is also a thing of the past. It is now standard behavior for senators to venture far from their committee's jurisdiction "to offer large numbers of amendments in a wide variety of issue areas." Senators are no longer reluctant to sponsor amendments to measures from committees on which they do not serve.[60] Even the norm of dedicating yourself to legislative work has receded. While senators in the past devoted themselves to "highly detailed, dull and politically unrewarding" legislative tasks, according to Donald Mathews, senators today leave that to their staff. Now senators are busy being show horses—running for president, attending fund-raisers, appearing on television—not workhorses—concentrating on legislation.

Finally, the reciprocity norm is also in eclipse. The Senate permits unlimited debate, allowing members to hold the Senate floor and tie up the Senate's business with filibusters. It was previously understood that individual senators would restrain themselves and not obstruct the work of the Senate with filibusters except when important principles were at stake. But filibusters are now more common than in the past. The average number of filibusters in the 1970s was five per year. Twenty years later, in the 1990s, the number of filibusters per year had increased by 300 percent. And instead of using them only on issues involving matters of principle, senators now filibuster relatively mundane concerns. Filibusters are now so common that the bar for passing legislation in the Senate has been raised in practice to 60 votes, the number you need to bring cloture, as opposed to the simple majority the Constitution requires to pass a bill. This is not immaterial. Bills that could get a majority of votes and would have passed the Senate cannot get 60 votes to invoke cloture and are thus defeated. For example, campaign finance reform was defeated twice in the Senate, first in 1998 and then again in 1999. Even though supporters had a majority of votes to pass these bills, they could not muster the supermajority of three-fifths required to stop a filibuster by the bill's opponents and bring campaign finance reform to the floor of the Senate for a vote.

Senators do not actually have to filibuster to get their desired results; often the application of what is called a 'hold'—a request not to bring legislation to the floor under the threat of a filibuster—is enough for Senate leaders to try and mollify a senator's concerns so that the rest of the Senate can proceed with its work. Barbara Sinclair found that, in 15 out of 37 filibusters

---

[59]Quoted in Alan Ehrenhalt, "The Senate of the '80s, Team Spirit Has Given Way to Rule by Individuals," *Congressional Quarterly Weekly Report,* September 4, 1982, 2176.

[60]Sinclair, *Transformation of the U.S. Senate,* p. 89.

between 1981 and 1986, senators who filibustered were rewarded for their efforts and received some concession. "When the chance of having such an impact is 40 percent," Sinclair concludes, "the incentives to engage in extended debate are obvious."[61] Consequently, more than one-third of all major legislation encounters some form of extended debate–related problem in the Senate today. But threats to extend debate create resentment against those senators who abuse their power to hold the Senate hostage until their individual concerns are satisfied. One senator told Sinclair that there is a third type of senator, the horse's ass, alongside the workhorse and the show horse. The problem, Sinclair writes, is that the "distinction between a show horse, now acceptable, and a horse's ass, unacceptable, is a good deal less clear than the old workhorse–show horse distinction."[62]

More than Senate customs have changed. First, senators are spread thinner than in the past, serving on many more committees and subcommittees. One result is that their staff, who are not elected and on whom they rely, have become increasingly important. Senators are now generalists, not specialists. [63] In the 106th Congress (1999–2000), the average Senator sat on 3.2 committees and 6.8 subcommittees.[64] When Republicans became the majority in 1994, they reduced the number of Senate subcommittees. But this did not alleviate greatly the scheduling problems (trying to be in two places at once when committee meetings overlapped) and workload problems that so many committee assignments create. But senators are reluctant to reduce their committee assignments. The more committees and subcommittees senators serve on, the more opportunities they have to pursue more issues and get their fingers into more pies.

Finally, central leadership within the Senate remains weak. The vice president is the official president of the Senate, but its real leader is the majority leader, selected by the majority party in the Senate. The majority leader's power is primarily procedural, such as scheduling the Senate's business. Former Senator Alan Cranston of California acknowledged, "A lot of leadership is just housekeeping now. Occasionally you have an opportunity to provide leadership but not that often. The weapons to keep people in line just aren't there."[65] With weak central leadership and the decline of committee chairs, the Senate is a more egalitarian institution than it used to be, with power distributed more evenly among senators than in the past. This has heightened the sense of individualism and independence among senators, with senators now pursuing their own agendas, voting, proposing

---

[61]Ibid., p. 136.

[62]Ibid., p. 97.

[63]Deering and Smith, *Committees in Congress*, pp. 80, 154.

[64]In comparison, the average House member had only half as many committee and subcommittee assignments as the average senator.

[65]Ehrenhalt, "The Senate of the '80s," p. 2179.

amendments to bills on the floor of the Senate, and filibustering according to their own inclinations.

The result of these changes, Sinclair offers, is that the Senate has become more adept at promoting issues and articulating demands. The more even distribution of resources among senators, including committee assignments and staff, as well as the decline of Senate norms that once inhibited certain activities, has empowered 100 senators to promote their own agendas. More issues are pushed than in the past. But such entrepreneurial activity by senators, with each one actively promoting a wide range of issues and threatening to use his or her full powers if the Senate is not accommodating them, may empower each individual senator at the expense of the Senate as an institution. As a result, Sinclair argues, the Senate has become more undisciplined and more inefficient.[66] According to journalist Alan Ehrenhalt, "The more individuals have to be personally satisfied for a bill to be enacted, the more likely it is that there will be none."[67] The unrestrained individualism of the Senate leads to obstructionism. Where it is every senator for himself or herself, it is difficult to legislate, to get things done. As one Republican senator lamented in frustration at the undisciplined, individualistic, inefficient ways of his own institution: "The Democrats are the opposition, but the Senate is the enemy."[68]

The 2000 election results first split the Senate evenly along partisan lines for the first time in the chamber's history as an elected body. With 50

Vice President Richard B. Cheney.

[66]Sinclair, *Transformation of the U.S. Senate,* p. 214.

[67]Ehrenhalt, "The Senate of the '80s," p. 2175.

[68]Quoted in Evans and Oleszek, *Congress Under Fire,* p. 178.

Democrats and 50 Republicans taking Senate seats, party leaders had to negotiate over how committee chairs, money, and staff would be distributed—issues normally decided by the majority party. Because vice president Dick Cheney could vote to break a tie, Senate Republicans were given a slight advantage, but still had to give ground to Democratic demands for equity. In May 2001, Senator James Jeffords of Vermont left the Republican Party to become an Independent, while caucusing with the Democrats for organizational purposes, giving the Democrats control of the chamber and initiating a period of divided government.

THE HOUSE OF REPRESENTATIVES

While the Senate has become less hierarchical, the House has become more so. A series of internal reforms initiated by House Democrats in the 1970s vested power in party leaders within the House of Representatives. The Speaker of the House; the House majority leader, who assists the Speaker in setting strategy; and the majority whip, who lines up votes among the party's rank and file, were empowered to promote goals supported by the Democratic House caucus.[69] Party leadership of the House accelerated when Republicans became the majority in 1994 for the first time in 40 years, permitting them to choose the Speaker. House Republicans selected Newt Gingrich as the new Speaker, and power was concentrated even further in the hands of party leaders under his tenure.[70]

According to political scientist Burdett A. Loomis, the new Republican House majority "centralized leadership authority more firmly than at any time since the overthrow [in 1910] of Speaker Joe Cannon."[71] Republican Party leaders set the agenda for the House, closely supervised the work of committees, and influenced the content of legislation. The shift in power to the party leadership under the Republicans did not depart from, but rather built on a trend that was already evident under the Democrats. However, this was now accentuated and accelerated under Republican control. For example, in a departure from past practices, Speaker Gingrich appointed each committee chair and exerted influence in assigning members to committees. When one committee chair informed Gingrich that he might not be able to meet the Speaker's deadline for getting legislation out of his committee, Gingrich threatened, "If you can't do it . . . I will find someone who will."[72]

---

[69]David W. Rohde, *Parties and Leaders in the Postreform House* (Chicago: University of Chicago Press, 1991).

[70]Evans and Oleszek, *Congress Under Fire*, p. 87.

[71]Burdett A. Loomis, *The Contemporary Congress* (New York: St. Martin's Press, 1996), pp. 128–29.

[72]Quoted in Paul S. Herrnson, "Directing 535 Leading Men and Leading Ladies: Party Leadership in the Modern Congress," in Herbert F. Weisberg and Samuel C. Patterson, eds., *Great Theatre: The American Congress in the 1990s* (New York: Cambridge University Press, 1998), p. 113.

The power concentrated in the hands of Republican Party leaders was to be used to advance only those issues that enjoyed widespread support within their congressional party. Members of the majority party invested power in party leaders in the expectation that centralizing power would move those bills the majority agreed on through the House expeditiously. They were also willing to cede power because they had faith and trust in their leaders. But when party leaders lose the confidence of their party caucus, they may be dethroned. For example, Republicans blamed Newt Gingrich for unexpected Republican losses in the 1998 elections and threatened to remove him from his post. Gingrich saved them the trouble by resigning his Speakership (and his congressional seat).

Party leadership has replaced committee leadership as the locus of power within the House. Prior to the 1970 reforms, committee chairs held power in the House, just as they did in the Senate. Chairs were petty tyrants who ruled over their committees, independent of the party leadership and even the majority sentiment of their own party members. In 1953, George Galloway provided a neat summary of the powers committee chairs wielded:

> Just as the standing committees control legislative action, so the chairmen are masters of their committee. . . . They arrange the agenda of the committees, appoint the subcommittees, and refer bills to them. They decide what pending measures shall be considered and when, call committee meetings, and decide whether or not to hold hearings and when. They approve the lists of scheduled witnesses and authorize staff studies, and preside at committee meetings. They handle reported bills on the floor and participate as principal managers in conference committees. They are in a position to expedite measures they favor and to retard or pigeonhole those they dislike.[73]

Committee members were in thrall to committee chairs, who determined the fate of legislation within their committee's jurisdiction.

Committee chairs were selected by the majority party in Congress on the basis of seniority. Previously, in the early twentieth century, the Speaker had selected committee chairs (a practice revived with Speaker Gingrich). But the House had revolted, stripping the Speaker of this power because it had been used to reward supporters and punish opponents. Contrary to the arbitrary way the Speaker abused this power, seniority was perceived as a fair, apolitical way to distribute influence within the House. The distribution of committee chairs would no longer depend on personal favors or political positions. Power would flow to the member of the majority party with the longest record of service on the committee.

But all rules, even those like seniority, that are designed to be neutral create winners and losers. An unintended consequence of the seniority rule was the distribution of the power in Congress to southern Democrats. Democrats were the majority party in the House for 40 consecutive years, from 1954 to

---

[73]Quoted in Deering and Smith, *Committees in Congress*, p. 32.

1994, and during those years had the votes to select committee chairs from among their members. Southern Democrats were able to build up more seniority in Congress than other Democrats because they came from uncompetitive districts where they faced token Republican opposition, if any at all. Consequently, southern Democrats came to dominate the committee chairs and the most important committees in Congress.

As chairs, southern Democrats used their power to block liberal legislation that northern Democrats supported. In addition, these Dixiecrats often crossed party lines to vote with Republicans. Together southern Democrats and conservative Republicans formed "the conservative coalition," which held the balance of power in Congress in the postwar period. Southern Democrats voted with Republicans against labor legislation and extensions of the welfare state in exchange for Republican votes against civil rights legislation.[74] By the 1960s, the conservative coalition "had become a regular feature of congressional voting and a powerful obstacle to liberal and social legislation," according to political scientist Alan I. Abramowitz.[75] The conservative coalition appeared frequently in congressional voting and often enjoyed success when it did so, thwarting the policy goals of liberal Democrats in Congress.[76]

Liberal Democrats in Congress were irate over the apostasy of their own party's southern congressional delegation. Northern Democrats were increasingly resentful that their numbers were responsible for making their party the majority in the House—and thus able to select the committee chairs—but that southern Democrats dominated these posts through seniority. To add insult to injury, southern Democrats then used their positions to block civil rights, labor, and welfare state legislation that northern Democrats supported. Northern Democrats felt they had done all the hard work of planting the crops, only to see them harvested by southern Democrats and used against them.

Consequently, nonsouthern Democrats sponsored a series of internal reforms that changed the procedures and organization of the House. New rules and procedures, it was hoped, would bring different legislative results. One goal of the reform movement was to reduce the power of committee chairs and make them more responsive to the Democratic House caucus. Committee chairs would now be elected by the entire Democratic caucus in

---

[74]Initially, southern Democrats voted with Republicans only on civil rights and labor issues, but the range of issues on which the conservative coalition appeared expanded in the 1950s and 1960s to include tax, welfare state, and economic policy—bedrock issues for American liberalism. See Ira Katznelson, Kim Geiger, and Daniel Kryder, "Limiting Liberalism: The Southern Veto in Congress," *Political Science Quarterly* 108, no. 2 (Summer 1993): 283–305.

[75]Alan I. Abramowitz, "Is the Revolt Fading: A Note on Party Loyalty Among Southern Congressmen," *Journal of Politics* 42 (May 1980): 568–72.

[76]Alan Draper, "Be Careful What You Wish For . . . : American Liberals and the South," *Southern Studies* 4 (Winter 1993): 309–25.

a secret ballot and would no longer be awarded automatically on the basis of seniority. In addition, the caucus passed a Subcommittee Bill of Rights, which restricted committee chair control over staff, their power to appoint subcommittee chairs, and their power to refer bills to subcommittees.

At the same time that reforms reduced the power of committee chairs and made them more responsive to the Democratic caucus, these changes sought to augment the power of the party leadership. According to Democratic Party rules, the Speaker was given the authority to appoint members from the Speaker's party to the important Rules Committee, effectively making that committee an arm of the Speaker, and to assign legislation to more than one committee. The party leadership was also given half the positions on the House Democratic Steering and Policy Committee, an executive committee of the entire caucus that would give out committee assignments to members and set legislative priorities.

While liberal Democratic reformers were trying to change policy results by tinkering with rules and procedures, removing the conservative veto that southern Democrats exercised as committee chairs, electoral forces were also making themselves felt. The Civil Rights movement precipitated an electoral realignment in the South, shifting its partisan sympathies from Democratic to Republican. This shift was first evident in presidential elections, but has since seeped down to the congressional level. In 1960, before the great civil rights struggles of that decade, the southern delegation in the House included only six Republicans from 106 congressional districts in the South. Since then, Republicans have become so competitive in southern congressional elections that they now comprise a majority of the southern House and Senate delegations. As southern Democrats lost seats to their Republican opponents, their proportion within the Democratic delegation in the House declined. In the 106th Congress (1999–2000), southerners comprised about 25 percent of the Democratic delegation in the House compared to 46 percent in the 83rd Congress (1953–54). Not only are there now fewer southern Democrats, but also they are different politically from the generation they succeeded. The remaining southern Democrats in the House are more liberal and more likely to vote with their party than were their conservative Dixiecrat forebears.[77] Southern Democrats have become national Democrats.

The decline and nationalization of the southern Democratic congressional delegation, leaving it with fewer and increasingly liberal members, spelled the end of the conservative coalition in Congress. The conservative coalition of southern Democrats and conservative Republicans that once held the balance of power in Congress is no longer as evident or as powerful as it once was. In 1987, the conservative coalition appeared in just 9 percent of all House votes—the lowest figure the *Congressional Quarterly Weekly Report*

---

[77]For party unity scores of southern Democrats, see Rohde, *Parties and Leaders in the Postreform House,* pp. 54–56. For the increasing liberalism of southern legislators, see Draper, "Be Careful What You Wish For . . . ," pp. 312–13.

ever recorded—where it has remained ever since.[78] But the South continued to haunt American liberalism, even as the Dixiecrat influence in Congress faded away. While the South no longer obstructed liberal programs in Congress from within the Democratic Party, it emerged as a new conservative and powerful obstacle to liberal legislation from outside the Democratic Party.

Just as party realignment turned southern Democrats into national Democrats, it recreated the spirit of the old conservative Dixiecrats in a newly revived southern Republican Party. As the Republican delegation from the South increased, so did its proportion within the Republican congressional delegation. In 1975, southerners comprised 19 percent of the Republican delegation in the House. In 1999, southerners comprised about one-third of all House Republicans. This increase in the proportion of southerners within the Republican congressional party has moved it further to the right. Political scientist Charles S. Bullock III found that southern Republicans "form an almost monolithic bloc" across a wide range of issues in Congress and score higher on conservative tests of ideological purity than nonsouthern Republican legislators do.[79] Finally, the 1994 election thrust the southern wing of House Republicans into leadership. House Speaker Newt Gingrich was from Georgia, while House Majority Leader Dick Armey and House Whip Tom DeLay were both from Texas. In 1998, the Republican House caucus elected another southern Republican, Bob Livingston from Louisiana, to replace Gingrich as Speaker. Livingston, however, was forced to step down even before he officially took the post when he admitted to several adulterous affairs. Livingston was then replaced as Speaker of the House by Dennis Hastert of Illinois. Although southerners could no longer boast they held the top post, their influence within the Republican House caucus remained strong. Southerners continued to hold leadership positions under the Speaker, and they continued to comprise the largest bloc among the House Republican membership.

The degree to which southerners now set the tone for House Republicans was never more evident than in their effort to impeach Bill Clinton in 1998. Southern Republicans led the effort to impeach the president and used their leadership positions to bring the rest of the Republican delegation along with them. While it used to be the case that presidents required the cooperation of southern Democrats in Congress in order to govern, now presidents must obtain the cooperation of southern Republicans. And the influence of

---

[78]Norman J. Ornstein, Thomas E. Mann, and Michael J. Malbin, *Vital Statistics on Congress, 1993–1994* (Washington, D.C.: American Enterprise Institute, 1994), p. 203, Table 8.5. See also Alan Ehrenhalt, "The Changing South Perils Conservative Coalition," *Congressional Quarterly Weekly Report*, August 1, 1987, 1699.

[79]Charles S. Bullock III, "Congressional Roll Call Voting in the Two-Party South," *Social Science Quarterly* 66 (December 1995): 803. For a similar analysis of the Senate, see Christopher J. Bailey, *The Republican Party in the Senate* (New York: Manchester University Press, 1988), p. 63.

southern Republicans in Congress today is based on some of the same sources as the old conservative Dixiecrats they replaced: their numbers, their unity, and their command of leadership posts in Congress.

The decline and liberalization of southern Democrats and the rise and growing conservatism of southern Republicans have produced ideologically polarized parties in Congress. The northern wing of the Democratic Party has acted as a pole of attraction, pulling southern Democrats in the House to the left; at the same time, the southern wing of the Republican Party acts as a pole of attraction, pulling the rest of the GOP to the right. The political differences *within* the parties have declined, while the political differences *separating* the parties in Congress have grown. Parties within the House have become more cohesive and more polarized.

As these ideological differences became clearer, the impact of party on congressional voting increased. Partisan voting, in which a majority of Democrats vote against a majority of Republicans, is now more evident than in the past. Party discipline, the degree to which representatives vote with a majority of their party, is also now more apparent than in the recent past.[80] Party unity and partisan conflict, which were increasing fairly steadily through the 1980s when the Democrats held power in the House, accelerated when the Republicans took over in 1994. The increasing partisanship in the House contributes to the public's lack of respect for Congress and its sense that Congress is out of touch. As partisan commitment declines and the number of independents in the electorate grows, the opposite is occurring in the House, where conflict increasingly occurs along party lines and party affiliation has become more meaningful. Much of the new partisan, ideologically polarized cast to Congress is the result of party realignment in the South. The least partisan and least ideological group of legislators, southern Democrats, is being replaced by the most partisan and most ideological group of legislators, southern Republicans.

Electoral forces—the triumph of Republican fortunes in the South and their decay in the Northeast—are invigorating partisan identification and conflict in the House, producing institutional changes within it. When members of the majority party agree on policy, strengthening party leaders increases the chances that the majority's policy goals will prevail.[81] House party leaders are strong because party members want them to be strong. Centralizing power, especially increasing the power of the Speaker's office, helps prevent defections from the party program, mitigating the competing pressures from constituencies, interest groups, and committees on a Congress member's vote. In addition, centralizing power permits the majority to focus on its agenda, as opposed to seeing it dissipated by the parochial tug of committees, interest groups, and constituents. Finally, centralizing power

---

[80]Rohde, *Parties and Leaders in the Postreform House.*

[81]Ibid., p. 172.

helps publicize the majority's agenda by giving the media a handful of party leaders to cover, as opposed to a larger group of committee and subcommittee chairs. When the majority can speak through one voice, the Speaker's, it can better focus public attention and debate around its priorities.[82]

The centralization of power within the House and the experience of party government probably reached their peak in the 104th Congress and the Speakership of Newt Gingrich. There has been retreat in subsequent Congresses from its excesses. Committees have already regained some of the autonomy they lost, and individual members are now more willing to resist party leaders. Following the failed Gingrich revolution, Republican representatives are now pursuing more traditional congressional strategies of burnishing their local image, bringing federal projects to their district, serving constituents, and devoting themselves to committee work—just as Democratic representatives did when they were in the majority.[83] But Republicans have diverged from past practice by setting term limits on committee chairs. In the Contract with America, House Republicans pledged that no committee chair would serve for more than six years. In 2000, the Republican House caucus partially set aside seniority and selected 13 new committee chairs to replace chairs whose term limits had expired.

If substantial policy divisions reemerge *within* the parties, the willingness of members to cede power and defer to the party leadership will diminish. But with the decline of moderate northeastern Republicans as the left in their party and the decline of southern Democrats as the right in their party, both congressional parties are drifting further apart and becoming more ideologically cohesive internally. So long as electoral forces continue to increase the divide between the parties and reduce the conflict within them, the impact of parties and centralization will continue to be felt within the House.

CONGRESS, THE BUREAUCRACY, AND INTEREST GROUPS

When we considered the presidency, we observed that the president manages the federal bureaucracy, but that Congress creates it. Each new federal agency originates with an act of Congress, which describes what the agency is supposed to do and provides the funding to do it. Congress is usually quite vague in its legislative instructions for agencies because it cannot anticipate all the contingencies an agency might encounter and because Congress hopes to avoid criticism and controversy by not being too specific. As a result, agencies have a great deal of discretion in interpreting the mandate they receive from Congress. Vague legislative instructions also give presidents an

---

[82]For the benefits of centralization, see Evans and Oleszek, *Congress Under Fire,* pp. 83–91.

[83]Rae, *Conservative Reformers,* p. x.

opportunity to use the discretion agencies have for their own ends—that is, to have the agencies interpret and implement the law in conformity with the administration's program—when managing the bureaucracy. To ensure that federal agencies interpret and implement the law as Congress intended, Congress engages in *oversight* of the bureaucracy.

As government has grown, Congress has come to spend more time on oversight. In addition, oversight has grown as a result of the frequency of divided government. Congress monitors the bureaucracy more carefully to see that the laws are executed to reflect Congress's intent when Congress and the president come from different parties. Oversight is performed by congressional subcommittees and committees, which review the activities of agencies under their jurisdiction. They hold hearings at which members of Congress remind agency heads that Congress is the boss, that they get their appropriations from Congress, and that Congress expects certain things of them.

Congress engages in more oversight than it did before, but it can cover only a small part of what the government is doing, and subcommittees and committees, far from being antagonistic to federal agencies under their jurisdiction, often form alliances with them. Congressional subcommittees and committees are typically a third partner in the clientelistic relationships that exist between federal agencies and interest groups. Mutually beneficial relationships among a government agency, a private interest group, and a congressional subcommittee are called *subgovernments* or *iron triangles*.[84] One of the most formidable subgovernments is found in the realm of defense contracting. All three participants in this subgovernment have an interest in increasing defense expenditures. For defense contractors, more military spending means more military orders and more profits. For the Defense Department, more military spending means more sophisticated weaponry and more career opportunities. For the House Armed Services Committee, more military spending means more military bases and defense contract work they can bring back to their districts and take credit for with voters.

Although this description of congressional subcommittees participating in their own exclusive subgovernments continues to be partially valid, the situation has become more complex. The stable worlds of subgovernments, in which congressional subcommittees operate in their own closed world without interference from the rest of Congress, have in many cases been jostled or replaced. New participants have forced their way into the game, and their goals often conflict with those of the established players. A host of grassroots activist groups—including consumer organizations, environmental groups, civil rights advocates, and women's groups—have used political pressure and legal skill to alter the geometry of iron triangles. In addition, much recent governmental activity cuts across established industry lines, threatening the cozy exclusiveness that private groups and government agencies previously

---

[84]See Gordon Adams, *The Iron Triangle: The Politics of Defense Contracting* (New York: Council on Economic Priorities, 1981).

enjoyed. Finally, subgovernments have been challenged from above. The congressional budget process, which sets overall spending targets, has brought subgovernments under closer scrutiny from the rest of Congress. The centralization of power in the House under party leadership has also curbed the independence of congressional subcommittees.

Subgovernments continue to flourish in some arenas. One political scientist found that "[s]ubgovernments are especially influential in affecting low visibility, noncontroversial routine policy making."[85] But Hugh Heclo suggests that what he calls "issue networks" are now more typical. Issue networks differ from subgovernments in that there are more participants and they come into conflict more often than was true when subgovernments dominated interest group–congressional relations.[86]

LOBBYING AND CONGRESS

Subgovernments and issue networks are linkages among participants that share a particular policy domain, such as defense or agricultural policy. Lobbying, on the other hand, is a more general process by which groups try to influence Congress. Lobbying has increased enormously as the reach of government has grown. In 1996, there were an estimated 80,000 people employed in the lobbying industry, working for 11,600 organizations whose combined annual operating costs were in the neighborhood of $12 billion.[87] In 1998, there were 18,590 lobbyists registered in Washington—38 lobbyists for each senator and representative.[88] When political scientists Kay Lehman Schlozman and John T. Tierney examined interest group presence in Washington, they found that 70 percent of all the organizations represented in their sample either were businesses and trade associations or were law and public relations firms hired by corporations to represent them in Washington.[89] The largest Fortune 500 companies were the best represented. They maintained their own lobbying arms in Washington, were members of their industrial trade group, and participated in peak organizations like the Business Roundtable. Moreover, the Washington corporate office was no longer a dumping ground where corporate executives placed their incompetent relatives to keep them out of harm's way. To the contrary, managers of corporate

[85]Joseph A. Pika, "Interest Groups and the Executive: Presidential Intervention," in *Interest Group Politics,* ed. Allan C. Cigler and Burdett A. Loomis (Washington, D.C.: Congressional Quarterly Press, 1983), p. 303.

[86]Hugh Heclo, "Issue Networks and the Executive Establishment," in *The New American Political System,* ed. Anthony King (Washington D.C.: American Enterprise Institute, 1978).

[87]These figures on the lobbying industry are from John R. Wright, *Interest Groups and Congress: Lobbying Contributions and Influence* (Boston: Allyn & Bacon, 1996), pp. 9–11.

[88]*New York Times,* July 29, 1999.

[89]Kay Lehman Schlozman and John T. Tierney, *Organized Interests and American Democracy* (New York: Harper & Row, 1986), p. 67.

public affairs departments gained status within the corporate hierarchy. The *Wall Street Journal* found "the post of government-affairs executive has taken on added luster. A tour through the government-affairs department can be a quick route to the top."[90] Indeed, many corporate lobbyists are former government officials who bring their privileged access to former colleagues and knowledge of agency or congressional procedures to their new jobs. Compared to other interest groups, business is the most organized, hires the most lobbyists, has the most contact, and devotes the most money to influencing policy-makers.

Lobbying is a sophisticated, multifaceted operation today and requires an extraordinary amount of money to be effective. Take, for example, the case of Microsoft Corporation, which initially ignored politics, but soon found it needed friends on Capitol Hill. Congress began to consider legislation affecting the technology industry, and the Justice Department sued the company for violating anti-trust laws. Microsoft's lobbying efforts included making campaign contributions to legislators, hiring expensive lobbyists, financing op-ed pieces and full-page advertisements in newspapers, underwriting the work of academics and research groups who advocated Microsoft's positions, giving money to local organizations that would defend Microsoft to make it appear that the company enjoyed grassroots support, creating new trade groups that generated support for the company through Web sites, and arranging meetings between Microsoft executives and congressional leaders. Microsoft, which made virtually no political contributions until the early 1990s, is now third on the list of corporate contributors, behind only AT&T and Philip Morris. Not taking any chances, the company gave $500,000 to both the Democratic and the Republican parties to help pay for each party's 2000 convention and has hired lobbyists who do work for both parties. Microsoft even went so far as to lobby Congress to trim the budget of the Justice Department's Antitrust Division after it successfully brought suit against Microsoft.[91] Such lobbying efforts cost Microsoft tens of millions of dollars, much more than what most other interests spend to influence policy.

Many Americans and some political scientists believe in a comforting picture of American politics. In their view, society is made up of relatively equal interests, with each one pursuing its own political goals and with government responding in an evenhanded way. But this is a partial picture, at best. Capitalist countries depend on business to invest and produce, creating what we called in Chapter 2 a "mobilization of bias" in its favor. The result is a privileged position for business that has come to be seen as so natural that business is often not regarded as a special interest at all.[92] Business's special

---

[90]Quoted in David Vogel, *Fluctuating Fortunes* (New York: Basic Books, 1989), pp. 196–98.

[91]*New York Times,* June 12, 2000.

[92]Mark Kesselman, "The Conflictual Evolution of American Political Science: From Apologetic Pluralism to Trilateralism and Marxism," in *Public Values of Private Power in American Democracy,* ed. J. David Greenstone (Chicago: University of Chicago Press, 1982), pp. 34–67.

position of privilege is augmented by a party system that is awash with corporate campaign contributions and by corporate lobbyists who are more organized and have more staff and money than any other interest group in Washington. That is, corporate capitalism enjoys a structural advantage (Chapter 2), an electoral advantage (Chapter 5), and an interest group advantage. These political advantages are cumulative, as they reinforce and augment each other.

CONCLUSION

Congress is decentralized and fragmented. It is separated into two chambers, a Senate and a House of Representatives. And within these chambers, power is dispersed widely, although this is much truer of the Senate than of the House. While Congress's decentralized structure makes it difficult for Congress to articulate a broad coherent program and to provide leadership to the government, except during unusual periods of party government, this structure is conducive to the expression of particularistic demands by organized groups. Congress is open to groups exerting influence on it because of the many points of contact and different power centers available within it. It is the country's most representative and accessible institution, which creates a certain irony. Its very openness to the social forces outside it means that the diversity and inequalities of the larger society are reflected within it. Those with the most political resources outside of Congress are in the best position to take advantage of Congress's accessibility, to cultivate relationships with its members, committee and subcommittee chairs, and party leaders. Inasmuch as business has more political resources than other groups, it can best take advantage of Congress's openness to influence the legislative process. The mobilization of bias, corporate lobbying, corporate campaign contributions, and the class background of members of Congress make Congress especially responsive to corporate concerns.

According to political scientist Nicol C. Rae, "Congress can delay and obstruct measures, and it can articulate the national mood, but except in highly unusual circumstances, it cannot lead."[93] Although Congress is usually unable to set the government's agenda, it remains a pivotal political institution. As Woodrow Wilson understood, Congress is central to policy making because of the powers conferred on it by the Constitution. It has the authority to delay, amend, or veto initiatives desired by the executive branch. As the world's most powerful legislature, its creative and disruptive capacities cannot be ignored.

---

[93] Rae, *Conservative Reformers,* p. 216.

8

THE JUDICIARY

Justice is not always simple to achieve; nor do we always recall its heroes. Together with 19 other brave individuals in Clarendon County, South Carolina, the Reverend J. A. DeLaine took to the courts in 1948 to resist discrimination in schooling on the basis of race. He was quickly fired from his job. Soon his wife and two sisters had lost theirs. He was sent threatening letters signed "the Ku Klux Klan" and run off the road. When he was not dissuaded, his house was burned to the ground and the church where he had pastored was torched as well. Shot at, he fired back. A warrant was issued for his arrest. Fearing for his life, he escaped across the state line. South Carolina's governor, happy to be rid of this fugitive from justice, did not pursue him any further.[1]

As it turned out, Reverend DeLaine became part of a momentous Supreme Court case. He and 19 others—dirt farmers, teachers, cleaning women, and car mechanics—possessed the courage of their convictions. They thought racial discrimination to be illegal. Simple justice, they believed, required the government to give black children the same educational opportunities it provided to whites. In Clarendon County, the local board of education maintained 12 schools for whites valued at $673,850 and 61 schools for blacks valued at $194,575. The white schools were equipped with toilets and drinking fountains. The black schools were equipped with outhouses and buckets with dippers for drinking water. White schoolchildren rode to school in buses. Invariably, they would pass black schoolchildren who had to walk because no school buses were provided for them.

Led by Reverend DeLaine and assisted by the National Association for the Advancement of Colored People (NAACP), this group filed suit in U.S. district court in Florence County, South Carolina, on March 16, 1948. They claimed that racial segregation, practiced by the Clarendon County Board of Education, violated the Equal Protection Clause of the Constitution's Fourteenth Amendment. The suit was filed under the name of Harry Briggs, the

---

[1]This paragraph draws from the beginning of Richard Kluger's prize-winning history of the *Brown* case, *Simple Justice: The History of* Brown v. Board of Education *and Black America's Struggle for Equality* (New York: Knopf, 1976).

The entrance to the U.S. Supreme Court Building.

first plaintiff in alphabetical order, who worked in a gas station. Before the litigation was finished, he would be fired. Maisie Solomon, another plaintiff, also lost her job. John McDonald could not get a loan for his tractor, Lee Richardson could not secure credit for his farm, and no one would rent land to William Ragin on which he could grow his cotton. The NAACP could provide the plaintiffs with legal counsel and assume their legal expenses, but it could not protect them from reprisals by whites out of court. The doors of justice were open, but it required money, professional skill, organization, and uncommon courage to walk through them.

After two years of delay and defeat in the lower courts, this school segregation case reached the Supreme Court of the United States, the court of last resort. There the suit from South Carolina joined two other school segregation cases, from Delaware and from Virginia, which the Court also was hearing on appeal. These cases were consolidated with a fourth school segregation case from Kansas. Called *Brown v. Board of Education of Topeka*, it was listed first because the justices did not want the issue of segregation to appear as purely a southern matter.

Seventeen months after hearing oral arguments on these school segregation cases known collectively as *Brown*, on May 17, 1954, Chief Justice Earl Warren read the Supreme Court's unanimous opinion. His delivery was spare and direct. So was the opinion he wrote. He told the assembled spectators and reporters that the Court had asked itself in *Brown* if racial segregation in public schools deprived black children of equal opportunity. Looking up from his text, the Chief Justice offered the Court's response: "We believe that it does." His closing remarks left no doubt where the Court stood: "We conclude that in the field of public education the doctrine of 'separate but equal' has no place. Separate educational facilities are inherently unequal. Therefore we hold that the plaintiffs . . . have been . . . deprived of the equal protection of the laws guaranteed by the Fourteenth Amendment."[2]

The *Brown* decision tore down the pernicious doctrine of "separate but equal" the Court had endorsed in 1896 in *Plessy v. Ferguson*, a case in which it had upheld the constitutionality of a Louisiana law that required railroads to provide "equal but separate accommodations for the white and colored races" and that barred persons from traveling in railcars other than those to which they had been assigned by race. Applied to education, this practice had relegated blacks not only to separate, but also to inferior schools. Backed by the authority of the Supreme Court, *Brown* represented the most powerful challenge to that date to racial segregation. Most legal scholars agree with Harvie J. Wilkinson III that "*Brown* may be the most important political, social, and legal event in America's twentieth century history," and many American historians trace the origins of the Civil Rights movement to this landmark Supreme Court decision.[3] The Court is credited with precipitating the revolution in race relations that occurred in the 1960s.

Today nowhere in the United States is racial segregation the law of the land. The process that shaped this racial revolution was not limited to the judiciary, of course. It was the result of a massive Civil Rights movement and congressional legislation. But there can be no doubt that *Brown* contributed to and symbolized the defeat of official, legal racism. Nonetheless, racial segregation has persisted. American schools, not only in the South, but also throughout the nation, remain divided along racial lines.[4] In Reverend De-Laine's home county of Clarendon, South Carolina, fifteen years after *Brown*, the public school system enrolled 3,000 black schoolchildren and just a single white child. Twenty-five years after the *Brown* decision, in 1979, a new school desegregation suit was filed in Topeka, Kansas, by Linda Brown, the original plaintiff in the landmark school desegregation suit that bears her name, on behalf of her own children! In 1989, the U.S. Court of Appeals for the Tenth

---

[2]This material on *Brown* draws on Kluger's unsurpassed history of the Supreme Court decision and Raymond Wolters, *The Burden of* Brown: *Thirty Years of School Desegregation* (Knoxville: University of Tennessee Press, 1984).

[3]Quoted in Gerald N. Rosenberg, *The Hollow Hope: Can Courts Bring About Social Change?* (Chicago: University of Chicago Press, 1991), p. 40.

[4]For a report that, after 20 years of progress following *Brown*, a pattern of school resegregation is advancing, see *New York Times*, June 13, 1999.

Circuit ruled that Topeka still had a long way to go in desegregating its schools.[5] Reflecting broadly on the impact of *Brown* and the courts more generally on racial change in the United States, one leading scholar has even gone so far as to argue that there is "little evidence that the judicial system, from the Supreme Court down, produced much of the massive change in civil rights that swept the United States in the 1960s."[6]

Is it possible that *Brown* could both be central to undermining legal racial segregation and yet fail to bring most white and black students together in the same schools? Or, more generally, is it possible that the courts are immensely powerful, yet are only limited actors in a much larger constellation of political institutions and social forces? This chapter argues that both are the case, simultaneously. The federal courts interpret the Constitution, the supreme law of the land. "We are under a Constitution," Chief Justice Charles Evans Hughes once remarked, and "the Constitution is what the judges say it is."[7] In addition, courts in the United States, unlike in many other countries, have the power of judicial review. That is, the courts can nullify or overturn any federal, state, or public law that conflicts with the Constitution. Judicial review permits the courts to overrule the decisions of other political institutions. Further, federal judges are appointed to life terms. They are free from pressures to raise funds and campaign for support to which other political actors are subject. Judges thus enjoy extraordinary independence and autonomy.

Yet, for all its power and prestige, the judiciary is often considered the weakest branch of government, less powerful than the legislative and executive branches. Since the founding of the Republic, leading political observers have pointed to the judiciary's limitations. Alexander Hamilton described the courts as the "least dangerous branch," having "no influence over either the sword or the purse; no direction either of the strength or of the wealth of the society; and can take no active resolution whatsoever." That is, the courts may rule on a case, but must depend on other political institutions to implement their decision. For example, when President Andrew Jackson disagreed with a Supreme Court ruling, he reportedly snickered, "[Chief Justice] John Marshall has made his decision, now let him enforce it."[8] Likewise, Justice Tom C. Clark once complained of the Court's powerlessness to make its decisions effective: "We don't have money at the Court to hire an army and we can't take out ads in the newspapers, and we don't want to go out on a picket line in our robes. We have to convince the nation by the force of our opinions."[9]

---

[5]Rosenberg, *Hollow Hope*, p. 40.

[6]Ibid., p. 157.

[7]Bernard Schwartz, *A Basic History of the U.S. Supreme Court* (Princeton: D. Van Nostrand Co., 1968), p. 9.

[8]Quoted in ibid., p. 15.

[9]Quoted in Kluger, *Simple Justice*, p. 706.

POLITICS AND THE LAW

The Supreme Court, and the judicial system more generally, is both a conservative and a radical instrument. Courts in the main are conservative institutions that usually confirm the status quo. By and large, they defer to legal precedent in reaching decisions and thus bind the present to the past. The legal process, with its constant motions and appeals, is designed to work slowly and deliberately. Often the pace is torturous. Only rarely, often slowly, and with great reluctance have American courts effectively produced social reform. Lacking power of the purse and power of the sword, courts are mostly dependent on other institutions to implement their decisions, and they usually defer to more democratic parts of the country's governing structure. Dependence and deference make the courts handmaidens of convention and conformity, reinforcing the disparities that existing economic arrangements and social patterns produce. Consequently, legal strategies that depend on the courts to right wrongs may be necessary to consolidate victories won in the voting booth, in the legislature, and in the streets, but they are no substitute for them.

The justice system is a system of written laws, legal procedures, and courts that resolve disputes and punish the guilty. Extending from the police walking their beat, to judges hearing cases, to jail guards locking down prisoners for the night, participants in the justice system often wear uniforms to signify that their actions are guided by the law, and not their private conscience or personal motives. The law thus presents itself as above politics and objective, with rules that apply to all citizens equally. This sentiment is captured in the words "Equal Justice Under the Law," which are engraved on the façade atop the columns of Italian marble at the entrance to the Supreme Court. Motivated by legal equality, the courts sometimes display independence and rule against the powers of the day. As in the case of Reverend DeLaine and his fellow litigants, the law can be liberal democracy's great equalizer. While whites and blacks, men and women, and the rich and the poor may have unequal resources in society, all citizens are equal before the law.

Most of the time, however, the law follows politics and power. It cannot erase inequalities of power, income, wealth, or social standing, whether they exist between races, between workers and employers, between men and women, or between other groups with uneven command of resources. Thus, while promoting equal citizenship, the law can mask inequality by giving the impression that all citizens stand before the law as equals. It also can reflect and reinforce inequalities of power. The individuals who sit on death row, for example, almost to a person are poor—not because rich or middle-class individuals never commit murder, but because the average number of hours of legal time assigned to defendants in capital cases who cannot afford a lawyer is just over 50 hours, hardly much time in trial preparation and the trial itself. Here the same basic procedures of trial by jury apply to all Americans, but the results are strongly shaped by the contrasting abilities of individuals to pay for defense lawyers. The illusion of justice, of formal equality under the law in a society marked with real, substantive inequalities, is captured best in Anatole France's famous remark: "The law in its majesty forbids the rich as well as the poor to sleep under bridges, to beg in the streets, and to steal bread."

Law and legal equality, nonetheless, are precious assets. When access to both is absent, as was the case in the segregated South, where intimidation and deep poverty prevented the vast majority of black citizens from exercising their legal rights, domination flourishes. By contrast, when citizens gain access to genuine procedural equality, their freedom widens. In a world marked by inequalities of many kinds, including those based on class, race, ethnicity, and gender, the justice system often protects, even re-creates, inequalities. But it also does more—for it creates a formal framework of rights and procedures, tangible resources that ordinary people can use to make claims against the rich and the powerful. In addition, the law sets limits on what the rich and the powerful may do.[10] They, too, must abide by the limits of the law. They cannot simply assert their naked power without limit. The law may suit them, but they are its willing or unwilling prisoners as well. Even presidents can be penalized for violating the law, as when President Richard Nixon was forced to resign in the aftermath of Watergate. His resignation, of course, was mainly the result of a political process, but the courts made it far easier for Congress to proceed against him, ultimately forcing a resignation, by requiring that incriminating tapes he made in the White House be turned over to investigators. It is the law under the Constitution that grants and protects freedom of speech, freedom from unreasonable search and seizure, and freedom of religion. And ordinary citizens can appeal to the law in order to assert their rights, as civil rights activists did in the 1960s.

A DUAL COURT SYSTEM

If we are to understand this combination of judicial effectiveness and limitations and how the courts both reinforce and counter inequality, we need first to understand how the courts are organized.

The United States has a dual court system; state and federal systems of justice exist side by side. Each of the 50 states and the federal government maintain their own systems of courts, for a total of 51 separate court systems in the United States. Federal courts hear criminal matters that concern federal law. They also hear noncriminal, or civil, cases that involve citizens of more than one state and complaints filed by the federal government. State courts hear all the rest. Sometimes there is conflict between federal and state courts over which has jurisdiction of a case. Although under the Constitution

---

[10]For a nuanced appreciation of the role the law plays, see E. P. Thompson, *Whigs and Hunters: The Origin of the Black Act* (New York: Pantheon Books, 1975).

a defendant cannot be tried twice for the same crime, sometimes defendants can be tried in both federal and state courts for the same incident if charged for different crimes. In 1992, four Los Angeles police officers were acquitted in California state court of assaulting Rodney King, a black man, even though a videotape appeared to provide ample documentation for the charge. The federal district attorney in Los Angeles then brought federal charges against the police officers for violating King's civil rights. Two of the four policemen subsequently were convicted on these charges in federal court.

State courts are the workhorses of the justice system. Ninety-nine percent of all legal cases are tried in state courts—from divorce and child custody matters to criminal cases; from wills, trusts, and estates issues to small claims disputes. Their role and the incarceration system they oversee at the state and local levels have become increasingly visible at a time when the population in prison has increased dramatically, nearly doubling to almost 2 million in the 1990s. Most of those behind bars are nonviolent offenders, about 70 percent are illiterate, 10 percent are afflicted with mental illness, and a disproportionate number are not white. Currently, 8 percent of African-American men in their late twenties are incarcerated (nearly 30 percent, at current rates, will spend some time in prison during their lives). The total population in American jails and prisons has grown at a rate exceeding 6 percent per year since 1970. Out of every 100,000 people in the country, 461 were behind bars in 2001. By way of comparison, from 1920 to 1970, the proportion behind bars was about 110 people per 100,000.

By contrast, the federal courts have much less routine criminal business to conduct. Federal court rulings interpret the Constitution and apply federal laws that apply to and govern all Americans. In addition, federal courts have the power to review the decisions of state courts to ensure they comply with federal law.

The federal court system is divided into three levels (see Figure 8–1). The lowest is comprised of 94 district courts. Most federal cases begin and end here. However, a litigant unhappy with a decision at the district court level may appeal it to the next level, the court of appeals. There is one U.S. court of appeals for each of the country's 12 judicial circuits. Most cases are heard on appeal from district courts in the states under their jurisdiction by panels of three judges (rather than by a single judge, as at the district level). Only about one in ten federal cases makes it to this level.

District and appellate courts play important policy-making roles. Once the Supreme Court rules on a case, it often turns the issue back to the district court to implement the actual decision. The Supreme Court will generally restrict itself in its decision to articulating the general principle of law involved in the case, giving the district court a great deal of discretion in how to apply its ruling. For example, in *Brown v. Board of Education of Topeka*, the Supreme Court did not fix a date for ending school segregation, but instead instructed the district courts to "act with all deliberate speed." But many district courts in the South reflected the region's opposition to *Brown* and used

THE U.S. FEDERAL COURTS

Supreme Court
U.S. Supreme Court

Appellate Courts
U.S. Courts of Appeals
■ 12 Regional Circuit Courts of Appeals
■ 1 U.S. Court of Appeals for the Federal Circuit

Trial Courts
U.S. District Courts
■ 94 judicial districts
■ U.S. Bankruptcy Courts
U.S. Court of International Trade
U.S. Court of Federal Claims

Federal Courts and Other Entities outside the Judicial Branch
Military Courts (Trial and Appellate)
Court of Veterans Appeals
U.S. Tax Court
Federal administrative agencies and boards

their discretion to forestall desegregation. They subsequently acted with "entirely too much deliberation and not enough speed," according to Justice Hugo Black, in requiring southern school districts to comply with the Court's ruling.[11]

Courts of appeals also are important policy-makers. Most of their decisions are final because the Supreme Court takes up so few cases—around 2 percent—that have been decided by these courts. But one important difference between the Supreme Court and courts of appeals is that decisions by appellate courts apply only to the specific states covered by the deciding court, not to the entire country. For example, in 1996, the Fifth Circuit Court of Appeals, covering Texas, Louisiana, and Mississippi, ruled that the University of Texas Law School discriminated against other applicants when it gave preference in admissions to Latino and black applicants. The court ruled that schools may not discriminate in admissions on the basis of race, and the Supreme Court refused to hear the case on appeal. This left the appeals court decision standing as the law in those states included within the Fifth Circuit's jurisdiction, but not elsewhere. Whether that decision becomes

---

[11]Quoted in David M. O'Brien, *Storm Center: The Supreme Court in American Politics* (New York: Norton, 1986), p. 290.

HOW CASES ASCEND TO THE SUPREME COURT

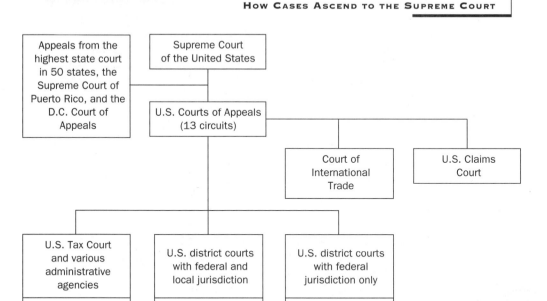

SOURCE: Administrative Office of the United States Courts.

the law of the land depends on whether another court of appeals from another circuit rules differently on the same question and the Supreme Court takes up the issue to settle the disputed matter.[12] (See Figure 8–2.)

Presidents appoint federal judges, subject to confirmation by the Senate. These appointments are especially consequential because federal judges have lifetime tenure. Presidents can thus leave a legacy regarding how laws are interpreted that extends far beyond the end of their term through the judges they appoint to the federal bench. Presidents generally appoint judges to federal courts who are from the same political party and who share their philosophy. With the exception of Franklin Roosevelt, who appointed more than 80 percent of federal judges over the course of his

[12]Robert A. Carp and Ronald Stidham, *Judicial Process in America,* 4th ed. (Washington, D.C.: Congressional Quarterly Press, 1998), p. 43.

three full terms, no presidents have been more assiduous and successful in staffing the federal judiciary with like-minded judges than Ronald Reagan and his successor, George Bush. For the first time in American history, White House aides were involved in the process of reviewing the credentials of potential judges, screening them to confirm their conservative values.[13] After twelve years of administrations led by Presidents Reagan and Bush, Republican appointees comprised just over 70 percent of the federal bench. These appointees did not disappoint their sponsors. As a group, they were among the most conservative jurists in this century. The Reagan and Bush appointments to the federal bench have consistently handed down decisions narrowing civil rights remedies and finding for the government against individual rights.[14]

The Clinton presidency did not do much to reverse this direction. The White House did not participate in the selection of judges to the extent it had under Presidents Reagan and Bush, nor did the Clinton administration screen judicial appointments ideologically to the degree its predecessors had. Rather, the judges Clinton chose reflected his centrist values. He made his mark, rather, by stressing judicial diversity, by appointing more women and minorities to judgeships than any previous president.[15] During his first term, only a minority of his appointments to the bench were white men. One aide in the Clinton White House explained, "We don't see courts as a vehicle for social change. It's enough to put people of demonstrated quality on the bench. We've done this across gender, race, and national origin lines. And that is a legacy the president is proud of."[16]

SUPREME COURT

At the top of the judicial system is the Supreme Court. It is the court of last resort; there is none higher. According to Justice Robert H. Jackson, "The Supreme Court is not final because it's infallible. It's infallible only because it's final." The Court receives the vast majority of its cases from the federal district and appellate courts, as well as from the state courts. In addition, in a

---

[13]Gregory A. Caldiera and John R. Wright, "Lobbying for Justice: The Rise of Organized Conflict in the Politics of Federal Judgeships," in *Contemplating Courts*, ed. Lee Epstein (Washington, D.C.: Congressional Quarterly Press, 1995), p. 54.

[14]Kenneth Jost, "The Federal Judiciary," *CQ Researcher*, March 13, 1998, 230. It is not clear they voted more conservatively than other Republican appointments; rather, they now formed a significant majority. See also Timothy B. Tomasi and Jess A. Velona, "All the President's Men?: A Study of Ronald Reagan's Appointments to the U.S. Courts of Appeals," *Columbia Law Review* 87 (1987): 766–93.

[15]David M. O'Brien, "Clinton's Legal Policy and the Courts: Rising from Disarray or Turning Around and Around?" in *The Clinton Presidency: First Appraisals*, ed. Colin A. Campbell and Bert A. Rothman (Chatham, N.J.: Chatham House Publishers, 1996), pp. 126–63. See also Carp and Stidham, *Judicial Process in America*, pp. 243–45.

[16]White House Deputy Counsel Joel Klein, quoted in O'Brien, "Clinton's Legal Policy and the Courts," p. 139.

Members of the U.S. Supreme Court.

very small number of cases involving foreign diplomats or a state as a party to a legal dispute, the Court has original jurisdiction and takes the case directly, without the dispute having to go through the lower courts first.

Many more cases are filed with the Court each year than it has the time or inclination to hear. For example, in 1999, over 7,000 petitions were received by the Court, but it agreed to decide only 75 of them with full signed, written opinions. The Court carefully chooses which cases to hear. Though the selection process is complicated, and scholars disagree about its principles, the Court broadly has followed guidelines expressed by Justice Fred Vinson in 1949:

> The Supreme Court is not, and never has been, primarily concerned with the correction of errors in lower court decisions. . . . The function of the Supreme Court is . . . to resolve conflicts of opinion on federal questions that have arisen among lower courts, to pass upon questions of wide import under the Constitution, laws and treaties of the United States, and to exercise supervisory power over lower courts. If we took every case in which an interesting legal question is raised, or our *prima facie* impression is that the decision below is erroneous, we could not fill the Constitutional and statutory responsibilities placed upon the Court. To remain effective, the Supreme Court must continue to decide only those cases which present questions whose resolution will have immediate importance far beyond the particular facts and parties involved.[17]

---

[17]Fred Vinson, "Work of the Federal Courts," *Supreme Court Reporter,* 1949, cited in Emmette S. Redford and Alan F. Westin, *Politics and Government of the United States* (New York: Harcourt, Brace & World, 1968), p. 474.

The Supreme Court has had as few as five justices, when it was first organized in 1789, and as many as ten. Its membership, set by Congress, has been fixed at nine since 1869. The head of the Court is the Chief Justice of the United States, who is appointed by the president, subject to confirmation by the Senate. The chief justice, who presides, is the leader of the Court in title. Actually, he is only first among equals in his relationship to the other eight justices. He cannot tell them what to do or how to decide a case. He is the leader of the orchestra, but he cannot tell the other justices what music to play. Some chief justices, however, are better conductors, getting the other justices to play the same tune, than others. For example, Chief Justice Earl Warren used every personal and political argument he could think of to convince two reluctant members of the Court to sign a unanimous opinion in the *Brown* decision. Other chief justices have not been so successful. The Court sometimes leads more than it is led by the chief justice.

Decision making on the Court begins after lawyers on each side plead their case. The justices then discuss the issues in completely private sessions. No outsiders are permitted to attend. The chief justice leads the discussion. Each justice reveals where he or she stands and gives reasons for his or her position. According to Justice Antonin Scalia, "[N]ot much conferencing goes on" at conference anymore.[18] Views are stated rather than argued. There is less collective deliberating and more expounding of individual views. After the conference reveals each justice's tentative vote on a case, the chief justice, if in the majority, assigns the writing of the Court's opinion to one of the justices who voted with the majority. (If the chief justice is not in the majority, the senior member of the majority assigns the opinion.) Here chief justices may use their power to assign a significant case to an ally who will write the decision in a way that conforms to their own views. Former Chief Justice Warren Burger was suspected by the other justices of going so far to protect his power to assign opinions that he would vote with the court majority even when he privately opposed it. The justice assigned to write the majority opinion then circulates a draft to the other justices, which elicits replies from them.

As a result of written exchanges among the justices, the rationale for the decision may be modified and votes may be switched, with a completely different decision emerging from the process. For example, the 1989 *Webster v. Reproductive Health Services* case threatened to overturn the 1973 *Roe v. Wade* decision, establishing a woman's constitutional right to an abortion. A majority of five justices at conference voted to uphold a Missouri law that would have placed restrictive conditions on abortions. Chief Justice William H. Rehnquist assigned writing the majority opinion to himself. But as memos circulated among the justices in response to Rehnquist's draft, Justice Sandra Day O'Connor switched her vote. What once was a 5–4 majority at conference to effectively overturn *Roe* became in the course of an exchange of views

---

[18]Schwartz, *Decisions: How the Supreme Court Decides Cases* (New York: Oxford University Press, 1996), p. 43.

among the justices a 5–4 majority to reaffirm *Roe* (while still upholding some of the restrictions in the Missouri law). The process leading to the *Webster* decision reveals that conference votes are tentative and not carved in stone.

Presidents select members to the Supreme Court whom they believe will reflect their views. Sometimes they are spectacularly wrong in their predictions. President Harry Truman, for example, did not mince words over his disappointment with Justice Tom Clark: "Tom Clark was my biggest mistake. No question about it. . . . I don't know what got into me. He was no damn good as Attorney General, and on the Supreme Court . . . it doesn't seem possible, but he's even worse. He hasn't made one right decision that I can think of . . . ."[19] When asked what the biggest mistake was that he made while in office, President Dwight Eisenhower replied, "The appointment of . . . Earl Warren."[20] More recently, conservatives have been disappointed by the liberal decisions of Justice David Souter, whom President Bush, a Republican, appointed to the Court in 1990. Sometimes presidents guess right, only to have their appointee change his or her views over time. Justice Harry Blackmun voted with his friend Chief Justice Warren Burger, another Nixon appointee, 90 percent of the time when he first came on the Court. But his views changed, and by the time he retired from the Court in 1994, he had become its most liberal member.[21] While these examples reveal that justices sometimes surprise a president, they are the exceptions that prove the rule. Most justices reflect pretty well the politics of the president who appoints them.

Political conflict surrounding presidential appointments to the Supreme Court grew in the late twentieth century, compared to the less contentious appointment processes of earlier decades. Prior to the Senate rejection of two of President Richard Nixon's Supreme Court nominees in 1969 and 1970, one had to go back to 1930 and the Hoover administration to find the last time the Senate rejected a presidential appointment to the Supreme Court. But, as we have indicated, conflict has escalated recently over presidential nominations to the Supreme Court. Pitched battles occurred over President Reagan's appointment of Robert Bork in 1987 and President Bush's nomination of Clarence Thomas in 1991. The former was rejected as too conservative by a Democratic Senate, while the latter was confirmed by the Senate despite charges of sexual harassment against him. Part of the reason Supreme Court appointments have drawn increasing scrutiny is because more political burdens are being placed at the Court's door. Groups are litigating what they cannot legislate, and Congress is unwilling to tackle issues such as abortion that have portentous electoral consequences. The Court increasingly is being called on to choose between competing policies in areas of

---

[19]Quoted in O'Brien, *Storm Center,* p. 81.

[20]Schwartz, *Decisions,* p. 184.

[21]O'Brien, *Storm Center,* p. 84.

wide disagreement. This has made the Court look less judicial and more political. This, in turn, calls attention to the people appointed to the Court, who are increasingly perceived as making public policy when they decide cases.

Who benefits when the Court engages in policy making? After examining cases where the Court invalidated federal law—an extreme case of policy making by the Court—political scientist Robert Dahl concluded that "the main task of the Court is to confer legitimacy on the fundamental policies" of the dominant coalition of groups and interests in control of the government. "Except for short-lived transitional periods," he wrote, "when the old alliance is disintegrating and the new one is struggling to take control of political institutions, the Supreme Court is inevitably a part of the dominant national alliance. As an element in the political leadership of the dominant alliance, the Court, of course, supports the major policies of the alliance. By itself, the Court is almost powerless to affect the course of national policy."[22]

According to Dahl, the Court is least effective when it decides cases against the dominant ruling coalition. In the few instances when it has done this, such as *Scott v. Sandford* in 1857 (when Dred Scott, who had fled slavery, was returned to his master) and cases rejecting New Deal legislation (when the Court cut against the grain of the dominant coalition), the Court paid a heavy price in terms of its autonomy and prestige. On the other hand, the Court is most effective when it acts within "the somewhat narrow limits set by the basic policy goals of the dominant alliance."[23]

Political scientist Richard Funston's research supported Dahl's thesis. Examining 168 laws the Court ruled unconstitutional within four years of their passage between 1801, when the first chief justice of the United States, John Marshall, was appointed, and 1969, when Chief Justice Earl Warren retired, Funston found that the Court's pattern of rejecting legislation was not random. Rather, "over long periods of time, the Supreme Court reflects the will of the dominant political forces." The Court strikes down national legislation far less frequently when governing coalitions are stable than it does during periods of partisan upheaval and electoral realignment.[24]

THE LAW AND THE DEVELOPMENT OF AMERICAN CAPITALISM

The development of a formal legal system, "a nation of laws, not men," was intimately bound up with revolutionary conceptions of liberty. The Constitution and the law, guarded by an independent judiciary and a system of

[22]Robert Dahl, "Decision Making in a Democracy: The Supreme Court as a National Policy-Maker," *Journal of Public Law* 6 (Fall 1957): 293.

[23]Dahl, "Decision Making in a Democracy," p. 294.

[24]Richard Funston, "The Supreme Court and Critical Elections," *American Political Science Review* 69 (September 1975): 796.

criminal law based on procedural rights and trial by jury, have underpinned popular sovereignty in the United States. Equally, the Constitution and the law have been fundamental to the development and success of the country's economic system. A capitalist economy that depends on economic exchanges via contracts cannot exist without the legitimacy, security, and stability that only a predictable legal system can provide. The first American government under the Articles of Confederation failed to provide these rudimentary conditions. The Articles reserved powers for the individual states. The new national government it created could neither tax nor regulate commerce. Different laws in different states led to costly economic disputes and deprived business of legal uniformity, certainty, and security. By contrast, the new Constitution drafted by the Founders did more than provide private citizens with a set of rights that protected them from unreasonable intrusions by the state, permitted them to select governments through elections, and furnished them with procedural guarantees. The Constitution also was designed to protect and secure private property. By creating a national government that had powers of taxation, sole control over a national monetary system, and the right to regulate interstate and foreign commerce, the new Constitution created an overarching legal framework for American capitalism.

If the new Constitution provided the hardware to promote capitalist development, changes in common law provided the software. Prior to the nineteenth century, common law regarding commercial activity, property rights, and contracts had expressed the moral sense of a rural community. The law had a paternalistic, regulative, and protective quality. For example, judges regularly held that the inherent fairness of a contract determined its legality. Contracts were void if they were found to be inequitable and unfair to one of the parties.

But from the ratification of the new Constitution up through the Civil War, common law doctrine changed dramatically. A new "instrumental" conception of the law prevailed, in which the growth of the market and economic development were regarded as the ends of justice. Law became separated from morality, from any community sense of what is fair and equitable. In its place, judges substituted the values of the marketplace, which was regarded as neutral because it was governed by the impersonal principles of supply and demand. Contracts arrived at in the market were allegedly fair because the parties were regarded as free and willing and as equal in the eyes of the law. Whereas the courts previously protected weaker parties to prevent them from being taken advantage of, the courts now followed the new doctrine of caveat emptor (buyer beware), which left the weaker parties on their own.

The law limited the ability of legislatures and courts to intervene substantively, to impose their own moral judgment on commercial transactions. The allegedly neutral principles of supply and demand would replace the politically tainted moral judgments rendered by government institutions. The only role left for the law and political institutions would be to perfect the rules under which economic activity occurred. Consequently, the law became formal and technical, indifferent to the results. The formal conception of the law as concerned only with rules and indifferent to results masked its role in perpetuating the fiction of fair contracts among unequal parties.

The priority that judges now gave to economic development and the growth of the market over other competing values was reflected in how the law dealt with such issues as usury, property rights, liability, and juries. For example, usury laws no longer restrained creditors from charging high rates of interest in a society where capital was scarce. Usury laws remained on the books, but the penalties for usury were weakened, and the circumstances in which such laws applied were reduced. Judges moved to promote market values on other legal fronts as well. Previously, property rights were absolute and exclusive, giving an owner the power to prevent economic improvements that injured his or her property. Now the test of property rights was productive use, freeing property owners to develop their land without concern for the injury it might cause another's property. This, for example, meant that a landowner could obstruct the flow of water by building a mill on his or her property. This obstruction, of course, hurt others downstream, but the courts now held that possession of property implied the right to develop it for business purposes even if it might harm another's enjoyment of his or her property. Moreover, strict liability and nuisance laws that had made it easy for people to win damages when they were injured by business were relaxed. This new reading of the law shifted the cost of economic improvements to those who were injured by them.

According to legal historian Morton Horwitz, these changes in the law "enabled mercantile and entrepreneurial groups to broadly advance their own interests through a transformed system of private law."[25] By redefining property rights and other commercial laws, the courts promoted economic development and the interests of those who benefited from it. These changes in common law were uneven, even quirky, with some judges responding to the pressures of economic development, while others remained rooted in an older, more regulative jurisprudence. But as the forces promoting a free market advanced up through the Civil War, the law changed, albeit faster in some areas than others, to accommodate them.

THE SUPREME COURT IN HISTORY

We have seen how the Constitution established the Supreme Court and left it to Congress to create lower federal courts as they might be needed. But the Constitution did not stipulate the number of members of the Supreme Court or what its specific powers would be. For example, the power of judicial

---

[25]Morton J. Horwitz, *The Transformation of American Law, 1780–1860* (Cambridge: Harvard University Press, 1977), p. 211.

review, in which the courts can nullify any federal, state, or public law that they believe conflicts with the Constitution, is not explicitly granted by the Constitution and cannot be found within it. This power first was asserted by the Supreme Court in the case of *Marbury v. Madison* (1803), in which the Court ruled that Thomas Jefferson's secretary of state, James Madison, had failed to properly convey the commission appointing William Marbury to a government post as a last-minute act of President John Adams. In his *Marbury* decision, Chief Justice John Marshall wrote, "It is emphatically the province and duty of the judicial department to say what the law is. . . . A law repugnant to the Constitution is void; . . . courts as well as other departments are bound by that instrument." Even after *Marbury*, however, judicial review was slow to institutionalize. The Court waited another 54 years before attempting to invalidate another act of Congress, in its infamous *Dred Scott* decision confirming black slavery, and it was not until the late nineteenth century that the principle was fully established.

The principle of judicial review is in tension with democratic theory inasmuch as it gives unelected judges the power to overrule laws made by a majority of elected officials. When courts overrule legislatures, it is regarded as an expression of judicial activism. Judicial restraint, its opposite, occurs when courts defer to the will of the people expressed through legislative majorities. Most expressions of judicial activism, of courts failing to defer to legislative judgment, have preserved and protected property rights. The Supreme Court's 1905 *Lochner v. New York* decision, which struck down a state law that restricted working hours, and its initial rulings that much New Deal legislation was unconstitutional are examples where judicial review overturned progressive social and economic legislation. But there is no automatic identification of judicial activism with conservative results or, correspondingly, judicial restraint with liberal outcomes. *Brown v. Board of Education*, which overruled state laws governing school segregation, shattered any illusion that judicial activism cuts only one way. Law professor Philip B. Kurland has suggested that "[a]n 'activist' court is essentially one that is out of step with legislative or executive branches of the government" and that it is liberal or conservative "depending which role its prime antagonist has adopted."[26] While judicial activism may be hard to reconcile with democratic theory, there may be circumstances in which it actually enhances democracy, such as when legislation violates one of the provisions of the Bill of Rights or subjects minorities to the tyranny of the majority, as was the case in *Brown*.[27]

Marbury v. Madison settled a question that had divided the country along clear partisan lines. Judicial review was supported by the Federalist Party, which was dominated by northern manufacturing, finance, and mercantile

---

[26]Philip B. Kurland, *Politics, the Constitution and the Warren Court* (Chicago: University of Chicago Press, 1970), pp. 17–18.

[27]Morton Horwitz, *The Warren Court and the Pursuit of Justice* (New York: Hill & Wang, 1998), pp. 76–82.

interests. Southern and western agrarian, planter, and small landowning interests in the Republican Party who favored the principle of legislative supremacy opposed it. But Federalists and Republicans were also divided over the scope of national, as opposed to state, power. This question came before the court in the form of *McCulloch v. Maryland* (1819). In *McCulloch,* the Court ruled that federal law was supreme. State law would have to give way when federal and state laws were in conflict. But not until *McCulloch* did the Court decisively rule in this manner. Thus, the *Marbury* case confirmed the power of the Supreme Court, and the *McCulloch* case confirmed the power of the national government. Both marked a triumph of national, industrial interests in the Federalist Party over local, agrarian interests in the Republican Party.

After Chief Justice John Marshall's death in 1835, President Andrew Jackson appointed Roger Taney to lead the Court. The Court over which he presided, in contrast to the Marshall Court, tilted toward states' rights and southern interests. This was particularly evident in its *Scott v. Sanford* (1857) decision, when the Court, by a 7–2 vote, ruled that no black could be an American citizen, that a black was "a person of an inferior order," that no individual of African descent was a "portion of this American people," and that blacks were slaves and possessions of their owners no matter whether they were in a slave or a free area of the country. The *Dred Scott* decision provoked an outcry in the North and hastened the onset of the Civil War.

Following the Civil War, the Court was in the hands of northern Republicans, who were chiefly concerned with safeguarding property and providing a legal environment for the development of capitalism. For example, the Fourteenth Amendment, adopted in 1868, was intended to protect black civil rights from hostile state actions. But its famous Due Process Clause—no state shall "deprive any person of life, liberty, or property, without due process of law"—served corporate interests more than it did blacks in the nineteenth century. The courts held that many laws regulating business were unconstitutional because they deprived corporations, which enjoyed the legal status of persons, of due process of law. This precipitated a wave of judicial activism by the Court, in which it repeatedly overturned state and federal laws designed to regulate business.[28] The Court used its laissez-faire interpretation of the Constitution to nullify so many laws that Justice Oliver Wendell Holmes complained there "was hardly any limit but the sky to the invalidating of [laws] if they happen to strike a majority of the Court as for any reason undesirable."[29] Not only did the courts protect business from most government regulation, but also they limited the reach of anti-trust laws and restricted the ability of unions to organize and to strike. In recognition of the

---

[28]James Q. Wilson and John J. Dilulio, Jr., *American Government,* 7th ed. (New York: Houghton Mifflin, 1998), p. 444.

[29]Quoted in Schwartz, *Decision,* p. 79.

Supreme Court's service to business, a New York bank president told an audience of capitalists in 1895: "I give you, gentlemen, the Supreme Court of the United States—guardian of the dollar, defender of private property, enemy of spoliation, sheet anchor of the Republic!"[30]

But the Court's defense of property rights and freedom of contract could not withstand the popular thrust of Franklin Roosevelt's New Deal. Initially, the Court repeatedly struck down New Deal legislation. It outlawed the Agricultural Adjustment Act, a New York State minimum wage law, and the National Industrial Recovery Act. The outlook was grim for other New Deal legislation whose constitutionality was also being challenged, such as the Social Security Act and the National Labor Relations Act. The more the Court stood as a roadblock in the way of the New Deal, the more popular frustration with the Court's undemocratic character grew. Senator George Norris of Nebraska expressed this common complaint when he denounced the Court on the Senate floor, saying, "The members of the Supreme Court are not elected by anybody. They are responsible to nobody. Yet they hold dominion over everybody."[31]

Roosevelt had the misfortune in his first term to be the first president ever to serve a full four years and not appoint someone to the Supreme Court. Unable to change the Court through appointment, he proposed to reform the Court by appointing justices who were sympathetic to the New Deal. He proposed "court packing" legislation, which would have permitted the president to appoint a new justice, up to a total of 15, for each justice who reached 70 and did not retire. Since six of the nine justices were over 70 at the time, this legislation would have let Roosevelt add six new like-minded justices to the Court. Roosevelt lost the battle to reform the Court in Congress, but he won the war. While Roosevelt was seeking acceptance for his plan to reform the Court and more court-curbing bills were proposed in Congress than ever before, Justice Owen Roberts, who had previously voted against New Deal legislation and had written some key opinions striking them down, now voted to uphold such legislation as constitutional.[32] One member of Congress noted that Justice Roberts had amended the Constitution and changed the lives of millions simply "by nodding his head instead of shaking it."[33] Justice Roberts's about-face is often referred to as the "switch in time that saved nine." This reversal provided Roosevelt with a majority on the Court, one he later expanded on. By the end of his presidency in 1945, he had filled eight Court vacancies, more than any president since George Washington.

---

[30]Quoted in Redford and Westin, *Politics and Government in the United States*, pp. 498–99.

[31]Quoted in William E. Leuchtenberg, *The Supreme Court Reborn: The Constitutional Revolution in the Age of Roosevelt* (New York: Oxford University Press, 1995), p. 103.

[32]For example, Justice Roberts wrote the majority opinion in *United States v. Butler* (1936), striking down the New Deal's Agricultural Adjustment Act.

[33]Congressman Maury Maverick, quoted in Leuchtenberg, *Supreme Court Reborn*, p. 176.

This reform episode reveals much about the power and limits of the Supreme Court. The Court can nullify the will of the people, as it did initially, at least, regarding New Deal legislation. But if the Court stands too hard and too long against public opinion, the Court's decisions risk losing legitimacy in the eyes of the public. The prestige and stature of the Court will suffer. This is particularly damaging because the Court does not derive legitimacy from democratic theory. Supreme Court justices are not elected and are not accountable to those affected by their decisions. Instead, the justices must depend on their eminence and prestige as the reasons why their decisions should be respected. The Court must constantly keep its reputation aloft, appearing above the political and partisan fray, since it cannot draw legitimacy for its decisions from democratic theory, as other American political institutions claim to do. This was precisely the point the minority tried to convey in their dissent to the Supreme Court decision that effectively made George W. Bush president in 2000. Justice Stevens wrote that the Court's action

> [c]an only lend credence to the most cynical appraisal of the work of judges throughout the land. . . . It is confidence in the men and women who administer the judicial system that is the true backbone of the rule of law. Time will one day heal the wound to that confidence that will be inflicted by today's decision. One thing, however, is certain. Although we may never know with complete certainty the identity of the winner of this year's presidential election, the identity of the loser is perfectly clear. It is the nation's confidence in the judge as an impartial guardian of the rule of law.[34]

After 1936, the Supreme Court upheld every New Deal statute whose constitutionality was challenged. Judicial supremacy gave way to deference to Congress and the president. Judicial activism was replaced with judicial restraint. In the course of confirming the New Deal, the Court initiated a constitutional revolution that greatly expanded the power of the federal government over business and the states. Previously, the national government had lacked power over business if it was not engaged in interstate commerce. The Court now defined interstate commerce so broadly that federal law applied to virtually all business transactions. It now interpreted the taxing and spending powers of the government so expansively that there were almost "no social welfare or regulatory statutes that the Courts would not validate."[35]

This constitutional revolution in 1937 replaced classical legal doctrines based on freedom of contract with a new jurisprudence that affirmed government regulation of business. Freedom of contract was just, according to the old classical legal theory, because it reflected the results arrived at in a neutral market among free and willing parties. But as legal scholar Roscoe Pound argued in 1903, the freedom of contract doctrine represented a conception of equal rights that was fraudulent to "everyone acquainted at first

---

[34]*New York Times*, December 13, 2000.

[35]Leuchtenberg, *Supreme Court Reborn*, p. 154.

hand with actual industrial conditions."[36] Employers enjoyed much more market power than individual workers in bargaining, for example, over the employment contract. Moreover, the Depression made it painfully clear that the interpretation of contractual freedom the Court wanted to protect rested on false assumptions about the ability of unregulated markets to satisfy people's needs. The formal, abstract, detached quality of classical legal doctrine was now replaced with one that was realistic and grounded in results. If the market was not neutral, if its results were harmful to society, then it was appropriate for government to intervene. The constitutional revolution of 1937 marked the rise of a new legal theory that could justify government interference in freedom of contract so as to require firms to pay minimum wages, bargain with their unionized workers, and stop hiring child labor. The Court finally acknowledged what had long been recognized everywhere outside of it: that laissez-faire capitalism was dead. (See Figure 8–3 for a graph of the number of economic and civil liberties laws overturned by the Supreme Court in the last century.)

THE MODERN COURT: FROM WARREN TO REHNQUIST

No Court has been so praised by liberals and so reviled by conservatives as the Warren Court, which takes its name from Earl Warren, who served as chief justice from 1954 to 1969. The Warren Court was liberal, in concert with the dominant coalition of liberal Democrats that governed in the 1960s. The issues confronting this coalition were no longer those related to government regulation of business, as they had been for the New Deal Democratic coalition that preceded it. Since 1937, the Court had decisively settled such issues in favor of regulation. Now the Court reflected concerns with civil rights and civil liberties.[37]

This focus entailed extending the promise of formal legal equality that most Americans took for granted to groups who had been excluded, such as blacks. The Warren Court proceeded to generate a more inclusive meaning of democracy, as was evident in its civil rights decisions, its rulings expanding freedom of speech and press protections, its voting rights decisions, and its application of the Bill of Rights to the states. These decisions provoked tremendous controversy. But the Warren Court prevailed because, according to two political scientists, "it enjoyed strong executive support

---

[36]Quoted in Morton Horwitz, *The Transformation of American Law, 1870–1960* (New York: Oxford University Press, 1992), p. 34.

[37]We might also add that the Warren Court reflected the Cold War consensus of the Democratic coalition as well as its domestic concern with rights. The Warren Court permitted the silencing of left-wing opinion with respect to admission to the bar and the conduct of congressional investigations.

■ FIGURE 8-3

ECONOMIC AND CIVIL LIBERTIES LAWS OVERTURNED BY
THE SUPREME COURT, 1900–1980

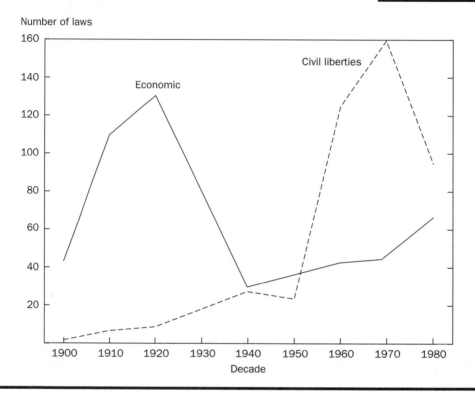

SOURCE: Lawrence Baum, *The Supreme Court* (Washington, D.C.: Congressional Quarterly Press, 1985), p. 188.

because its activism served the interests of the occupants of the White House."[38]

The Warren Court's effort to realize the promise of legal equality for all Americans was evident in a number of landmark decisions. *Brown*, of course, led the way in civil rights. But until Congress got serious about civil rights, the Court moved slowly, denying a hearing to many cases. Once Congress took the lead, the Court, in 1964, announced that the time for school districts to show deliberate speed in desegregating schools had run out *(Griffin v. County School Board of Prince Edward County)*. Four years later, in *Green v. County School Board of New Kent County*, the Court required school districts

---

[38]Mark Silverstein and Benjamin Ginsberg, "The Supreme Court and the New Politics of Judicial Power," *Political Science Quarterly* 102 (Fall 1987): 379.

that had practiced segregation in the past to not only stop discriminating, but to take affirmative action to achieve racial balance in their schools. Nor did the civil rights legislation of the 1960s suffer the same fate at the hands of the Warren Court that the legislation passed by the Reconstruction Congress of the 1860s had suffered at the hands of earlier Supreme Courts. In the 1870s and 1880s, the Supreme Court had vitiated the intent of the Reconstruction Congress to protect the rights of newly freed slaves. A century later the Warren Court reinforced the will of Congress when it upheld the constitutionality of the Civil Rights Act of 1964 and the Voting Rights Act of 1965. Opponents of civil rights legislation, racist or otherwise, who looked to the Supreme Court to restrict or undermine its effect, as opponents of the Reconstruction Congress had done, would have to look elsewhere.

The Warren Court also acted to expand the notion of legal equality and ensure the effectiveness of each citizen's vote by requiring equally apportioned legislative districts. Some state legislative districts included many more voters than others. Some legislative districts were so malapportioned that only 20 percent of the population was sufficient to elect a majority in some state legislatures. In *Baker v. Carr* (1962), the Court ruled that it was appropriate for federal courts to hear cases challenging malapportioned state election districts. Two years later, in *Reynolds v. Sims*, the Court took the next step on the road to making the promise of political equality a reality. It declared that the "one person, one vote" principle, which governs congressional districting, also applies to state legislatures. Writing for the majority on the Court in requiring states to apportion their legislative districts fairly by population, Warren wrote, "Legislators represent people, not trees or acres."[39]

The Warren Court also was responsible for extending the boundaries of democracy by requiring states to abide by virtually every provision of the Bill of Rights. State law enforcement and criminal procedures would now have to meet federal due process requirements, giving defendants charged with crimes certain procedural rights and protections. In *Mapp v. Ohio* (1961), the Court ruled, in the words of two experienced reporters, "that evidence obtained in violation of the Fourth Amendment guarantee against unreasonable search and seizure must be excluded from use in state, as well as federal courts." Two years later in *Gideon v. Wainwright* (1963), the Court declared that states must provide legal counsel to all defendants charged with serious crimes. In 1966, the Court handed down its *Miranda* decision, which stated that a confession obtained from a criminal suspect during interrogation is not admissible as evidence in court unless the accused person has been informed of his or her rights to remain silent and to be represented by a lawyer. The Warren Court accelerated the process of creating a "second Bill of

---

[39]Quoted in Schwartz, *Decision*, p. 105.

Rights" that now applied to the states, alongside the original document that applied to the federal government. [40]

Finally, the Warren Court extended citizens' personal rights and protections. In *Griswold v. Connecticut* (1965), the Court recognized a constitutional right to privacy, striking down a state law barring the use of contraceptives. The right to privacy first enumerated in *Griswold* under Chief Justice Earl Warren was later extended by the Court after he retired to include a woman's right to an abortion in *Roe v. Wade* (1973).

Some of the Warren Court's decisions have become national standards and accepted democratic principles. It is hard to imagine the law today tolerating government-sanctioned racial segregation, as it once did, or deviating from the principle of one person, one vote, as it once also did. While Supreme Court decisions have chipped away at the Warren Court's jurisprudence in recent years, its legacy lives on.

The Warren Court's decisions drew the ire of conservatives, who attacked it for coddling criminals, tying the hands of police and prosecutors, being irreligious, violating states' rights, and promoting civil unrest. Richard Nixon pledged to remold the Court in his 1968 presidential campaign, and within a year of his election, he had a chance to deliver on that promise. In 1969, Earl Warren retired, and President Nixon appointed Warren E. Burger, a known critic of many Warren Court decisions, to replace him as chief justice. By the end of Warren Burger's service as chief justice in 1986, Republican presidents had appointed six members to the Supreme Court. Only two members of the liberal faction from the Warren Court, Justices William Brennan and Thurgood Marshall, remained on the bench, along with Byron White.

Circumstances were ripe for conservatives to undo the work of the Warren Court. Yet the Burger Court was a disappointment to all those who believed it would overturn the decisions of the Warren Court. The counterrevolution many anticipated never happened. Indeed, it would be inaccurate even to describe the Supreme Court as the Burger Court during the years he served as chief justice (1969–86). Despite his title, Burger never led the Court intellectually or put his personal stamp on it to the extent that Earl Warren, his predecessor, had. To the dismay and disappointment of conservatives, the Burger Court was caught in the backdraft of the Court it had succeeded. The power of judicial precedent, the lack of leadership exuded by Burger, and the skill of liberal Justice William Brennan in coaxing a majority of justices to follow the Warren Court's lead were enough to hold the line. Reviewing the Burger Court, political scientists Mark Silverstein and Benjamin Ginsberg concluded in 1987: "The most controversial decisions of the Warren era involving school prayer, reapportionment, desegregation, and

---

[40]This paragraph draws on the description of the "due process revolution" in Joan Biskopic and Elder Witt, *Guide to the U.S. Supreme Court,* 3rd ed. (Washington, D.C.: Congressional Quarterly Press, 1997), pp. 52–53. See also Leuchtenberg, *Supreme Court Reborn,* pp. 237–58.

criminal procedure remain the law of the land. The Burger Court nibbled at the edges of several Warren Court precedents, often seeking to confine their application, but overt attempts at overruling were either avoided or defeated."[41] Even though conservatives pilloried the Warren Court for judicial activism in invalidating state and federal laws as unconstitutional, the Burger Court was actually more guilty of this alleged sin than its predecessor, showing even less judicial restraint, less deference to legislatures, than the Warren Court it followed.

Nowhere was the Burger Court more faithful to its predecessor than in the area of civil rights. In *Swann v. Charlotte-Mecklenberg County Board of Education* (1970), the Court made clear there would be no retreat from *Brown*. The Court unanimously upheld the use of busing to achieve racially balanced schools. The Court also gave constitutional approval to affirmative action plans as a way to remedy past discrimination against minorities and other protected groups. Thus, for example, in *Fullilove v. Klutznick* (1979), the Court upheld the provisions of the Public Works Employment Act of 1977, providing for a 10 percent "'set-aside" for minority business enterprises. In *United Steelworkers of America v. Weber,* the first case in which the Court specifically addressed affirmative action in employment, it rejected the argument of a white complainant that Title VII of the Civil Rights Act of 1964 outlawed any grant of preferential treatment to racial minorities.

But the Burger Court's most famous decision, *Roe v. Wade* (1973), most clearly expresses the degree to which the Court drew on the legal reasoning of the Warren Court. In *Roe v. Wade,* the Burger Court applied the Warren Court's logic of a constitutional right to privacy in order to strike down state laws denying a woman's right to an abortion.[42] This was judicial activism of the highest order.

But as the number of liberal holdovers from the Warren Court decreased and the decline of the Democratic governing coalition became more evident, the Burger Court, over time, became more conservative. The drift to the right was particularly apparent in criminal law, where the Burger Court began to chip away at the Warren Court's revolution in due process, reducing defendants' procedural rights and protections.

In 1986, Republicans pulled the equivalent of a double steal in baseball. Justice Burger retired and was replaced as chief justice by William Rehnquist, the most conservative member of the Court. Rehnquist was so at odds with the basically liberal thrust of the Burger Court that he wrote a record number of single dissents to its decisions, earning him the nickname "The Lone Ranger." Now as chief justice, he could use the real, if limited, leverage the position afforded to move the Court in his direction. When Rehnquist

[41]Silverstein and Ginsberg, "Supreme Court and the New Politics," p. 372.

[42]Many legal experts believe that there was less logic than invention involved in the Warren Court's holding that a constitutional right to privacy existed.

became chief justice, Antonin Scalia, a conservative law professor and judge, took the seat Rehnquist formerly had occupied.

William Brennan, the most liberal member of the Court, stepped down in 1990. President George Bush replaced him with David H. Souter. Thurgood Marshall, the last liberal holdover from the Warren Court, resigned a year later in 1991. President Bush replaced him with another African American, Clarence Thomas. Skin color may have been the only thing that Marshall and Thomas had in common. Marshall opposed the death penalty and supported affirmative action and a woman's right to an abortion. Thomas, on the other hand, favored the death penalty and opposed abortion and government programs to remedy the effects of discrimination. His appointment was the last in an unbroken string of 11 Supreme Court appointments by Republican presidents (Republicans controlled the presidency for all but four years from 1968 through 1992).[43] They thus were able to use their power to transform the Court politically, appointing justices who would reflect their basically conservative values.

The Rehnquist Court has had a solid right wing, composed of the chief justice, Scalia, and Thomas, which has perceived its role as undoing the work of the Warren and Burger Courts. The other Supreme Court justices appointed by Republican presidents—Sandra Day O'Connor, David Souter, and Anthony Kennedy—have resisted too great a turn away from the precedents built up by their predecessors. To simply discard the legal legacy of those Courts, this group believes, would damage the Supreme Court as an institution. Thus, in 1991, Justices O'Connor, Souter, and Kennedy wrote an unusual joint opinion upholding *Roe* in the abortion case *Planned Parenthood of Southeastern Pennsylvania v. Casey*. They were aware that, if the Court overturned *Roe*, this would be perceived, quite accurately, as due simply to the fact that membership on the Court had changed. It would expose the Court to the charge that its decisions reflect election results, rather than the Constitution, and that the law mirrors the personal values of whomever the president appoints to the Court, rather than legal precedent or reasoning. The joint opinion of O'Connor, Souter, and Kennedy argued that, since *Roe* had been decided, people "had ordered their thinking and living around that case" and that no legal principle weakening *Roe*'s constitutional basis had occurred since 1973. "A decision to overrule *Roe*'s essential holding under the existing circumstances," their opinion continued, would be "at the cost of both profound and unnecessary damage to the Court's legitimacy and to the rule of law."[44] Thus, one survey that described the early terms of the Rehnquist Court was called *The Center Holds*.[45]

---

[43]The only Democratic president elected between 1968 and 1992 was President Jimmy Carter, who had the misfortune of never having the chance to appoint anyone to the Supreme Court.

[44]See James F. Simon, *The Center Holds: The Power Struggle Inside the Rehnquist Court* (New York: Simon & Schuster, 1995), pp. 144–67, for the Rehnquist Court's process of decision making in *Casey*.

[45]Simon, *The Center Holds*.

With more of the Rehnquist Court's record available now, it is clear that the center that once existed within the Court has collapsed. Nowhere has the contrast between the Warren and Rehnquist Courts been greater than in the area of civil rights. While the Warren Court's finest hour came with *Brown* and the principle of school desegregation, the Rehnquist Court has retreated from this commitment. It has limited lower federal courts in imposing plans that would achieve racial integration. The Rehnquist Court also has begun to back away from affirmative action, requiring a far stricter standard to justify such programs than had been used before. Finally, the Rehnquist Court has shifted the burden of proof from the employers who are charged with discrimination to the employees who are its victims (Congress overturned the Court in this regard in the Civil Rights Restoration Act of 1991).

The law has begun to change subtly, and not so subtly, in other areas as well. As we have already seen in abortion cases, the Rehnquist Court did not go so far as to repudiate *Roe*, but it did permit states to place more obstacles in the way of women who sought abortions. In criminal law, the Court has made it easier for states to impose the death penalty. It also has been much less vigilant in requiring that the due process rights of criminal defendants be respected. But the Rehnquist Court did not stop at challenging some of the Warren Court's legacy. It also struck at legal doctrines regarding federalism that go back to the New Deal. After Rehnquist joined the Court in 1971, he issued lonely dissents on behalf of states' rights and limits to federal power. Now a majority on the Court agrees with him, reducing the authority of Congress over the states. The Court's devotion to states' rights has had a profound impact, resulting in reversal of civil rights rulings, due process decisions, and even precedents upholding the separation of church and state. According to Edward P. Lazarus, who once clerked for Justice Harry Blackmun, "The Court today . . . is riven between those who see the federal government as the primary guarantor of constitutional rights and those who do not; between those Justices who still think the federal government must intervene to achieve racial equality and those who do not; and between those who for whom 'states' rights' still carries the taint of the slaveholder and those for whom it does not."[46]

President Bill Clinton was the first Democrat to appoint a justice to the Supreme Court in 26 years. In 1993, Byron White retired. President Clinton replaced him with Ruth Bader Ginsburg, the second woman appointed to the Court, following Sandra Day O'Connor. In 1994, Harry Blackmun retired, giving Clinton the chance to make another appointment. He chose Stephen Breyer. Both Ginsburg and Breyer were former judges who fit the mold of Clinton's judicial appointments to the lower courts: They were political moderates who would not counterbalance the strict conservatives who now composed a plurality in the lower courts, just as they did on the Supreme Court. With Scalia, Rehnquist, and Thomas voting together as a

[46]Edward P. Lazarus, *Closed Chambers: The First Eyewitness Account of the Epic Struggles Inside the Supreme Court* (New York: Random House, 1998), p. 512.

bloc on almost all cases before the Court—and no bloc on the left to offset them, as there had been when Brennan, Marshall, and Blackmun were on the Court—it only takes two defections from among the centrists for the conservatives on the Court to win. As William Brennan, the liberal jurist, was fond of saying, "It takes five votes to do anything in the Supreme Court."[47]

POLITICS BY LAWSUIT

Americans are known to be litigious, settling their disputes in court rather than among themselves. The degree to which Americans engage in lawsuits is not a cultural trait, but a reflection of the individual rights we enjoy and the openness of the judicial system to assertions of those rights. Recently, corporate America has tried to reduce the prevalence of lawsuits, claiming they are frivolous and expensive and hamper innovation. It has tried to pass bills that would cap punitive damages awards by juries and discourage lawsuits by making plaintiffs pay if they lose. Its most telling example of a justice system that is out of control is the 1994 case of a woman who won a multimillion-dollar award from McDonald's after she spilled coffee on herself. But the common perception that her claim was trivial is a myth. In fact, McDonald's had received over 700 complaints about burns from their coffee, which was 20 degrees hotter than in most other restaurants, and the woman in question required skin grafts for the third-degree burns she suffered. While the $2.9 million jury award received extensive coverage in the media, not many newspapers covered the story of how the woman later settled for $600,000 after the judge reduced the jury's punitive damages award. Corporations have mounted an effective public relations campaign against "frivolous" lawsuits, like that against McDonald's, which often are not frivolous at all. While the law may serve the interests of corporations, it can also be used to hold them accountable for unsafe cars, cancerous cigarettes, dangerous drugs, and risky products.

The same rush to the courts for judgment and restitution is occurring in politics as well as outside of it. More and more groups are looking to the courts to settle political issues. At no time was this more evident than when Al Gore and George W. Bush appealed to the courts to settle questions surrounding the 2000 presidential election. Or take the example of how environmentalists shifted tactics once George W. Bush became president. They filed expensive lawsuits against polluters because they had little faith the Bush administration would enforce environmental regulations.[48] Environmentalists hoped to make policy through lawsuits in the courts as opposed

---

[47]Quoted in David G. Savage, *Turning Right: The Making of the Rehnquist Court* (New York: John Wiley and Sons, 1992), p. 12.

[48]*New York Times,* December 2, 2000.

to legislation by Congress or regulation by federal agencies. The courtroom has become simply another extension of the political battle once it moves past the electoral, legislative, and administrative arenas. More than a century and a half ago, Alexis de Tocqueville noted this peculiar trait when he observed, "There is hardly a political question in the United States that does not sooner or later turn into a judicial one."[49]

While the courts have always been a strategic political option, this has been particularly so since the 1960s. In the 1960s, Supreme Court rulings made federal courts more open and inviting to those who wanted to bring suit in them. Previous restrictions regarding the kinds of cases that could be brought and the parties who could legally bring them in federal courts were relaxed. This change, according to two political scientists, Benjamin Ginsberg and Martin Shefter, has "given a wider range of litigants access to the courts, has rendered a broader range of issues subject to judicial settlement, and so has greatly increased the reach of the courts in American life."[50] As the courts have expanded their jurisdiction, making themselves open to a wider array of interests and issues, their power has increased. The federal courts have become more involved in policy issues that groups now bring to them in the form of litigation.

According to legal scholar Martin Shapiro, the new openness of the courts has contributed to a broader involvement of the courts in policy and politics. Nowhere is this more evident than in the growth of judicial activism. Nullifying laws as unconstitutional has become more frequent under both liberal and conservative Supreme Courts, from Warren to Rehnquist. Judge-made law substitutes for legislature-made law. Second, the courts have become more engaged in policy and politics through their greater role in implementing the law. For example, federal district courts have gone so far as to take over local school systems, constructing elaborate plans for their desegregation when local school boards have dragged their feet. Courts have become involved in such matters as what schools would close, where new ones would be constructed, and to which schools students would be assigned. In the 1970s, people in Alabama joked that the real executive leader of the state was Federal District Court Judge Frank M. Johnson, Jr., and not Governor George Wallace. Johnson earned such notoriety because his appointees oversaw Alabama schools, prisons, mental hospitals, and elections when state agencies failed to perform their constitutional duties.

Finally, the courts' growing involvement in policy and politics is evident in the lack of deference courts now show to federal administrative agencies. The courts, of course, have the final say over the meaning of legislation. They have, however, previously deferred to the expertise of administrative

---

[49]Alexis de Tocqueville, *Democracy in America* (New York: Knopf, 1946), p. 280.

[50]Benjamin Ginsberg and Martin Shefter, *Politics by Other Means: The Declining Importance of Elections in America* (New York: Basic Books, 1990), p. 150.

agencies in how legislation is to be interpreted and implemented. But courts today are more willing to invoke their authority, to have the final word on legislative meaning, and to overrule administrative agencies. For example, the U.S. Court of Appeals for the District of Columbia Circuit, which handles most challenges to federal regulations, recently prevented the Environmental Protection Agency (EPA) from implementing new, more stringent clean air standards. Such standards had been developed over two years in which interested parties had made their case to the EPA, an independent panel of scientists had confirmed the health effects of the new standard, and the new standard passed legislative scrutiny when Congress failed to overturn it. This did not prevent the American Trucking Association from challenging the stricter standards in court by bringing suit against the EPA. And it won.[51] Of course, the more courts substitute their judgment for that of administrative agencies, the more they invite litigation. Groups seeking vigorous enforcement of the law and groups resisting regulation now engage in politics by lawsuit in order to shape court decisions as much as they previously engaged in lobbying in order to influence agency rule making.[52]

Yet, as much as the courts have grown in power, so have the other branches of the government, Congress and the executive, with which they compete. Moreover, as we have already noted, the courts tend to reflect the politics of ruling coalitions, reaffirming as opposed to challenging them. The courts are powerful so long as they blow with the prevailing wind and not against it. Consequently, while public-interest advocacy groups have had some success in appealing to the courts and getting the law changed, what happens in the real world is often another matter. Schools remain segregated despite *Brown*, and the number of abortions grew faster in the years preceding *Roe* than they did in those afterward. Changing the law is often only one step in the larger quest for social change.

CONCLUSION

Courts are, at times, both conservative institutions, backing the status quo, and innovative institutions, promoting change. On the side of preserving existing patterns, courts play an important role in confirming the power and legitimacy of corporate capitalism. Their decisions usually follow and confirm reforms rather than causing them. On the basis of a study of civil rights, women's rights, and reapportionment, among other subjects, political

---

[51]John B. Judis, "Deregulation Run Riot," *American Prospect*, September–October 1999, 16–19. Later, in 2001, the Supreme Court reversed the court of appeals ruling that had overturned the EPA clean air standards.

[52]Martin Shapiro, "The Juridicalization of Politics in the United States," *International Political Science Review* 15 (April 1994): 101–12.

scientist Gerald Rosenberg concluded that, in the United States, "courts can *almost never* be effective producers of significant social reform. At best, they can second the social reform acts of other branches of government."[53] Lacking influence over the budget and control over administrative agencies, courts cannot enforce their decisions on their own. In addition, the deference courts show to legal precedent in reaching their decisions tends to bind them to the past. Finally, the legal process, with its constant motions and appeals, is slow and tedious. The law usually follows politics, not the other way around. Consequently, courts may confirm victories won by voters, social movements, and legislators, but rarely do they spearhead such advances.

Yet Rosenberg and other constitutional scholars who caution that we must not overestimate the contributions of the judicial system to social change also know that at some historical moments the constraints on court action are overcome and the judicial system becomes a key part of change and reform. While it would be misleading to identify *Brown* as the main cause of the Civil Rights movement, it would equally misrepresent the historical record to put the court-centered strategy of the Civil Rights movement aside as if it had no bearing on the monumental changes that were to follow. At an earlier point of large-scale change, Franklin Roosevelt's New Deal, a constitutional impasse was overcome by changes in the views, decisions, and membership of the Supreme Court. By the early 1940s, in the space of a single decade, the Court had switched from a red light to a green light with respect to authorizing a strong governmental role in shaping and regulating modern capitalism.

---

[53]Rosenberg, *Hollow Hope*, p. 338 (emphasis in original).

PUBLIC POLICY

Trying to Resolve the Tension Between Capitalism and Democracy

Political institutions are the motor that drives the political machine. Policies represent the programs that dictate in which direction the machine moves. The government pursues policies on an endless array of topics, ranging from the most minute to the most important. In Part IV, we analyze two of the most important policy areas, foreign policy and social policy. We chose them because they connect closely with our central themes, they consume a large share of federal expenditures, and they heavily influence the entire practice of American politics. (Note that we analyzed economic policy in Chapter 3.)

Government policies are both a result and a cause. They result from struggles among private groups and political officials. And policies matter because they help shape future political outcomes. They involve what Harold Lasswell described as the stuff of politics: who gets what, where, and how.[1] It is no wonder that political debate so frequently revolves around what policies the government should and should not pursue.

Our discussions of foreign policy and social policy highlight the tense interrelationship of capitalism and democracy. Policies are not made in a vacuum. The context in which they occur is a country's political economy—the particular features of capitalist democracy in the United States that we analyzed in Chapters 2 through 4—as well as its political institutions, analyzed in later chapters. The democratic features of American politics mean that policies are widely debated and partially responsive to what mobilized groups demand. However, the fact that American democracy is incomplete heavily affects which demands are considered and what happens when government debates those select few demands.

In our discussions of foreign policy and social policy, we will continually see how public policy represents changing ways to work out the connections between capitalism and democracy, to provide specific and changing form to the American version of capitalist democracy. We will highlight both that there is considerable space for democratic debate and practice to alter the contours of policy and that policy choices are severely constrained by the organization of the political economy and the design of political institutions.

---

[1]Harold Lasswell, *Politics: Who Gets What, Where, and How* (New York: Meridian Books, 1958).

9

Corporate Capitalism, Foreign Policy, and the Global Political Economy

INTRODUCTION

Some statistics provide the context for understanding American foreign policy: With just less than 5 percent of the world's population in 1995, the United States accounted for more than one-quarter of the world's gross domestic product (GDP). Income in the United States alone is 4 times as large as the combined income of all the countries in East Asia and the Pacific and 14 times as large as the combined income of all the countries in the Middle East and North Africa. The United States also has almost twice as many televisions per thousand citizens as the world average and 34 percent of all radio receivers in the world. It consumes more oil than Germany, France, China, and India combined.[1] Overall, most Americans are wealthier (as can be seen in Table 9–1), enjoy better housing, suffer less from hunger, and receive more education and services than most people in the world. These figures are averages for all Americans and do not take note of the extensive inequalities *within* the United States, which is the subject of other chapters. But they suggest how deep the inequalities are between American citizens and much of the world's population. When American political leaders talk of the need to maintain world order and stability, they are referring to the order and stability of a world based on fundamental inequalities, in which the United States enjoys a vastly disproportionate share of the world's resources.

In order to understand the position of the United States in the world today, and the aims and process of making foreign policy, it is useful to establish a baseline. Later in the chapter, we will describe the historical evolution of the United States's position in the world since the early years of the Republic. We open this chapter by reviewing a watershed period in American foreign

---

[1]Income estimate from the World Bank Group, "Development Data, 2000 World Development Indicators," p. 12, at *http://www.worldbank.org/data/wdi:2000/pdfs/tab_1.pdf*. See also *UNESCO Statistical Yearbook* (Paris: UNESCO Publishing and Bernan Press, 1999), sec. I.V. On oil consumption, see *Key World Energy Statistics from the IEA*, 1999 ed. (Paris: International Energy Association, 1999), p. 10.

■ TABLE 9-1

PER CAPITA INCOME, SELECTED COUNTRIES, 1998

Country	Per Capita Income ($)
Brazil	4,630
Canada	19,170
China	750
Dominican Republic	1,770
Ghana	390
Hungary	4,510
India	440
Italy	20,090
Mexico	3,840
Philippines	1,050
Russian Federation	2,260
Senegal	520
Sweden	25,580
United States	29,240

SOURCE: World Bank Group, Development Data, 2000 World Development Indicators, pp. 10–12, *http://www.worldbank.org/data/wd:2000/pdfs/tabl_1.pdf.*

policy, the Cold War, which began in 1945, just after World War II, and came to a close in the 1990s, when the Soviet regime crumbled.

The major goal of American foreign policy during the Cold War was to check the power of the Union of Soviet Socialist Republics—the USSR or Soviet Union. World politics was structured by the conflict between the two superpowers. Each one was dominant in its sphere of influence: the United States in Western Europe, North America, and Latin America; the Soviet Union in Eastern and Central Europe, Cuba, and the People's Republic of China. Each country also had client states in the less-developed regions of Africa, Asia, and Latin America—often referred to as the Third World, to distinguish it from the industrialized capitalist world (the First World) and the Soviet bloc (the Second World).

Foreign policy during the Cold War contrasted sharply with the more restrained foreign policy that the United States pursued in its early years. During the Cold War, the United States devoted enormous political, military, and economic resources to checking the Soviet Union, maintaining regimes friendly to the United States throughout the world, and weakening movements and regimes allied with the Soviet Union.

A common view is that the United States was dragged reluctantly into the Cold War and only grudgingly accepted the responsibility of world leadership that was thrust on it. According to an influential foreign policy analyst and official, the United States did not deliberately seek to extend its power at the end of World War II, but, "having many obligations and vast responsibilities in the world," it was forced to "adopt a policy not dictated by any American material needs and certainly not in response to any American ambition or desire."[2] As President Lyndon B. Johnson proudly stated, "History and our own achievements have thrust upon us the principal responsibility for the protection of freedom on Earth."[3] Writing in the fiscal 1975 annual Defense Department report, the secretary of defense observed: "The United States today, as opposed to the period before 1945, bears the principal burden of maintaining the worldwide military equilibrium, which is the foundation for the security and the survival of the free world. This is not a role we have welcomed; it is a role that historical necessity has thrust upon us. . . . There is nobody else to pick up the torch."

Critics question this portrait of the United States as a reluctant superpower that hesitated to accept leadership in world affairs. For example, historian David Callahan suggests that the United States played a less active role in world affairs throughout the nineteenth and early twentieth centuries because it was able to rely on Britain, the dominant world power at the time, to provide a framework of order and stability in the world. The United States could depend on Britain to do the heavy lifting for it. But by the end of World War II, Britain's power had declined noticeably, and it could no longer ensure world order. Both the Great Depression of the 1930s and the deadly conflict of World War II had created a power vacuum—that is, the absence of a hegemonic power that could provide global economic and political stability. Callahan suggests: "Whether the Cold War had occurred or not, it is clear that the United States would still have played a much greater global leadership role after World War II than it did after World War I. . . . For quite apart from the problem of security, postwar U.S. economic growth was seen as requiring international economic order that could only be guaranteed if the United States took over the position of a declining Britain."[4]

This does not mean that the Soviet Union's communist ideology and attempt to extend its own power did not affect how the United States sought to exercise dominance. According to Callahan, Cold War superpower rivalry between the United States and the Soviet Union meant that "America's global leadership role was far more militarized and far-reaching than it might otherwise have been, and it served to entrench and sustain the consensus [within the United States] that U.S. engagement was needed to assure balanced power abroad."[5]

---

[2]Charles E. Bohlen, *The Transformation of American Foreign Policy* (New York: Norton, 1969), p. 124.
[3]Quoted in Richard J. Barnet, *Roots of War* (New York: Penguin, 1972), p. 19.
[4]David Callahan, *Between Two Worlds: Realism, Idealism, and American Foreign Policy After the Cold War* (New York: HarperCollins, 1994), p. 30.
[5]Ibid.

The Cold War period was unique in one respect. Ever since the United States developed and used atomic weapons against Japan, in the closing months of World War II, the world has faced the awful possibility that nuclear weapons will cause unparalleled devastation. For decades (and to a lesser extent continuing into the present), the future of the world has hung by a thread. With thousands of nuclear-equipped intercontinental ballistic missiles targeted on opposing armed forces and civilian populations, there is the possibility that, by accident or irresponsible design, nuclear catastrophe could endanger the entire planet. Indeed, the two superpowers approached the brink of nuclear war on several occasions—most notably, during the Cuban missile crisis of 1963. (Documents recently revealed just how close the two sides were to ordering their nuclear-tipped missiles to fly.) Nor was the Cold War always cold. The two countries fought a series of "proxy wars" in the Third World, in which their client states and movements engaged in armed conflict. And the United States was directly involved in two hot wars during the period of the Cold War—in Korea and Vietnam—and intervened in less open ways in countless other conflicts to counter what it claimed was a Soviet threat.

Beginning in the late 1980s, however, momentous changes occurred on the Soviet side, culminating in the dissolution of the Soviet Union in 1991 and the emergence of a noncommunist Russia and a variety of independent states formerly incorporated within the Soviet Union. With the crumbling of the Second World (although China and Cuba continue to profess allegiance to communism), the Cold War has been succeeded by a new era in which the United States is the only remaining superpower. As a result, the United States now has immensely greater power than any other country in the world and has attempted to use that power to shape a global framework in America's image.

The United States seeks to foster a stable world order in which global capitalism and liberal democracy can thrive. Not coincidentally, with the United States as the world leader, powerful U.S. interests benefit most from this situation. A major question in world politics today is whether subordinate groups and movements in the United States and elsewhere, as well as the many countries and regions receiving few benefits and paying heavy costs in the new world order, will have a say in shaping decisions about production, consumption, and social life in an interconnected world.

AMERICAN FOREIGN POLICY BEFORE WORLD WAR II

During the eighteenth and nineteenth centuries, the United States was far removed from world power struggles. In his presidential farewell address, George Washington urged Americans to profit from the good fortune that geography provided, in the form of an ocean separating it from Europe, and to avoid "entangling alliances" with other countries. For much of the nineteenth century, the United States was able to remain isolated from European intrigues. Instead, the United States practiced a policy of expansion into its vast western frontier, resulting in the decimation, conquest, and forced resettlement of native Indian populations, the taking of Florida from Spain in 1819, the annexation of Texas in 1845, and war with Mexico in 1846. (The Mexican-American War resulted in the annexation of a substantial portion of Mexico, including the area that is now California, New Mexico, Utah, Arizona, and Nevada.)

Furthermore, being isolated from Europe did not mean abstaining from foreign intervention. Although the United States remained distant from Europe's struggles, it staked out its own sphere of influence close to home. In 1823, President Monroe issued what came to be known as the Monroe Doctrine, in which he warned European powers not to intervene in Latin America. According to historian Richard Van Alstyne, "[I]t is not the negatives [in the Monroe Doctrine] that really count. It is the hidden positive to the effect that the United States shall be the only colonizing power and the sole directing power in both North and South America."[6]

The orientation of the United States began to change around 1900 as Britain's power waned. In the period between the Spanish-American War in 1898 and World War II, the United States was divided between its traditional isolationism and a new expansionism overseas. War with Spain enabled the United States to gain control over the Philippines, Puerto Rico, and Guam. The United States practiced what came to be called gunboat diplomacy in Latin America, in which it sent the navy to install and protect regimes favorable to American business interests. President Theodore Roosevelt connived to build the Panama Canal by carving out the client state of Panama from Colombia and pressuring Panama to grant the United States sovereignty over the land for the canal. (Nearly a century later, on December 31, 2000, the United States turned over control of the canal to Panama, at last closing the books on a flagrant instance of American imperialism.)

Until the early twentieth century, U.S. influence was mostly confined to the Western Hemisphere. But the two world wars enormously weakened the leading European nations. In particular, World War II brought the irrevocable decline of Great Britain as the dominant capitalist power and the hub of world manufacturing, commerce, and banking. The Soviet Union, Japan, Germany, Britain, and France—the only major industrialized countries other than the United States—all suffered heavy damage from the war. By contrast, the United States was unscathed by the war. Indeed, the war gave the U.S. economy a shot in the arm, and the United States emerged as the world's preeminent economic, military, and political power.

After World War II, Europe's decline, the existence of a political and ideological rival in the form of the Soviet Union, and the fear of American officials that a domestic depression would recur if the world was unstable produced

[6]Richard W. Van Alstyne, *The Rising American Empire* (Chicago: Quadrangle, 1965), p. 99.

a basic reorientation in U.S. foreign policy. Movements for independence in colonies of Western powers in Asia and Africa, as well as demands for economic development and social justice from these peoples and from groups in Latin America, also encouraged the United States to play a leading role in steering the world into a new era. The result was to transform the United States from a powerful, but insular country into a dominant force throughout the world.

COLD WAR RIVALRY

At the conclusion of World War II, U.S. officials hoped to create a peaceful, stable world free for international trade, where American industry would have easy access to raw materials and markets throughout the world. At the same time, the United States sought to achieve formal equality among nations, both for idealistic reasons and because of the calculation that a world of independent nations was more likely to promote stability. Like President Woodrow Wilson after World War I, American leaders after World War II pressed the colonial powers (Great Britain, France, and the Netherlands) to dismantle their empires. Only one country posed a massive threat to the vision of an integrated capitalist world order: the USSR.

Although the Soviet Union played a crucial role in the Allied coalition during World War II, it was prostrate after the war. According to Soviet expert Adam Ulam, "The moment of victory was to find the Soviet Union enfeebled and devastated on a scale unprecedented in the past by countries *defeated* in a major war."[7] John Lewis Gaddis recounts how Soviet losses far exceeded those of the other Allied powers:

> For three years, from June of 1941 to June of 1944, the Soviet Union carried the main burden of the fight against Hitler. . . . Partly because of Russian military successes, the United States Army got through the war with less than half the number of divisions prewar plans had indicated would be necessary for victory. Casualty figures reflect with particular vividness the disproportionate amount of fighting which went on in the east. A conservative estimate places Soviet war deaths—civilian and military—at approximately 16 million. Total Anglo-American losses in all theaters came to less than a million.[8]

Most historians "now generally agree on the limited nature of Stalin's [postwar] objectives."[9] Invaded twice from the West within a generation, Russia aimed to create a buffer zone under its control in Eastern Europe. In

---

[7]Adam Ulam, *The Rivals: America and Russia Since World War II* (New York: Viking Press, 1971), p. 11.

[8]John Lewis Gaddis, *The United States and the Origins of the Cold War, 1941–1947* (New York: Columbia University Press, 1972), pp. 79–80.

[9]Ibid., p. 355, fn. 2.

its zone of influence, the Soviet Union stationed hundreds of thousands of troops and exercised extensive repression to prevent opposition to its vision of central planning and single-party rule. Yet, regardless of the ethics, legality, or wisdom of Soviet practice, it was far from an attempt to foment global revolution, as American officials described it. Indeed, Premier Joseph Stalin restrained Communists in Western Europe, Yugoslavia, and China from seeking power.

American political leaders probably sincerely misjudged Soviet intentions after World War II, when they continually alarmed Americans with the prospect of a Soviet invasion of Western Europe.[10] In part, however, the Soviet threat was used to frighten Americans into supporting new, activist foreign policies. The only way to get Americans to accept the United States's new role as world leader, Senator Arthur Vandenberg advised President Harry Truman, was "to scare the hell out of the country." The president heeded this advice and proposed the Truman Doctrine, which justified American intervention in other countries' affairs in order to contain communism. Military aid to the governments of Greece and Turkey was justified in global terms. President Truman explained the need for such aid by insisting "that it must be the policy of the United States to support free peoples who are resisting attempted subjugation by outside minorities or by outside pressures."[11] Historian Stephen Ambrose comments that Truman's statement "was all-encompassing. In a single sentence Truman had defined American policy for the next thirty years. . . . The Truman Doctrine came close to shutting the door against any revolution, since the terms 'free peoples' and 'anti-Communist' were thought to be synonymous. All the Greek government, or any dictatorship, had to do to get American aid was to claim that its opponents were Communist."[12]

More important than the question of which country "started" the Cold War was the ensuing and continuing destructive spiral of arms production, which maintained world tensions at a dangerous pitch. The most important military development in the Cold War period was the creation of a vast arsenal of nuclear warheads and long-range intercontinental missiles able to deliver these weapons within minutes to destinations halfway around the globe. The costs associated with the research, development, production, and maintenance of the nuclear program have been tremendous. Scholars at the Brookings Institution estimate that, between 1940 and 1996, the nuclear

---

[10]Many of those influential in shaping the containment policy have subsequently admitted their error in judgment. See, for example, Dean Acheson, *Present at the Creation* (New York: Norton, 1969), p. 753; George Kennan, "'X' plus 25: Interview with George F. Kennan," *Foreign Policy* no. 7 (Summer 1972): 14; and others cited in Ronald Steele, "The Power and the Glory," *New York Review of Books*, May 31, 1973, 30, fn. 3.

[11]Stephen E. Ambrose, *Rise to Globalism: America's Foreign Policy, 1938–1980*, 2nd. ed. (New York: Penguin, 1980), p. 132.

[12]Ibid.

program cost almost $5.5 trillion, or over 40 percent of all defense expenditures during that period.[13] For well over half a century, continuing into the present, the world has lived in the shadow of nuclear devastation.

The damage that nuclear weapons can inflict is beyond imagination. The initial blast will kill, burn, and maim millions of people. But this is only the beginning. Summing up the wider effects, astrophysicist Carl Sagan suggests that "the long-term consequence of a nuclear war could constitute a global climatic catastrophe."[14] About half the world's population would be immediately affected by a major nuclear exchange, and the remaining half would be affected within a short time. A major nuclear war would provoke widespread fires that would cause immense clouds of radioactive dust, soot, and smoke. These would block sunlight, causing a drop in temperature ("nuclear winter"), which would destroy crops. Moreover, the firestorms would reduce the earth's protective ozone shield in the stratosphere, enabling the sun's ultraviolet rays to penetrate the earth's surface. This, in turn, would endanger nucleic acids and proteins, the "fundamental molecules for life on Earth."[15]

Although the end of the Cold War has vastly reduced the risk that nuclear war will be initiated through conscious decision, Russia, the United States, and several other countries continue to maintain large nuclear arsenals. The risk of a nuclear device being detonated by accident remains significant. Further, several smaller countries have developed nuclear weapons. The Cold War has ended, and several important nuclear arms limitation agreements have been concluded, but the nuclear genie has not been put back in the bottle.

GLOBAL EXPANSION AND THE INVISIBLE EMPIRE

Focusing on the Cold War rivalry—important as that issue is—may obscure another key development following World War II, the emergence of the United States as the dominant power in the world. In 1970, foreign policy analyst Graham Allison observed, in words that prove remarkably accurate in hindsight: "Historians in the year 2000, looking back with detachment on the cold war, are apt to conclude that the main feature of international life in the period 1945–1970 was neither the expansion of the Soviet Union nor Communist China. Instead, it was the global expansion of American influence: military, economic, political and cultural."[16]

---

[13]Stephen I. Schwartz, *Atomic Audit: The Costs and Consequences of U.S. Nuclear Weapons Since 1940* (Washington, D.C.: Brookings Institution Press, 1998), Fig. 1, p. xxii; Fig. 2, p. 5.

[14]Carl Sagan, "Nuclear War and Climatic Catastrophe," *Foreign Affairs* 62, no. 2 (Winter 1983/84): 259. Also see *New York Times*, September 22, 1985.

[15]Sagan, "Nuclear War," p. 263.

[16]Graham Allison, "Cool It: The Foreign Policy of Young America," *Foreign Policy* no. 1 (Winter 1970–71): 144–45.

Achieving and maintaining global dominance has required a 24-hour-a-day, 52-week-a-year effort, involving an enormous expenditure of American resources. The American-Soviet rivalry can be better understood when placed in this context, for the Soviet Union opposed the two key elements of American foreign policy: support for a global capitalist economy and for pro-capitalist governments. In response, the Soviet Union erected a rival noncapitalist military and trading bloc.

The American "empire" was not one formed through traditional imperialism or colonialism. With the exception of a few outright protectorates— Puerto Rico, the Virgin Islands, and some Pacific possessions—the United States did not establish legal custody over territory. Although American power is both more global in scope and more intensive within individual countries than was the case in past imperial situations, this power is exercised through political, military, and economic influence, not formal legal control.

The first priority in creating the postwar American empire was rebuilding war-torn Europe. In 1948, Secretary of State George Marshall proposed a program of American financial and technical aid to Europe. Marshall defended his plan to Congress on the humanitarian ground that the destruction from the war threatened to produce famine in Europe. This was surely part of the explanation, given Europe's inability to restore agricultural and industrial production.

But the Marshall Plan was not driven simply by humanitarian concerns. Unless the United States helped other countries to recover, Marshall warned, "the cumulative loss of foreign markets and sources of supply would unquestionably have a depressing influence on our domestic economy."[17] The Marshall Plan was further justified as a way to prevent radical regimes from taking power in Western Europe. At the same time that the Marshall Plan was launched, the North Atlantic Treaty Organization (NATO) was formed, which linked the United States and Western Europe in a military alliance to check Soviet forces in Europe.

Given the shattered state of Europe's economy, American business was uniquely situated to expand into other regions of the world. The U.S. policy toward the rural, poor countries in Asia, Africa, and Latin America, which were aligned with neither the Communist bloc nor the Western capitalist bloc—the Third World—was designed to open up these areas to investment by American corporations and to prevent regimes from reaching power that might challenge foreign (particularly American) interests.

With Latin America already largely under informal American control, the United States expanded into other resource-rich areas. Particularly important was the Middle East, which contained vast petroleum deposits. American oil companies soon gained control of this vital ingredient of an industrial

---

[17]William Appleman Williams, *The Tragedy of American Diplomacy* (Cleveland, Ohio: World, 1959), p. 177.

economy. In 1940, Great Britain controlled 72 percent of Middle East oil reserves; the United States, 10 percent; and other countries, the rest. By 1967, Great Britain controlled 29 percent; the United States, 59 percent; and other countries, the remainder.[18]

American expansion abroad took two major forms: economic penetration by multinational corporations into Europe and the developing world, and political and military influence exercised by the American government. The two are distinct, yet intertwined, and each has contributed to advancing the other. According to political economist Robert Gilpin, the income generated by American business investments abroad in the postwar period was used "to finance America's global political and military position. The income from foreign investments, in other words, had become an important factor in American global hegemony."[19] It should be noted that, although these twin processes flourished during the Cold War, they did not disappear after the Cold War ended. In this respect, there is important continuity from 1945 to the present.

In recent decades, however, some analysts claim that a new era has begun, as the result of a substantial increase in international economic and political integration, which is commonly described as globalization. Has globalization replaced the Cold War era? What is the political impact of globalization?

A NEW ERA OF GLOBALIZATION?

One can distinguish two opposing groups, which we will label the globalists and the critics, regarding the extent and character of globalization. Globalists claim that, in the title of one influential account, we are living in "One World, Ready or Not."[20] According to globalists, for better or worse (and there is debate among globalists on this issue), the world has entered a fundamentally new phase. Rapid means of transportation and communication enable people, commodities, capital, and information to circle the globe at vastly greater speeds. The result is exponential increases in the linkages among citizens, localities, companies, and governments throughout the world. The political consequences of globalization are similarly vast. States no longer can effectively police their borders, in part because physical borders become meaningless in an electronically interconnected world. At best, states can try

---

[18]Harry Magdoff, *The Age of Imperialism: The Economics of U.S. Foreign Policy* (New York: Monthly Review Press, 1969), p. 43.

[19]Robert Gilpin, *U.S. Power and the Multinational Corporation: The Political Economy of Direct Foreign Investment* (New York: Basic Books, 1975), p. 161.

[20]William Greider, *One World, Ready or Not: The Manic Logic of Global Capitalism* (New York: Simon & Schuster, 1997). For an influential account of globalization from this perspective, see Thomas L. Friedman, *The Lexus and the Olive Tree: Understanding Globalization* (New York: Farrar, Straus and Giroux, 1999).

to devise policies that help position their economies at the cutting edge internationally, as well as help their citizens adjust to globalization; at worst, states can send their economies into a downward spiral by refusing to accept the harsh realities of global competition.

Critics question some of the globalists' key claims and differ in their evaluation of the political conclusions that follow from globalization. The two camps do not totally disagree: Critics agree about the importance of qualitatively new developments within the global economy, especially the development of high-speed information processing and transportation, which have enormously increased cross-border communication. But they suggest that some changes are less dramatic than meets the eye, and they point out that the increase in transnational flows that we designate as globalization refers to a diverse number of changes that are not necessarily a single phenomenon. Finally, they warn that one should not mistake description for cause. Many of the changes we associate with globalization may be as much a product of political decisions as of economic or technological forces.

The increase in some global flows is dramatic. Exports of the 24 members of the Organization for Economic Cooperation and Development (OECD), the most industrialized and richest countries in the world, increased from 9.5 percent of their GDP in 1960 to 20.5 percent in 1990. Foreign direct investment grew three times faster than international trade. Multinational corporations (MNCs)—firms with significant foreign operations—now control a third of the world's privately owned productive assets. However, the greatest increases in transnational economic flows are found in financial assets, including loans and the exchange of foreign currency and government bonds. The increased volume of financial flows is truly astonishing: from several billion dollars daily in the 1970s to around $2 trillion a day today! In the 1990s alone, international bank loans rose from 4 percent to 44 percent of the GDP of the OECD countries.[21]

There is no disagreement between the two camps about these statistics. What does divide the two sides is how to evaluate their importance. For example, critics of the globalist position regard present-day globalization as one phase in a larger story of capitalist development. When one views the present from a historical perspective, the current era is not unprecedented. In the past, too, periods of greater political and economic interdependence developed and were reversed by war or economic crisis.

Consider foreign trade. As a portion of the world's economic output, foreign trade was as high in the period before World War I as in the current period (admittedly in an era when total production was much smaller). Indeed, the high point of international economic integration in the modern era may

---

[21]The data in this and the following paragraph are from Robert Wade, "Globalization and Its Limits: Reports of the Death of the National Economy Are Greatly Exaggerated," in *National Diversity and Global Capitalism*, ed. Suzanne Berger and Ronald Dore (Ithaca, N.Y.: Cornell University Press, 1996), ch. 2.

have occurred not in the present period, but in the nineteenth century—the age of colonialism—when the imperialist powers of Western Europe, especially Britain, forged close (and highly exploitative) economic and political links among regions of the world.[22] This great interdependence and integration were abruptly reversed from 1914 to 1945 by two world wars and the Great Depression. As a result of military conflict and economic instability, the dense international political and trade networks constructed in the nineteenth century were destroyed. When globalists stress the rapid increase in international trade since the 1970s, they select the period following World War II—a low point in international trade—as the baseline, not the period prior to World War I.

Another important qualification to the globalization argument is that the bulk of production in the world remains geared to domestic production. Consider the United States, a global economic leader. Guess what proportion of U.S. GDP is exported: less than one-fifth, about half, over half? The first answer is correct: around 12 percent of GDP is exported. Most U.S. production is destined for domestic markets. Similarly, the vast bulk of what American consumers buy is produced at home. Nor should one assume that international investment and trade will continually increase. When a number of East Asian, East European, and Latin American countries experienced economic crises in the 1990s, international investment and trade stagnated.

Even granting that the world is highly integrated economically, the political implications of the change are complex. Globalists usually see increased globalization as a product of technology and economics. Further, they argue, political decisions cannot much alter the contours of globalization. Critics often stress the importance of politics. Political decisions were essential in constructing the framework of international financial treaties and organizations that have enabled globalization to develop, and political decisions can alter the future direction and character of globalization.[23]

We believe that there is much merit to the critics' arguments. Globalization is not an impersonal, transhistorical, and irreversible force. It does not just happen; it has been made to happen as the result of decisions by corporate and government leaders. We can gain a better understanding of this process by examining the strategies of U.S. corporations and the govern-

---

[22]For some fine arguments along these lines, see Suzanne Berger and Ronald Dore, eds., *National Diversity and Global Capitalism* (Ithaca, N.Y.: Cornell University Press, 1996), chs. 1–2, and Robert Boyer and Daniel Drache, eds., *States Against Markets: The Limits of Globalization* (London: Routledge, 1996), chs. 7–9.

[23]For several approaches to this issue, see Geoffrey Garrett, *Partisan Politics in the Global Economy* (Cambridge: Cambridge University Press, 1998); David Held, Anthony McGrew, David Goldblatt, and Jonathan Perraton, *Global Transformations: Politics, Economics and Culture* (Stanford, Calif.: Stanford University Press, 1999); Dean Baker, Gerald Epstein, and Robert Pollin, eds., *Globalization and Progressive Economic Policy* (Cambridge: Cambridge University Press, 1998); and Daniel Singer, *Whose Millennium? Theirs or Ours?* (New York: Monthly Review Press, 1999).

ment, which promoted globalization in the recent past. Decisions and policies promoting globalization were a response to specific economic and political problems. No doubt globalization will be altered in the future by other political decisions and policies.

GLOBALIZATION AND MULTINATIONAL CORPORATIONS

Globalization is not simply a cause. It is a response to challenges. American corporate capitalism has expanded outside the United States in response to four internal dilemmas: dependence on raw materials, dependence on open markets, dependence on foreign investment, and dependence on workers.

DEPENDENCE ON RAW MATERIALS

The United States is among the countries best endowed with natural resources. It has some of the world's largest deposits of coal, copper, natural gas, iron, petroleum, and aluminum. The United States is also among the world's leading food producers; for example, it is the largest producer of corn, soybeans, cotton, and oranges and the largest exporter of wheat and rice.[24] However, no country is fortunate enough to contain within its borders all the raw materials it needs for modern industrial production—and the United States is no exception. Moreover, the United States has begun to deplete many of the natural resources it once contained in abundance. Both factors produce a growing dependence on other countries for essential raw materials.

The speed with which the United States has come to rely on other countries for raw materials can be seen from the following figures: Of the 13 minerals considered essential for a modern industrial economy, the United States had to import more than half its supplies of only 4 in 1950; since then, that figure has climbed to 12.[25] Most of these raw materials come from less developed countries in Latin America, Asia, the Middle East, and Africa.

American corporations and the U.S. government seek to assure a cheap and adequate supply of minerals and other natural resources flowing to the United States. The most effective way to do this in the past was for American corporations to invest in the Third World and to gain direct control over foreign raw materials. Thus, Kennecott and Anaconda control much of the world's copper deposits, located in Zambia, Chile, and elsewhere. And a handful of American petroleum corporations (along with a few foreign companies) control most of the capitalist world's petroleum supplies, located in the United States, the Middle East, Nigeria, Mexico, and Venezuela.

---

[24]*New York Times*, January 6, 1974; Emma Rothschild, "The Politics of Food," *New York Review of Books*, May 16, 1974, 17.

[25]*New York Times*, November 5, 1972; and December 22, 1973.

DEPENDENCE ON FOREIGN TRADE

The United States is the largest exporter of agricultural products, industrial goods, and services in the world. Although, as we shall see, some of the rhetoric about the importance of globalization is overblown, global markets are essential to the prosperity of American business. Encouraged by government tax incentives, technical assistance, insurance against political difficulties, and, most important, a foreign policy that aims at opening foreign markets to American exports, the expansion of America's foreign trade has been rapid. In 1960, U.S. exports were valued at $26 billion; by 1980, their value had increased to $272 billion; and by 1999, they were valued at over $956 billion—more than 36 times their value in 1960.[26] Imports of goods into the United States increased even faster: $22 billion in 1960, $291 billion in 1980, and $1.2 trillion by 1999.

DEPENDENCE ON FOREIGN INVESTMENT

American corporations often find it more profitable to invest capital in building new plants abroad to produce and assemble products than to expand manufacturing at home. When manufactured products or food is exported, the transaction ends once the goods are purchased by foreign customers. However, when an American corporation creates a foreign subsidiary, the transaction only begins with the initial investment: The foreign subsidiary remains year after year, continuing to produce and sell goods that make a profit for the American home company. American corporations began investing heavily in foreign subsidiaries during the 1950s and have piled up substantial investments abroad since then. In 1979, U.S.-owned assets abroad were valued at $786 billion. Ten years later, as Figure 9–1 shows, international assets of American companies had grown to over $2 trillion. By 1999, the foreign assets of American companies had more than tripled in value to $6 trillion.

Profits generated from foreign investments represent a substantial and growing proportion of total American corporate profits. The share of after-tax corporate profits accounted for by foreign investment rose from 7 percent of all corporate profits in 1950 to 18 percent in 1998.[27] The 100 largest corporations obtain considerably more of their profits from overseas investment.[28]

---

[26]U.S. Department of Commerce, International Trade Administration, "U.S. International Trade in Goods and Services, Balance of Payment Basis," at http://www.ita.doc.gov/td/industry/otea/usfth.

[27]Richard C. Edwards, Michael Reich, and Thomas E. Weisskopf, eds., *The Capitalist System: A Radical Analysis of American Society*, 2nd ed. (Englewood Cliffs, N.J: Prentice-Hall., 1978), Table 13-B, p. 477; and for 1998, Department of Commerce, Bureau of Economic Analysis, *Survey of Current Business*, April 2000, p. 89.

[28]Barry Bluestone and Bennett Harrison, *The Deindustrialization of America: Plant Closings, Community Abandonment, and the Dismantling of Basic Industry* (New York: Basic Books, 1982), p. 42.

■ **FIGURE 9-1**

U.S. INTERNATIONAL ASSETS, 1976–1999

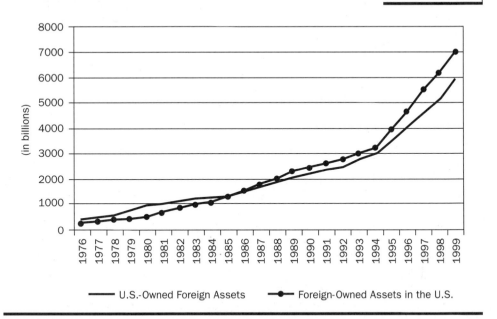

SOURCE: Russel B. Scholl, "The International Investment Position of the United States at Yearend 1999," *Survey of Current Business,* Department of Commerce, Bureau of Economic Analysis, July 2000.

DEPENDENCE ON WORKERS

A key reason why corporations invest abroad is to end-run American workers and recruit compliant and low-paid workers abroad. As two economists observe, "Production of the traditional industrial goods that have been the mainstay of the U.S. economy is being transferred from . . . factories in New England to . . . factories in the 'export platforms' of Hong Kong and Taiwan."[29] To illustrate, in 2000, the Zebco Corporation announced that it was relocating most of its fishing reel production from Tulsa, Oklahoma, to China. For some time, the company had threatened to pull out of Tulsa unless workers increased their output. A memorandum that management sent workers earlier in the year was blunt: "When we don't get quota, it is another day closer to China taking our jobs."[30] Despite workers increasing their output, management decided that it could squeeze Chinese workers more effectively and pulled up stakes in Tulsa.

---

[29]Richard J. Barnet and Ronald E. Muller, *Global Reach: The Power of Multinational Corporations* (New York: Simon & Schuster, 1974), p. 216.

[30]*New York Times,* July 7, 2000.

Companies create runaway shops, as they are called, to slash wage costs and recruit workers who will not talk back. Not only are the effects of job loss severe for displaced workers, but also the threat of runaway shops has a chilling effect on the working class as a whole. The movement of capital overseas heightens insecurity among all workers because of the potential threat that they may be next. As a result, plant closures and capital movements depress overall wage levels and weaken union bargaining power. This was one reason why workers did not use tight labor markets in the 1990s to press for higher wages and better working conditions. The result was to sustain the American economic boom—but in a way that provided meager benefits to millions of workers and their families. Former Labor Secretary Robert Reich has documented how the prosperity of American multinational corporations has become relatively decoupled from that of American workers.[31] These developments make it understandable why the American labor movement has militantly opposed agreements (such as the North American Free Trade Agreement [NAFTA], reviewed in Chapter 3) that promote international capital movement and do not provide adequate protection—for example, the requirement of a living wage and the right to form independent labor unions—for American and foreign workers.

Multinational corporate investments in poor countries, such as Bangladesh, Indonesia, Malaysia, and the Philippines, create jobs that people eagerly seek in the absence of adequate alternatives. Globalization can promote development as well as underdevelopment. But there is no dispute that multinationals invest in poor countries to secure access to workers willing to work for low wages. And, often in alliance with governments who are authoritarian and corrupt, multinationals impose harsh restrictions on workers' freedom to organize.

This situation has provoked extensive strikes and protests from workers in poor countries, as well as consumer boycotts and efforts by unions and other groups in the United States and elsewhere to force MNCs to accept fair labor standards. The White House urged a group of American manufacturers to form the Fair Labor Association, which has developed a code of conduct and provided for overseas monitoring. However, these efforts are too timid, according to some critics. Charles Kernaghan, director of the National Labor Committee, suggests, "I think the Fair Labor Association is just window-dressing. You don't have full disclosure of what's found, and it doesn't require that factories pay a living wage."[32] Students on many college campuses have joined together to form such organizations as United Students Against Sweatshops and the Workers Rights Consortium to improve conditions in factories where apparel is manufactured carrying college logos. More generally, students on American college campuses have been active and influential in the anti-sweatshop movement to promote fair labor

---

[31]Robert B. Reich, *The Work of Nations: Preparing Ourselves for 21st Century Capitalism* (New York: Knopf, 1991), chs. 10–12.

[32]*New York Times,* July 9, 2000.

standards for workers hired by MNCs in poor countries in Africa, Asia, and Latin America.

MULTINATIONAL CORPORATIONS

Any discussion of American foreign policy must deal with the immensely important role that MNCs play in the United States and abroad. Just as is the case in American domestic affairs, MNCs seek to present their interests as identical to the interests of the American people as a whole. In both cases, this obscures the significant conflicts between what is good for business and what is good for people.

Multinational corporations are businesses with extensive foreign operations. They are the new Goliaths of the present era. In 1998, three-quarters of all multinationals were U.S. corporations. By 2000, multinational corporations outnumbered countries on the list of the world's 100 largest entities. The parent companies of American multinationals had a gross product (the total value of their combined goods and services) valued at over $1.6 trillion in 1998, more than the GNP of all the countries in the Middle East, Central and South Asia, and Africa.[33] Multinationals make decisions about research, investment, manufacturing, and sales without much regard for national boundaries; decisions are governed by profitability. According to economist Daniel R. Fusfeld, the emergence of multinational corporations "was made possible by advances in the technology of transportation and communication after World War II (jet aircraft and automatic data communication, for example). U.S. corporations were able to take advantage of the new technology much more readily than foreign corporations, in part because much of that technology was developed here, but chiefly because of the predominance of the United States in world trade and international finance."[34]

Multinational corporations can integrate far-flung operations as a result of technological advances in communications and information processing. A multinational corporation may carry out product research in one country, obtain raw materials from another, manufacture parts in a third country, assemble the product in several other countries, and market the resulting commodities throughout the world.

The economies of Third World nations have to a considerable extent been shaped to serve the needs of multinational corporations. Their natural resources fall under foreign ownership and control; they serve as low-cost manufacturing bases, while research and development are located in the home country; local entrepreneurs that compete with multinationals tend to be squeezed out of business; and wealth generated locally is transferred by

---

[33]Raymond J. Mataloni, Jr., "U.S. Multinational Companies: Operations in 1998," *Survey of Current Business* (Department of Commerce, Bureau of Economic Analysis), July 2000.

[34]Daniel R. Fusfeld, *The Rise of the Corporate State in America* (Andover, Mass: Warner Modular Publishers, 1973), p. 3.

multinationals back to the United States, further draining Third World countries of resources.

Take the example of multinational investment in agriculture in Third World countries. Agribusiness transforms patterns of land use in ways that are the opposite of what is needed by the people of these areas. Rather than being devoted to raising staple foods for local consumption, land is devoted to raising cash crops for export, with agribusiness taking the profits. Throughout the Third World, local farmers have become hired help for the United States's and other Western nations' agribusiness or have been thrown off the land altogether. In some Third World countries, the rate of rural unemployment has reached 40 percent, and the vicious cycle continues when the surplus agricultural population migrates to cities to seek jobs, swelling the ranks of the urban unemployed.

Perhaps even more than in the case of the United States, in evaluating growth in poor countries one must go beyond statistics measuring the expansion of GDP to analyze the kind of growth that occurs, its negative effects, who controls productive resources, and who benefits. Often, the main beneficiaries of economic growth in poor countries of the world are Western-based MNCs; and economic development often fuels economic inequality and environmental devastation.

Consider the burgeoning growth of aquaculture, the raising of seafood in coastal areas, much of which is controlled by multinational food processors. Indian environmental activist Vandana Shiva reports, "For every acre of an industrial shrimp farm, 200 acres of productive ecosystems are destroyed. For every dollar earned as foreign exchange from exports, six to ten dollars' worth of destruction takes place in the local economy. . . . In India, intensive shrimp cultivation has turned fertile coastal tracts into graveyards, destroying both fisheries and agriculture. . . . Shrimp cultivation destroys 15 jobs for each job it creates."[35]

For multinational expansion to occur, friendly policies are necessary from the American as well as foreign governments. But resistance to the alliance between multinationals and the American government has come under strain both within the United States and overseas. One response has been a restructuring of the U.S. military to deal with opposition to corporate capitalism.

THE MILITARY ESTABLISHMENT

The United States has a vast military establishment, the largest and most powerful in the world. It maintains 61 major military bases overseas. Over one-quarter million troops are stationed abroad; the navy has patrols in

---

[35]Vandana Shiva, *Stolen Harvest: The Hijacking of the Global Food Supply* (Boston: South End Press, 2000), p. 15.

The nuclear-powered aircraft carrier, USS Vinson, and some of its fighter planes.

every ocean; reconnaissance satellites circle the world; American warplanes enjoy uncontested supremacy in the skies; and the United States has the best trained, best equipped army in the world, and ready to be dispatched at a moment's notice.[36] The army would not have to go far because American troops are already stationed in over 70 foreign nations. In addition, military treaties link the United States to the regimes of over 40 countries in Europe, Asia, and Latin America. In fiscal year 1999, the United States spent $292 billion on defense, three times the combined military budgets of Russia and China. The United States spends more on defense than the next 12 highest-spending nations put together. According to journalist George Easterbrook, the American military is the only military in the world "whose primary military mission is not defense. Practically the entire military is an expeditionary force, designed not to guard borders—a duty that ties down most units of other militaries, including China's—but to 'project power' elsewhere in the world."[37]

---

[36]Adam Yarmolinsky, *The Military Establishment* (New York: Harper & Row, 1971), p. 115.

[37]George Easterbrook, "Apocryphal Now," *New Republic*, September 11, 2000, 24.

During the Cold War, this immense military force was justified on the grounds that it was necessary to contain Soviet expansion and maintain peace. Both the United States and the Soviet Union possessed a staggering "overkill" capacity: The United States had a stockpile of over 9,000 strategic nuclear warheads (the Soviet Union had over 7,000) and several times that number of tactical nuclear weapons.

As a result of popular and congressional pressure, attempts were initiated in the 1970s to limit new weaponry. Strategic arms limitation talks between the United States and the Soviet Union resulted in a treaty signed in 1972 (SALT I), extended by accords concluded in 1974; a second SALT treaty negotiated (but never ratified); and the Anti-ballistic Missile Treaty of 1972 (ABM). These agreements to limit arms buildups were part of a broader process of accommodation between the United States and Soviet Union in the 1970s that was termed détente. Although both nations continued to increase their military arsenals, the trend shifted from military confrontation to limited economic and political accommodation.

Under President Ronald Reagan, the United States embarked on the most substantial peacetime military buildup in history. Defense expenditures increased by 51 percent by 1984, after just three years under Reagan, surpassing defense spending at the height of the Vietnam War. The aim of this buildup was to achieve decisive superiority over the Soviet Union and, hopefully, force it to spend itself into bankruptcy trying to match the American military effort. The arms buildup achieved its purpose, and by the end of the decade, the Soviet Union was in shambles. (The result was also to increase the danger of thermonuclear war.) When the Soviet Union crumbled in the 1990s, the Cold War ended.

One might have expected that, with its adversary no longer a threat, the United States would fundamentally reorient its military and foreign policy. But instead, it has continued many of those same policies. About 1.3 million Americans serve in the armed forces, while 4.5 million Americans are employed in defense-related industries.[38] As Retired Admiral Eugene Carroll, Jr., Deputy Director of the Center for Defense Information, put it, "For 45 years we were in an arms race with the Soviet Union. Now it appears we're in an arms race with ourselves."[39] What is most striking about U.S. foreign policy in the post–Cold War period is the continuity with the past. This leads one to speculate whether an even more fundamental aim than containing the Soviet threat existed throughout the entire postwar period.

---

[38]Department of Defense, Washington Headquarters Service, Directorate for Information and Reports, "DOD Active Duty Personnel Strength Levels Fiscal Years 1950–1999," http://web./.whs.osd.mil/mmid/military/ms9.pdf. Total personnel estimates from U.S. Census Bureau, Statistical Abstract of the United States: 1999, p. 369, Table 577.

[39]Quoted at http://www.cdi.org/issues/wme/spendersFY00b.html.

POLITICAL AND ECONOMIC INFLUENCE

The government does not rely exclusively on military power to project American power on the world stage. The U.S. government's financial agencies, including the Agency for International Development (AID) and the Export Import Bank, provide aid and loans to foreign governments and technical help and insurance to American businesses in an attempt to facilitate American business operations abroad. The United States's participation in NATO and other international organizations, including the Organization of American States, the United Nations General Assembly, and the United Nations Security Council, leverages U.S. influence. The United States uses its preponderant influence within international financial institutions, including the International Monetary Fund (IMF), the Organization for Economic Cooperation and Development (OECD), and the International Bank for Reconstruction and Development (commonly known as the World Bank), to regulate an international capitalist order within which American business can prosper.

Maintaining international economic stability is no easy task. In the 1980s, a debt crisis that threatened the entire international capitalist system erupted when several nations, including Poland, Mexico, and Argentina, were unable to meet repayment schedules. If they had declared bankruptcy and refused to repay their debts, most major U.S. banks (who are the major creditors of these nations) would also have been jeopardized. Intricate maneuvers by international and American financial agencies narrowly averted economic chaos. As will be discussed later in this chapter, financial crisis again broke out in the 1990s, in East Asia and elsewhere.

Military power, participation in international agencies, and foreign aid are routine, visible ways the United States seeks to influence other countries. But the United States also engages in covert operations through the Central Intelligence Agency (CIA) to protect and defend its interests. On numerous occasions in the past, the United States has intervened when democratically chosen governments pursued policies opposed by the American government. The CIA has secretly funded pro-American political parties, labor unions, and media in foreign countries. It has sponsored political assassinations. It carried on a secret war in Laos, subverted the government of Guatemala (1954), helped plan the 1961 Bay of Pigs invasion of Cuba, and organized the murder of Ernesto "Che" Guevara in Bolivia (1967). In the 1980s, the CIA trained and equipped mercenaries and provided covert aid and equipment in an illegal attempt to overthrow the Sandinista government of Nicaragua.

THE MILITARY-INDUSTRIAL COMPLEX

The growth of a powerful domestic military sector is quite recent. Through the 1930s, except during wartime, the armed forces were small, and few resources were devoted to their maintenance. Planning and preparing for war were relatively easy because military technology was simple, and a wartime economy was quickly demobilized when peace arrived. World War II represented a transition in the history of warfare. Military technology advanced enormously, with such innovations as radar, missiles, mechanized warfare, and, perhaps the greatest advance in the science of destruction, atomic weapons. General Dwight D. Eisenhower, the top-ranking U.S. Army officer after World War II, understood the fundamental implications of the change in military technology that had occurred as a result of the war. In a memorandum entitled "Scientific and Technological Resources as Military Assets," he wrote: "The recent conflict has demonstrated more convincingly than ever before the strength our nation can best derive from the integration of all of our national resources in time of war. It is of the utmost importance that the lessons of this experience be not forgotten in the peacetime planning and training of the Army. The future security of the nation demands that all those civilian resources which by conversion or redirection constitute our main support in time of emergency be associated closely with the activities of the Army in time of peace. . . ."[40] The peacetime cooperation among the armed forces, business, and science advocated by General Eisenhower began soon after World War II. Ever since then, the new partnership is a key element of the American political and economic system.

Fifteen years after he had written his memorandum, General Eisenhower returned to the subject. Yet this time, in his farewell address after eight years as president, he expressed alarm about the new trend:

> Our military organization today bears little relation to that known by any of my predecessors in peacetime, or indeed by the fighting men of World War II and Korea.
>
> Until the latest of world conflicts, the United States had no armaments industry. American makers of plowshares could, with time and as required, make swords as well. But now we can no longer risk emergency improvisation of national defense; we have been compelled to create a permanent armaments industry of vast proportions. . . .
>
> The conjunction of an immense Military Establishment and large arms industry is new in the American experience. . . . In the councils of government we must guard against the acquisition of unwarranted influence, whether sought or unsought, by the military-industrial complex. The potential for the disastrous rise of misplaced power exists and will persist.

The term *military-industrial complex (MIC)* refers to the alliance of government, business, and science devoted to war preparation. Producing for war is the biggest industry in the United States: Over 2 percent of the labor force is engaged in military activity. More than 1.3 million Americans serve in the armed forces, and over 4.5 million are engaged in defense-related occupations. The military sector has close links with corporate capitalism and reaches throughout American society. The Department of Defense (DOD) is

---

[40]As noted in Seymour Melman, *Pentagon Capitalism* (New York: McGraw-Hill, 1970), pp. 231–32.

the single largest consumer in the world: It purchases 15 percent of American manufactured goods,[41] and in 1999, it awarded $118 billion to defense contractors for weapons and services. The three largest defense contractors—Lockheed Martin, Boeing, and Raytheon—alone accounted for one-quarter of all defense contracts, and all appear on the Fortune 500 list of the biggest American corporations.

Military spending is concentrated in the most technologically advanced sectors. Two-thirds of defense spending in the civilian sector is located in three industries: aircraft and missiles, electronics and communications, and shipbuilding and repairing.[42]

Many large corporations benefit greatly from military contracts. Among the 25 largest corporations, all but 5 were on the list of the top 100 firms receiving DOD contracts. Thus, there is extensive overlap between the largest DOD contractors and the largest firms in the country.

Military production is a lucrative business. This is primarily the result of government generosity. Payments for cost overruns, which total billions of dollars, are the most dramatic example. Focusing on costs, however, misses the major point. Neither the Pentagon nor military producers have an incentive to keep costs low. Quite the contrary. The Pentagon is mainly interested in ensuring a steady flow of funds to military producers. These payments can be considered a subsidy to support a constituency for militarism. Both the Pentagon and military contractors share an interest in maximizing the threat of war—which, in turn, generates support for more military spending.[43]

Although the largest firms derive immense profits from military production, small companies throughout the United States also benefit because giant firms subcontract out much of the actual work on prime contracts. Twenty thousand firms throughout the country are engaged in production for the military, integrating communities and small business into the war economy. Military spending is high in part because it provides jobs and business to corporations and communities all over the country. Military spending represents subsidies to both large and small businesses and the people who work for them. Thus, the lobby for militarism includes labor unions, local businesspeople, local political officials, and corporate executives.

Thanks to government sponsorship of arms sales, means of destruction have become one of America's major exports. As Figure 9–2 shows, the United States is by far the world's largest arms exporter. In 1999, American contractors sold nearly $11.8 billion worth of weapons—more than a third of

---

[41]Tom Christoffel, David Finklehor, and Dan Gilbarg, "Corporations and Government," in Christoffel, Finklehor, and Gilbarg, eds., *Up Against the American Myth* (New York: Holt, Rinehart & Winston, 1970), p. 101.

[42]*U.S. Statistical Abstract, 1985* (Washington, D.C.: Bureau of the Census, 1985), p. 334.

[43]Melman, *Pentagon Capitalism, passim; The Permanent War Economy* (New York: Simon & Schuster, 1974); and *Profits Without Production* (New York: Knopf, 1983).

■ FIGURE 9–2

THE WORLD'S LEADING SUPPLIERS OF NEW WEAPONS
IN 1999

In millions of dollars

United States	**11,768**
Russia	4,800
Germany	4,000
China	1,900
France	900
Britain	800
Italy	600
All other European countries	4,600
All other countries	900

SOURCE: *Congressional Research Service*. In the *New York Times*, August 21, 2000.

the world's total and more than all the European countries combined.[44] In 1997, arms trading amounted to 4.6 percent of American exports, more than four times the world's average. Whenever there is an armed conflict anywhere in the world, it is a safe bet that American-made arms will be used— often by both sides. The United States's military sales have contributed to militarizing the entire world, fueling regional arms races, increasing the risks of war, and tying up resources that might go for productive purposes.

The MIC represents the most powerful influence on the shape and conduct of U.S. foreign policy. More than is the case for domestic policy making, American foreign policy making is decided behind closed doors by a small number of key participants. There is generally much less partisan and public debate about foreign policy than about domestic policy. Foreign policy is often considered a relatively closed, technical preserve of the political and economic elite, ruled off-limits to democratic debate and decision making. The president is the key decision-maker in foreign policy, assisted by advisers in the executive branch—notably, the president's national security adviser, the director of the CIA, and the secretaries of defense and state. These officials serve on the National Security Council, the top executive agency responsible for developing and overseeing American foreign policy. Other powerful officials who help shape foreign policy include the military heads of the armed forces, leaders of Congress and the congressional military affairs committees, and executives of aerospace corporations and weapons manufacturers. Think tanks, such as the Council on Foreign Affairs and the

[44]*New York Times*, August 21, 2000.

Rand Corporation, provide forums for informal discussion of foreign policy options by members of the political and economic elite.

With the end of the Cold War, there has been a broadening of debate and participation concerning foreign policy. Congress has claimed a greater role. So, too, have social movement activists in the fields of human rights, labor, and the environment. The field is more crowded and noisy than in the past, just as the goals of foreign policy have also widened and become more complex.

FOREIGN POLICY IN THE POST–COLD WAR ERA

When the Soviet Union imploded, beginning in 1989, it became necessary to formulate a foreign policy orientation for a world in which the United States was the sole superpower. For nearly half a century, the United States had organized a permanent war economy, as one observer described it, to counter the Soviet threat.[45] The end of the Cold War provided a golden opportunity for the United States to reorient foreign policy. But in which direction?

At first glance, it might seem surprising that there has been relatively little reorientation. The world has changed, but the fundamentals of American foreign policy have not. What is perhaps most striking about American foreign policy since 1990 is the degree of continuity, not contrast, with the Cold War period. One foreign policy analyst described the current "consensus among foreign policy elites . . . over the most basic objective of American post–Cold War foreign policy: that the United States must maintain a position of undisputed primacy to ensure global order. . . ."[46]

Historian David Callahan summarizes the thinking of government officials and foreign policy experts outside of government: "U.S. primacy was needed to combat the disorder that was likely to dominate the new post–Cold War era."[47] George H. W. Bush was the first president in the new post–Cold War era. Perhaps in part because of his many years helping to direct American foreign policy in the Cold War era—e.g., he served as director of the CIA and its headquarters has been officially named the George Bush Building—he did little to change the traditional foreign policy stance. Bush's major foreign policy initiative was to coordinate a massive attack on Iraq following that country's invasion of its oil-rich neighbor Kuwait in 1990. Iraq's ill-considered and aggressive action, directed by its president, Saddam Hussein, represented a brazen challenge to American dominance and international law. It was especially dangerous because it occurred in the unstable Middle East, with its vast supply of petroleum resources on which the United States depended. Rather than risking a protracted land war, the

---

[45]Melman, *Permanent War Economy.*

[46]Callahan, *Between Two Worlds*, p. 1.

[47]Ibid., pp. 65–66.

United States launched a massive missile and bombing campaign to destroy Iraq's military capability and its civilian economy. The result was swift military victory.

Governor of a small landlocked state, Bill Clinton took office with little experience in foreign affairs. A generation younger than Bush, he was less steeped in the culture of the Cold War. Indeed, like many of those who came to adulthood in the 1960s, as a college student he had opposed American militarism in general and U.S. involvement in the war in Vietnam in particular. Yet Clinton learned to make his peace with the MIC. Shortly before assuming office, President-Elect Clinton declared, "The American people have called for a new administration, yet there is essential continuity in our foreign policy."[48]

The powerful interests comprising the military-industrial complex make it unlikely that any president can reorient American foreign policy in significant ways. Members of Congress boast at their success in lobbying the Pentagon to land contracts for military producers in their districts. The Pentagon itself—the single largest organization in the world—is a formidable machine for lobbying Congress and the president to maintain military spending at high levels. Military producers, from large aerospace corporations to small subcontractors scattered throughout the country, benefit handsomely from America's militarist orientation. This mighty lobby is mobilized to promote military spending. And no president wants to be regarded as "soft" in the area of military preparedness.

Yet Clinton's foreign policy was not simply more of the same. To assess what is both similar and different in American foreign policy in the years since the fall of the Soviet Union, it helps to recognize that postwar American foreign policy was not driven exclusively by rivalry with the Soviet Union, important as that was. At an even deeper level, American political leaders sought to maintain American global supremacy in the face of any and all challenges. Although the Soviet Union represented the most visible and dangerous threat, it was far from the only one. Thus, although the end of the Cold War signified the end of a major challenge to American supremacy, it left others unresolved.

This interpretation helps make sense of President Clinton's three major foreign policy initiatives, summarized by one scholar as "updating and restructuring American military and security capabilities, elevating the role of economics in international affairs, and promoting democracy abroad."[49] The Bush administration that took office in 2001 mostly accepted Clinton's foreign policy objectives. Thus, these three elements, which we will now analyze, constitute the U.S. foreign policy agenda for the early years of the twenty-first century.

---

[48]Ibid., p. 66, quoting from a State Department dispatch.

[49]Douglas Brinkley, "Democratic Enlargement: The Clinton Doctrine," *Foreign Policy* no. 106 (Spring 1997): 112. We draw on Brinkley's summary of Clinton's foreign policy aims to organize this discussion.

RATIONALIZING AND RESTRUCTURING AMERICAN MILITARY DOMINANCE

In the period following the Cold War, the United States is the only super-power. Indeed, it is so clearly dominant that the French have coined a new term—*hyperpower*—to describe the unrivaled power of the United States. Even though the Cold War is over, U.S. military spending remains at a high level, reaching $292 billion in 1999. The "peace dividend" generated by the end of the Cold War—which was supposed to help finance American health care, welfare, and education—turned out to be relatively small, since military spending remained at high levels. American policy-makers justify maintaining such a high rate of military expenditures by warning of new threats to American security in the post–Cold War era. These include (1) nuclear weapons possessed by Russia, (2) nuclear proliferation and potential attack from other countries, (3) military hostilities throughout the world, (4) international terrorist activity, and (5) unconventional threats to American dominance.

(1) Although the Soviet Union has disappeared, policy-makers fear that Russia, which emerged from the ashes of the Soviet Union and which retains the nuclear arsenal of the former Soviet Union, potentially poses a nuclear threat. As a result, the United States continues to maintain and upgrade an enormous strategic nuclear force. Although Russia and the United States have negotiated arms limitations treaties to dismantle some nuclear weapons, each country continues to possess 3,500 strategic nuclear weapons, enough to cause devastation on a scale beyond the imagination.[50]

(2) Nuclear war could occur in other ways than confrontation between the United States and Russia. A large group of countries possesses nuclear weapons. The first tier, including China, Britain, France, Russia, and the United States, is made up of what American policy-makers consider to be "responsible" nuclear states. All five countries are permanent members of the UN Security Council and have possessed nuclear weapons for decades. The second tier consists of India, Pakistan, and possibly Israel. These states more or less openly acknowledge possessing nuclear weapons and have openly or tacitly threatened to use them against a regional opponent, but are not hostile toward the United States. A third tier of the nuclear club includes Iran, Iraq, and North Korea, which probably possess the capability to make and deliver nuclear weapons. Until 2000, the American government designated them as "rogue states" and sought to isolate them as irresponsible and dangerous members of the international community. The United States abandoned the term *rogue state* in 2000, when Iran became more moderate in its internal and foreign policy and when North Korea engaged in negotiations with South Korea to end their long conflict.

---

[50]Michael Cox, *U.S. Foreign Policy After the Cold War: Superpower Without a Mission* (London: Pinter, 1995), p. 51.

In order to counter the threat of nuclear attack from small states, U.S. policy-makers began planning a $90 billion project in 1999 that resembled President Reagan's Star Wars initiative of the 1980s. The goal was to develop a ballistic missile defense system, a "shield" to destroy incoming nuclear-tipped missiles. Reagan's plan—which was begun and then abandoned because of its cost and technical difficulties—was directed against the Soviet Union. President Clinton proclaimed that the scaled-down version was designed to defend the United States against attack by small and irresponsible nuclear powers, like North Korea. But China and Russia were not persuaded. They warned that constructing the proposed system would change the global balance of power and violate the letter and spirit of previous arms limitations agreements. During his first months in office, President George W. Bush proposed expanding the project.

Ironically, the missile defense system might achieve the worst of both worlds. On the one hand, influential technical experts charged that, in light of the immense technical difficulties involved, the project might be ineffective. For example, even assuming that interceptors could be devised that could destroy incoming missiles, a hostile power could outsmart the system by launching a swarm of decoys to mislead interceptors. On the other hand, Russia and China questioned American assurances that the system was not designed as a shield against their nuclear forces and warned that launching the project risked provoking another nuclear arms race.

If the proposed system held out little promise of increasing American security, what was the rationale for the plan? The answer appears to involve domestic political considerations. Military producers and congressional representatives lobbied hard for a project that would provide lavish defense contracts. It provides a case study of how the MIC remains alive and well although the Cold War has become a distant memory.

Nuclear threats are not confined to states that have developed nuclear capability. Terrorist groups might succeed in developing crude (but deadly) nuclear weapons; purchase or steal radioactive material, such as plutonium; or hijack a nuclear installation in order to engage in nuclear blackmail or aggression. Given these horrifying possibilities, it seems clear that the United States should place the highest priority on limiting the proliferation of nuclear weapons and dismantling the vast arsenals possessed by established and new nuclear powers. Beginning in the 1960s, as a key element that helped to cool Cold War tensions between the United States and the Soviet Union, a number of treaties were negotiated that regulated the size of the nuclear arsenal, as well as limited providing nuclear weapons technology to other countries. The U.S. ratified several of these, notably the Nonproliferation Treaty (NPT), the Anti-Ballistic Treaty (ABM), and the Strategic Arms Limitation Treaty (SALT I). However, it refused to sign SALT II, which provided for sweeping strategic arms control with Russia, as well as the Comprehensive Test Ban Treaty, which banned all nuclear testing.

Soon after taking office in 2001, the Bush administration adopted policies that many claim may unleash a fresh round of nuclear arms buildup around the world. For example, as was mentioned earlier in the chapter, it proposed expanding a version of the ballistic missile defense system first proposed by President Reagan and later revived (in much more limited form) by President Clinton. Although the official reason given was to provide protection against terrorist states and groups, it may be that (despite official assurances to the contrary) the real aim is to construct a system to counteract a potential Chinese nuclear threat. Because building a ballistic missile defense system would violate the ABM treaty between the U.S. and Russia, President Bush declared that the U.S. might opt out of the treaty if it actually begins to build such a system.

(3) American policy-makers justify maintaining American military dominance in the post–Cold War era by pointing to the increased potential for regional conflicts to occur. The Cold War imposed a rigidity and stability in the international arena. Both superpowers exerted a tight grip on client states and movements, calibrating their actions to minimize the chance of outright confrontation. The end of the Cold War enlarged the space for local and regional conflict. One result has been an increase in the number of regional wars, including hostilities between Eritrea and Ethiopia, Pakistan and India, and Iraq and Iran and civil wars in Angola, Rwanda, Sierra Leone, Somalia, Sri Lanka, and the Balkans. The United States has intervened in such conflicts, sometimes acting on its own, as when it dispatched troops to Haiti, and sometimes sending troops under NATO or UN auspices, as it did in Bosnia and Iraq.

The United States has, in effect, come to define its role as the sole global authority, responsible for making and executing laws for the entire world. Yet there is intense public opposition to committing American forces abroad, and popular movements in the United States and elsewhere reject the idea that the United States has the right to dictate what is appropriate for others.

(4) The attempt to maintain American security has become even more problematic in the face of unconventional threats, including narco-trafficking, undocumented immigration, and international terrorism, involving the possible use of chemical, radioactive, or biological weapons. There have been several violent attacks against U.S. civilian targets in recent years. There is a flourishing international arms trade in sophisticated guns, bombs, and missiles.

A recent unconventional threat is cybercrime—for example, the interception or disruption of global electronic communication. American policy-makers warn that the government must engage in heightened surveillance and control in order to safeguard against these dislocations. At the same time, critics charge that the U.S. government is among those most heavily involved in spying and snooping. For example, the European Union (EU), a political and economic organization closely linking European states, opened an official inquiry in 2000 into charges that the U.S. government engaged in electronic spying for the purpose of industrial espionage. The U.S. government monitors billions of telecommunications daily by law-abiding citizens of the United States and other countries. Thus, in the name of maintaining law and order, the U.S. government has substantially increased its capacity to control social life.

(5) Those who determine U.S. foreign policy warn about growth in the world's population, increased economic inequality and poverty around the world, global epidemics like AIDS, and environmental hazards like deforestation and global warming. These developments do not necessarily involve armed conflict but may represent longer-run and more deeply rooted challenges to the planet. At the same time, U.S. practices are partly to blame for several of these dangers. Along with those in other industrialized countries— but more than most—U.S. companies and consumers engage in wasteful use of resources. American-based MNCs plunder the world's natural resources and promote "development" that may involve devastating consequences. Economic globalization, with MNCs in the lead, contributes to deepening inequalities on a global scale. Thus, in order to address some of the most important problems confronting the world in the twenty-first century, we would do well to rethink American economic, political, and social practices.

THE NEW GLOBAL ECONOMY: WHOSE GLOBALIZATION?

President Clinton placed unusual emphasis on promoting American economic interests abroad. As one account observed, the Clinton administration believed that "economic policy was the means to global leverage."[51] Clinton's foreign policy sought to integrate domestic and foreign policy, as well as foreign security and economic concerns. This approach assumed, according to foreign policy analyst Michael Cox, that "in an era of geo-economics no distinction could be drawn between domestic politics and foreign policy."[52] Cox suggests that, for the Clinton administration, "promoting trade almost seemed to become synonymous with U.S. foreign policy itself."[53] Indeed, a *New York Times* reporter suggests that "Mr. Clinton's lasting imprint on American diplomacy may well be his recognition that preserving and creating a stable global economic system are two sides of the same coin."[54] President Clinton believed that American domestic prosperity was heavily dependent on American exports. As he declared in his 1994 budget address to Congress: "We have put our economic competitiveness at the heart of our foreign policy."[55]

---

[51]Brinkley, "Democratic Enlargement," p. 117.

[52]Cox, *U.S. Foreign Policy After the Cold War*, p. 23.

[53]Ibid.

[54]*New York Times*, July 9, 2000.

[55]Brinkley, "Democratic Enlargement," p. 117.

An important reason for the booming American economy in the 1990s was a sharp increase in foreign trade. Particularly noteworthy was an increase in services exported to other countries, including cultural production—notably, films and television broadcasts—as well as computer programs and financial services. Clinton sought to promote an open international economy, in which capital and goods could move freely throughout the world. In his first term, he negotiated more than 200 new market-opening agreements. He also supported strengthening the authority of international economic organizations and agreements, including NAFTA and the World Trade Organization (WTO). These institutions seek to promote the free flow of capital and trade transnationally and to promote such goals as privatization, deregulation, open markets, low taxes, and low social spending.

The U.S. government did not give equal priority to economic ties to all regions. For example, it devoted little effort to Africa, which contains among the highest rates of poverty and disease in the world. Indeed, the United States allots the smallest proportion of foreign assistance to poor countries of any member state of the OECD. Further, the United States has been the stingiest of all OECD countries in helping impoverished nations repay debts on past loans.

The Clinton administration designated ten less-industrialized countries as Big Emerging Markets and accorded them priority treatment.[56] The U.S. government pressured the governments of these countries to end restrictions on foreign investments in order to allow foreign (often U.S.-based) companies to invest in facilities and to purchase stocks and bonds, as well as to enable companies in these countries to borrow abroad. In the absence of an adequate banking system and governmental financial oversight, these countries were vulnerable to corruption and "crony capitalism," in which members of the ruling elite siphoned off large sums.

The policies of the U.S. government and the international banks and investors that promoted large-scale investments and loans with little oversight and regulation produced a series of severe financial crises in the mid- and late 1990s. As mentioned earlier in this chapter, the pattern was similar in Mexico, Thailand, South Korea, Malaysia, Indonesia, the Philippines, Taiwan, and Russia. Foreign investors who had poured large sums into the country would suddenly become fearful and withdraw their holdings. Overnight, the value of the national currency would sink, prices soar, and living standards plummet. George Soros, a wealthy investor whose own actions powerfully contributed to global financial instability, ruefully observes, "Instead of acting like a pendulum, financial markets can act like a wrecking

---

[56]Robin Broad and John Cavanaugh describe the pattern in which the bulk of multinational corporate investment is channeled to a few countries, as "global apartheid." Robin Broad and John Cavanaugh, "Don't Neglect the Impoverished South," *Foreign Policy* no. 101 (Winter 1995–96): 24.

ball, swinging from country to country and destroying everything that stands in their way."[57]

The consequences are particularly grave for poorer groups. In order to prop up their economies, governments were forced to obtain loans from the IMF and other international financial agencies. In return, they were forced to slash social spending and sponsor other austerity measures. Thus, the poor received few benefits from the sudden creation of new wealth, but paid a heavy price for the financial panic and resulting austerity measures. These developments dramatically and tragically highlight the impact of the American model on countries that have adopted it, as well as the way that globalization has made countries throughout the world dependent on decisions made in New York, Frankfurt, Tokyo, and other financial centers.

Globalization has intensified political and economic inequalities within and across nations and has produced catastrophic environmental damage around the world. Robin Broad and John Cavanaugh provide a few illustrations of the economic consequences of globalization. In the 1960s, the richest fifth in the world had 30 times more income than the poorest fifth; in the 1990s, the income gap was 60 times greater. In the 1960s, the richest fifth controlled 70 percent of the world's income; this rose to 85 percent of the world's total at the end of the century. During this period, the share of the poorest fifth declined from 2.3 percent of the world's income to 1.4 percent. In 1994, the world's 358 billionaires were worth about $752 billion, which was about the same amount as the combined income that year of the world's 2.5 billion poorest people—about 45 percent of the world's population.[58]

Critics claim that the WTO and other international financial institutions, like the IMF and the World Bank, provide benefits for transnational corporations at the expense of the vast majority of the world's population. These organizations issue regulations facilitating MNC trade and investment, but restrict the ability of governments (including the American government) to regulate food supplies, the environment, labor standards, human rights, and product safety.

In the new global economic order being constructed by the WTO and other international agreements, the rights of property are heavily protected. For example, multinational pharmaceutical companies can patent herbs and traditional methods of treatment, thereby prohibiting others from marketing them. Agribusiness firms can prevent governments from limiting the importation of genetically modified seeds and food. The North American Free Trade Agreement (NAFTA), which links Canada, Mexico, and the United States, prohibits governments from requiring that companies purchase a share of materials locally or that they invest a share of profits locally.[59] The

---

[57]George Soros, "Capitalism's Last Chance," *Foreign Policy* 113 (Winter 1998–99): 58.

[58]Robin Broad and John Cavanaugh, "Don't Neglect the Impoverished South," p. 26.

[59]Eric Alterman, *Who Speaks for America: Why Democracy Matters in Foreign Policy* (Ithaca, N.Y.: Cornell University Press, 1998), p. 115.

Protesters at the 1999 World Trade Organization meeting in Seattle.

web of international organizations and treaties represents the foundation of a new world economic order. If unchallenged, the result will tip the world-wide balance of power toward private property and reduce the possibilities for political participation and democratic decision making.

Yet this new world order is not unchallenged. Initiatives by the Clinton and Bush administrations to promote globalization and economic liberal-ization provoked intense political opposition within the United States and abroad. For example, when trade representatives from governments around the world met in Seattle in late 1999 to seek to expand the WTO's powers, over 40,000 protested, including activists from unions, environmental groups, human rights organizations, and churches. The protest closed down the city and made the hitherto unknown WTO a household name. Not long after, other protests occurred in Davos, Switzerland; in Washing-ton, D.C.; in Prague, the Czech Republic; in Québec, Canada; and at the two parties' 2000 nominating conventions. Indeed, no international economic summit takes place nowadays without protestors challenging business as usual.

The grassroots movements opposing free-market globalization demon-strated that determined popular movements can have an important impact. The debate over whose globalization—that is, the form that international co-operation will take and the groups that will benefit from increased global economic ties—remains very much alive.

PROMOTING DEMOCRACY ABROAD

Secretary of State Warren Christopher declared in 1993, "The promotion of democracy is the frontline of global security. A world of democracies would be a safer world."[60] Such a view was based on an influential theory within international relations that claims that democratic governments do not wage war against each other. In part, recent governments have accorded higher priority to promoting democracy and human rights because progressive social movements like Amnesty International and Physicians for Social Responsibility have been highly successful in dramatizing issues of democracy and human rights. For example, a Vermont citizen, Jody Williams, launched a successful international campaign for a treaty banning the use of land mines—which kill and maim countless civilians each year throughout the world. (Williams was awarded the Nobel Peace Prize in 1997.) Ironically, the U.S. government has refused to ratify the treaty on the grounds that it will not accept limits on its use of land mines.

The Clinton and Bush administrations have promoted democracy and human rights on the grounds that it made good economic sense for the United States to promote a world of capitalist democracies. As Douglas Brinkley puts it, "Clinton was quick to understand that . . . the presence of market-based democracies plausibly would render the world a safer, richer place."[61] Political scientist William Robinson put it even more bluntly. After studying cases of authoritarian countries in which the United States intervened (Chile, Haiti, Nicaragua, and the Philippines), he concluded, "The immediate purpose of U.S. intervention in national democratization movements was to gain influence over and to try to shape their outcomes in such a way as to preempt more radical political change, to preserve the social order and international relations of asymmetry."[62]

The United States targeted regimes throughout the world for democratic reform, including the countries of the former Soviet Union, Africa, and East Asia. However, Brinkley observes, the United States distinguished between countries that held out the promise of providing better economic opportunities and the others. "Relations with countries with bright economic futures such as Mexico and South Korea would thus be placed on the front burner; poor, blighted nations, particularly in sub-Saharan Africa and Central America, would receive back-burner attention at best."[63]

In similar fashion, human rights activist Aryeh Neier suggests that the United States employs double standards in its human rights policy. It rarely condemns human rights abuses against powerful countries. For example,

---

[60]Callahan, *Between Two Worlds*, p. 119.

[61]Brinkley, "Democratic Enlargement," p. 117.

[62]William I. Robinson, *Promoting Polyarchy: Globalization, U.S. Intervention, and Hegemony* (Cambridge: Cambridge University Press, 1996), pp. 318–19.

[63]Brinkley, "Democratic Enlargement," p. 117.

although Russia's armed forces committed human rights violations on a large scale in Chechnya in the 1990s and 2000, U.S. reaction was mild. Further, Neier observes, "the United States would not press human rights concerns where important economic interests are at stake."[64] When he sought to persuade Congress to approve most-favored-nation (MFN) trading status for China and supported China's application for membership in the WTO in 2000, President Clinton minimized the importance of China's violations of human rights, including its suppression of dissidents and use of prison labor in its factories. Neier labels as "false" the Clinton administration's claim that "maintaining trade [with China] will be more effective in promoting human rights than will issuing sanctions."[65] Likewise, the United States minimized the importance of human rights abuses by its allies, including Egypt, Israel, Mexico, Saudi Arabia, and Turkey, yet condemned abuses by its opponents, including Cuba, Iran, Iraq, Libya, North Korea, Sudan, and Syria.

The United States practiced a more extreme double standard by refusing to comply in its own behavior with international agreements and norms that it pressed on others. For decades, Congress refused to ratify the UN treaty on human rights because it would subject U.S. citizens to international jurisdiction for human rights violations. Similarly, the United States has refused to recognize the jurisdiction of a UN-sponsored international criminal court. As Kenneth Roth, executive director of Human Rights Watch, pointed out, "The United States is increasingly being viewed as a government that preaches to the rest of the world but is unwilling to be bound by international standards."[66]

Although there is great continuity in foreign policy between the Clinton and Bush administrations, they differ in significant respects. George W. Bush has given lower priority than did his predecessor to promoting human rights, international cooperation, and international environment protection, as evidenced by two examples:

- Soon after taking office, President Bush announced that the U.S. government did not plan to implement the international accords negotiated at Kyoto, Japan, in 1992 to limit greenhouse gases to prevent global warming. The president defended his decision on the grounds that complying with the accords was not in the "economic interest" of the U.S. Bush's announcement provoked a firestorm of protest among citizens and governments throughout the world.

- As mentioned earlier, when President Bush proposed an expanded plan to construct a missile defense system, he declared that the ABM treaty with Russia, which prohibits constructing intercontinental

---

[64]Aryeh Neier, "The New Double Standard," *Foreign Policy* no. 105 (Winter 1996–97): 97.

[65]Ibid.

[66]*New York Times*, July 3, 2000.

ballistic missile systems, was outdated. This move was also widely criticized abroad.

Bush's actions isolated the United States within the world community. For example, in 2001 the U.S. was defeated for re-election to the UN Commission on Human Rights (a seat it had held since the creation of the Commission) and the International Narcotics Control Board. These developments reflected a widely held belief around the world that the Bush administration was acting in an arrogant and reckless fashion.

CONCLUSION

The United States is by far the most powerful country in the world. In addition to military supremacy, especially noteworthy following the end of the Cold War, the United States's economic might has grown enormously since the 1990s. And American cultural influence is apparent around the world, from the Pizza Huts and McDonald's found in countless foreign cities to the American clothing styles, rock stars, movies, and television programming. These apparently apolitical artifacts, in fact, convey a political message about what counts in life: a lifestyle dedicated to ever more consumption organized by global corporations often based in the United States.

American influence is evident in more overtly political ways as well. The United States plays a key role in setting the global agenda on trade, investment, human rights, environmental regulation, and nuclear weapons. Not that the American government always carries the day. But it is the government to which all others look, with either admiration or hostility.

What goals does the United States seek in deploying its vast power? American foreign policy goals are largely shaped by the balance of domestic political forces within the United States. The highly integrated system of political and economic power described elsewhere in this book deeply affects what American policy-makers define as American interests abroad. The result is that the military-industrial complex, of which President Eisenhower warned a half century ago, equates its interests with America's national interests. American policy-makers claim that the U.S. government pursues foreign policies that serve the interests of all Americans—indeed, of citizens throughout the world. Yet, as with the costs and benefits that flow from domestic policy, the costs and benefits generated by foreign policy are distributed highly unequally in terms of class, race, and gender.

"Tip" O'Neill, Speaker of the House of Representatives in the 1970s and 1980s, famously remarked that all politics is local. He meant that people tend to judge the merits of a policy by its impact on their own lives. He might have added that all politics is also global, in that local and domestic political decisions affect the fate of the world. This interdependence represents one of the most pressing reasons to promote fuller democracy within the United States.

10

THE WELFARE STATE

"This isn't welfare reform," Senator Daniel Patrick Moynihan of New York thundered in dismay as an overhaul of the existing welfare system wound its way through Congress in 1996. "This is welfare repeal."[1] Republicans in Congress seized the initiative President Bill Clinton had given them when he promised the American people in his 1992 campaign "to end welfare as we know it." In August 1996, Congress sent the president a welfare bill that did what he promised, but in ways he probably never had intended. Forced to choose between breaking his campaign promise to reform welfare and repudiating his own more generous welfare proposals, President Clinton chose the latter and signed the Personal Responsibility and Work Opportunity Reconciliation Act of 1996 (PRWORA). This legislation created a new welfare program, Temporary Assistance to Needy Families (TANF), to replace the old one, Aid to Families with Dependent Children (AFDC), which had been the country's main instrument for helping impoverished children and their families since 1935. With the stroke of his pen, President Clinton annulled the promise that the federal and state governments would assist all poor children and their families who qualified for welfare.

Since the 1960s, AFDC essentially had become an entitlement program that provided cash assistance to poor families. This meant that states were required to provide grants to families that qualified for welfare for as long as they were eligible. The amount of federal money for welfare would adjust automatically to cover a portion of the benefits states gave to poor families regardless of the number of families on the rolls and regardless of how long they had been there.[2]

Under the new law, states receive fixed lump sums of money from the federal government in the form of block grants to pay for welfare. Federal money to pay for welfare no longer increases automatically with the welfare rolls, but now as a block grant to each state, it remains a set amount, even if

---

[1] Quoted in "Moynihan Turns Up the Heat," *Economist* 337 (November 11, 1995): 32.

[2] In *Goldberg v. Kelly* (1970), the Supreme Court ruled that beneficiaries, once eligible, could not lose their grants without a due process hearing.

the number of people on welfare increases. This means that if welfare rolls rise and states spend all of their federal money and choose not to supplement it, poor families that are eligible for income support may not receive any. Guarantees of cash assistance to poor families are now gone. The new law also gives states more discretion on how to spend the federal money they receive, to devise their own welfare policies, but with one important condition required by Congress. PRWORA imposes a work requirement on all welfare recipients by time-limiting welfare. The new law sets a limit of two years on welfare, after which recipients must work, and sets a lifetime limit of five years during which recipients may receive welfare. The promise of a Democratic president and a Republican Congress to "end welfare as we know it" thus was redeemed. Welfare as an entitlement was eliminated by setting time limits to benefits and by removing the guarantee the federal government would reimburse the various states for each eligible recipient regardless of how many there were.

The 1996 debate over welfare policy in Congress was as charged as any in recent memory. Conflict on the House Ways and Means Committee over eliminating the guarantee of welfare benefits to every eligible poor American was so furious that the sergeant-at-arms had to be called to restore order. When the bill reached the floor of the House, the debate reached uncommon levels of acrimony. Some Democrats compared Republican welfare proposals to Nazism, while some Republicans likened welfare recipients to wild animals.

The debate over welfare became so overwrought because, more than most policy issues, personal values and public morality move close to the surface when considering welfare policy for the poor. Policy-makers and social analysts are not shy about projecting their personal values onto the poor through welfare policy because that group is often too weak, too vulnerable, and too outside the mainstream of political life to resist. Consequently, welfare policy often combines with other issues that are reflected through it. For example, the proper role of women in society has been projected through welfare policy. Some scholars argue that welfare policy has been used to reinforce the virtues of motherhood and discourage women from entering the labor force, or today, just the opposite by forcing women to work, but only if they are poor.[3] Others argue that welfare policy is about race. From the start, welfare policy has treated blacks differently, making it harder for them to receive grants and offering less help in counties with large African-American populations. Welfare policy in this view is about maintaining racial subordination.[4] Some believe welfare policy is about

---

[3] Gwendolyn Mink, *The Wages of Motherhood: Inequality in the Welfare State, 1917–1942* (Ithaca, N.Y.: Cornell University Press, 1995).

[4] Jill Quadagno, *The Color of Welfare: How Racism Undermined the War on Poverty* (New York: Oxford University Press, 1994).

class, perceiving the welfare state as another terrain of class struggle between workers and capitalists.[5] Workers seek protection from the insecurity and rigor of the market through the welfare state, while employers try to use the welfare state to supplement and reinforce market discipline. Still others believe the welfare state is about federalism and which level of government works best. [6] Some prefer to locate authority with state governments, which can experiment with different approaches to welfare that reflect local conditions. Others prefer federal control, believing that citizens in every state should be treated equally and that states, if left to themselves, will compete to see which can be the most stingy. Finally, some argue that welfare is not about what level of government should respond to the problem of poverty, but whether government should respond at all. Welfare policy is about the proper balance between the obligations citizens owe each other and the responsibility they should take for themselves.[7]

Cash assistance to the poor is emotionally charged and engenders so much conflict because it is freighted with so many meanings, from relationships between the sexes to relationships between the states. Since less than 2 percent of the federal budget is spent on welfare, it is clear the symbolic significance attached to the issue is out of all proportion to the actual money spent on it.[8] Welfare policy has attracted so much attention not because we invest a significant amount of money to implement it, but because it embodies our deepest public values.

But welfare policy extends beyond programs intended for poor families—which is what we have been referring to so far and is a distinctively modern American understanding of the term. In the United States, the welfare state is divided into two parts, only one of which is oriented to the poor. Indeed, the largest part of the welfare state is not targeted at the poor at all. Most welfare state spending goes to the working middle class through *social insurance* programs. These are programs based on contributions workers make in the form of payroll taxes to the government, which holds these funds in trust in the event of a worker's death, injury, unemployment, or retirement. The best known and most inclusive social insurance programs are Old Age and Survivors and Disability Insurance, under Social Security, and Medicare, which provides government health insurance for all elderly Americans. These programs, which enjoy widespread popular and bipartisan support, are universal, covering almost all those in the labor force and

---

[5] Charles Noble, *Welfare as We Knew It: A Political History of the American Welfare State* (New York: Oxford University Press, 1997).

[6] Sanford F. Schram and Samuel H. Beer, *Welfare Reform: A Race to the Bottom?* (Baltimore, Md.: Johns Hopkins University, 1999).

[7] Alan Wolfe, *Whose Keeper: Social Science and Moral Obligation* (Berkeley: University of California Press, 1989).

[8] Gary Bryner, *Politics and Public Morality: The Great American Welfare Reform Debate* (New York: Norton, 1998), p. xi.

their families. Moreover, their benefit levels tend to keep up with the cost of living. Since the early 1970s, Social Security benefits have been indexed; that is, they are increased to keep up with the previous year's rate of inflation. Finally, clients of these welfare programs tend to be perceived as "deserving," since they worked and contributed toward their benefits through the payroll taxes they paid.

The second, smaller category of the welfare state is composed of *public assistance* programs directed to poor people, such as TANF, a part of the new welfare law we described earlier. These are programs for citizens whom social insurance programs miss. They include Medicaid, which offers health insurance to the needy, and Food Stamps, which offers coupons that the poor can redeem for food in grocery stores. In contrast to social insurance programs, these programs are selective, or means-tested. These programs are available only to Americans whose income or wealth is below the level set by law. Also, unlike Social Security, public assistance program benefits are not indexed, nor is there a national standard of support. That is, benefit levels in public assistance programs can be eroded by inflation and are vastly unequal across the states. Finally, unlike the aura surrounding recipients of social insurance programs, persons receiving public assistance are viewed with suspicion, even as undeserving, because they are thought to be responsible for their plight, they often are outside the labor market, and they do not contribute money toward their benefits. Thus, the country's welfare state is split between social insurance programs, which have public approval, and public assistance programs, which offend dominant values regarding the work ethic and individual responsibility.[9] We can see this uneven history reflected in the spending patterns noted in Figure 10–1.

The division of the welfare state into social insurance and public assistance is reflected in the meaning we now give to the term *welfare*. Welfare was once viewed favorably and referred to all sorts of programs that promoted economic security for everyone. However, once the welfare state was divided into social insurance programs for those who worked and public assistance programs for the poor, the term *welfare* came to be associated only with the latter.[10] Welfare's original positive and inclusive meanings now turned into their opposites. The shift in the meaning of welfare and its contemporary reference only to public assistance programs were evident in President Clinton's promise "to end welfare as we know it." No one presumed that Clinton was thinking about ending social insurance programs

---

[9] Nathan Glazer, "Welfare and 'Welfare' in America," in *The Welfare State East and West*, ed. Richard Rose and Rei Shiratori (New York: Oxford University Press, 1986), pp. 41–63. See also Michael K. Brown, "The Segmented Welfare System: Distributive Conflict and Retrenchment in the United States, 1968–84," in *Remaking the Welfare State*, ed. Michael K. Brown (Philadelphia: Temple University Press, 1988), pp. 182–210.

[10] Indeed, a 1995 Kaiser Family Foundation survey found that people associate the term *welfare* only with means-tested programs for the poor and do not apply the term to such social insurance programs as Social Security and Medicare. Cited in R. Kent Weaver, *Ending Welfare as We Know It* (Washington, D.C: Brookings, 2000), p. 172.

■ FIGURE 10–1

MEANS- VS. NON-MEANS-TESTED SPENDING AS A PERCENTAGE
OF GROSS DOMESTIC PRODUCT, 1962–1999

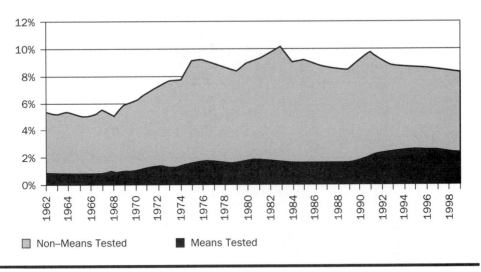

SOURCE: Department of Health and Human Services, 2000.

like Social Security and not public assistance programs for the poor when he made that promise.[11]

Spending on welfare state social insurance and public assistance programs has expanded dramatically since World War II. Regardless of whether Republicans or Democrats have been in office, welfare state expenditures have steadily grown. In 1980, President Ronald Reagan came into office determined to shrink the welfare state. But welfare state spending continued to grow inexorably even under his reproving administration. Total social welfare expenditures in 1980 were $3,700 billion. At the end of the decade, after Reagan's two terms and halfway through the term of his successor, George H. W. Bush, welfare state spending had risen 25 percent to $4,631 billion in constant dollars (that is, after taking inflation into account). Social welfare expenditures continued to increase in the 1990s, rising to $5,442 billion in 1994.[12]

Despite this growth in welfare state spending, the United States actually is near the bottom of the league standings for welfare state spending compared to European countries (see Figure 10–2). In 1994, welfare state spending accounted for 22 percent of the American gross domestic product. This was

[11] Michael B. Katz and Lorrin R. Thomas, "The Invention of 'Welfare,'" *Journal of Policy History* 10, no. 4 (1998): 399–418.

[12] U.S. Department of Commerce, *Statistical Abstract of the United States, 1998* (Washington, D.C.: U.S. Government Printing Office, 1998), p. 376.

■ FIGURE 10-2

COMPARATIVE WELFARE STATE SPENDING AS A PERCENTAGE
OF GROSS DOMESTIC PRODUCT

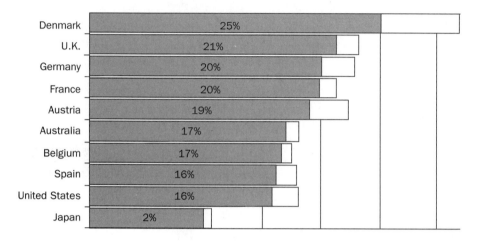

Denmark	25%
U.K.	21%
Germany	20%
France	20%
Austria	19%
Australia	17%
Belgium	17%
Spain	16%
United States	16%
Japan	2%

■ Government Expenditures as a Percentage of GDP

□ Social Security and Welfare as a Percentage of GDP

SOURCE: National Accounts, OECD, Paris, 1998, *http://www.oecd.org*.

about 25 percent less than the average that the 15 members of the European Union spent on the welfare state as a proportion of their economies. Our welfare state spending is on par with Spain, Portugal, and Greece, which are not nearly as wealthy as the United States, and lags far behind more developed, industrialized societies, such as Germany and France, which more nearly resemble the United States. Comparatively, America's welfare state is small, capturing a more limited share of tax revenues and national wealth than welfare spending in comparable advanced capitalist countries. One reason for this divergence is the absence in the United States of many welfare state programs available elsewhere, including universal health care and family allowances.

But the American welfare state is distinctive in ways other than its low score on spending and the absence of programs that are available elsewhere. Welfare states can also be compared in the degree to which they detach a person's well-being from dependence on the labor market. Some societies provide social rights, such as a right to health care, as part of the package of rights granted to all its citizens. Where a social right to health care exists, workers do not have to depend on employment in the labor market to afford or receive health care; it is available automatically as a right of citizenship. Social rights may not relieve the whip of necessity that the market imposes on workers, but they do relieve the sting—and thereby the significance—

of the blows. Americans, however, enjoy fewer and less generous social rights than can be found in other industrial societies. Social rights in the United States are not extensive enough to detach the well-being of citizens from their class position or their place in the labor market. The relative absence of social rights in the United States means that American workers are penalized heavily for failing in the labor market. Because U.S. welfare state benefits are relatively low, stigmatizing, and of short duration, they effectively reinforce the discipline of the marketplace rather than offer an alternative to it.[13]

Throughout the West, welfare states are under tremendous pressure as a result of globalization and capital mobility. Employers are tempted to move their investments to locations where tax rates are relatively low and welfare states are relatively puny. When they do so, they take jobs with them. Globalization thus can threaten a "race to the bottom," in which societies compete to reduce their welfare state costs in order to attract investment. Under this scenario, the American welfare state may be a model to which more extensive welfare states in Western Europe will conform. But there are countertrends. Globalization also creates pressures to maintain, even expand, the welfare state. Globalization increases the number of citizens who feel economically insecure, building pressures on governments in democratic countries to respond to their unease. When economic insecurity is growing, politicians are pressured by voters to keep the welfare state intact. In recent years, workers in France and Germany have taken to the streets to defend their welfare state benefits and have elected governments that promise to protect them. And in the United States, now that welfare reform has been enacted, both major parties try to outdo each other in support of the social insurance parts of the welfare state.

Welfare states also gain vitality from their economic role. It is far too simple to think of social policies merely as a drag on economic investment, productivity, and economic growth. To be sure, welfare states may impose high taxes, which discourage investment, but they also increase the quality of the labor force, promote citizens' efficient integration into the labor market, and furnish essential services that cannot be obtained from the market. Extensive and generous welfare states can help promote economic competitiveness, increase labor productivity, and spur production. Large welfare states with an array of social rights that distributes benefits to all citizens can be an advantage in the global marketplace.[14]

This chapter will examine the history of the American welfare state, the forces that have shaped it, and the politics surrounding it.

---

[13] Gosta Esping-Andersen, *The Three Worlds of Welfare Capitalism* (Princeton, N.J.: Princeton University Press, 1990).

[14] Geoffrey Garrett, *Partisan Politics in the Global Economy* (New York: Cambridge University Press, 1998).

THE HISTORICAL WELFARE STATE

The history of American social policy is not simply a story of slow development. The perception that the American welfare state is a laggard, a late and stunted addition to the family of welfare states, is based on when the "big four" welfare state programs—unemployment insurance, workers' compensation, disability insurance, and pensions—first were enacted. These welfare programs were first founded at the federal level in the United States in 1935 with the passage of the Social Security Act, well after they were established in many European countries.

But this comparison gives a false impression that the federal government was not involved in social assistance prior to the enactment of Social Security. In fact, an unusual sort of welfare state, one that diverged from what existed in Europe, did exist prior to 1935. The American welfare state appears as a laggard only if we use the "big four" as the standard of comparison. In other words, the American welfare state did not arrive late; it just did not develop along the same lines as those that existed in Western Europe.

Western European welfare states were aimed at workers, from unemployment insurance in the event of layoffs to workers' compensation in the event of an industrial accident. A consequence of targeting workers was that these welfare programs predominantly covered men, who were far more likely to participate in the labor force than women. In the United States, on the other hand, the early American welfare state did not target working men, but rather extended social protection to soldiers and mothers.

Between 1880 and 1910—well before the passage of Social Security in 1935—the federal government spent more than a quarter of its entire budget on pensions for Union Civil War veterans and their dependents. In fact, the federal government expended more money on pensions for former Union Army soldiers and their dependents than on any other spending category, with the exception of interest payments on the national debt. By 1910, 28 percent of all men over age 65—more than 500,000 Americans—received federal benefits averaging $189 per year, a tidy sum at the time (approximately $3,000 today). An additional 300,000 orphans, widows, and dependents also received payments from the federal government.[15] Coverage rates were as high as those in some European old-age programs, and the benefits Americans received were more generous than what some pensioners received in Europe.

This unusual social assistance program in the form of veteran's pensions died of natural causes; the generation of Civil War veterans eligible to draw a pension passed. As Civil War pensions faded away, the American welfare state took a new turn, one that would again distinguish it from Europe. In Europe, the early welfare state was inclined to support men who worked. In the United States, the early welfare state was intended to discourage mothers from working.

---

[15] Theda Skocpol, *Protecting Soldiers and Mothers: The Political Origins of Social Policy in the United States* (Cambridge: Harvard University Press, 1992), p. 65.

During the Progressive era, in the first two decades of the twentieth century, a "maternalist" welfare state developed that promoted the cult of motherhood. Social benefits were contingent on women conforming to traditional norms of domestic motherhood, thus reaffirming the strict separation of gender roles, in which men worked and women took care of the home. For example, mother's pensions provided income assistance to single, poor, deserving mothers so they could stay home and raise their children. At the time, this was widely perceived by both men and women as preferable to the other alternatives: having a woman work for a wage outside the home to support her family or give up her children to an orphanage or foster home because she could not provide for them. Each of these options would have undermined the mother's role, which advocates of mother's pensions sought to preserve.

But not all mothers were treated alike. To qualify for assistance, they had to prove themselves worthy. Widows could easily do this, since they were not regarded as responsible for their plight, but unwed mothers, who could be blamed for their distress, were often excluded. Benefits, moreover, were made contingent on the behavior of mothers. They had to display moral character by showing "intelligence, willingness to learn English, piety, celibacy," compliance with directions from social workers, and dedication to "full-time child-centered domesticity."[16] The price of accepting mother's pensions was state regulation over the lives of women to ensure they conformed to the gender roles dictated by the dominant culture. We also know that these pensions were differentially made available to white and black women. States with the highest concentrations of African-American women, mainly in the South, were among the last to inaugurate such pensions, and their benefit levels were unusually meager.

Mother's pensions are an example of how certain roles—in this case, roles based on gender—can be inscribed by social policy. According to the defenders of mother's pensions, mothers earned their benefits because caring for children was the natural, appropriate way for women to contribute to the well-being of society. Mother's pensions were defended as "the wages of motherhood," in Gwendolyn Mink's artful phrase. Society would profit from this investment in motherhood through the benefits children derived from it.

THE NEW DEAL

Mother's pensions reached only one in four women who were eligible. They were so underfunded that recipients had to take jobs outside the home in order to make ends meet. This, of course, undermined the very principle of domestic motherhood the program was supposed to promote. But even this

---

[16] Mink, *The Wages of Motherhood*, p. 33.

modest effort on behalf of mothers was more than the early American welfare state provided to adult working men. Unemployment insurance to tide workers over from one job to the next did not exist. A minimum wage to ensure a modest income for those who worked was not available. Disability insurance for those too sick to work had not yet been legislated. There were no legal restrictions on working hours, except for a few workers in hazardous occupations, and there was no pension system for workers who were too old to work. The only social protection available to a few workers was that provided by employers. In the 1920s, many of the nation's most prominent corporations practiced welfare capitalism, offering retirement pensions, health care, housing, and community services to their employees.[17]

Welfare capitalism was more developed in the United States than in other nations because it fit well within a "distinctive American environment composed of large firms, weak unions, and small government," according to historian Sanford M. Jacoby.[18] Welfare capitalism assumed that employers, not the government, would take care of the labor force. But even during the 1920s, the heyday of welfare capitalism, employer-based welfare benefits never extended beyond workers in a few progressive corporations. Fewer than 10 percent of all companies offered significant welfare benefits to their employees. Even where corporations practiced welfare capitalism, firms tried to buy the loyalty of their workers on the cheap by spending as little as possible on employee benefits, which cut into profits. Eligibility requirements were stringent and benefit levels were low. In fact, most workers and the poor were left to their own devices when it came to providing for their own welfare. There was no safety net other than local charities, family and friends, and poorly funded local public relief agencies to break their fall. When the Great Depression arrived in 1929, these provisions were grossly inadequate. The Depression swept away not only those who could barely keep their heads above water, but also all the life rafts—employer-based welfare programs, personal savings, private charities, and local public relief efforts—designed to save them.[19]

When President Franklin Roosevelt stated in 1937 that "one-third of [the] nation" was "ill-housed, ill-clad, ill nourished," his estimate understated the problem. The proportion of the population that fit this description in the midst of the Depression, contemporaries agreed, was actually closer to one-half.[20] The main source of this distress was the staggering unemployment that afflicted the nation. In 1933, almost 13 million workers—a quarter of the

---

[17] Stuart Brandes, *American Welfare Capitalism* (Chicago: University of Chicago Press, 1976).

[18] Sanford M. Jacoby, *Modern Manors: Welfare Capitalism Since the New Deal* (Princeton, N.J.: Princeton University Press, 1997), p. 4.

[19] Lisbeth Cohen, *Making a New Deal* (New York: Cambridge University Press, 1990).

[20] James T. Patterson, *America's Struggle Against Poverty, 1900–1994* (Cambridge: Harvard University Press, 1994), p. 42.

workforce—were jobless, looking for work. Unemployment bred poverty and poverty bred despair. One man wrote relief officials in Washington, "Can you advise me as to which would be the most humane way to dispose of myself and family, as this is about the only thing that I can see left to do."[21]

Poverty, low wages, and unemployment led some to despair, but others to political action. Thousands of workers sat down in factories to demand union recognition, the unemployed marched to demand food and shelter, and farmers dumped their produce to demand higher prices. The Roosevelt administration tried to blunt these challenges by offering federally funded jobs and social welfare programs to help those in need. The corporate community balked at these reforms, claiming they were a threat to private enterprise. But with the prospect of mass unrest growing, Roosevelt ignored their misgivings. The president recognized that concessions were necessary to save capitalism, even if this meant opposing capitalists who urged thrift and passivity in the face of the economic calamity.

While conservatives strenuously opposed the New Deal, there was an element to it they could sympathize with, even if they could not appreciate it at the time. In 1935, *Fortune* magazine noted that "it was fairly evident to most disinterested critics" that the New Deal "had the preservation of capitalism at all times in view." Social reform was part of the administration's strategy to keep the market economy functioning. When the threat of civil disorder arose, the federal government expanded work relief programs. When the threat of disorder waned, federally funded jobs diminished. Some social welfare concessions were extended when the poor disrupted the status quo and were later retracted once the threat passed.[22]

But the New Deal also left an enduring liberal legacy in the form of the 1935 Social Security Act, which forms the basic legislative framework of the American welfare state even today. This landmark legislation offered pensions and unemployment compensation to qualified workers, provided public assistance to the elderly and the blind, and created a new national program for poor, single mothers, called Aid to Dependent Children (ADC). The range of social welfare activities the government was now engaged in and the money committed to them in the 1930s were scarcely imaginable ten years earlier. The various protections and support the government provided through the Social Security program for the blind, the unemployed, the elderly, and poor single mothers now made it possible for people to live with a modicum of security and dignity. Moreover, as the government expanded its social welfare activities, people's expectations about the role and responsibilities of government grew.

---

[21] Quoted in Patterson, *America's Struggle Against Poverty*, p. 52.

[22] Francis Fox Piven and Richard Cloward, *Regulating the Poor: The Functions of Public Welfare* (New York: Pantheon, 1971).

But even as the liberalism of the Social Security Act blazed new paths, it carried many conservative ideas about poverty from the previous period into the future with it. First, it continued the American tradition of localism. States were given the authority to set benefit levels and eligibility requirements for ADC and unemployment insurance. This discretion led to wide variations in benefits between states. Citizens in identical circumstances were treated differently depending solely on where they lived. Benefit levels were particularly low in the South so as not to compete with or undermine the low wages paid by employers in that region.

Second, benefit levels may have been lower in the South than in other regions, but they were meager everywhere. Benefit levels continued to follow the "least eligibility" principle, which held that no one should be better off on welfare than in work. Benefits should be set below the wage of the lowest paid worker so that the poor would rather offer themselves to any employer on any terms than accept relief.[23] Welfare should be made as undesirable as possible in order to reinforce the work ethic and ensure an abundant supply of cheap labor.

Third, the Social Security Act institutionalized the invidious distinction between deserving and undeserving welfare recipients. Programs organized on the principle of social insurance, like Social Security, were for workers who deserved them. These programs were financed through the private sector by payroll taxes on employers and employees. Recipients "earned" their benefits through their contributions while they worked. Public assistance programs, on the other hand, were for the less deserving poor. These programs were not financed on a contributory basis from the private sector like social insurance programs. Instead, they were financed out of general tax revenues. This pattern of funding bred resentment, since many taxpayers came to consider these programs to be governmental handouts to the poor, who did nothing to earn their benefits. The poor thus were separated from mainstream workers and placed in means-tested public assistance programs that stigmatized them.

Finally, the Social Security Act reinforced racial and gender inequalities. The separation of the poor and workers into different welfare state programs had the effect of segregating men from women and whites from blacks in different parts of the welfare state. For example, men were more likely to work than women and thus qualify for social insurance programs, like Social

---

[23] An example of the least eligibility principle can be found in the British *Poor Law Report of 1834*. For "able-bodied labourers who apply for relief," the *Poor Law Report* recommended "hard work at low wages by the piece, and extracting more work at a lower price than is paid for any other labour in the parish". . . . In short, . . . let the labourer find that the parish is the hardest taskmaster and the worst paymaster he can find, and thus induce him to make his application to the parish his last and not his first resort." Quoted in David Schmidtz and Robert E. Goodin, *Social Welfare and Individual Responsibility* (New York: Cambridge University Press, 1998), p. 173.

Security and unemployment compensation, which depended on labor force participation in order to draw benefits. In addition, whites were more likely to work in occupations covered under Social Security, as opposed to disproportionately black occupations, such as agricultural workers and domestics, which were not originally included under the Social Security Act's coverage. Consequently, many blacks and women did not qualify for pensions or unemployment compensation even though they were often the lowest paid and most irregularly employed groups in the entire nation.[24]

The distinction between social insurance and public assistance programs, which separated workers from the poor and white men from minorities and women, was an important legacy of the New Deal. The degree to which the American welfare state separates these groups into different programs is much more extreme than in other Western countries. Many European welfare states, by contrast, developed a blend of more comprehensive and universal welfare programs that included workers with the poor. But the United States segregated these groups from each other, putting them in different programs organized according to different principles. The result was a dual welfare state in which social insurance programs for workers enjoyed political support, while public assistance programs for the poor, which included a disproportionate number of blacks and women, were suspect as handouts for the unworthy.

CONSERVATIVE AND LIBERAL WELFARE STATES

The conservative and liberal aspects of the New Deal reveal the two sides of the welfare state. On the one hand, the welfare state is conservative, stabilizing the corporate capitalist system. Welfare, British politician Joseph Chamberlain once said, is the ransom the rich must pay in order to sleep peacefully in their beds at night. The welfare state alleviates, but does not correct the basic structural inequalities that are part and parcel of American capitalism. It reinforces the market by making the inequalities and insecurities of a capitalist economy tolerable.

On the other hand, the welfare state is a progressive force, offering an egalitarian alternative to the market. A generous welfare state allows workers to obtain basic needs without succumbing to the demands of employers. The welfare state can provide workers with enough economic security that they are less susceptible to the "whip of necessity" if they do not accept the terms employers offer. The welfare state can make workers' standards of living less dependent on the wages they receive, thus reducing the power that employers exercise over their employees. For this reason, business generally

---

[24] Charles Houston, a black lawyer, described the Social Security bill as a "sieve with holes just big enough for the majority of Negroes to fall through." Quoted in Michael K. Brown, *Race, Money and the American Welfare State* (Ithaca, N.Y.: Cornell University Press, 1999), p. 61.

has opposed extensions of the welfare state, while working-class and poor people's movements have supported it. In addition, where welfare states are extensive, as they are in Scandinavia, providing such benefits as health care and a modest income to all citizens, workers are less tolerant of inequality.[25] The egalitarian logic of the welfare state may spread to other activities, progressively infringing on areas that once operated according to market principles based on the ability to pay.[26]

Welfare states always are both conservative, reinforcing capitalism, and progressive, providing workers with an alternative to dependence on employers and the market. The mix of effects in different countries and at different historical moments depends on the precise kind of welfare state on offer. Some are quite limited, extending only the minimum required to maintain social peace and the status quo.[27] In this model, the welfare state functions as a safety net. Benefits are set low, below the lowest wage that workers could earn, in order to encourage the poor to work. The process of applying for benefits is made as demeaning and degrading as possible in order to discourage applications and stigmatize those who do apply. Benefits are of short duration in order to force people back into the labor market as soon as possible on whatever terms are available. Government services are inferior to those available in the private sector so as not to compete with profit-making firms. Finally, benefits are targeted to the poor, segregating them from workers, whose well-being is tied to the private economy. Since public assistance programs are for poor people, most workers and members of the middle class do not have a stake in defending them. Consequently, these welfare programs are vulnerable politically to cutbacks.

More progressive welfare states, by contrast, provide more than a safety net for those unfortunate enough to fall out of the labor market. Such welfare states distribute more generous benefits to all citizens on a more equal basis, making it unnecessary for citizens to go to the market for their needs. Benefits are not targeted to the poor, but are available as social rights to all citizens and long-term residents. Benefits are extensive and of long duration so that workers do not suffer a steep drop in living standards when they are out of the labor market. These programs enjoy broad political support because so many citizens are included within them.

Though there are liberal, even progressive, features of the U.S. welfare state, overall it is set apart by the degree to which it approaches the more conservative, safety-net model. It is organized to provide the minimum necessary to support the market, stabilize capitalism, and ensure social peace.

---

[25] Richard Scase, *Social Democracy in Capitalist Society* (Totowa, N.J.: Rowman & Littlefield, 1977).

[26] John D. Stephens, *The Transition from Capitalism to Socialism* (Urbana: University of Illinois Press, 1986).

[27] Georg Simmel, "The Poor," in *Poverty: Power and Politics,* ed. Chaim I. Waxman (New York: Grosset & Dunlop, 1968), pp. 3–9.

It does not go beyond this minimum to pose for workers an egalitarian alternative to dependence on employers and the market, like progressive welfare states do.[28]

Comparatively, the U.S. rate of poverty is higher than the rates in Western Europe, not because our economy produces more poverty, but because our politics does.[29] Before government taxes and welfare programs are factored in, measures of relative poverty in the United States are approximately the same as those in Australia, Canada, Italy, the Netherlands, and Sweden, and they are lower than those in Britain, Ireland, France, and Denmark. But the United States diverges from all these countries, with more than twice and sometimes three times the rate of relative poverty, after government taxes and welfare programs are taken into account. Table 10–1 indicates that the United States eliminates less poverty through its government taxing and spending programs than does any other country to which it is compared. In other words, capitalism left to itself pretty much produces the same results everywhere. What matters in creating greater social equity is politics, and it is this that accounts for America's rate of relative poverty.[30]

BEYOND THE NEW DEAL

With the New Deal, the federal government now took responsibility for social welfare, which it had never done before. But as much as the New Deal signified a dramatic break with the past, it also contained traditional elements that reduced its progressive thrust. Conservatives in Congress and corporate opponents of the welfare state ensured that benefits were meager, that the poor were segregated in different programs from workers, that racial and gender hierarchies were not disturbed, and that the states would play a prominent role in administering social welfare programs.

The last major New Deal social policy initiative was the Fair Labor Standards Act of 1938, a law that established the first national minimum wage (25 cents per hour) and a 40-hour work week. Soon, World War II brought a halt to social reform, as the country's attention turned decisively to the war against Germany, Italy, and Japan. When the war ended, liberals hoped, in vain, to restore the momentum of the New Deal. But a politically resurgent business community in tandem with an increasingly conservative Congress resisted

---

[28] Ira Katznelson, "Considerations on Social Democracy in the United States," *Comparative Politics*, October 1978, 77–99.

[29] Relative poverty, which is the standard measure used in comparisons of poverty rates across countries, is the number of families with incomes 50 percent below the median family income.

[30] See L. Kenworthy, "Do Social Welfare Policies Reduce Poverty? A Cross-National Assessment," Working Paper No. 188, Luxembourg Income Study, 1998, in Robert M. Solow, "Review of *The Real Worlds of Welfare Capitalism*," *New York Review of Books*, March 23, 2000, 20–24.

■ TABLE 10–1

RELATIVE POVERTY RATES (PERCENT), 1991

	Post-tax/transfer Relative Poverty	Pre-tax/transfer Relative Poverty
Australia	6.4	21.3
Belgium	2.2	23.9
Canada	5.6	21.6
Denmark	3.5	23.9
Finland	2.3	9.8
France	4.8	27.5
Germany	2.4	14.1
Ireland	4.7	25.8
Italy	5.0	21.8
Netherlands	4.3	20.5
Norway	1.7	9.3
Sweden	3.1	20.4
Switzerland	4.1	12.1
United Kingdom	3.3	25.7
United States	11.7	21.0

SOURCE: L. Kenworthy, "Do Social Welfare Policies Reduce Poverty? A Cross-National Assessment," Working Paper No. 188, Luxembourg Income Study, 1998, in Robert M. Solow, "Review of *The Real Worlds of Welfare Capitalism*," *New York Review of Books*, March 23, 2000, 20–24.

new social initiatives. Federal welfare programs were thrown on the defensive and effectively denounced in the early years of the Cold War as the opening wedge of communism and a threat to freedom. In 1946, conservatives in Congress weakened a bill that would have committed the government to a full-employment policy. In 1949, a national health insurance bill proposed by the Truman administration was defeated in Congress. The American Medical Association effectively denounced the measure as "socialized medicine." Business groups joined the opposition, criticizing the bill as "big government."[31] Other parts of President Harry Truman's Fair Deal met a similar fate.

Defeated politically, unions and other liberals who supported national health insurance tried to obtain from employers what they could not secure from Congress. Unions began to negotiate fringe benefits packages in

---

[31] Edmund F. Wehrle, "For a Healthy America: Labor's Struggle for National Health Insurance, 1943–1949," *Labor's Heritage*, Summer 1993, 28–44.

collective bargaining with employers that included health insurance, employer-funded pensions, and supplementary unemployment benefits for their members. Between 1948 and 1959, the number of workers receiving health insurance and private pensions as part of their employment contracts tripled. A private welfare system in which social protections, such as health insurance and pensions, were tied to the job, through the labor contract between employers and employees, began to develop. This private welfare system comprises the third leg of the American system of social provision, alongside government social insurance and public assistance programs. Indeed, the United States is distinctive in the degree to which its mix of public- and private-sector welfare spending is weighted toward the latter. Approximately one-quarter of all welfare spending in the country comes from the private sector, compared to just 5 percent in France and Sweden. Welfare benefits, such as health insurance, that are provided by the government as a right of citizenship elsewhere are offered by American employers, but only to those workers with enough economic clout to win them.

The private welfare system of employer-based benefits became a new form of welfare capitalism, reminiscent of what had existed in the 1920s— only now it was more generous and inclusive. Just as it was designed to do in the 1920s, modern welfare capitalism made workers dependent for their social protection—health insurance and pensions—on the firms that employed them. This pattern of social provision not only tied workers to their employers, but also divided workers from each other. Only workers employed in the corporate sector of the economy received extensive social protections from their employers. Workers who toiled for firms in the competitive sector of the economy often did not receive such fringe benefits because small firms could not afford to pay health insurance costs or contribute to private pensions for their workers. Consequently, workers in the corporate sector of the economy, who were receiving social protection from their employers, had less of a stake in improving, expanding, and adding new government programs that workers in the competitive sector and the poor depended on. The private welfare system of employer-based benefits siphoned off political pressure from corporate-sector workers—the most organized and politically powerful section of the American working class—to increase the level of protection the American welfare state provided beyond the minimum necessary for social peace.

While the New Deal may not have gone forward under President Truman, a Democrat, neither did it go backward under his successor, President Dwight Eisenhower, a Republican. Under Eisenhower, conservatives did not try to revoke the Social Security Act or return to pre-Depression-style minimal government.[32] Corporations that had adamantly opposed Social

---

[32] In fact, Social Security coverage expanded in the 1950s under President Eisenhower to include farm workers and maids, who initially had been left out of Social Security at the insistence of the segregated South.

Security in the 1930s now acknowledged that it could help stabilize the economy and was preferable to more radical, or conservative, alternatives. The issue for Republicans was striking the proper balance between private welfare plans run by employers and public welfare programs run by the government. Republicans were determined that the welfare state not displace welfare capitalism in the form of private, employer-based welfare plans. According to Marion B. Folsom, an Eastman Kodak executive who became secretary of health, education, and welfare in Eisenhower's cabinet, government should provide only "basic minimum protection and it should not be intended to cover all the needs of everyone."[33] He argued that benefits in government programs should be low and that business should be offered tax incentives to subsidize their own employer-based welfare plans. Limited public benefits would encourage the need for and reliance on private, corporate welfare plans. These private, corporate plans, in turn, would act as a brake on the further extension of public welfare state programs.[34]

The publication in 1962 of *The Other America: Poverty in the United States* by Michael Harrington, a democratic socialist, roused the nation's conscience and became a best-seller. Using statistics that were widely available, but that previously had drawn little attention, Harrington bemoaned a disturbing truth: Despite unprecedented prosperity, 40 to 50 million people—one-quarter of all Americans—remained mired in poverty. Postwar economic growth, a rising tide, had not lifted all boats. Rather, an unevenly rising tide was putting more distance between the boats, leaving some farther behind than they were before. The president's Council of Economic Advisors acknowledged in 1964 that, "in the future, economic growth alone will provide relatively fewer escapes from poverty."[35] In previous decades, full employment had reduced poverty. But by the mid-1960s, the traditional correlation between low unemployment and low AFDC welfare rates no longer applied. Throughout the 1960s, in the midst of one of the most prosperous decades in the nation's history, the number of welfare recipients grew by almost 10 percent per year.[36]

One reason that welfare caseloads grew even as the country experienced near full employment was the changing color of poverty. A disproportionate and increasing number of the poor now were African Americans who lived in urban ghettos. By 1997, the proportion of black families living in poverty was one in four compared to one out of every ten white families.[37] Once

---

[33] Quoted in Sanford M. Jacoby, "Employers and the Welfare State: The Role of Marion B. Folsom," *Journal of American History* 80, no. 2 (1993): 526.

[34] Ibid., p. 527.

[35] Quoted in Patterson, *America's Struggle Against Poverty*, p. 12.

[36] *Wall Street Journal*, April 24, 1969.

[37] U.S. Bureau of the Census, *Current Population Reports, P60-203, Measuring 50 Years of Economic Change Using the Current Population Survey* (Washington, D.C.: U.S. Government Printing Office, 1998), Table C-22, pp. C-38 to C-46.

blacks migrated from the South to join the modern industrial economy in northern cities like Cleveland, New York, and Chicago, they faced greater discrimination and larger obstacles to social mobility than did the immigrant groups, such as Italians, Poles, and Jews, who preceded them. Race proved a more visible and powerful marker of difference than ethnicity and nationality.[38]

Blacks, moreover, entered the modern industrial economy at the very moment it was passing from the scene, having been replaced by a postindustrial economy that had less use for the unskilled labor they offered. A postindustrial economy of white-collar jobs that required skills and education was replacing an industrial economy of blue-collar jobs that required little of either. When previous immigrant groups had arrived with little education, the economy needed their unskilled labor to dig canals, lay railroad tracks, and work in the industrial plants of Detroit, Philadelphia, and Chicago. When black newcomers entered the northern nonagricultural labor force, the economy no longer called for the physical labor they had to offer. Technology had reduced the need for labor in manufacturing. Capital had replaced labor in production. Economic restructuring now put a premium on high-order skills that many urban blacks lacked. In addition, factories no longer were located in cities accessible to blacks. Manufacturing plants were now located in the suburbs, where taxes and land were cheaper. This put many blue-collar manufacturing jobs beyond the reach of poor black residents located in center cities.[39]

At the same time postindustrial capitalism was producing well-compensated white-collar jobs requiring education, it was also creating service-sector jobs that failed to pay a living wage. As we showed in Chapter 2, both good and bad jobs in postindustrial capitalism are growing at the expense of blue-collar jobs in the middle. The service-sector jobs available to unskilled blacks, such as fast-food worker, maid, and security guard, are characterized by low wages, as well as irregular and temporary employment, without the payment of fringe benefits. The rewards of such jobs are so meager that what President Clinton called "playing by the rules" is no assurance of escaping poverty. A person in a family of four who works 40 hours a week, 52 weeks a year, at a minimum-wage job paying $5.15 per hour earns $10,700 annually. This income provides less than three-quarters of the poverty threshold for a family of this size.[40] For this reason, the remarkable number of jobs created in the 1990s by the American economy, which created 1.6 million new jobs *per year* from 1989 to 1996, had only a modest impact on poverty rates. This led comedians to joke that members of the working poor could now say with

---

[38] Stanley Lieberson, *A Piece of the Pie* (Berkeley: University of California Press, 1980).

[39] William Julius Wilson, *The Declining Significance of Race: Blacks and Changing American Institutions* (Chicago: University of Chicago Press, 1978).

[40] We should note that the poverty threshold presumes an unrealistically sparse family budget that includes no expenses for savings, emergencies, or entertainment.

pride that the Clinton administration created one million new jobs last year and I have four of them. After nearly a decade of sustained job creation, the poverty rate, which stood at 13.1 percent in 1989, had declined only to 12.7 percent by 1998. While many of these new jobs required skills and education that many of the poor lacked, the rest were either jobs that failed to pay a living wage or temporary and part-time jobs that did not lift families out of poverty. As the century drew to a close, four in ten workers were earning less than $10 an hour. The lack of unions that could bargain up wages on their behalf and the lack of government regulations that could assure them an adequate income consigned a great many working Americans to poverty.[41]

Not only was the color of welfare changing, becoming darker as job discrimination and economic changes conspired to restrain black mobility, but so was its sex. Women now increasingly filled the ranks of the poor. Poverty became feminized. Almost one-third of all female-headed households are poor. These families comprise more than one-half of all families in poverty, a significant increase from 30 years ago, when female-headed households accounted for only one-third of all poor families.[42] Single mothers are likely to be poor either because women earn lower wages when they work or because they need to stay home to care for their children and are unable to work.

Two factors contributed to the growth in the number of single mothers. One was economic. Men who were unemployed, underemployed, or unable to find jobs that paid adequate wages deserted their families, leaving single mothers to go on welfare in order to provide for their children. Divorce and abandonment deprived these families of a male breadwinner's income, leaving single mothers and their children in poverty. But if family breakup led to poverty, the reverse is also true: Poverty caused family breakup. This pattern was confirmed by a Census Bureau report that found that two-parent families who were poor were twice as likely to break up within a few years as two-parent families who were not poor. The rise in the number of poor female-headed households was caused by poverty as much as poverty was its consequence.

The increase in the number of poor single mothers was also due to cultural factors. More women were willing to have babies out of wedlock. Illegitimacy no longer carried the stigma that it once had. The proportion of babies born to unmarried women climbed not only among the poor, but also among women in all social classes and racial groups.

Finally, the poor are younger—much younger than they once were. The great success of the American welfare state in reducing the poverty rate among the elderly has only underlined its greatest failure, the high and persistent poverty rate that remains among children. The poverty among those

---

[41] Laurence E. Lynn, Jr., "Ending Welfare Reform as We Know It," *American Prospect*, Fall 1993, 83–90.

[42] U.S. Bureau of the Census, *Measuring Fifty Years of Economic Change Using the March Current Population Survey*, Table C23, pp. C-40 to C-41.

who are 65 years of age and older has declined by almost two-thirds in just 30 years, from 29.5 percent in 1967 to 10.5 percent in 1997. In the same period, the poverty rate among children has hovered stubbornly around 20 percent—almost twice the current poverty rate for the elderly.[43] In 1995, federal, state, and local governments spent about $15,000 for every American over 65, while spending only about $6,000, including school costs, for each child. The American poverty rate among children is three times the rate in Western Europe. Poverty among children in Europe is so much lower than in the United States because European countries spend more money on more programs for families with children, raising children above the poverty line who otherwise would be below it. No other developed welfare state is as generationally skewed as that of the United States, where benefits flow to the elderly through such relatively expensive programs as Medicare and Social Security, with no comparable effort made on behalf of children to insulate them from deprivation and its corrosive effects.[44] Indeed, after Congress enacted the new welfare law and repealed AFDC in 1996, the number of children living in deep poverty, defined as below half the poverty line, jumped by nearly 500,000, despite the country's strong economy. This startling increase was directly related to cuts in public assistance and Food Stamps.

THE GREAT SOCIETY AND ITS BACKLASH

Just as the New Deal welfare reforms were made possible by the sweeping Democratic electoral realignment spearheaded by President Roosevelt in the 1930s, so were the social policy reforms associated with the Great Society made possible by President Lyndon Johnson's landslide victory in the 1964 election. In 1964, 51 freshmen Democrats were elected to Congress on President Johnson's coattails. Liberals now had enough votes to overcome the veto that the conservative coalition of Republicans and southern Democrats in Congress had exercised over social welfare legislation in the 1950s. A liberal Democratic president with concurring supermajorities in the Senate and the House could now overcome the obstacles that conservative opponents had used to stymie welfare state initiatives in the past.[45]

In his 1964 State of the Union address, President Johnson declared a War on Poverty that would result in a Great Society, free of hunger and privation. Delighted by this commitment, the AFL–CIO reflected the sentiment of other

---

[43] Ibid., Table C-21, p. C-37.

[44] Barbara R. Bergmann, *Saving Our Children from Poverty: What the United States Can Learn from France* (New York: Russell Sage Foundation, 1996).

[45] James C. Sundquist, *Politics and Policy: The Eisenhower, Kennedy, and Johnson Years* (Washington, D.C: Brookings, 1968).

Poverty and homelessness amidst wealth and affluence in America.

liberals when it crowed, "The New Deal proclaimed in 1933 has come to a belated maturity now under LBJ in 1965."[46] After a 39-year hiatus, the federal government was building on the legacy of the New Deal and assuming new responsibilities in almost every area of social welfare. Federally funded health insurance for the aged and the poor in the form of Medicare and Medicaid was passed. New educational opportunities for the disadvantaged, such as Head Start and Upward Bound, were enacted. Job-training programs, such as the Job Corps, were legislated. New initiatives in housing and urban development, such as the Model Cities program, followed suit. The thrust of these initiatives was to enhance the poor's opportunities, "to open up doors, not set down floors; to offer a hand up, not a handout," according to historian James T. Patterson.[47] Federal social welfare expenditures almost doubled from 1965 to 1975 in support of these efforts. Social welfare costs, which amounted to one-third of the entire federal budget in 1965, accounted for more than one-half ten years later.[48]

But like the social reform period of the New Deal, the War on Poverty was short-lived. Initially, the War on Poverty drew its moral and political energy

---

[46] *AFL–CIO Convention Proceedings, 1965* (1965), pp. 2:1–6.

[47] Patterson, *America's Struggle Against Poverty*, p. 136.

[48] Sar A. Levitan and Robert Taggert, *The Promise of Greatness* (Cambridge: Harvard University Press, 1976), p. 20.

from the Civil Rights movement. But as that social movement splintered, portions of it becoming radical and advocating violence, it lost broad support. As its moral power declined, so did the impetus behind the Great Society. Equally important, the Johnson administration became distracted by the war in Vietnam. The more the war against communism in Asia escalated, the more the war against poverty at home lost momentum. A conservative backlash to the Great Society first appeared in the 1966 congressional election, which restored the blocking power of the conservative coalition of Republicans and southern Democrats within Congress.[49] Two years later, in 1968, Richard Nixon, a Republican, was elected president, effectively bringing the moment of social reform to an end.

According to conservatives, the War on Poverty had failed; worse, the various poverty programs had been harmful. Welfare rolls continued to increase, not decrease; crime became worse, not better; more single mothers appeared, not fewer; and illegitimacy rates continued to rise, not decline. The country's cities burned as violent urban protests rocked the nation in the late 1960s. During his 1968 presidential campaign, Nixon captured this sense of disappointment when he charged, "For the past five years we have been deluged by government programs for the unemployed, programs for cities, programs for the poor, and we have reaped from these programs an ugly harvest of frustration, violence and failure across the land."[50]

Backlash to the Great Society also developed because the War on Poverty had polarized the electorate along the fault lines of the dual welfare state. Workers covered by social insurance programs had little stake in the Great Society programs that aided the poor. As the prosperity of the 1960s turned into the stagflation of the 1970s, resentment over these expenditures and their tax burden grew. Race compounded this resentment. While many New Deal programs purposely had excluded blacks, the War on Poverty purposely had targeted them for inclusion.[51] The more welfare as public assistance was identified with racial minorities, the more Great Society programs took on a combustible racial dimension. The political consequences of the Great Society program pitted taxpayers, who were part of the social insurance system, against tax recipients, who received public assistance; the private sector was set against the public sector, workers against the jobless, and whites against blacks.[52] Many politicians in both parties exploited and exacerbated these tensions, using welfare as a code word to appeal to some voters' fears concerning crime, taxes, morality, and race.

---

[49] For the consequences of the 1966 election for the welfare state, see Alan Draper, "Labor and the 1966 Elections," *Labor History*, Winter 1989, 76–93.

[50] Quoted in Levitan and Taggert, *The Promise of Greatness*, pp. 3–4.

[51] Brown, *Race, Money and the American Welfare State*, p. 325.

[52] Thomas Byrne Edsall and Mary D. Edsall, *Chain Reaction: The Impact of Race, Rights, and Taxes on American Politics* (New York: Norton, 1991).

The recoil against the Great Society reached its peak during the Reagan administration (1981–1989). President Ronald Reagan came to office pledging to shrink the federal government. His administration quickly aimed its fire at the poor and the Great Society programs on which they depended. Domestic programs suffering the largest cuts under Reagan were those targeted to the low-income population. Some federal programs, such as funding for public service jobs and revenue sharing for the states, were eliminated completely, while other poverty programs were cut back drastically. Food Stamp expenditures were cut by 14 percent, child nutrition programs by 28 percent, and AFDC by 14 percent from 1981 to 1984.[53] Budget cuts were accompanied by reductions in benefit levels and more stringent eligibility requirements.[54]

The Reagan attack on the welfare state overreached, however. Tax cuts for the rich and spending cuts for the poor exposed the administration to charges of unfairness, even meanness. As poverty became more visible due to government cutbacks and rising unemployment, the public became more upset with the results. Poll after poll indicated that the administration had gone too far in cutting social programs for the poor. Congress soon balked at any further reductions. As David Stockman, Reagan's budget director, observed, "The abortive Reagan revolution proved that the American electorate wants a moderate social democracy to shield it from capitalism's rough edges."[55]

The president's attempt to scale back the American welfare state was finally checked when his administration turned its attention from cutting public assistance programs for the poor, in which it had some success, to cutting social insurance programs for the working middle class. Spending cuts needed to balance the budget and pay for tax cuts could not be obtained from gutting discretionary programs for the poor alone. To keep the federal budget from mushrooming out of control, social insurance programs for the working middle class, such as Medicare and Social Security, would have to be pared as well. When the Reagan administration proposed cutting Social Security benefits, the outcry was harsh and swift. The Republican-controlled Senate rejected Reagan's proposal on a 99–0 vote. Democrats took the issue with them into the 1982 elections, claiming only they could be trusted to protect social insurance programs. Voters rewarded the Democrats with a majority in the 1982 congressional elections and broke the momentum of Reagan's attack on the welfare state.

Critics of the War on Poverty underestimated the American public's attachment to that effort. While Americans had qualms about how those

---

[53] Lee Bawden and Frank Levy, "The Economic Well-Being of Families and Individuals," in John L. Palmer and Isabel V. Sawhill, eds., *The Reagan Experiment* (Washington, D.C.: Urban Institute Press, 1982), Table 6.1, p. 185.

[54] James Midgeley, "Society, Social Policy and the Ideology of Reaganism," *Journal of Sociology and Social Welfare,* March 1992, 24–25.

[55] David Stockman, *The Triumph of Politics* (New York: Harper & Row, 1986), p. 394.

programs were executed, they were committed to the principle underlying them: that the federal government had an obligation to assist the poor. A 1986 CBS/*New York Times* survey found that "fully 66 percent think the Government should spend money now on efforts similar to those of the Great Society programs to help the poor people in the United States."[56] Americans were simply not willing to leave the poor to the mercilessness of the market.

Far from being a failure, the War on Poverty had enormous success in reducing the number of people living in poverty. The poverty rate dropped from 19 percent in 1964 to less than 12 percent in 1979. The number of people living below the poverty line was declining until President Reagan signaled retreat in a war we were winning. Government income support programs, not economic growth, accounted for a large part of this decline in the poverty rate. Between 1965 and 1971, the number of households in poverty fell by only 900,000 before government income supports were factored in. When government income transfers to the poor were included, the number of poor families declined by 2.6 million, nearly three times the drop in the number of poor before receiving aid.[57] Government poverty programs not only lifted families out of poverty, but also raised the quality of their lives, reducing malnutrition, increasing access to medical care, improving housing, and opening up educational opportunities that previously had not been available.[58]

Despite these dramatic changes, critics of the War on Poverty were suspicious of the type of difference such programs made in poor people's lives. Poverty programs, they argued, may have improved poor people's lives materially, but they did not change their behavior—welfare dependency, illegitimate babies, and family breakup. More of the poor's basic needs may have been met as a result of Great Society initiatives, but at the cost of their character. This seductive line of argument, however, does not hold up to close scrutiny. Larger cultural forces regarding sexuality and parenthood, not welfare policy, drove the trend toward more female-headed households. Moreover, poverty, low wages, and the growing insecurity of the market weakened the ties that bound families together. As noted economist Lester Thurow stated the point, "The traditional family is being destroyed not by misguided social welfare programs coming from Washington . . . but by a modern economic system that is not congruent with 'family values.'"[59]

---

[56] Poll results are mentioned in Thomas Ferguson and Joel Rogers, "The Myth of America's Turn to the Right," *Atlantic Monthly*, May 1986, 43–53.

[57] Levitan and Taggert, *The Promise of Greatness*, pp. 200–1.

[58] John E. Schwarz, *America's Hidden Success: A Reassessment of Twenty Years of Public Policy* (New York: Norton, 1984).

[59] *New York Times*, September 3, 1995.

Inaccurate impressions of welfare dependency also abound. In fact, four in ten welfare recipients left the rolls within one year; another 28 percent left within two years. Sociologist Mark Rank writes, "To be sure, some individuals do abuse the welfare system . . . [but] such cases constitute a very small fraction of the overall welfare population. Most welfare recipients want a better life for themselves and their children; they don't enjoy being on government assistance; and they persevere in the face of countless hardships and handicaps."[60] There were many more people on welfare who received benefits episodically than who were long-term users. They moved in and out of the rolls not because they wanted to be there, but because personal and economic setbacks, such as divorce, abandonment, unemployment, lack of child care, or sickness, placed them there. And all the disadvantages of being poor that afflict one generation affect the next. What gets passed from one generation to the next among the poor is their poverty, not welfare dependency.[61] This was evident in the classic study of black urban men by anthropologist Eliot Liebow. Liebow found black street-corner men had followed in the failed footsteps of their fathers not because a culture of poverty had been handed down, but because the same social and educational deficits of poverty that had prevented their fathers from succeeding were visited on their sons. Liebow wrote in 1967 in his classic work of ethnography: "No doubt, each generation does provide role models for each succeeding one. . . . However . . . many similarities between the lower-class Negro father and son (or mother and daughter) do not result from 'cultural transmission' but from the fact that the son goes out and independently experiences the same failures, in the same areas, and for much the same reasons as his father. What appears as a dynamic, self-sustaining cultural process is, in part at least, a relatively simple piece of social machinery which turns out, in a rather mechanical fashion, independently produced look alikes."[62]

The argument that welfare creates perverse incentives that sustain a culture of poverty among the poor is a prisoner of its own cramped view of human behavior. In this view, the poor are regarded as self-interested, income-maximizing individuals whose behavior can be regulated with the right economic incentives. This view is twice wrong. The poor—like everyone else—respond to incentives other than economic ones, and the main problem is not the behavior of the poor, but the social and economic constraints they face.[63]

---

[60] Mark Rank, *Living on the Edge: The Realities of Welfare in America* (New York: Columbia University Press, 1994), p. 5.

[61] Randy Albelda, Nancy Folbre, and the Center for Public Economics, *The War on the Poor: A Defense Manual* (New York: New Press, 1996), p. 82.

[62] Eliot Liebow, *Tally's Corner: A Study of Streetcorner Men* (New York: Little, Brown, 1967), p. 223.

[63] Sanford Schram, *Words of Welfare: The Poverty of Social Science and the Social Science of Poverty* (Minneapolis: University of Minnesota Press, 1995).

CLINTON DEMOCRATS AND THE WELFARE STATE

The Reagan attack on the welfare state proved a partial success. Welfare state spending was slowed, but not reversed. The Reagan administration did succeed, however, in shifting the internal balance of welfare state spending between social insurance and public assistance programs in the direction of the former. Its greatest successes came in paring the most politically vulnerable programs, those targeted to the poor. Great Society poverty programs took heavy cuts, mostly surviving in truncated form, while New Deal social insurance programs emerged relatively unscathed.[64]

But the Reagan administration's impact on the welfare state was more profound than can be gleaned from looking at welfare state spending alone. Republicans succeeded in placing the welfare state on the defensive. Conservatives now set the terms of debate over social policy, redefining the problem from reducing poverty to changing the behavior of the poor, from blaming poverty on the inadequacies of the economy to blaming it on the perverse incentives of the welfare state. The public mood changed so much that even Democrats were prepared to renounce their own New Deal and Great Society legacies. In March 1990, members of the Democratic Leadership Council (DLC), a group of conservative Democrats, announced they were ready to bury their party's past. Meeting in New Orleans, they dismissed the relevance of New Deal and Great Society programs, claiming that "the political ideas and passions of the 1930s and 1960s cannot guide us in the 1990s." At that meeting, the DLC selected a new president to present this view, putting a little-known governor from a small southern state on the national stage for the first time. His name was William Jefferson Clinton.[65]

Republican presidents produced another legacy that would haunt welfare policy after they were gone. Ronald Reagan and George Bush left massive budget deficits that would reach $4.3 trillion by the time President Clinton took office in 1993. Oversized budget deficits are not neutral in their political impact. According to political scientist Paul Pierson, they create a demand for deficit reduction that "favored those who opposed an activist federal government."[66] The priority given to deficit reduction made it hard to argue for new social programs or increases in social welfare spending. Quite the reverse: Demands to reduce the deficit create fierce pressure to cut back social programs.

---

[64] See Bawden and Levy, "Economic Well-Being of Families and Individuals," Table 16-5, p. 469.

[65] Howard Jacob Karger, "Responding to the Crisis: Liberal Prescriptions," in David Stoesz and Howard Jacob Karger, *Reconstructing the American Welfare State* (Lanham, Md.: Rowman & Littlefield, 1992), pp. 92–93.

[66] Paul Pierson, "The Deficit and the Politics of Domestic Reform," in *The Social Divide: Political Parties and the Future of Activist Government*, ed. Margaret Weir (Washington, D.C.: Brookings, 1998), p. 171.

President Clinton's social policy was shaped decisively by these two inheritances from previous Republican administrations: the need for deficit reduction and a conservative definition of the welfare problem. To reassure financial markets that he was serious about cutting the deficit, Clinton sacrificed his 1992 campaign promise to invest in domestic programs. His failed health care plan also fell victim to fighting the deficit, relying on government regulation to control costs rather than new taxes and new spending to pay for it. Even as the budget began to run surpluses toward the end of the 1990s, the Clinton administration continued to give priority to reducing the deficit. Its budget for 2000 promised to use billions of dollars in surplus revenue to drive down the federal debt rather than restore cuts to the welfare state. Consequently, Clinton's budget requests fell far short of the demonstrated need for them. According to Michael M. Weinstein of the *New York Times,* "Mr. Clinton resorted to doling out spoonfuls of money where shovels were needed."[67]

President Clinton's social policy was not simply mortgaged to deficit reduction, but also conducted within a conservative definition of the welfare problem that the president adopted as his own—a view that public assistance programs undermined the character of the poor. From this perspective, the best way to build their character was to remove the welfare crutch on which they depended. This view was embodied in the Personal Responsibility and Work Opportunity Reconciliation Act (PRWORA), which President Clinton signed in 1996, and with which we began this chapter. Under the new law, welfare is time limited. Recipients have to be participating in work activities within two years and cannot receive federally funded aid for more than five years. In addition, the new law gives states much greater authority to run their own welfare programs, receiving fixed lump sums of federal money in the form of block grants to pay for them. But the change to block grants means federal money for welfare no longer increases automatically to provide for all the poor families who are entitled to and legally eligible for it. Guarantees of assistance now are gone. Should a recession occur that creates high unemployment and increases the number of poor families who qualify for welfare, there no longer is any guarantee that such families will receive cash assistance. The growth in welfare recipients from 1960 to 1999 is shown in Figure 10–3.

Proponents of the new welfare law point to declining welfare rolls as a sign that the work deterrent in the new law is effective. Since welfare reform was enacted, welfare caseloads have dropped dramatically, down by more than half, with fewer people on welfare than at any point in the last three decades.[68] But the welfare rolls had begun to decrease in 1993, well before the new welfare bill was signed. Most of the credit must go to record lows in unemployment; increases in the earned income tax credit, which subsidizes

---

[67] *New York Times,* February 4, 1999.

[68] *New York Times,* April 11, 1999.

■ FIGURE 10-3

GROWTH IN U.S. WELFARE RECIPIENTS, 1960–1999

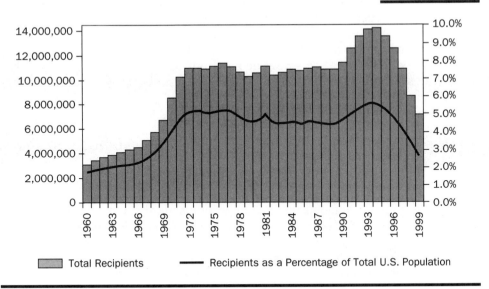

Total Recipients   ——— Recipients as a Percentage of Total U.S. Population

SOURCE: Department of Health and Human Services, 2000.

the wages of low-wage workers; and increases in the minimum wage—not to new welfare policies. Moreover, research conflicts about whether those who have left welfare have actually found work. Some studies have found more evidence of the move from welfare to work than others.[69] But all agree that those formerly on welfare who have found jobs are those who are most employable. It is not clear whether it will be so easy to move from welfare to work those individuals with physical and mental problems who remain on the rolls. It also is clear that some of the decrease in welfare has resulted from caseworkers simply dropping welfare recipients from the rolls for the slightest infraction.[70]

While we really do not know yet whether the millions of people who have left or been cut from the welfare rolls since the new welfare law took effect are any better off, some early reports are disturbing. As welfare rolls have decreased, lines at soup kitchens around the country have gotten longer.[71] In effect, the purge of the welfare rolls under the new welfare law has simply transferred the financial burden of caring for the poor from the government to poor families and local private charities. As the number of people on

[69] *New York Times*, June 19, 1998, and April 12, 1998.

[70] *New York Times*, April 15, 1998.

[71] *New York Times*, February 26, 1999.

welfare has plunged, the number of children left with relatives because their parents no longer could afford to care for them has risen. In 1996, family income from Food Stamps and cash assistance kept more than 3.6 million children out of deep poverty. A year later, as welfare reform took effect, this number fell to 3 million.[72]

Aside from the poor, the new law ironically has hurt those who work and are not on welfare. By pushing people from welfare to work, PRWORA has created a larger pool of low-skill workers competing for jobs. This competition has reduced the bargaining power of workers who are already at the bottom of the economic order and whose wages are already inadequate. In addition, local governments sometimes have used programs employing welfare recipients to replace jobs performed by civil servants. In these instances, moving people from welfare to work has come at the expense of workers who already have jobs, while employers have profited and local governments have been able to reduce their expenses.

The biggest winners from welfare reform so far have been the budgets of the fifty states. States have experienced a financial windfall, as the federal block grants for welfare have remained the same even as welfare caseloads have declined. With fewer families on welfare, states now have more federal money to spend on each of them. But they are not doing so. Federal subsidies for each family on welfare have risen by 64 percent, but the states have increased actual spending by only 28 percent per welfare family. Fully 45 states have not spent the available anti-poverty monies on the poor, and 49 states spent less on the poor in 1999 than in 1994.

These savings have come, of course, because fewer people are receiving welfare benefits. But the poverty rate has hardly changed. If indigent individuals and families are to become more self-sufficient, they have to grapple with increased costs in housing, transportation, clothing, and child care. But the funds and programs with which to do so have yet to be forthcoming.

CONCLUSION

By the end of the 1990s, when the stock market soared to new highs, when the American economy far outpaced that of any rival, when unemployment and inflation were at 40-year lows, and when the economy was creating 1 million jobs per year, more Americans were without health insurance than at the beginning of the decade, more children grew up in poor families than in any other Western industrialized nation, and the poverty rate hovered stubbornly around 12 percent. Thirty-four million Americans remained in poverty, more than at any point in the 1970s. At the end of the longest economic expansion in postwar history, little of the prosperity that the top fifth

---

[72]*New York Times,* February 21, 1999.

of income earners enjoyed over the course of the 1990s trickled down to the bottom fifth.

Economic growth alone cannot reduce poverty. Only government programs in tandem with a successful economy can do that. Poverty rates are sensitive to political choices governments make about the welfare state. Yet, rather than providing expanded social policy offerings at a time of prosperity, the welfare state was retrenched in the 1980s and 1990s under both Republican and Democratic administrations. Public assistance programs for the poor suffered most of these cuts, but social insurance programs for the working middle class were not entirely immune. Some welfare programs have been eliminated completely; in others, eligibility requirements have become more stringent, benefit levels have failed to keep pace with inflation, program budgets have been cut, and administrative rules have been more strictly enforced.

Conservatives and liberals agree the welfare state is here to stay. Less clear is the kind of welfare state the United States will now come to have. Will the gap between the social insurance and public assistance parts of the welfare state widen or close? Will poverty, especially child poverty, emerge as a major public issue? Will the big social insurance programs—Social Security and Medicare—be changed to accommodate a larger role for private, rather than public, investment? Will the private welfare system of welfare capitalism grow further to displace and undermine support for the public welfare state? These choices are just around the corner.

11

CONCLUSION: AMERICAN POLITICS, PAST, PRESENT, AND FUTURE

Introduction

We conclude this book soon after George W. Bush's contested election ushered in a new Republican administration. There is a remarkable parallel between the Bush presidency and that of Ronald Reagan, twenty years earlier. Both presidents succeeded moderate southern Democrats—Reagan followed Jimmy Carter, from Plains, Georgia; and Bush followed Bill Clinton, from Little Rock, Arkansas. In both cases, moderate Democrats forged policies that broke with the traditional New Deal orientation of Presidents FDR, Truman, Kennedy, and Johnson. Both presidents sought to attract centrist groups by diluting the Democratic stance of using government to provide benefits to working-class Americans. But neither president succeeded in generating sufficient Democratic party support to consolidate electoral dominance.

The parallel on the Republican side is also remarkably similar. As Yogi Berra, that gifted social analyst, might have remarked, it was déja vu all over again. Both Ronald Reagan and George W. Bush talked the talk of generosity and compassion toward the less fortunate (Reagan spoke of "morning in America"; Bush, of "compassionate conservatism"). But in their foreign and domestic policies, both presidents walked the walk of redistributing power and material resources in a manner that benefited the more fortunate. Both presidents significantly increased military spending and sponsored initiatives that increased military tensions. In Reagan's case, the gamble succeeded, in that the arms buildup helped drive the Soviet Union into bankruptcy, which resulted in the dissolution of the country and the demise of communism. The returns are not yet in on the consequences of President Bush's initiative to upgrade U.S. military capabilities. But, in the short run, the effect has been to isolate the United States and increase anti-U.S. sentiment among its allies and opponents alike.

The parallel between the domestic policy initiatives of Reagan and Bush are equally striking. Within a year after taking office, Presidents Reagan and Bush sponsored a massive restructuring of the tax system. Both presidents defended their plan on the grounds that it would help the entire economy and benefit all Americans. In both cases, however, the major consequence of the reform was to deliver generous tax breaks for affluent Americans. Under

Bush's tax plan, the top fifth of earners garners 70 percent of the total tax breaks.[1] Like the Reagan tax reform, Bush's plan shrunk federal revenue, thus necessitating spending cuts that primarily lowered government benefits for lower income Americans.

In trying to explain presidential actions, it helps to follow the money trail: both presidents Reagan and Bush were beholden to the most powerful, organized, and affluent groups in the country. At the moment that Congress was voting on the Bush tax plan, the Republican party was holding a fundraiser in Washington, D.C., addressed by the president, that boosted party coffers by $24 million. The guest list read like a who's who of corporate and affluent America, with energy industry executives playing a particularly prominent role. As a *New York Times* reporter noted, "The event comes less than a week after Mr. Bush outlined a comprehensive energy policy that was shaped in part by the same lobbyists and executives [who helped organize the fund-raiser]."[2]

What will be the impact of the Bush presidency on American politics? Although we provide a brief analysis at the end of this chapter, it would be perilous, during the early years of the new administration, to venture a prediction. As an old saw among historians has it, it's easier to predict the past than the future. However, one way to seek answers is to analyze a debate about the impact of the Reagan presidency, following which we will evaluate the Clinton presidency. Although our analysis here is linked to recent presidents, we do not mean to imply that American politics is exclusively the story of particular presidents, or even the groups or advisers and broad coalitions that presidents assemble. As this book has documented, many aspects of the politics of power have little directly or even indirectly to do with who occupies the White House. Yet presidential terms can provide a handy shorthand reference for identifying important periods in American politics, and we follow a typical convention here in focusing on presidential administrations.

Our agenda in this concluding chapter is to analyze how much the Reagan years of the 1980s reshaped American politics since the New Deal and to use our findings as a baseline against which to measure the extent of change wrought by Clinton in the 1990s. We conclude with a discussion of where American politics is going—and of our (and our readers') relationship to the American political system.

There are dramatically different views on the impact of the Reagan presidency. *The Triumph of Politics*, written by David Stockman, President Reagan's first director of the Office of Management and Budget, claimed that the Reagan Revolution to dismantle the welfare state failed because of bedrock

---

[1] Citizens for Tax Justice, "Distributional Effects of the Senate Finance Committee–Passed Version of the Bush Tax Plan," May 16, 2001, at *http://www.ctj.prg/html1/senmark.htm*.

[2] *New York Times*, May 23, 2001.

realities and continuities within American politics. *Washington Post* columnist Thomas Byrne Edsall, in *The New Politics of Inequality*, argued that, on the contrary, Reagan administration policies substantially altered the New Deal legacy and brought about an extensive redistribution of income and power from workers, the poor, and the middle class to America's affluent minority.[3] After reviewing this debate, we address a similar question regarding the relationship of the Reagan-Bush era to that of Clinton, and we close by analyzing the Bush administration's policy orientation.

THE REAGAN REVOLUTION?

David Stockman began his term as President Reagan's budget director as a true believer in the Reagan Revolution. More capitalism and less government would permit free markets to produce the most efficient outcome, since government regulations and spending impede free enterprise and thereby reduce efficiency. According to Stockman, ever since the New Deal first promoted the welfare state, government spending has imposed massive burdens on market forces.

The Reagan Revolution promised a break with the legacy of government intervention it inherited from the New Deal. In its place, President Reagan advocated "minimalist government—a spare and stingy creature, which offered even-handed public justice, but no more. Its vision of the good society rested on the strength and productive potential of free men in free markets. . . . It envisioned a land the opposite of the coast-to-coast patchwork of dependencies, shelters, protections, and redistributions that the nation's politicians had brokered over the decades."[4]

The revolution initially appeared to be a brilliant success. By the end of his first years in office, President Reagan achieved his principal goals of reducing taxes and increasing military spending. However, Stockman soon became disillusioned because, in his view, the extent of actual change fell far short of what the Reagan team planned. According to Stockman, the revolution soon foundered on the shoals of American politics. Powerful interest groups were able to prevent cuts in government programs in which they had an interest. At the same time, tax cuts (which went mainly to the rich and to business) reduced the government's ability to raise money. As Stockman recalled to a reporter for *Rolling Stone,* he was shocked at the greed of business interests and their power to block tax increases or cuts in pro-business government programs. He recalled, "The hogs were really feeding. The

[3]David A. Stockman, *The Triumph of Politics: Why the Reagan Revolution Failed* (New York: Harper & Row, 1986); Thomas Byrne Edsall, *The New Politics of Inequality* (New York: W. W. Norton, 1984).

[4]Stockman, *Triumph of Politics,* p. 8.

greed level, the level of opportunism, just got out of control."[5] The inevitable result of enacting tax cuts that considerably exceeded spending cuts was soaring federal deficits—well over $100 billion annually—and economic instability.[6] A title that would better reflect Stockman's insight than *The Triumph of Politics* might be *The Triumph of Business*.

Yet Stockman does emphasize the importance of politics in blocking change. In order to succeed, he notes, "[t]he Reagan Revolution . . . required a frontal assault on the American welfare state. That was the only way to pay for the massive [personal income] tax cut. Accordingly, forty years' worth of promises, subventions, entitlements, and safety nets issued by the federal government to every component and stratum of American society would have to be scrapped. . . ."[7] Instead, only modest cuts were made. The revolution foundered on the conservative institutional forces of American politics: the system of divided powers, checks and balances, congressional power, and the like. However, more fundamentally, he observes, the revolution failed for deeper reasons than the specific institutional features of American government. It proved impossible to gut the bulk of programs comprising the welfare state because of the democratic character of American politics. Not only elected politicians, but also, and more important, the American people opposed the basic goal of the Reagan Revolution: to dismantle the welfare state and return to a situation of unfettered capitalism. The Reagan Revolution was blind to a fundamental political reality: that citizens were unwilling to scrap government programs and leave their fate to the marketplace. Stockman later ruefully admits, "The Reagan Revolution was radical, imprudent, and arrogant. . . . It mistakenly presumed that a handful of ideologues were right and all the politicians were wrong about what the American people wanted from government." As a result, Stockman implies, relatively little changed within American politics during the 1980s. The Reagan administration's attempt to dismantle the welfare state failed; thus, the collision between the Reagan Revolution and the American political system left the latter intact.

THE NEW POLITICS OF INEQUALITY

While Stockman sees continuity from the New Deal through Reagan, Thomas Byrne Edsall sees things quite differently. Edsall's argument is concisely summarized on the cover of *The New Politics of Inequality*: "A quiet transfer of power has taken place in the nation's capital." According to

---

[5] Quoted in William Greider, "The Education of David Stockman," *Atlantic Monthly*, December 1981, 51.

[6] Ibid., p. 8. For a parallel analysis, see Paul Pierson, *Dismantling the Welfare State? Reagan, Thatcher, and the Politics of Retrenchment* (Cambridge: Cambridge University Press, 1994).

[7] Stockman, *Triumph of Politics*, p. 8.

Edsall, "For nearly fifty years, since the formation of the New Deal coalition in the 1930s, there had been a sustained base of support for both social spending programs and a tax system that modestly redistributed income and restricted the concentration of wealth in the hands of the few. These deeply rooted liberal traditions were abandoned during the late 1970s in favor of policies calling for a major reduction of the tax burden on income derived from capital, and for reductions in domestic spending programs directed toward the poor and the working poor."[8]

Edsall accords close attention to the tax cuts described in *The Triumph of Politics*. Yet whereas Stockman considers that their major significance was to feed budget deficits, Edsall emphasizes the degree to which tax reform benefited the wealthiest 15 percent of the population, and especially the few percent at the very top of the income pyramid.

A similar difference between Stockman and Edsall is found in their analyses of budget cuts. Whereas Stockman minimizes the importance of their impact, Edsall emphasizes the selective nature and magnitude of the cuts, which "eliminated the entire public service jobs program, eliminated the Social Security minimum benefit, and reduced or eliminated welfare and Medicaid benefits for the working poor. . . . The cuts, in effect, chipped away at the margin of the most marginal incomes." In contrast to Stockman, Edsall interprets the Reagan Revolution in class terms. For example, he identifies an overall goal of the Reagan Revolution—one that Stockman does not even mention: "More than any other president since Franklin Delano Roosevelt [but in an opposite manner], Ronald Reagan has consciously set out to use the federal government to alter the balance of power between labor and management. . . ." Thus, Edsall sees a class bias, ignored by Stockman, associated with Reagan's policy orientation. For example, "[t]he cuts in food stamps and welfare were just a part of a much larger pattern of spending reductions, reductions that functioned more to alter the political balance of power than to reduce the size of the deficit." In brief, Edsall squarely challenges Stockman's argument that the forces supporting Reagan failed to achieve their fiscal goal: "From the vantage point of those seeking a reversal of past progressive redistributional policies in both tax and spending programs, this drive was an extraordinary success."[9]

One can highlight the change by referring to changes in income inequality during the Reagan years. Shortly before President Reagan was elected in 1980, the wealthiest 5 percent of American households received 15.3 percent of the income pie; the top fifth of all households received 41.4 percent of the pie. When President Reagan left office, the top 5 percent had increased their share to 17.9 percent, while the share of the top fifth increased to 44.6 percent.[10]

---

[8] Edsall, *New Politics*, p. 15.

[9] Ibid., pp. 28, 204, 228.

[10] Lawrence Mishel, Jared Bernstein, and John Schmitt, *The State of Working America 1998–99* (Ithaca, New York: ILR Press, 1999), p. 49.

Edsall points to other changes, further intensifying class inequalities, that were wrought by the Reagan Revolution, but that do not figure in Stockman's account. Reagan successfully increased the power of management over labor and deregulated industry, reducing the "scope and content of the federal regulation of industry, the environment, the workplace, health care, and the relationship between buyer and seller."[11] In brief, rather than a revolution, the Reagan program might better be interpreted as a *counter*revolution that aimed to replace the New Deal alliance of organized labor and large-scale capital with a pro-business governing coalition. This counterrevolution, Edsall argues, was the result of distortions in our political system created by pervasive social inequalities. Moreover, Edsall presciently predicts, in an observation that will help illuminate our understanding of the constraints facing Bill Clinton: "The Reagan administration achieved a number of key, long-range victories, changes that will survive to influence policy significantly no matter what the elective future of the GOP. . . . The most important of these victories was . . . what amounts to continued conservative domination of the federal agenda. . . . Even if the Democratic party were to regain power, the centrality of the deficit will obstruct all efforts to seek to provide benefits to such key Democratic voting blocks as blacks, women, and workers in distressed industries."[12]

Edsall concludes his account with an observation that goes far beyond the Reagan presidency: "As long as the balance of political power remains so heavily weighted toward those with economic power, national economic policy will remain distorted, regardless of which party is in control of the federal government."[13] This prediction provides a useful guide to assessing the Clinton presidency.

THE CLINTON-GORE ADMINISTRATION: BOLD CENTRISM OR BROKEN COMPACT?

As President Clinton prepared to leave the White House after eight years as president, historians began to explore the ambiguous nature of his legacy. For example, the title of a fine study by presidential scholars James MacGregor Burns and Georgia Sorenson captured an important feature of Clinton's presidency: *Dead Center: Clinton-Gore Leadership and the Perils of Moderation.*[14] Burns and Sorenson claim that Clinton "seemed to want to make his mark as the kind of president who does more than administer. . . . He wanted to be

---

[11] Edsall, *New Politics*, p. 66. We analyze deregulation in Chapter 3.

[12] Edsall, *New Politics*, pp. 231–32.

[13] Ibid., p. 242.

[14] James MacGregor Burns and Georgia Sorenson, *Dead Center: Clinton-Gore Leadership and the Perils of Moderation* (New York: Scribner, 1999).

Bill and Hillary Clinton.

a president who changed the character of government and citizens' perception of it."[15] They describe Clinton's presidential strategy as centrism. "The strategy in essence was sincere on its face—Clinton would position himself, his administration, and his party at the center of the ideological and policy spectrum. From that center he could move left or right as day-to-day needs arose, but he would always return to the middle. . . . Thus Clinton's presidency would be a test of political and philosophical centrism as a strategy of leadership."[16]

Clinton shared the Republican Party's aversion to using the L word (liberal). When he announced his candidacy for president, Clinton declared, "The change I seek . . . isn't liberal or conservative. It's different and it's both."[17] Clinton himself described his approach as that of a New Democrat—that is, one that did not fit the mold of a classical left-leaning New Deal Democrat. He wanted to exercise bold leadership to move America forward. But moving forward would require leaving behind the New Deal approach of expanding government responsibility for the economy. "Most of the good

---

[15] Ibid., p. 125.

[16] Ibid., p. 77.

[17] Quoted in Jon F. Hale, "The Making of the New Democrats," *Political Science Quarterly* 110 (Summer 1995): 226.

ideas are ones that move us into the future, not to the left or right," he proclaimed, and he invited Republicans to "join me in the center of the debate."[18]

If Clinton was not an old-style Democrat, he also sought to demarcate his
presidency from the 12 years of Republican administrations that ended
when he took office. The generational, partisan, and ideological gulf that
separated Clinton from the Republicans was symbolized by the fact that
Clinton was the first truly post–Cold War president. Ronald Reagan's presidency was marked by his passionate commitment to weakening Soviet
power, which produced the largest peacetime military buildup in U.S. history. George H. W. Bush was steeped in the postwar culture of the Cold War.
A youthful opponent of America's involvement in Vietnam and a president
whose mental map of the world highlighted its economic and political connections, Clinton often spoke of wanting to help build a bridge into the new
millennium. Where, then, would the bridge lead?

Clinton's centrist vision or philosophy of government was a contradictory
mixture. As a political aide, George Stephanopoulos, commented, "There is
always a tension between wanting to get this big program and knowing you
have to reduce the deficit and get future growth. . . . It's a conflict among
several sides of him: the part of him that's committed to children's programs
and investing in jobs and highways; . . . the part of him that's cut spending
time and time again in Arkansas [when Clinton was governor of the state],
but also the part of him that knows the intense pain caused by each cut; the
part of him that understands the role of Wall Street, and the part of him that
knows that ordinary people have been screwed by those sources."[19] Thus, a
key question, when Clinton first assumed the presidential office, was, which
element would predominate in his presidency?

According to Burns and Sorenson, the conservative tendency soon triumphed. For example, Clinton chose as his first priority the attempt to reduce the budget deficit, dear to the hearts of fiscal conservatives. Inevitably,
the choice required him to ignore campaign promises to increase social
spending. Those advisers urging a more activist course knew they had lost
"when they saw [Clinton's first] State of the Union speech draft, and even
more when they spotted [Alan] Greenspan [head of the Fed] sitting next to
the First Lady [when Clinton delivered the speech to Congress]. . . .
Greenspan as guest of honor! . . . Clinton's hour-long [State of the Union]
address was an oratorical triumph for deficit reduction."[20]

Burns and Sorenson claim that Clinton lurched from one policy defeat
and compromise to the next, beginning with the defeat of his first legislative
proposal in 1993, a modest spending bill designed to revive the ailing
economy. (When Clinton was elected in 1992, unemployment was inching

---

[18] Text of a 1994 news conference, quoted in Burns and Sorenson, *Dead Center*, p. 139.

[19] Elizabeth Drew, *On the Edge: The Clinton Presidency* (New York: Simon & Schuster, 1994),
p. 64, quoted in Burns and Sorenson, *Dead Center*, p. 101.

[20] Burns and Sorenson, *Dead Center*, p. 102.

toward the alarmingly high level of 8 percent. Indeed, this was a major reason for Clinton's defeat of incumbent president George H. W. Bush.)

Clinton's next battle was the budget. In order to gain congressional approval of the budget, he abandoned some of his pet proposals, strengthening the impression that principle took a back seat to pragmatism.

Clinton's most important defeat during the early years of his presidency, however, was the disastrous defeat of his signature reform proposal: a program that would guarantee all Americans access to affordable health care. When Clinton took office, reform of the sprawling, unfair, and expensive system of health care in the United States was long overdue. Health care consumed $800 billion yearly in 1991, one-seventh of America's entire gross national product. While health care costs were soaring, the number of those who had no health care safety net—who lacked any kind of health insurance—was increasing by millions yearly. Clinton's health care reform proposal was intended both to control the burgeoning costs of health care and to extend the guarantee of affordable health care to all Americans.

Burns and Sorenson argue that Clinton's health care reform failed in part because he staked out "a prematurely centrist position."[21] The result: "Setting off to achieve the greatest effort by government on behalf of its citizens in thirty years, Clinton chose compromise as his compass."[22] The reform was soon forced to compete for public attention with other high-priority proposals (for example, passage of the North America Free Trade Agreement—NAFTA); foreign policy crises in Russia, Haiti, and Somalia; and Bill and Hillary Clinton's personal political difficulties (the Whitewater controversy erupted in 1993, involving allegations of the Clintons' financial misconduct during their Arkansas days). As a result, the momentum for passing health care reform soon petered out. Along with it went Clinton's dream of becoming a powerful reform-minded president. His fate was sealed when Republicans won the 1994 congressional elections and gained control of both houses of Congress.

It is instructive to reflect on why the health care reform plan was defeated. Poor tactics by the Clinton administration—for example, developing the plan behind closed doors in a way calculated to infuriate influential groups like doctors—are part of the explanation. Another tactical error was Clinton's drawing a line in the sand by warning that he would not retreat if his proposal was modified—which he later ignored when, in fact, he accepted compromises that moved him considerably back from the line. A second level of explanation is that the push and pull of American interest group politics was responsible for defeating health care reform. Whereas large numbers of Americans would have benefited if health care coverage had

---

[21] Ibid., p. 125.
[22] Ibid.

been broadened, they were dispersed, were unorganized, and possessed relatively few resources. By contrast, although opponents of the plan, including doctors, hospitals, and the insurance and pharmaceutical industries, were fewer in number, they were rich, powerful, well organized, and intensely motivated. Their massive lobbying and publicity campaign succeeded in defeating the proposal.

There is an even deeper level of analysis, ignored by Burns and Sorenson, that helps explain why equalizing access to affordable, quality health care is so difficult. In order to identify this level, we must connect the unequal distribution of health care to the larger class structure of the American political economy and the way that interests are organized. The United States is alone among industrialized countries in lacking broad public health care coverage. The largely private and inequitable health care system is part of a political economy in which markets are given a free hand in producing and distributing an unusually large proportion of goods and services, with relatively little public regulation to assure universal and equal access by all citizens. Specific features of this system can be altered by determined reform efforts—witness how the environmental movement has succeeded in introducing a host of public regulations in areas concerning the environment and consumer safety, from fuel efficiency and safety standards in automobiles to the requirement that industries install technology to minimize pollution. But as this book has described, key features of the American political institutions and class structure make the playing field on which political struggles are waged highly uneven. Progressive reforms face a very steep uphill battle. Change is difficult, especially when it involves challenges to those in positions of wealth and power. The failure of health care reform becomes more understandable when viewed from a structural perspective. It is helpful—indeed, even essential—to focus on the specific ways in which interests are organized and how political battles are fought. But it is important to go further and analyze how interests are connected into broader coalitions. Otherwise, one risks missing the forest for the trees.

The failure of health care reform is part of a larger story, analyzed in earlier chapters, that involves the fragmentation of working-class and poor groups in the United States. Conversely, the greater cohesion of these groups in other industrialized capitalist nations during much of the twentieth century provided political energy propelling the creation of larger and more egalitarian welfare states. The different way that interests get defined and aggregated in the United States—notably, the rhetoric of class has played a far smaller role—has had important political consequences. The impact can be seen both in the lack of a broad public program of universal health care in the past and in the failure of the push to promote one in the 1990s.

Returning to the Clinton presidency, just as success begets success in politics, so failure begets failure. Once the Clinton administration failed to pass its health care plan, it gained the reputation of being ineffective, and its standing in the polls sagged considerably below 50 percent at the time of the 1994 midterm congressional elections. Democratic candidates distanced themselves from their relatively unpopular president, and Republican candidates united under the strong leadership of House Minority Leader Newt Gingrich, who sponsored a Contract with America, which set out a bold conservative reform agenda (so brashly conservative that some renamed it the "Contract on America,"—that is, a contract to assassinate America). The Republicans relentlessly attacked Clinton and linked the unpopular president to Democrats running for Congress. The degree of animosity toward Clinton was unusually intense and exceeded the usual level of party conflict. The added dose of partisanship, which prevailed in Washington throughout the Clinton years, may have been a result of generational conflict—with Clinton, the first postwar, baby boomer president, inspiring distrust among older Americans. It was to some extent a cultural split, pitting Clinton, who opposed the American war in Vietnam and who confessed to having tried marijuana (although, he reassured the country, he had not inhaled), against cultural conservatives. This cultural opposition later developed into outright hatred of the president during the Monica Lewinsky scandal and helps explain why Clinton was impeached.

The groundwork for Clinton's impeachment in 1999 was the 1994 congressional election, when Republicans wrested control of both houses of Congress from the Democrats. The swing was far larger than the usual midterm shift away from incumbent presidents and their party. Indeed, the Republican Party had not controlled the House of Representatives for 40 years.

Divided government decisively limited Clinton's prospects for exercising bold leadership. The midterm election outcome, and the fact that, from 1994 until the end of his presidency, Clinton had to face a Republican-controlled Congress, created strong pressure to move toward the right. As a former member of George H. W. Bush's cabinet chortled, "We're dragging the Clinton administration to the center-right, where most of the people of this country are."[23] Clinton's reform proposals—as well as the defeat of these proposals—alienated diverse groups of voters. The largest disaffected groups were white, working-class and middle-class men, as well as southern voters. (Large majorities of southerners voted for Republican congressional candidates in 1994, the first time since Reconstruction, despite the presence of Arkansas-born Bill Clinton in the White House.)

Following the 1994 elections, Clinton wavered between trying to placate conservatives—with increases in military spending, support for welfare "reform" that gutted one of the New Deal's signature programs, and priority given to balancing the budget—and defending liberal elements of the status quo, including affirmative action and existing social programs. At the same time, Clinton proposed low-cost, incremental reforms intended to symbolize his commitment to bold forward movement. Examples included campaigns against teenage pregnancy, national standards for collecting child support, and federally mandated unpaid family and medical leave.

---

[23] Quoted in ibid., p. 139.

Nonetheless, modest reform efforts, even when launched by a president of extraordinary intelligence and oratorical ability, were hardly likely to mobilize and bring people to their feet—or to the voting booth. As Burns and Sorenson point out, Clinton "played to, and played up, the mainstream forces, often at the expense of the traditional Democratic labor, urban, women, consumer, and African-American constituencies. Election results proved he had not mobilized a true 'constituency of the middle,' partly because these elements were unorganized, uncommitted, and lacking in any conviction except for a mood of 'agin the government.'"[24]

Clinton's new-style centrism borrowed from both Republican and Democratic approaches. He accepted the Republicans' insistence that priority be put on reducing budgetary deficits and the national debt—at the same time that he stoutly opposed Republican cutbacks in Medicare, Medicaid, education, and the environment. Clinton demonstrated great political savvy when he succeeded in pinning blame on the Republicans in Congress for shutting down the government. When in 1995 he vetoed funding bills that provided for cuts in public services and programs, some high-profile government agencies like the national parks were forced to close. Public outrage forced the Republicans to restore the cuts, and Clinton temporarily gained a reputation for being principled and courageous in the face of a stingy and mean-spirited Republican-controlled Congress. By boxing the Republicans into a corner, and successfully portraying them as dogmatic and unreasonable, Clinton was able to position himself favorably for the 1996 presidential election.

Clinton's policy of seeking accommodation with the Republicans paid off when he agreed to a Republican proposal—which he appropriated as his own—to reform "welfare as we know it," in his words, by ending a major New Deal form of federal welfare assistance to mothers and dependent children. As we describe in Chapter 10, the reform involved transforming direct federal welfare payments into block grants to states and requiring those receiving welfare to seek work, as well as limiting welfare payments to a total of five years. The reform also involved ending Food Stamps and other assistance to legal immigrants and cutting cash assistance to the poor who were aged, blind, and disabled. The reform was a fundamental restructuring of the American welfare state. Although Clinton announced while signing the bill that it was flawed and should immediately be altered, the fact remained that he praised a reform that many interpreted as an assault on a core element of the American welfare state dating from the New Deal. Opponents noted that the reform forced mothers to accept jobs offering low wages and substandard conditions. Moreover, the reform was doubly cruel given the meager supply of adequate and affordable day care in the United States. Senator Edward Kennedy described the legislation as "legislative child abuse."[25]

---

[24] Quoted in ibid., p. 162.

[25] Quoted in ibid., p. 227.

Although sustained economic growth in the years after the reform was enacted enabled many of those eliminated from the welfare rolls to find jobs, many others did not. The welfare reform also coincided with a rise in the number of working poor: those who, despite holding down full-time jobs, earn wages below the federally defined economic threshold. Moreover, these developments occurred during good times. An economic downturn would strike most directly at those who had been pruned from the welfare rolls and who risked losing their jobs.

Another way to chart the impact of the Clinton presidency is to revisit statistics on income inequality. During the 1990s, economic inequality increased substantially beyond the point it had reached during the two preceding Republican administrations.[26]

Clinton's centrist (that is, conservative) approach was also evident in his actions in regard to race. Although he made some high-profile administrative appointments of African Americans, he launched no bold legislative and administrative programs to counter deepening racial inequalities in American society. "Unlike under [President Lyndon B. Johnson], there were no legislative milestones or executive acts creating entities to address racial disparities or inequities. No Great Societies or Wars on Poverty. No Voting Rights Acts or Equal Employment Opportunity Commissions."[27] Clinton sponsored the President's Initiative on Race, in which meetings were sponsored around the country to discuss race relations. But as in so many other areas, so on race: "In the end, Clinton was content to tinker, when he had had a genuine opportunity to transform."[28]

Burns and Sorenson observe: "A contradiction lay at the heart of Clinton's leadership: if he truly aspired to presidential greatness, the strategy he had chosen ensured that he would never achieve it. Rather, long before his presidency he had resolved on a centrist path that called for the kind of transactional leadership that he would exercise in abundance. . . . As a master broker he raised the art of the deal to world-class levels. But he rejected the kind of transformational leadership that might have placed him among the historic 'greats.'"[29] The dilemma was both that Clinton displayed a passionate, principled conviction to change in order to achieve his centrist vision *and* that the content of this vision—"centrism"—was inherently uncertain and confusing. Since it could mean nearly anything and everything, in the end it meant nothing much. Without a sharply etched vision of change, Burns and Sorenson contend, Clinton's presidency was inherently doomed to zigzag and drift. Hence, rather than pointing toward a bold vision transcending traditional divisions, centrism soon became little more than marginal incrementalism.

---

[26]Mishel, Bernstein, and Schmitt, *The State of Working America*, p. 49.

[27]Burns and Sorenson, *Dead Center*, p. 256.

[28]Ibid., p. 258.

[29]Ibid., p. 326.

The major theme in many accounts of the Clinton years is the president's failure to exercise forceful leadership to sponsor substantial changes. Yet these analyses do not stress sufficiently both the obstacles to promoting change and the fact that important changes have occurred in the United States, for better and for worse. For example, Burns and Sorenson rightly note that the explanation for Clinton's meager achievements includes the hostile treatment that he received from the media, the deeply rooted institutional barriers to change (notably, divided government—especially after the Republicans captured Congress in 1994), and the deep wounds inflicted by the impeachment scandal. However, by focusing on tactical errors and not ascribing sufficient importance to institutional design and the connection between the economy and the political sphere, Burns and Sorenson underestimate Clinton's margin for exercising new initiatives. Their implicit model is President Franklin D. Roosevelt. But FDR's bold innovations were made possible by the severe economic crisis of the 1930s.

A full analysis of the Clinton presidency should do more than identify enduring continuities in American politics, located at a far deeper level than presidential personality. It should also stress the important changes that occurred during the Clinton presidency. On the economic level, the longest economic boom in American history occurred during the 1990s and early 2000s, producing low unemployment and substantial economic growth. The United States was catapulted to preeminence where once many regarded it as faltering in international economic competition with Japan and Germany. During Clinton's presidency, the United States leaped into the world of high tech with a vengeance. When he entered the White House, few Americans possessed a personal computer, and the Internet and cellular telephones were oddities. When Clinton left office, a large proportion of Americans were passionately participating in the wireless society. Clinton never lost an opportunity to praise the virtues of technological change. Some critics charged that the occupant of the White House had little to do with the technological innovations that occurred; others charged that Clinton was too ready to promote technological change without paying sufficient attention to its costs for less advantaged Americans. But more generally, ample grounds seem to justify regarding the United States, as it entered the new millennium, as a model for the world to emulate. What continuities and changes in American politics warrant our critical review?

What, then, was the domestic impact of the Clinton presidency? We do not intend to engage in the game of president-rating—an exercise that is highly subjective and superficial. Clinton was the object of intense criticism, although we believe that Clinton-bashers were often motivated by mean-spirited moralizing about his character. A balanced view of his presidency requires highlighting that the 1990s were among the longest periods of sustained economic growth in world history. Our critical evaluation of Clinton reflects our judgment that the unparalleled prosperity occurring in the 1990s might have been better directed to realizing the egalitarian promise of American democracy. Not only did Clinton's economic and social policies fail to promote this progressive goal, but they contributed to increasing inequalities in American society.

THE COMPASSIONATE CONSERVATISM OF THE BUSH PRESIDENCY

George W. Bush's activism after becoming president was in sharp contrast to Clinton's centrism and relative passivity. Although Bush received fewer votes than his major opponent Al Gore and Republicans divided control of Congress with the Democrats, the new president sponsored several bold initiatives in his first months in office:

- *Tax reform.* Although income taxes were reduced for all taxpayers, the tax cut was sharply skewed toward the wealthy. At the same time, payroll taxes, which fall most heavily on working families, were not reduced at all. One tax was not only reduced but eliminated altogether: the estate tax, which is levied on the wealthiest 2 percent of Americans. Indeed, the wealthiest 1 percent of Americans have paid $32 billion of the $35 billion annually generated by this tax.[30] Eliminating the tax substantially increases the prospect that the class privileges of the wealthiest Americans will be passed from one generation to another. While the repeal of the tax was being debated, a newspaper ad criticized the move in the following terms: "Repealing the estate tax would enrich the heirs of Americas' millionaires and billionaires while hurting families who struggle to make ends meet."[31] Guess which extremist group placed such a partisan ad? The answer: a group of 120 super-wealthy Americans, including David Rockefeller, Warren Buffett, George Soros, and Bill Gates, Sr. (father of Microsoft's founder Bill Gates).

- *Energy policy.* The Bush administration energy plan suggests that they who pay the piper call the tune. The president and vice president amassed their personal fortunes from the petroleum industry, and top energy company executives and lobbyists have been among the most lavish donors to the Republican party. At a time when, thanks to the booming demand for gas-guzzling sport-utility vehicles (SUVs), automobile efficiency has slipped, the Bush administration concentrated its efforts on increasing energy supplies at all costs. Although

---

[30] Citizens for Tax Justice, "Distributional Effects."

[31] The ad appeared in the *New York Times,* February 18, 2001. The ad explained that the revenue lost by abolishing the estate tax would have to be made up by increases in taxes paid by working Americans or by cutting social programs.

energy consumption in the United States is far higher than in any other country in the world, Vice President Richard Cheney dismissed energy conservation as "personal virtue." Nor did the Bush administration simply promote market solutions as a way to increase energy sufficiency. The libertarian Cato Institute described the energy plan as a "smorgasbord of handouts and subsidies for virtually every energy lobby in Washington."[32] Princeton economist and *New York Times* columnist Paul Krugman observes that the implicit message behind the Bush administration's dire warnings of an energy crisis was to "scare us into relaxing environmental regulation."[33] A case in point of this pro–energy industry approach is President Bush's announcement that the United States would not comply with the Kyoto accords to set ceilings on greenhouse gases that contribute to global warming. (The accords require countries to increase energy efficiency and reduce energy consumption.)

■ *An expanded missile defense system.* As described in Chapter 9, President Bush proposed an expanded version of an earlier plan to develop a missile defense system. This provides yet another example of pork barrel politics in that, if implemented, the project will provide tens of billions of dollars in contracts for weapons companies. Although it is not clear whether the added expense will purchase greater security for the United States, it is very clear that the project has provoked intense opposition to the United States around the world.

Thus, the Bush administration has charted a bold new conservative course. How does it compare with the trends analyzed in this book? One way to tell is to revisit the four important changes identified in Chapter 1 in light of the analysis we have developed.

1. THE UNITED STATES IS THE LONE SUPERPOWER IN A MORE INTERCONNECTED WORLD. We described in Chapter 9 the position of the United States as the most powerful country in a world intensely interconnected as a result of technological, economic, and political changes. How the United States directs its vast power affects billions of people throughout the world. We suggested that a major aim of American foreign policy is to maintain the United States's unique advantage in order to reap the benefits of being number one. We question whether the United States has used its power in ways that will promote peaceful, equitable arrangements throughout the world, as well as protect a planet whose ecosystem is under increasing stress. Unless the United States does so, it is predictable that there will be increasing challenges to U.S. dominance. When grassroots movements throughout the world mobilize to contest the way in which globalization is being organized,

---

[32] Quoted in Paul Krugman, "Burn, Baby, Burn," *New York Times*, May 20, 2001.
[33] Ibid.

they do so in the name of more democratic arrangements. All too often such groups perceive the United States as a major obstacle, not an ally.

2. *Money Has Become Vastly More Important to Political Debate and Outcomes.* We documented at many points the vast amounts of money spent to shape election returns and political decisions. We also stressed that political contributions are highly concentrated: A small number of private individuals and corporations give very large contributions to purchase political access and influence. Judging by the benefits these investments generate, it is money well spent. Meanwhile, there is an increasingly widespread belief among rank-and-file Americans that corporate money has corrupted our core democratic processes.

Periodically in American history, reform movements have mobilized to check the power of what was called in the early twentieth century the "moneyed interests." Such movements exist today. But given the extent to which political institutions and policies have been reshaped by the power of political contributions, much remains to be done.

3. *Politics Has Become More Polarized in Terms Defined by the Interplay of Party, Class, Race, and Region.* We analyzed in several chapters the curious double movement in the United States toward ideological convergence and partisan polarization. At the same time that the two major parties have become more homogenous ideologically, they have converged toward a promarket approach—and yet they clash bitterly within institutions like Congress and elsewhere on some important issues, such as abortion rights and environmental protection. For example, a *New York Times*/CBS poll conducted during the 2000 presidential campaign found that over 70 percent of the electorate perceived the two parties' presidential candidates as differing significantly on important issues.[34] An important illustration of how the two parties have become more polarized was provided by Vermont Senator James Jeffords' decision, less than six months after his election to a third senatorial term in 2000, to resign from the Republican Party and become an independent. Jeffords explained that he no longer believed there was room in the party for a moderate like himself. The result of his decision was to upset the 50–50 party split in the Senate following the 2000 elections, thereby enabling the Democrats to gain control of the Senate for the first time since 1994.

When citizens find parties quite unrepresentative and unresponsive, they pursue their interests in other ways. As described in Chapter 4, the result is to fuel the rise of social movements outside the party system.

4. *Americans Demonstrate a Stronger Belief in the Virtue of Markets.* We studied in Chapters 3, 5, 6, and 10 how, as a result of ideological and partisan changes closely linked to the increased influence of political money, the

---

[34] *New York Times*/CBS News Poll reported in *New York Times*, July 25, 2000.

balance between government and market forces has shifted. Compared to the situation in other capitalist countries, private enterprise has always enjoyed great freedom from government regulation in the United States. However, since the 1980s, market forces have obtained an even more secure position.

At the same time, there is widespread discontent about the results of market-based production, among groups ranging from elderly citizens who pay inflated prices for essential medications to college students who challenge multinational corporations when they engage in violations of human rights and labor rights in industrialized and less developed countries.

CONCLUSION

We have analyzed in this book how political outcomes are a result of both the broad structural framework of American politics and the political struggles that occur within that framework. The two levels are analytically distinct, but interrelated, for political struggles are affected by the structural framework and the outcome of political struggles affects the framework. Indeed, the structural framework is nothing more—although this is saying quite a lot—than the cumulative result of past political struggles. Why is this so important? Because, however incomplete American democracy is, it provides ample space for political activism. Indeed, every one of the four important changes in American politics identified in Chapter 1 and restated in the preceding section has recently been challenged. Just as there have been momentous changes in the past, we can be confident that the future will be very different from the present.

But in what ways? The answer depends in large part on political participation—or nonparticipation. We urge students of American politics to be both critical and engaged: critical because, as this book has demonstrated, the promise of American democracy is far from being fulfilled; engaged because, without robust critical engagement, inequalities will intensify and produce an even more constricted form of democracy.

Critical engagement can be both politically effective and politically infectious. An essential element that preceded the Reagan Revolution in the 1980s, and helped make it possible, was a wave of conservative scholarship challenging established policies and ideas associated with the welfare state and proposing alternative policy directions. Similarly, the time is ripe for fresh ideas and proposals to revitalize the theory and practice of American democracy. Although much work is required to develop feasible proposals, the broad direction is clear: Just as the New Right successfully proposed to resolve the strain between capitalism and democracy by restricting the public, democratic sphere, so the opportunity exists to extend and deepen democratic possibilities. We hope that we have sufficiently informed readers about the politics of power that they can work to realize the thrilling promise of American democracy.

CREDITS

INDEX